ASP.NET Website Programming

Problem – Design – Solution

Marco Bellinaso

Kevin Hoffman

Wrox Press Ltd. ®

ASP.NET Website Programming

Problem – Design – Solution

© 2002 Wrox Press

First Printed in March 2002
Latest Reprint : November 2002

Published by Wrox Press Ltd,
Arden House, 1102 Warwick Road, Acocks Green,
Birmingham, B27 6BH, UK
Printed in the United States
ISBN 1-861006-93-4

Trademark Acknowledgements

Wrox has endeavored to provide trademark information about all the companies and products mentioned in this book by the appropriate use of capitals. However, Wrox cannot guarantee the accuracy of this information.

Credits

Authors
Marco Bellinaso
Kevin Hoffman

Commissioning Editor
Dan Kent

Technical Editors
Dianne Arrow
David Barnes

Index
Andrew Criddle

Managing Editor
Viv Emery

Project Manager
Helen Cuthill

Production Coordinator
Abbie Forletta

Cover
Chris Morris

Technical Reviewers
Don Lee
Dan Maharry
Christophe Nasarre
Matthew Rabinowitz
Marc H Simkin

Proof Reader
Dev Lunsford

About the Authors

Marco Bellinaso

Marco Bellinaso is a freelance software developer. He lives in a small town close to Venice, Italy. He has been working with VB, C/C++, ASP and other Microsoft tools for several years, specializing in User Interface, API, ActiveX/COM design and programming. He is now spending all his time on the .NET Framework, using C# and VB.NET.

He is particularly interested in e-commerce design and implementation solutions with SQL Server, ASP.NET, and web services. He is a team member at www.vb2themax.com, for which he writes articles and commercial software, such as add-ins for MS Visual Studio and other utilities for VB and .NET developers.

Marco recently co-authored "Beginning C#" from Wrox Press, and is also a contributing editor for two leading Italian programming magazines: Computer Programming and Visual Basic Journal (Italian licensee for Visual Studio Magazine). Reach him at mbellinaso@vb2themax.com.

Acknowledgments

Writing this book has been a real pleasure to me. It gave me the opportunity to work with ASP.NET on a good project, and to improve my knowledge of the technology along the way. So it surely has been worth the effort! And of course, everyone likes to be published writing about what they like to do and how to do it. :-)

I owe many thanks to Wrox Press for giving me the opportunity to write the book: this is the most English I've ever written, so I guess the editors and reviewers had some extra work with me, although they were so kind as to never confess it. Some of these people are Daniel Kent, David Barnes, and Dianne Arrow.

Other people contributed to this project, in a way or another, now or in the past, and I'd like to mention at least a few names. First of all a really big thank you goes to Francesco Balena, famous speaker and author, and editor in chief of the Italian licensee of VBPJ (now Visual Studio Magazine). He reviewed and published an article about VB subclassing that I wrote some years ago, when I had no editorial experience at all. Since that moment he has continued to help me by advising how to improve my writing style, pushing me to start writing in English, suggesting the hottest technology to study, and giving the opportunity to work on some cool software projects as part of the VB-2-The-Max team. Francesco, all this is greatly appreciated!

Two other developers I work with for the Italian magazines, who helped me in different ways, are Dino Esposito and Alberto Falossi.

Giovanni - Gianni - Artico is the person who initiated me in the programming art, suggesting to start with VB and then to learn C/C++ as well. Thank you for answering my questions when I was at the beginning, and for still helping me in some situations.

A mention goes also to my closest friends. They still remember me after several "sorry, I can't come today" rebuttals, and have put up with me when I was under pressure and not the nicest person possible.

Last but not least I have to say thank you to my family, who bought my first computer and a lot of programming books when I was in high school and couldn't buy all that stuff by myself. They didn't offer much moral support during the work – mostly because they didn't have a clue of what I was doing! I kept it a secret to almost everybody – I hope it will be a nice surprise. :-)

Kevin Hoffman

Kevin has always loved computers and computer programming. He first got hooked when he received a Commodore VIC-20 from his grandfather, who had repaired it after finding it in the trash. He then started a prolific but unprofitable career writing shareware games and utilities for electronic bulletin board systems.

He started working as a programmer while still in college, writing computer interfaces to solar measurement devices and various other scientific instruments. Moving to Oregon, he did everything from technical support to tuning Unix kernels, and eventually working as an ASP programmer for 800.COM, a popular on-line electronics retailer. From there he moved on to working on large, enterprise ASP applications.

Then he finally found .NET, which he now spends 100% of his programming and learning efforts on. A big C# fan, who would use it to do everything including brush my teeth if only he could figure out how, Kevin has been writing on .NET for Wrox since the middle of Beta 1. He plans to continue until we get tired of him. He's currently in Houston, Texas sweating a lot and working on web services and other large-scale .NET applications.

Acknowledgments

I'd like to dedicate this book to the rest of my "family", without whom I could not have accomplished many of the things I am proud of today. I would like to thank Gerald for all his support – a best friend in every sense of the word – and his daughter Keely for making me laugh. I would also like to thank Jen, Jocelyn, and Emily for their support and being there for me. And as always I want to dedicate my work to my wife, Connie – without her support I would never have published a single word.

Table of Contents

Table of Contents

Table of Contents

Table of Contents

Table of Contents

Introduction

Welcome to ASP.NET Website Programming. In this book we will build an interactive, content-based website using expandable, interchangeable modules. By the end of the book you will have developed your ASP.NET skills for producing effective, well-engineered, extendable websites.

ASP.NET is a great tool for building websites. It contains many built-in features that would take thousands of lines of code in classic ASP. And it does not require admin rights in order to deploy compiled components – your whole site can be deployed in one folder.

This book will guide you through the bewildering features available to ASP.NET developers, highlighting the most useful and exciting.

The book concentrates on websites that focus on content. It does not show how to produce an e-commerce system, although a lot of the advice will apply to e-commerce sites. We could add a shopping basket module using the same foundations, for example.

This book is different to most Wrox books, because we build a single working website throughout the book. However, each chapter stands alone and shows how to develop individual modules, which you can adapt for your own websites. We also suggest a framework that allows us to create modules and slot them in to the website quickly and easily.

What Does This Book Cover?

The chapters in this book follow a problem-design-solution pattern. First we identify what we need to achieve, then we sketch out how we will achieve it, and finally we will build the software in Visual Studio .NET.

Most chapters involve building a 3-tier system, with data, business, and presentation layers. We will also see how to build separate modules so that they integrate well into the whole site.

Chapter 1 looks at the website as a whole. We identify the problem that it is trying to solve, and discuss how we will go about solving it. We then come up with a solution – which involves building and integrating the modules detailed in the other chapters.

Chapter 2 builds the foundations of our site. We set coding standards and design our folder and namespace structure. We create our initial database – although at this stage we have no data to put in it. We also build site-wide error handling code and base classes for our data and business layer objects.

Chapter 3 extends our foundations to the presentation layer. We will build base classes for the ASP.NET pages in the site, a custom error page, and site wide navigation, header, and footer controls.

Chapter 4 presents a file management module, which we can use to download and upload source code for the site, and make changes online. We will also look at Microsoft's Data Manager, which enables us to manage SQL Server databases through our website.

Chapter 5 covers user accounts. We look at how to create a powerful role-based security system, and integrate it with ASP.NET's built-in authentication features.

Chapter 6 shows how to provide regularly changing news content through a website. We also build a web service to expose news headlines to other sites and applications, and a Windows news ticker that uses this web service.

Chapter 7 looks at advertising. We create our advertising system by extending the ASP.NET `AdRotator` control to provide the power we need. We look at logging *hits* and *impressions*, and providing reports to advertisers.

Chapter 8 covers opinion polls and voting. We look at how to administer questions, log votes, and collate them into useful reports.

Chapter 9 provides the tools to create e-mail newsletters. We will look at how to create messages in plain text and HTML, and how to administer lists and set up new ones.

Chapter 10 looks at forums. We create everything you need to post and read messages, and give administrators special permissions. Along the way, there is some powerful use of the `DataList` and `DataGrid` controls. We also look at how to use regular expressions to provide limited HTML support, without opening our forum to the risk of cross-site scripting.

Chapter 11 shows how to deploy the site. We will look at the ways Visual Studio .NET allows us to provide source-free distributable versions of our software, and how to deploy our sites onto hosting services.

Chapter 12 looks to the future. We've only just begun our lives as ASP.NET website developers and here we will look at ways in which Wrox can support your continued development. In particular this includes the book's P2P list, where you can work together with fellow readers and benefit from each other's ideas and experience.

Who Is This Book For?

The book is for developers who have a reasonable knowledge of ASP.NET, and want to apply that knowledge to building websites. You will get the most from this book if you have read a decent amount of Wrox's Beginning ASP.NET using C#, or Professional ASP.NET and a C# book.

You should be comfortable using Visual Studio .NET to create ASP.NET projects, and that you know C#.

What You Need To Use This Book

To run the samples in this book you need to have the following:

- ❑ Windows 2000 or Windows XP.

- ❑ Visual Studio .NET 1.0. We have tested the code for version 1.0, although most of the code should work in late pre-release versions. Nearly everything will also work in Visual C# .NET Standard.

- ❑ SQL Server 2000 – although most of the techniques we use could apply to any database system, including Access.

To get the site working you may also need an ASP.NET web host. We will give some guidance on choosing one towards the end of the book.

Conventions

We've used a number of different styles of text and layout in this book to help differentiate between the different kinds of information. Here are examples of the styles we used and an explanation of what they mean.

Code has several fonts. If it's a word that we're talking about in the text – for example, when discussing a `For...Next` loop, it's in this font. If it's a block of code that can be typed as a program and run, then it's also in a gray box:

```
<?xml version 1.0?>
```

Sometimes we'll see code in a mixture of styles, like this:

```
<?xml version 1.0?>
<Invoice>
```

```
<part>
    <name>Widget</name>
    <price>$10.00</price>
</part>
</invoice>
```

In cases like this, the code with a white background is code we are already familiar with; the line highlighted in gray is a new addition to the code since we last looked at it.

Advice, hints, and background information comes in this type of font.

> **Important pieces of information come in boxes like this.**

Bullets appear indented, with each new bullet marked as follows:

- ❏ **Important Words** are in a bold type font.
- ❏ Words that appear on the screen, or in menus like the File or Window, are in a similar font to the one you would see on a Windows desktop.
- ❏ Keys that you press on the keyboard, such as *Ctrl* and *Enter*, are in italics.

Customer Support

We want to hear from you! We want to know what you think about this book: what you liked, what you didn't like, and what you think we can do better next time. Please send us your comments, either by returning the reply card in the back of the book, or by e-mailing feedback@wrox.com. Please mention the book title in your message.

We do listen to these comments, and we do take them into account on future books.

How to Download the Code for the Website

It is well worth getting the website working on your own machine before reading too much of this book. It will help you follow the descriptions, because you will be able to see how code snippets relate to the whole application, and experience the modular approach first hand.

To get the code, visit www.wrox.com and navigate to ASP.NET Website Programming. Click on Download in the Code column, or on Download Code on the book's detail page.

The files are in ZIP format. Windows XP recognizes these automatically, but Windows 2000 requires a de-compression program such as WinZip or PKUnzip. The archive contains the whole site, plus a readme describing how to get it up and running.

Errata

We've made every effort to make sure that there are no errors in the text or in the code. If you do find an error, such as a spelling mistake, faulty piece of code, or any inaccuracy, we would appreciate feedback. By sending in errata you may save another reader hours of frustration, and help us provide even higher quality information.

E-mail your comments to support@wrox.com. Your information will be checked and if correct, posted to the errata page for that title, and used in subsequent editions of the book.

To find errata for this title, go to www.wrox.com and locate ASP.NET Website Programming. Click on the Book Errata link, which is below the cover graphic on the book's detail page.

E-mail Support

If you wish to directly query a problem in the book with an expert who knows the book in detail then e-mail support@wrox.com, with the title of the book and the last four numbers of the ISBN in the subject field of the e-mail. Please include the following things in your e-mail:

- ❏ The **title of the book**, **last four digits of the ISBN**, and **page number** of the problem in the Subject field.
- ❏ Your **name**, **contact information**, and the **problem** in the body of the message.

We *won't* send you junk mail. We need the details to save your time and ours. When you send an e-mail message, it will go through the following chain of support:

- ❏ Customer Support – Your message is delivered to our customer support staff, who are the first people to read it. They have files on most frequently asked questions and will answer anything general about the book or the website immediately.
- ❏ Editorial – Deeper queries are forwarded to the technical editor responsible for that book. They have experience with the programming language or particular product, and are able to answer detailed technical questions on the subject.
- ❏ The Authors – If even the editor cannot answer your problem, he or she will forward the request to the author. We do try to protect the author from any distractions to their writing, but we are happy to forward specific requests to them. All Wrox authors help with the support on their books. They will e-mail the customer and the editor with their response, and again all readers should benefit.

The Wrox Support process can only offer support to issues that directly relate to the content of the book. Support for questions that fall outside the scope of normal book support, is provided via the community lists of our http://p2p.wrox.com/ forum.

p2p.wrox.com

For author and peer discussion join the P2P mailing lists. Our unique system provides **programmer to programmer**™ contact on mailing lists, forums, and newsgroups, all in addition to our one-to-one e-mail support system. If you post a query to P2P, you can be confident that the many Wrox authors and industry experts who use our mailing lists will examine it. At p2p.wrox.com you will find a number of different lists that will help you, not only while you read this book, but also as you develop your own applications.

This book has its own list called aspdotnet_website_programming. Using this, you can talk to other people who are developing websites using the methods and framework presented here. You can share ideas and code for new and improved modules, get help with programming headaches, and show off the sites you've written!

To subscribe to a mailing list just follow these steps:

1. Go to http://p2p.wrox.com/.

2. Choose the appropriate category from the left menu bar.

3. Click on the mailing list you wish to join.

4. Follow the instructions to subscribe and fill in your e-mail address and password.

5. Reply to the confirmation e-mail you receive.

6. Use the subscription manager to join more lists and set your e-mail preferences.

Why this System Offers the Best Support

You can choose to join the mailing lists or you can receive them as a weekly digest. If you don't have the time, or facility, to receive the mailing list, then you can search our online archives. Junk and spam mails are deleted, and the unique Lyris system protects your e-mail address. Queries about joining or leaving lists, and any other general queries about lists, should be sent to listsupport@p2p.wrox.com.

Building an ASP.NET Website

In this book we are going to build a content-based ASP.NET website. This website will consist of a number of modules, which will all fit together to produce the finished product.

We will build each module in a standard order:

- ❑ Identify the **problem** – What do we want to do? What restrictions or other factors do we need to take into account?

- ❑ Produce a **design** – Decide what features we need to solve the problem. Get a broad idea of how the solution will work.

- ❑ Build the **solution** – Produce the code, and any other material, that will realize the design.

This book focuses on programming. When we talk about design, we generally mean designing the software – we will not be looking at graphic or user interface design.

Your website will not be solving all of the same problems as ours, but many of the modules we build – and the programming techniques we use – are very transferable.

In this chapter we will take a high-level look at the whole site – what it needs to do, and how it will do it.

The Problem

We will be building a website for DVD and book enthusiasts. In outlining the site's problem, we need to consider the purpose and audience. In real life this stage would be business-oriented – taking into account things like advertising demographics, competition, and availability of funding. These processes need to be analyzed rigorously, but we will leave all that to the managers.

Our site will cater for lovers of books and DVDs. It will provide useful content and try to build community. Our visitors will want to read about these things, and contribute their opinions, but each visit will be fairly short – this will not be a huge database in the style of the Internet Movie Database (www.imdb.com). It will be funded by advertising, and will rely on repeated (but fairly short) visits from its readers.

We also need to consider constraints. These are more practical. One of the major constraints that this site faced was the development team – the members would never meet, because they were on opposite sides of the world. This meant that the design must allow one developer to work on sections of the site without interfering with other developers working on different sections. But all of the sections needed to eventually work together smoothly. In most cases the separation between developers will be less extreme, but giving each developer the ability to work independently is very useful. We need to design and build methods to enable this.

Site development never really finishes – sites tend to be tweaked frequently. Another key to successful websites is to design them in a way that makes modification easy. We will need to find ways to do this.

> We will call our site ThePhile.com, because it is a site for lovers of books (bibliophiles) and DVDs (DVD-philes). It's also a play on the word 'file', because our website will be a definitive source of information.

The Design

We have outlined what our site needs – now let's look at how we can provide it. The main points raised in the problem section were:

- ❑ Enable developers to work from many different locations
- ❑ Build a maintainable, extendable site
- ❑ Build community
- ❑ Provide interesting content
- ❑ Provide revenue through advertising
- ❑ Encourage frequent visits

Let's discuss each of these in turn.

Working From Different Locations

Our developers need to work on sections of the site with relatively little communication. Our developers are in different countries so face-to-face meetings are impossible. Telephone conversations can be expensive, and different time zones cause problems.

We need to design the system so that developers can work on their own section of the site, knowing that they will not damage the work of others.

A good way to solve this is to develop the site as a series of **modules**, with each module being fairly independent. Of course there will be shared components, but changes to these will be rare and can be done in a controlled way. In this book, we work in modules. We also make frequent use of **controls**. This means that components for a page can be developed independently, and easily 'dropped in' as needed – changes to the actual pages of the site are kept to a minimum.

A Maintainable, Extendable Site

Most websites have new features added quite frequently. This means that from the start the site needs to be designed to make that easy.

Working in modules and using controls already goes some way towards this. Particularly, using controls means that non-programmers can edit the pages of our site more easily – nearly all they see is HTML code. A control just looks like another HTML tag.

Working in modules means that new modules can be added to the site at any time, with minimum disruption. All modules are fairly independent, so new ones can be added – and changes made – pretty easily.

Each individual module needs to be easy to change. A good way to do this is to work in layers, or 'tiers'. We will be using a three-layer design for most modules. We have a data layer, a business layer, and a presentation layer. Data passes from **data layer** to **business layer**, and from business layer to **presentation layer**, and back again. Each layer has a job to do. Underneath the data layer is a data source, which it is the data layer's job to access.

The data layer obtains fairly raw data from the database (for example, "-10"). The business layer turns that data into information that makes sense from the perspective of business rules (for example, "-10 degrees centigrade"). The presentation layer turns this into something that makes sense to users (for example, "strewth! It's freezing!").

It's useful to do this, because each layer can be modified independently. We can modify the business layer, and provided we continue to accept the same data from the data layer, and provide the same data to the presentation layer, we don't need to worry about wider implications. We can modify the presentation layer to change the look of the site without changing the underlying business logic.

This means we can provide versions of the site for different audiences. We just need new presentation layers that call the same business objects. For example, providing different languages: "zut alors! Comme il fait froid", "allora, fa freddo", and so on.

We need methods to get changes we make onto the live site. This could be through FTP uploads, but in many circumstances it is better to work through a web interface.

We will also need tools to administer the other sections – ban problem users, add news articles, and so on. This is all part of providing a maintainable site.

Community

Sites generally benefit from allowing readers to contribute. Because our site is not intended for users to spend hours looking at, our community features must not require a lot of users' time.

There are two ways that we will build our community: through polls and forums. Polls give users the opportunity to give their opinion in a single click – so they require very little time from the user, but can make a site seem far more alive.

Forums enable users to discuss topics with other users. Messages remain in the system, and replies are posted. Readers can leave a post, and then come back later to see if there are replies. This is more appropriate for our purposes than a chat room, which requires the reader to concentrate on the site for the whole duration of the chat.

Community can really give a site a life of its own. Over time, strong characters, heroes, and villains emerge. Many sites depend entirely on community, and become extremely popular – for example www.plastic.com.

For any of this to work, we need to identify users and provide them with unique logons. So our system will need some form of user accounts system.

Interesting Content

The content most relevant to our users will be movie and book related news and reviews. This content tends to be highly relevant for a short period of time: after a story has broken, or immediately after a release. Our site will need tools to manage news in this way.

Another way to provide interesting content is to get somebody else to provide it! This is part of what we're doing with our community section. Part of the purpose of building community is to get people contributing content.

Advertising

Advertising generates revenue (or in some cases it is used to exchange banners with other sites). We need to display adverts, and record data about how often each advert has been displayed and clicked on.

We also need to gather information about what the users of the site like, so we can target our advertising content. Polls and forums can provide us with useful information when finding products to advertise.

The biggest sites target individual users based on their demographic and any other information gathered about them (for example, Yahoo! and Amazon.com target advertising and product recommendations to the demographic and buying habits of each user). Our site already has a fairly narrow target demographic, and is not particularly big, so we don't need to do this.

Frequent Visits

A good site will make people want to return. If the content is compelling, and there's plenty of discussion going on, then people visit again and again.

It's still a good idea to remind users from time to time. We want to draw attention back to the site, even when the user isn't viewing it. One way we'll be doing this is through an e-mail newsletter, which gives users useful information and subtly reminds them to visit the site.

We will also build a Windows application that acts as a news ticker, with automatically updating news headlines. Users can click a headline to view the full story on the site.

The Solution

We've seen what we want the site to do, and sketched out some rough ideas of how we might provide it. Now we'll look at how to build our solution. This really encompasses the whole of the book. Here we'll look at how each chapter relates to our initial problem and design.

Working From Different Locations

In the next two chapters, we will provide a framework for development. This will lay down coding standards, and a framework for organizing the modules into folders and Visual Studio .NET projects.

We will decide what namespaces we will use for each module, and all the other things that will make team working as hassle-free as possible. We will also develop some initial UI features to use across the site, promoting a unified feel. These include a header, footer, and navigation control, and stylesheets.

Building A Maintainable, Extendable Site

Chapters 2 and 3 will also set us on the road to a maintainable site. We will develop base classes, giving each new module a solid foundation to build on.

We will develop a web-based file manager in Chapter 4. Through this we can download and upload files, create new ones, move them, change their attributes, and even edit files online with a built-in, web-based text editor. If you've ever wanted to provide file upload facilities, offer source code for download, or provide online editing tools then this is the place to look!

Most of the modules we develop will have administration features. For these to be useful, we need to identify administrators. In Chapter 5 we will develop a user accounts system. Using this, we can collect user information and give different users different privileges. Our final site will support full role-based security, with login details stored in a SQL Server database.

Providing Interesting Content

In Chapter 6 we create a news management system. This will enable our administrators to add and edit news articles, receive and approve suggested articles from readers, and place new articles in categories. And, of course, it lets users read the news. We will create a control so that we can easily display headlines on any page that we like.

The news system will be flexible enough to also cover reviews, which will eventually form the core of our site.

Managing Adverts

Advertising will be covered in Chapter 7. We will develop a system to display adverts, and log impressions (when an ad is displayed) and hits (when an ad is clicked). This will allow us to create reports from this data to give to advertisers.

There will be admin facilities to create adverts, select how frequently they should be displayed, and start and end campaigns.

Encouraging Community

Chapter 8 will cover our voting system, and forums will be covered in Chapter 10. The voting system will allow administrators to create new questions to vote on. Answers will be recorded and displayed, and an archive of old results maintained – accessible from a standalone Windows application. We guard against multiple votes from the same user by using cookies and IP number.

The forums system will let each user choose an avatar image to represent them, and start posting. Discussion will be organized into categories, and within them there will be various topics. Users can post new topics, and reply to existing topics. We use regular expressions to allow formatting tags in messages, but prevent images or JavaScript.

Getting Repeat Visitors

As well as providing all this great content, we will include two features specifically for getting visitors back to the site.

The first is covered in Chapter 6 where we look at news. We will develop a web service that exposes our news headlines. We will then build a Windows client that displays the headlines, updating itself regularly. Clicking a headline will open a browser on the correct page for the full story.

The second is covered in Chapter 9. We will create the facility for visitors to subscribe to receive e-mail updates from us. Once they are subscribed, we send a mail out regularly to encourage repeat visits. This mail will include highlighted news and features, and links back to the site. We will develop a system that enables administrators to create plain text and HTML messages. We then develop a mailing list admin module for creating subscription forms for new mailing lists, administering list members, adding newsletters, and managing subscriptions. Messages can include custom tags so that each list member receives an e-mail tailored to their own details.

Deploying the Site

Although we haven't mentioned it before, we will eventually need to move the site from our production machine to the live server. This can be a complex task, because we need to separate the files needed for the site to run from the source code files that we only need for development. We will look at this in Chapter 11, and see how Visual Studio .NET gives us tools to make the process easy.

Summary

We're now ready to look at the site in detail. Before reading the following chapters, it's worth getting hold of the code download and seeing how the final site fits together. This book does not describe every detail of the website, and it will be a lot clearer if you look at the final site first.

> **The code and database is available from www.wrox.com. Once you've downloaded and unzipped it, look at the readme file to see how to get it working in Visual Studio .NET. You will get far more from the book if you look at the project *before* reading on.**

In the next chapter we will start to build the foundations for the rest of the site.

2

Foundations

Laying foundations is one of the first steps we need to take when starting any non-trivial programming project. Foundations include things like code and documentation conventions, and the structure and design of the backend. In a formal development process, the foundations also typically include a vision statement of some kind, and a project plan.

Developers often have opposing views on how much work to do at this stage. Many want to sit in front of a keyboard and start coding straight away, while others want to spend weeks developing pages of rules and standards. Somewhere between the two extremes lies a fairly good medium. We don't want to get caught in an endless loop of designing, but we also don't want to write any code before we've figured out what our architecture and design is going to be like.

If we are building a house, and we build the foundations on sand, the house is likely to come tumbling down before the building is finished. On the other hand, if the ground is too hard then laying the foundations can be a major task in itself, placing unnecessary restrictions on the rest of the project.

This chapter will demonstrate a sensible compromise between the two extremes – building a solid but unrestrictive foundation for an ASP.NET website. First we will discuss the common problems facing an ASP.NET website architect in building the foundation. Then we will delve into designing a solution to these problems. Finally we'll implement these designs, and even get to work on some code. This chapter is geared towards both architects and developers alike. We will cover broad, high-level issues such as design and architecture, and we will also take a look at the code used to implement a solid foundation for an ASP.NET website.

The Problem

Building a solid foundation can be a daunting task. It requires a good understanding of how the application will operate before we go into the detailed design of each component. If we build a good foundation, everything else will seem to fall into place. But if the foundation is poor, the site will take an extraordinary amount of work and time to complete, if it's completed at all.

Building the foundation of a website is really a collection of smaller, inter-related tasks. There are many aspects of the website's development that need to be part of the initial foundation's design. One such aspect is the development environment – for example team size and working style, and the tools that will be used to build the site. The type of team that will work on the project is an important factor in developing the foundation, as the latter should be developed to support the needs of the team. For example, a small team in a single office might work well with a fairly loose foundation, because they can easily make small changes here and there. But a large, distributed team will benefit if the foundation is set in stone, since negotiating a change could be a mammoth task. For the website in this book, the development team consisted of only two people. However, these two people were on opposite sides of the world. For this reason, the foundation needed to provide a stable basis for plugging in the different modules that each developer was working on.

In addition to the *development* needs, we need to determine the requirements of the website in its *deployment* environment. A website can have many different types of requirements, including:

- ❏ Physical – the software and hardware environment in which the final website will run. Requirements such as these typically dictate whether the website needs to be in a certain directory, or on a certain machine, or in a certain network infrastructure. Physical requirements also dictate the specific type of database to be used to support the system. We need to plan ahead for what type of system we're going to use to store our back-end data. Will it be a relational database management system (RDBMS) like Oracle or SQL Server, or are we pulling information from a mainframe, from a web service, or even from a collection of XML files? While you can code your data services tier to be as source-agnostic as possible, it isn't an excuse to spend less time on the definition of your data requirements.

- ❏ Architectural – we need to know how we plan on structuring our application. We need to know where the physical and logical separations are, and we need to consider things like firewalls and networking considerations. The website may need to be designed to support a certain type of development style, or modification by authorized third parties.

- ❏ Logical – these requirements are those that, for example, dictate that a website will consist of three layers of servicing components on top of a layer of database stored procedures.

The deployment environment includes both the server and the client browser. Many websites recommend, or even require, a particular browser in order to function correctly. Sometimes this is appropriate, but often it isn't. When laying the foundations of the site, a strategic decision needs to be made about what type and version of browser your website must support. This will affect the HTML and client-side scripts that your developers can work with, and hence be part of the coding standard. As far as ThePhile.com is concerned, we will not be dictating the use of any particular browser. We will try to code the pages so that any recent browser that supports the latest HTML standards can use them.

We also need to consider what the purpose of the website is, and who will be the users. Many businesses, ranging from the small start-up business to the huge worldwide corporation, provide services and applications for their employees on their intranet. There are many different types of applications that fall into this category, including:

❑ HR applications – many large corporations provide systems on the web to automate many tasks for dealing with the employee's day-to-day business, such as time sheets and benefits tracking. These applications require high security and availability.

❑ Internal support applications – as well as creating software that is deployed to their customers, companies have various departments that often have 'in-house' software designed to support their own needs. These applications require security, reliability, availability, and often a high degree of support from the programming staff.

These types of applications have specific deployment issues, which often arise due to a wide disparity in system configuration and type across the employees requiring the software. Other deployment concerns arise simply due to the large number of employees that must make use of this software. It is also becoming more common for web application vendors to create an application, build a deployment program, place it on a CD, and then sell that CD to customers who then deploy that application throughout *their* intranet. For example, there are several companies that provide defect tracking solutions that are essentially websites you install from a CD to support your programming intranet. The possibilities are extremely wide and varied. You may not know your particular solution for deployment at the time you are defining your problem, but you should definitely be aware that it must be a core part of the design of your website foundation.

Finally, our website wouldn't look very much like a website without a user interface. So we obviously need some type of UI. Putting some effort into the design of the user interface before a lot of code has been written can have extremely large payoffs. We will need to take into consideration our audience when we design the look and feel of our website, as well as the navigation and flow of the site, to make it easy for the target audience to use and traverse.

Now that we've covered a little bit about the overall problems that face ASP.NET website architects, let's take a look at the problem statement we came up with for the foundation of our website. We had special needs for ours, because the developers of our website have never physically been in the same room.

The Problem Statement

For our purposes the problem statement includes stating the problem we are attempting to solve, and the constraints that we must conform to in solving that problem. Our problem statement is divided into two sections: a vision (or purpose) and a set of requirements. Depending on what particular software development process you use, your problem statements may vary significantly from the one we will present here. If you are a fan of the Microsoft Solutions Framework (MSF) then you might already be used to producing a vision statement and a requirements document.

We'll present our vision statement and then list the requirements for our product. It is absolutely imperative that you do not start a single line of code or actual design until you have adequately defined these for your project. In many iterative processes, you may be satisfied with only partially defining the requirements, because you know you will revisit the requirements document multiple times throughout the lifetime of your project.

The Vision

We are endeavoring to build a complete, content-driven website that illustrates the importance of modular building and will hopefully illustrate a few ASP.NET 'best practices' along the way. We will develop a solid, scalable foundation on which to build the modules that will be developed throughout the rest of this book. A secondary goal is to provide a foundation that can be used by multiple programmers with diverse experience and still produce a coherent, cohesive solution.

The Requirements

It is important that we keep our requirements separate from our purpose. The requirements are the rules to which our design must conform in order to produce the solution we set out to create. In an iterative process, the requirements generally change with each iteration. In our small development environment, we won't need an iterative process, so the following is the list of requirements that we defined for our project:

❑ Scalability – our solution must be scalable. It must be able to expand to meet increasing performance demands with a minimum of extra coding required. It's a lofty goal, but it is quite possible with the right design.

❑ Flexibility – our solution must be *agile*. This may be a buzzword, but there is some validity behind it. We must try to make the foundation of our website agile so that changes that require modification of the foundation will not drastically impact the rest of the site.

❑ Reusability – our solution for the core foundation of our website must be designed in such a way that it promotes code reuse. A strong emphasis should be placed on object hierarchies, inheritance, and reuse, starting with the foundation and carrying on through all of the modules in the website.

❑ Separation – our core foundation code should provide a solid foundation for the rest of the website, but it should not be so closely tied to it that changes to individual modules will have an impact on the core foundation code.

❑ Deployment – our application should be coded in such a way that it can be deployed on the Internet for public use, and also to workstations running Windows 2000 and XP to allow programmers to examine and learn from the source code.

❑ Test plan – as experienced programmers we know that developing a large project, even one that may appear simple on the outside, is going to be a difficult process. As such, we need to make sure that we have an organized way in which we test our code so that we can be reasonably confident that there are no bugs in it when it is released to production.

In summary, the foundation for our website, ThePhile.com, needs to provide a stable, solid, scalable foundation that will give us the flexibility to make changes throughout the development process and later, as well as providing enough standardization and convention to allow a team of programmers to build portions of the website separately, allowing for easy integration of individual modules.

The Design

Now that we have formally defined the problem of building our application's foundation, we can begin the design process. Our design should reach a happy medium, providing enough foundation and structure to produce cohesive results, without getting so bogged down in design that we end up producing nothing.

Our discussion of the design process is going to look at some of the most common tasks in building the foundation of a website. Then we'll apply that general concept to our specific application by actually designing the various pieces of The Phile's foundation. The following list of items illustrates some of the concepts at the core of good foundation design:

- ❑   Naming and coding conventions
- ❑   Programming language choice
- ❑   Folder structure
- ❑   Designing the database(s)
- ❑   Building a data services tier
- ❑   Building a business services tier
- ❑   Providing for effective error handling
- ❑   Deployment and maintenance
- ❑   User interface design

Naming and Coding Conventions

Coding conventions can be unpopular, particularly where they are imposed on a team by a non-programmer and contain dated or restrictive rules. Every programmer has their own opinion about the usefulness of naming guidelines, coding conventions, and other code-related rules. The opinions range from those who think that any coding convention ruins the programmer's creative style, to those who thrive on the structure that conventions and standards provide.

Once again, we're faced with finding a compromise that benefits everybody. Standardization not only allows teams of programmers to produce code that follows the same conventions, making it easier to read and maintain, but it allows for the same programmer to write consistent code. Far more often than we like to admit, programmers will use one convention one day, and another convention the next. Without some sense of enforced structure to the programming, the infamous spaghetti code will rear its ugly head and make life miserable for everyone involved. Another common practice that ensures solid, standardized code is the use of **code reviews**. Code reviews are where other programmers (or managers, depending on skill distribution) review their peers' code for accuracy, efficiency, and compliance to coding standards and conventions. Some programmers resist this kind of practice, but it can be extremely valuable and productive.

The guidelines here tend to match the recommendations that Microsoft issues to its own .NET development teams. If we haven't pointed out a difference between our standards and Microsoft's, then they're essentially the same. When in doubt, it is generally a good idea to favor established methods that developers are already familiar with. Change can often bring with it benefits; but it can also be something that programmers resist strongly.

Naming Guidelines

Naming guidelines actually cover two things: **naming** and **casing**. The following is a list of generic guidelines that apply to both naming and casing. Microsoft strongly recommends the use of a capitalization scheme called **Pascal casing**. Pascal casing is a scheme where all words in an identifier have the first letter capitalized and there is no separation character between words. Another type of capitalization scheme is called **camel casing**. This is where the first letter of the identifier is lowercased, and thereafter the first letter of each word is capitalized. The following table is a summary of Microsoft's capitalization suggestions:

Type	Case	Additional Information
Class	PascalCase	Examples: *MyClass, Utility, DataHelper*
Enum value	PascalCase	Examples: *Colors.Red, PossibleValues.ValueOff*
Enum type	PascalCase	Examples: *Colors, PossibleValues*
Event	PascalCase	Examples: *MouseClick, ButtonDown*
Exception class	PascalCase	Class name ends with `Exception` suffix, for example: *MyCustomException, WebServiceException*
Interface	PascalCase	Interface name is prefixed with the letter `I`, for example: *ICar, ISerializable*
Method	PascalCase	Examples: *GetItemData, UpdateModifiedValue*
Namespace	PascalCase	Examples: *Company.NewApplication.DataTier*
Property	PascalCase	Examples: *ItemValue*
Parameter	camelCase	Examples: *itemArray, valueData, purchasePrice*
Private member variable	camelCase	Microsoft makes no recommendation on this; however, it is useful to distinguish private member variables from other identifiers.

In addition to the above summary of capitalization rules, the following guidelines apply to naming classes, interfaces, and namespaces:

❑ Do *not* use class names that overlap with namespaces, especially those namespaces that are supplied by Microsoft. So stay away from naming your classes things like `System`, `UI`, `Collections`, or `Forms`.

❑ Do *not* use the underscore character. Many of us who have been writing C++ code for a long time have developed the habit of using a preceding underscore to indicate a private member variable within a class. This practice has fallen from grace, and is now discouraged.

❑ Do *not* use identifier names that conflict with keywords. Most languages won't let you anyway!

❑ Do *not* use abbreviations in your identifiers. Also, where you use an acronym, treat it as a word – don't use all uppercase. For example, the .NET Framework has namespaces such as `SqlClient` (not `SQLClient`).

❑ *Do* follow the casing conventions in brand names. For example, if you place your company name in a namespace, and your company name has a specifically branded capitalization scheme (for example NeXT or IBM, both of which have a capitalization scheme that doesn't coincide with the casing recommendations) you should retain your company's branding. So, you would not reduce IBM in a namespace to `Ibm`, nor would you reduce NeXT in a namespace to `Next`.

❑ *Do* use nouns and noun phrases when naming your classes and namespaces. This is highly recommended and preferred over using verbs. For example, use `Parser` as a namespace or class name, rather than `Parse` or `Parsing`. Verbs should be used for method names only.

❑ Do *not* use Hungarian notation when naming things. For example, in classic VB, controls were often given names like `btnConfirm`, which would immediately tell the reader that it was a button. Microsoft's style guidelines are now recommending that people do not prefix their variable names with anything related to that variable's data type. Microsoft feels that the development tools (specifically VS .NET) should provide information pertaining to a given member's data type by such means as intelligent hovering pop-up dialogs. A better purpose for a variable name is to describe its use rather than its data type. Interestingly enough, Microsoft *does* recommend the usage of Hungarian notation prefixes on static member names.

There are a lot of code conventions to remember, and for some people it is a radical switch in development style. The important thing is to have guidelines, even if they are different from those given here. If two programmers agree to follow guidelines, then there is a very good chance that they will produce code that looks similar and is just as easy to read. You can find all the information you need on Microsoft's recommended design, naming, and coding convention guidelines in the MSDN documentation that comes with the .NET Framework SDK. Some topic names to look up include:

❑ Parameter naming guidelines

❑ Property naming guidelines

❑ Event usage guidelines

❑ Method usage guidelines

❑ Field usage guidelines

❑ Static field naming guidelines

It's a good idea to follow the Microsoft guidelines wherever possible. Microsoft code samples all follow these guidelines, including those in the .NET documentation. Writing code using this style will make it easier to read other code in that style.

Namespace Hierarchy

If you haven't worked on large projects with .NET, designing the **namespace** hierarchy may seem alien. Namespaces in .NET are logical containers for classes, enumerations, and so on. One namespace can span multiple assemblies and modules.

An assembly is essentially a container for .NET components. Multiple .NET components can reside in a single assembly. To keep things familiar and to provide easier backwards compatibility, typical assemblies retain the familiar DLL extension.

Modules are collections of components that can be compiled outside an assembly and then merged into an assembly later. For the most part (especially if you're using Visual Studio .NET) you will be working in a model that only has one module per assembly.

Namespaces are conceptually similar to folders. One useful purpose of folders is to distinguish between two files of the same name – two classes with the same name can be distinguished by their namespace. For example, if we have a class named `Car`, and some other vendor has a class named `Car`, we can distinguish our car from theirs by using a different namespace.

However, folders are also useful because they enable us to organize our files. Namespaces allow us to organize our classes in a logical, memorable way. If all of the developers on the team know the namespace hierarchy, and the namespace hierarchy is logical and consistent, then any developer sitting down to start working on the application should have no trouble finding any code they need to get their job done. A well-organized namespace hierarchy can be a massive help towards building an application that is easy to maintain and enhance.

Now that we've determined that a well-organized namespace hierarchy is essential to any good core foundation design, let's design the namespace hierarchy for ThePhile.com.

Before we actually try to draw out the tree structure, we'll identify the primary areas of our website's functionality. These areas should give us an idea of what kind of namespaces we will need, and from there we can organize them into a tree and further subdivide them if needed. One thing to be aware of when building a namespace hierarchy is that it is very easy to go overboard. Detailing namespaces down to too fine a degree of granularity will actually hinder the development process rather than enhance it. It is best to find a middle ground where there is enough categorization to make sense, but not so much that it confuses the programmers.

The areas of functionality are listed below in no particular order:

❑ Email newsletter

❑ News and content system

❑ Opinion polls (voting)

❑ Forums

❑ Users and security (accounting)

❑ Advertising

❑ Web site basics (homepage, navigation, headers, footers, etc.)

❑ Administration (uploading changes to files)

Microsoft recommends that the namespace hierarchy strategy should always begin with the company name. In our case, the company name is "Wrox", so we're going to make sure that `Wrox` is our root namespace. Then, the second recommendation is that immediately beneath the company name should be the application (or technology) name. In our case, our application is called "The Phile", so we'll have another namespace underneath `Wrox` called `ThePhile`. Note that we're keeping in line with our naming convention rules and using Pascal casing and no underscores.

As we mentioned in the requirements listing, our design must allow us to separate the core functionality of the website (for example the core server controls, navigation, and pages) from the extra modules that we are building into it (forums, advertising, etc.). This way, we can logically separate each individual module from the core of the website, creating a plug-in feel for the other modules.

In order to do this, we'll create another namespace for all of the additional modules being developed for this application throughout this book. We're going to call this namespace WebModules. We are trying to make sure that everything we do conforms to the standards and casing conventions we came up with earlier. This namespace will be underneath the main root of Wrox.

If we take the above list of features and turn them into namespace names by following our naming convention, we get the following namespaces:

- ❑ MailingLists
- ❑ NewsManager
- ❑ Polls
- ❑ Forums
- ❑ Accounts
- ❑ AdsManager
- ❑ FileManager

So underneath our root namespace we have the namespace WebModules, beneath which we will have a namespace for each web module. Within each of these we will have a namespace called Web for our website skeleton. This namespace will hold each of the code-behind classes. Each of the Web namespaces can have a child namespace called Controls that will hold all of the user or server controls for that module. The Wrox.ThePhile namespace is structured in a similar way to an individual web module. There's room for expansion here, too – if we decide to make room for webservices, we can add another child namespace to the Web namespace and call it Services. It could hold all the code-behind classes for the web services functionality for a given module.

Now that we've decided on the names, and we have some idea of where we want everything to flow, let's take a look at the diagram that our website designers came up with for the namespace hierarchy:

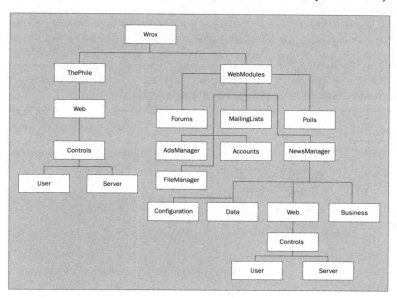

This diagram only fully expands the namespace for the `NewsManager` *module, but other modules will have a similar structure.*

The fact that we have three namespaces under each module looking very much like a standard three-tier architecture (with a presentation, business services tier, and data services tier) is far from coincidence. We also have the `Configuration` namespace, which we can use to logically contain any code that is required for the configuration of that particular module.

Having this hierarchy laid out early in the development can help with documenting and planning the project. For example, we can use the namespace hierarchy as a to-do list of things to design, implement, and document.

The modules we're building in this book are designed to be easily reusable so they can be plugged into other websites with little or no work and hassle, which will become more evident as we look into each module throughout this book. That is the main reason why the additional modules have been separated into their own namespaces, so they have no direct requirement of belonging to any given website.

Microsoft provides a few guidelines for building a namespace hierarchy. Their general format is `Company.Technology.Product`. *Therefore, you might see a namespace like* `Microsoft.Office.Word` *at some point in the future.*

Programming Language

One of the things we need to decide early in our design phase is which programming language to use. With the CLR and .NET, the choice of programming language has become one of personal preference rather than necessity. With certain exceptions, most languages running under the CLR will perform similarly, so the choice is less driven by performance requirements than in previous legacy projects.

In our case, both of the programmers thoroughly enjoy the C# language, and we've decided to use that as the only language for the project development. In a real-world environment, however, it is entirely possible that a project team might choose to use both VB.NET and C#, with the language choice left up to each individual programmer. Most of the components should cooperate just fine even if their main language is different.

There will be exceptions to this, if components make use of language features that are not supported by the CLR, or CLR features not supported by the language. For example, VB.NET does not have support for operator overloading, while it's an almost natural process in C#.

Folder Structure

Just like a poorly organized namespace hierarchy, or a poorly defined set of coding standards, a poorly organized folder structure can hinder the maintainability of the application.

The easiest thing to do is take the namespace hierarchy diagram that we produced for the previous step and simply convert it into a tree of directories, making allowances for a few things like directories for images, stylesheets, XSLT files, and such like.

The following directory structure is the result of converting the namespace hierarchy into a directory:

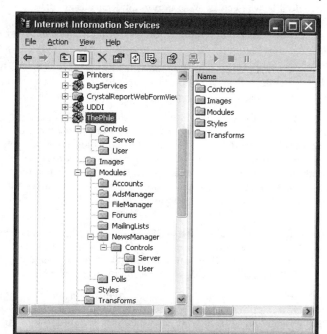

This doesn't include all of the repetitive subdirectories (Controls and Services) for each of the solutions we'll be building for the website. Only the NewsManager directory appears in full.

If you've worked with Visual Studio .NET for creating an ASP.NET application, you will know that any time you create a web form, the code-behind class is created in the same directory as that form. This will be the case for our solution too (at least in the version we distribute with source code). As you can tell, the ThePhile directory is the main application root. Below that, we have a directory that will house the code and .ascx files for our server and user controls. Also, there is a generic Images directory that is, obviously, designed to house our graphics. Each of the modules we will be developing throughout the rest of this book will be primarily contained in its own subdirectory in the Modules directory. There is a Styles directory that will contain any stylesheets we use, and a Transforms directory for our XSLT files.

Designing the Database

When we come to design the core components of the website, we will look at database design – the tables and relationships that we need to model. Each new module will lead to different demands, so new tables and relationships will be added as the site progresses.

At this stage we need to make the decisions that will leave us with an appropriately constructed empty database. Before we can do this, we need to make important decisions about:

❑ Hardware – typically this covers the machine and what kind of hardware it sports, such as RAID hardware, hot-swappable drives, and multiple processors.

❑ Network topology – this covers considerations such as firewalls, security, backbone bandwidth, and speed (for example, will your middle tier encounter bandwidth bottlenecks in trying to reach your RDBMS?), and isolation to prevent various forms of network attacks and intrusions.

❑ Database size and growth rate – this is one area that is typically managed by the database administrator (DBA), but we aren't all fortunate enough to have a DBA around to do this for us. If you are warehousing data then you need to consider extreme growth rates in your data, whereas if you're serving up a fixed product catalog and not much else, you don't need to be too worried about database growth and size. In the past this was a huge concern, but in these modern days where we can simply drop another massive hard drive into a logical partition, it is becoming less and less of a concern in terms of space. However, there are performance concerns with data growth that we won't go into here.

❑ Disaster recovery – every good database needs a backup. There needs to be some kind of plan in place that will allow for failures in the system so we can restore data to a previous good state. This can be done with full or differential backups, redundant storage, and other options that might be RDBMS-specific, such as clustering or managing mirrored tables.

❑ Database quantity – one decision that often gets overlooked in the design phase is whether or not everything you're going to need will be in the same physical database. With many modern RDBMSs like Oracle and SQL Server, each database is handled by a different running process (often referred to as an *instance* of the database), offering a potentially very large performance benefit if your web application needs access to two different stores of data, but not necessarily at the same time (for example, when you don't need to join data from one source to the other).

❑ Security – one thing you definitely don't want is people having unauthorized access to your system. Even if your database is safely tucked away behind a firewall, there are still ways of hijacking trusted resources on the other side that can 'spoof' their way into your database. A good way of preventing this kind of thing is by securing your database. For example, one *really* good idea might be to change the default password of the system administrator accounts for your RDBMS (such as 'sa' for MS SQL Server).

Now that we've looked at some database creation issues, we'll go over what we did for our particular application. It is important that third-party hosting companies and home-office Windows 2000 Professional machines can host ThePhile. This makes MS SQL Server an obvious choice.

All we need to do is create a database called ThePhile with all of the default options (meaning that it will automatically grow and automatically truncate the log file when necessary). Later on, as we develop the individual modules of the application, we'll start creating data structures in the database.

ThePhile.com uses a single database for the whole site, rather than a different one for each module. This is because third party application hosts usually provide their customers with only a single database. We'll design our application modules so that they can easily be configured to run on their own separate databases if those resources are available, however.

> In order to install and run the application we'll be developing throughout this book, you'll need to have at least an evaluation copy of SQL Server 7 or SQL Server 2000 installed on your machine. These are available from the Microsoft website.

Building the Data Services Tier

In many applications, programmers will often have a single tier between the presentation logic and the actual back-end database. They tend to lump both business logic and data access into the same logical tier. This will work, but it's usually a bad idea. It's better to separate the code that enforces business rules and performs multi-step business processes from the database access code. This leaves us with a data services tier, giving many benefits, including:

❑ Scalability – using a data services tier can make an application far more scalable. Even if the data services tier isn't hosted in COM+ or MTS, there is still a large added benefit. Let's say we have a data services component that obtains inventory information by simply querying the database. Because our business logic is separate from the data component, we can upgrade the data component to use a stored procedure without changing any of the business code. Now assume we want to upgrade it even further by adding in the summary of transactions stored in an MSMQ queue; again all we need to do is place the new code into the data services component and drop it in. The user interface and the business rules are still the same and require no changes. Distinctly separating your code across tiers also allows you to scale the solution by adding more hardware to handle increased demand without having to modify existing code.

❑ Availability – separating the data services from the business services can help an application to be more fault-tolerant, and so more available to clients. By distinguishing separate units of business and data logic and placing them in separate components, you further separate your application from the classic "monolithic" application model (which can tear everything down even if only a small problem occurs in a small subsystem). If a portion of your application breaks using an n-tier architecture, you will be able to isolate, identify, and replace the defective component far more easily and with less disruption than if you had been working with a monolithic application.

❑ Maintainability – as we mentioned when we talked about scalability, if you need to make a change to your data back end, all you need do is make the change to the data services tier components that are affected and you're all set. If coded properly, the business tier and presentation tiers should be entirely unaffected by this change. For example, if you suddenly decided that your user information needed to come from an Oracle database, while your purchase history information needed to come from a DB2 database on a Unix mainframe, you could easily make the changes to the data services components and not have to worry about crashing the rest of your application. Another benefit in terms of development is the fact that the data source is literally plug-and-play. You can, for instance, make a minor configuration change and move a test application to a production database, or a production application to a test database, without significant impact to the overall application.

❏ Performance – in classic ASP, three tiers was almost a requirement because of the limitations of VBScript in the presentation tier (such as not being able to early bind to COM objects). With .NET there really is no performance benefit from splitting into the third tier, unless we're using COM+. Hosting business and/or data services components with COM+ allows us to pool our objects and take advantage of services like just-in-time (JIT) activation and object pooling. COM+ and related concepts are a little out of scope for this book, as our simple content application is just going to use standard components.

In the following sections we will look at creating a single base class for every object in a given tier. What this essentially means is that every data access object will inherit from a common data access object. In addition, every business class will inherit from a common business class. Typically, when designing a data services tier, there are two main ideas people adopt: building a single helper class which performs all data access on behalf of all components in the data tier, or building a data object for every type of entity that needs access to the database. For our purposes, we're going to go with the latter method. An entire book could be written about all of the different arguments people have both for and against each of these methods.

This technique further enhances scalability and maintainability. For example, if we want to change where every single data services component obtains its connection string, we just make a single change to the base class for the data services tier.

For more information on the benefits of creating base classes for related or similar groups of classes, consult a good object-oriented programming manual. There are many examples of these, including *Object-Oriented Analysis and Design with Applications* by Grady Booch (ISBN 0-805353-40-2).

We will look at creating the base class for our data services tier in the *Solution* section of this chapter.

Building the Business Services Tier

The business services tier provides a layer of abstraction that rests atop the low-level components that comprise the data services tier. It is often hard to see the purpose in splitting the business logic from the data services tier. But once it's done, the benefits are massive. Keep in mind that we are talking about layers of abstraction, not actual physical layers or separations between components and component tiers.

We've already discussed maintainability as one of the benefits of this split. If the business rules and business logic rests in a layer above the data services, then the underlying data access mechanisms, code, and even server or server location can all change without breaking any of the code in the business services tier. As we mentioned earlier, this ability often produces the useful side effect of being able to 'switch' an application from a live data source to a debug or test data source with little or no visible consequence to the application itself.

The other main benefit is for modeling of business processes and rules. By separating your data access from your business tier, your designers can devote their full attention to determining how the application should function with the business rules in place. They won't need to concern themselves with whether or not a given field in a database table is a short or a long integer.

The bonus is in the modeling and design. The presentation tier is modeled to be close to what the user expects to see, for example, we have a class for each page the user can see. The data services tier often ends up producing a close ratio of components to tables. The business services tier generally produces something in the middle, modeling processes, rules, and logical abstractions rather than data-dependent components.

This diagram is a typical example of the dispersal of components across a three-tier model. It shows the difference in design patterns used in developing classes, or components, for each of the tiers:

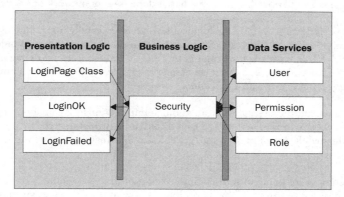

As we can see from the above example, a sample user might hit the login page for a simple web application. From there, an instance of the LoginPage class might invoke the Authenticate method in the business class for a particular username and password combination. The Security class is a model for the business processes relating to security. It first requests that an instance of the data services class User validate that a given user exists with that username and password combination. Again, keep in mind that if we changed where and how we were storing user information, all we'd have to do is change our User component, leaving the business and presentation tiers unharmed. Then, assuming we have a fairly robust security scheme, the Security class instance checks to see what roles that user belongs to, and whether any of those roles has been given permission to log in.

From all this, the key point is that the presentation logic is modeled to be very close to what the user sees and interacts with; the business tier is modeled around business processes and rules; and the data services tier is modeled around finite sets of data.

Even with these benefits, it might seem tedious to take on this extra work when modeling simple processes. However, applications grow – sometimes into things we never intended (this is typically where marketing and sales get involved). With a solid architecture, we have the room to scale our application with the demand of our customers, consumers, and even our sales department!

We are building our application in a number of modules. Each module will have its own presentation, business, and data tiers. This way we can drop a complete module into other web applications. Each chapter that deals with a specific module will cover the classes for that module.

Error Handling and Fault Tolerance

If we have been following good software development practices, then our code has received extensive testing before we release it to the public or to production. Typically, each individual component receives unit testing that is outlined in the project plan, and then each component is integration-tested in the larger application as a whole. However, no matter how good our testing plans are, we can't account for all possible unexpected occurrences. We can't program to expect hardware failures or other failures caused by effects that weren't part of our testing lab scenario. In these cases, we rely on the last resort: **exception handling**.

Many websites do not handle exceptions well. This results in users seeing low-level error messages, including the line number within the ASP page that caused the exception. This kind of thing is highly unprofessional, and any time you see it, you know that someone hasn't done their homework or enough testing.

If something unexpected happens, then the application should gracefully inform the user. It might also give them a phone number or e-mail address to send information about the problem. Windows XP, Office XP, and Visual Studio .NET all have a feature built in that allows users to transmit debug information directly to Microsoft. While we can't all aspire to this level of fault tolerance, we should take a hint from this and strive for the best we can get out of our web application.

When an error does occur, the site should store as much information as it can about the error and inform the user that something went wrong. This way the user is told politely that an error occurred, without seeing any technical detail. Meanwhile, the administrators get detailed information that helps to track down and repair the failure.

In the *Solution* section we're going to start coding. As part of that, we will look at what kind of information we can store and how we can store it. We'll also look at how to provide an environment where programmers can track down bugs, even in a live system that can't be brought down for debugging.

Deployment and Maintenance

You might be wondering why you need to consider deployment at the design stage. Isn't deploying the application done after you've completed all of the code? Well, yes and no. The physical deployment of the application does indeed take place when an iteration of the development phase has completed.

However, the choice of development design can radically impact the options available when building the application itself. There are many things to consider when designing your deployment strategy, such as the target platform, hardware requirements, software prerequisites (such as requiring the .NET Framework or XML v3.0 on the destination machine), network deployment, and much, much more. We won't cover all the possible things you can consider when designing a deployment strategy here, as that could fill a book of its own.

For our deployment design, we decided to keep it as simple as possible. We are going to allow our application to be deployed via the Windows Installer to a programmer's machine. In addition, you can use XCopy deployment and some supplied database scripts to deploy the system to a third party hosting company. We'll discuss all this and actually show you the solution to our deployment design at the end of the book, in Chapter 11, once we've developed all of the modules.

User Interface Design

We won't go into too much detail here, as we're just building the non-visible core foundation of code for this chapter. However, in the next chapter we'll take a look at some in-depth design of user interface elements and we'll cover some ideas for designing reusable interface controls. For now, it's sufficient to include in our design the requirement that our user interface should be professional and easy to navigate, but not so professional that our site looks like an accounting application.

The Solution

Now that the foundation has been designed, we can start writing some code. To recap, a few of the things that we covered in our design were:

❑ Naming and coding guidelines – we set out the conventions to be used throughout the project

❑ Programming language choice – we chose C# as our development language

❑ Folder structure – we designed a namespace hierarchy and a corresponding folder structure for all the modules of the website

❑ Designing the database – we chose SQL Server as our core database

❑ Building the data services tier and the business services tier – we talked about the importance of n-tier design and architecture, and about the usefulness of creating a base class for each tier

This next section will cover the code and implementation of each tier's base class, as well as a custom exception class that we're going to build.

Of course, the implementation we create here might have unforeseen limitations that we will discover later. We might find ourselves changing these classes throughout the development. At this point, we have to continue with what we already know, and build what's best at this point.

To create the solution for this chapter, we're going to create a new C# Class Library project in Visual Studio .NET, and name it Core. We're going to make some minor changes to its properties and to the AssemblyInfo.cs file. Right-click the project and choose **Properties**. Then make sure that the **Assembly Name** property is set to Wrox.WebModules.Core, and the **Default Namespace** property is set to Wrox.WebModules.

The next thing we need to do is make sure that our project is **strong-named**. Since this is the first project in the entire web application, we get to make our **SNK file**. The SNK file is a file that contains a digital signature encrypted using the RSA algorithm. In order to make sure that all of our assemblies appear as though they're coming from the same vendor, they all need to have the same **public key**. The only way to accomplish this is to compile each of the assemblies against the same SNK file.

To create our digital signature file, we go to the command prompt and type:

SN –k ThePhile.SNK

> Note that you won't be able to use **SN** from any directory unless you've launched the Visual Studio .NET command prompt, which pre-configures your path statement to allow you access to all of the useful .NET command-line tools.

The above command creates a new digital signature file. Copy this file to some safe, common location on your hard drive. All of our samples use \Wrox\Keys\ThePhile.SNK as the location. This way we don't have to worry about the drive letter, only that the file is in the \Wrox\Keys directory on the same physical drive as the project.

We can now modify our `AssemblyInfo.cs` file to include a full version number and a reference to the digital signature file, which is required in order to create a strongly named assembly. `AssemblyInfo.cs` should contain the following (the comments have been removed to save space, but otherwise this is the complete file):

```
[assembly: AssemblyTitle("ThePhile.COM Core")]
[assembly: AssemblyDescription("Foundation Code for ThePhile.COM")]
[assembly: AssemblyConfiguration("")]
[assembly: AssemblyCompany("Wrox Press Ltd")]
[assembly: AssemblyProduct("ThePhile.COM")]
[assembly: AssemblyCopyright("(C) 2001 Wrox Press Ltd")]
[assembly: AssemblyTrademark("")]
[assembly: AssemblyCulture("")]
[assembly: AssemblyVersion("1.0.0.0")]
[assembly: AssemblyDelaySign(false)]
[assembly: AssemblyKeyFile(@"\Wrox\Keys\ThePhile.snk")]
[assembly: AssemblyKeyName("")]
```

As well as the usual description and a title, there is an entry for company, product, and copyright. This is all just additional information that can be useful, but non-essential. The key components of the strong name are `Culture`, `Version`, and `KeyFile`. Our assembly isn't language-specific, so we've left the culture blank. An assembly built for the "en-us" culture is *not* considered the same as an identically versioned assembly built for the "en-uk" culture. These two assemblies would have different strong names, and components that reference the assemblies will be able to tell the difference between the two.

Each of the next three classes we're going to cover will be in the `Wrox.WebModules.Core.DLL` assembly that we just set up.

The DbObject Class

The first set of code we're going to produce is a base class for the data services tier. We've already explored the benefits of using a base class – it enables us to rapidly and easily change an aspect of behavior that is common to all data services classes, without having to change the code in every single class.

For our class we are going to provide a couple of support functions, as well as automatic instantiation and configuration of the `SqlConnection` object. One of the things we have already mentioned in our design is a preference for not using in-line SQL, and using stored procedures instead. In addition to speed improvements, the use of stored procedures allows us to make changes to the SQL and low-level data access code without having to modify any classes in our core component library. In a situation where in-line SQL queries are not being used, it becomes apparent that there are two activities that most data services classes will need to do:

❑   Execute a stored procedure and obtain a number – for inserting, updating, or deleting records. The number usually represents the number of records modified.

❑   Execute a stored procedure and obtain a `SqlDataReader` – for selecting records. This kind of stored procedure is typically executed with the `ExecuteReader` method of a `SqlCommand` instance. We're going to use a `SqlDataReader` for our core functions because our data needs are simple. We'll never be returning more than one related table from any given method, so we can make do with the faster, leaner `DataReader` object.

To create this class, remove the default one created with the Class Library project, and add a new one called `DbObject`. Let's take a look at the code for our `DbObject` base class. Inline comments have been removed to save space. We start by declaring it as an abstract class, which means that this class can act as a basis for other classes, but that we cannot instantiate it:

```
using System;
using System.Data;
using System.Data.SqlClient;

namespace Wrox.WebModules.Data
{
    public abstract class DbObject
    {
```

In the code below, we create two member variables. The first is to hold our SQL connection. It is protected, which means that only those classes deriving from this class can access this variable. If a class inherits from this one, it may provide a method that requires the `Connection`. The connection string is completely hidden from child classes, preventing them from too closely relying on any given underlying implementation:

```
        protected SqlConnection Connection;
        private string connectionString;
```

Next we see our constructor. This constructor takes a connection string and instantiates a new connection based on that string. We don't open the connection at this point. Leaving a connection open for longer than required for the operation is wasteful and could slow down the application:

```
        public DbObject( string newConnectionString )
        {
            connectionString = newConnectionString;
            Connection = new SqlConnection( connectionString );
        }

        /// <summary>
        /// Protected property that exposes the connection string
        /// to inheriting classes. Read-Only.
        /// </summary>
        protected string ConnectionString
        {
            get
            {
                return connectionString;
            }
        }
```

This next routine, `BuildIntCommand`, automates the instantiation of a `SqlCommand` object. It does this by taking the name of the stored procedure and an array of `IDataParameter` objects. From there, it builds a SQL command using those parameters. Then, once those parameters have been added, it creates a new parameter to store the numeric return value of the stored procedure. The method returns the new command after it has been built:

```
private SqlCommand BuildIntCommand(string storedProcName,
                                  IDataParameter[] parameters)
{
  SqlCommand command = BuildQueryCommand( storedProcName, parameters );

  command.Parameters.Add( new SqlParameter ( "ReturnValue",
      SqlDbType.Int, 4, /* Size */
      ParameterDirection.ReturnValue, false, /* is nullable */
      0, /* byte precision */
      0, /* byte scale */
      string.Empty, DataRowVersion.Default, null ));

  return command;
}
```

The above method calls `BuildQueryCommand` to create a new SQL command object. This new command will typically be used for returning the results of SELECT statements in stored procedures to either a `DataSet` or a `DataReader`. The following is the listing for the `BuildQueryCommand` method:

```
private SqlCommand BuildQueryCommand(string storedProcName,
                                    IDataParameter[] parameters)
{
  SqlCommand command =
      new SqlCommand( storedProcName, Connection );
  command.CommandType = CommandType.StoredProcedure;

  foreach (SqlParameter parameter in parameters)
  {
    command.Parameters.Add( parameter );
  }

  return command;
}
```

The method below, `RunProcedure`, takes as arguments the name of the stored procedure to execute, an array of parameters, and an out integer parameter. The out parameter will contain the number of rows affected by the stored procedure after the method completes. This method helps execute Insert, Update, or Delete queries, and returns a numeric condition code that indicates success or some degree of failure. This method does not interpret these codes, so the class inheriting from DbObject can use any enumerations for its status codes and not interfere with any other classes. Calling `BuildIntCommand` will enable us to do this, as we've just seen. Then, the `ExecuteNonQuery` method is invoked, which returns the number of rows affected by the stored procedure. Finally, the method returns the value in the `ReturnValue` parameter (we saw that this parameter is added automatically by the `BuildIntCommand` method).

```
protected int RunProcedure(string storedProcName,
                           IDataParameter[] parameters,
                           out int rowsAffected )
{
  int result;
```

```
         Connection.Open();
         SqlCommand command = BuildIntCommand( storedProcName, parameters );
         rowsAffected = command.ExecuteNonQuery();
         result = (int)command.Parameters["ReturnValue"].Value;
         Connection.Close();

         return result;
      }
```

The next code snippet contains an overload of the RunProcedure method. This overload is responsible for creating a SQL command (using BuildQueryCommand), executing it, and placing the results of the executed stored procedure into a SqlDataReader. This method will be called by inheriting classes that need fast, high-performance, forward-only access to data:

```
      protected SqlDataReader RunProcedure(string storedProcName,
                                           IDataParameter[] parameters )
      {
         SqlDataReader returnReader;

         Connection.Open();
         SqlCommand command = BuildQueryCommand( storedProcName, parameters );
         command.CommandType = CommandType.StoredProcedure;

         returnReader = command.ExecuteReader( CommandBehavior.CloseConnection );
         return returnReader;
      }
```

The next overload of the RunProcedure method (shown below) takes the usual arguments of the name of the stored procedure and the IDataParameter array. However, this one also takes the name of a table as an argument. This method runs the stored procedure, obtains the result set, and then stores that result set in a newly instantiated DataSet, in a table with the name indicated by the tableName parameter. A DataSet provides a read-write cache of data in a database, useful for more complex data manipulation. Here is the code:

```
      protected DataSet RunProcedure(string storedProcName,
                                     IDataParameter[] parameters,
                                     string tableName )
      {
        DataSet dataSet = new DataSet();
        Connection.Open();
        SqlDataAdapter sqlDA = new SqlDataAdapter();
        sqlDA.SelectCommand = BuildQueryCommand( storedProcName, parameters );
        sqlDA.Fill( dataSet, tableName );
        Connection.Close();
        return dataSet;
      }
```

The fourth and final RunProcedure overload (shown on the following page) is very similar. However, in this case the code assumes that the DataSet has already been created, and simply adds the result set to a table within the previously existing DataSet. This allows for incredible flexibility, because an object can fill one table from one source and another table from another source. Relationships between the different sources can then be established using the DataSet object's Relations collection. Here is the code:

```
protected void RunProcedure(string storedProcName,
                            IDataParameter[] parameters,
                            DataSet dataSet,
                            string tableName )
{
  Connection.Open();
  SqlDataAdapter sqlDA = new SqlDataAdapter();
  sqlDA.SelectCommand = BuildIntCommand( storedProcName, parameters );
  sqlDA.Fill( dataSet, tableName );
  Connection.Close ();
}
}
}
```

So that's the code for our DbObject abstract base class. One thing you might have noticed is that for our data services base class we didn't do anything with MTS or COM+. This was intentional. One of the design goals of ThePhile.com is to make it easy to deploy the site onto one of the many third party hosting services that offer .NET and SQL Server support. If the site depended on COM+ services it would be harder to deploy on those systems. Most third party .NET hosting companies don't provide any ability to access COM+, so we decided to not implement it in our solution in order to keep things simple. However, in your own solution you might want to upgrade to a COM+ solution to gain object pooling, JIT activation, and transaction support.

If we did want to convert this base class from what we have now into a ServicedComponent class (the base class for COM+/MTS components), it wouldn't take much effort. The next section will look at how we would do that.

Converting to a ServicedComponent

To convert our base class to a COM+/MTS ServicedComponent, we would take the following steps:

- ❏ Change the class to inherit from ServicedComponent (found in System.EnterpriseServices)
- ❏ Implement the following methods: Construct, Activate, Deactivate
- ❏ Remove all code from the standard constructor (DbObject())

Let's look at the shell of a COM+ base class called ServicedDbObject that inherits from ServicedComponent:

```
using System;
using System.Data;
using System.Data.SqlClient;
using System.EnterpriseServices;

namespace Wrox.WebModules.Data
{
  public abstract class ServicedDbObject : ServicedComponent
  {
    protected SqlConnection Connection;
    private string connectionString;
```

```
    protected string ConnectionString
    {
      get
      {
        return connectionString;
      }
    }

    // place all of the helper methods from DbObject here.
```

At this point in the code, we can simply copy and paste the helper methods from the DbObject class into this class, and everything will still work. You can see below that rather than using the constructor to obtain the connection string, we're using a COM+ concept called **object construction**. Essentially, this just means that when an object is instantiated by COM+, it can be given a string construction argument. In our case, this string will be the connection string. We'll see how we can use this shortly:

```
    protected override void Construct( string constructString )
    {
      connectionString = constructString;
    }

    protected override void Activate()
    {
      Connection = new SqlConnection( connectionString );
    }

    protected override void Deactivate()
    {
      Connection = null;
    }
  }
}
```

So, the only other difference between the two classes is that classes inheriting from ServicedDbObject need a couple of extra code attributes in order to function properly. Let's take a look at just the very top of a class definition that inherits from ServicedDbObject:

```
namespace Wrox.WebModules.ServicedSample
{
  using System;
  using System.EnterpriseServices;
  using System.Data;
  using System.Data.SqlClient;
  using System.Data.SqlTypes;

  [Transaction( TransactionOption.Supported )]
  [ConstructionEnabled( Default = "Data Source=localhost; Initial
                       Catalog=ThePhile; User id=ThePhile;
                       Password=philer1;")]
  sealed public class SampleCOMPlusObject : ServicedDbObject
  {
```

The `ConstructionEnabled` attribute is essential for the `ServicedDbObject` to be able to configure its connection. The `Transaction` attribute is used to indicate what level of transactional support the particular component wants or needs. We won't need to worry about these attributes for the rest of the code in the book, however. We could spend another chapter or so going into all of the other considerations when programming for COM+ or MTS, but that's beyond the scope of this book. The rest of this book will use `DbObject`. If you feel comfortable with your COM+ skills, you can simply change your own copy of the code to use `ServicedDbObject` and supply the appropriate attributes.

The BizObject Class

Right now, we're not sure what kind of common functionality we want to supply to the business services tier, so we're essentially just going to create an empty shell of a base class, called `BizObject`. It is pretty straightforward at this point. This base class is, of course, abstract and public, allowing any class from any assembly to inherit from it.

If we were worried about others potentially abusing our code, then we could place code attributes into our code that would restrict inheritance of this class to only those assemblies that have a certain public key, and so come from a specific vendor. This would restrict inheritance of our unsealed classes to classes we write ourselves. Techniques like this are covered in other books such as *Professional .NET Framework* (ISBN 1-861005-56-3) and *Professional ADO.NET* (ISBN 1-861005-27-X).

Here's the code for the `BizObject` class:

```
using System;

namespace Wrox.WebModules.Business
{
  /// <summary>
  /// The class from which all classes in the business tier inherit.
  /// </summary>
  public class BizObject
  {
    public BizObject()
    {   }
  }
}
```

The AppException Class

Many times, in many different programming languages, error-handling routines have become enormous, cumbersome, and difficult to maintain. Even in modern languages that support the throwing of exceptions, one problem remains: how do we make sure that there is a persistent record of every exception the system throws? This is an absolute necessity for a website on the Internet where the users may not see the problem (it could be something internal that causes subtle failures, such as rounding problems or bad numbers). Even if the user sees the problem, most will either log off the website angry, or hit the back button and move on to some other feature of the website. We cannot rely on users to detect our errors.

To get around this, we will create our own custom derivative of `System.ApplicationException`. This custom exception class will place an entry in the NT/2000 Application Event Log every single time an exception is thrown. This way, the website administrator and the programmers can find out the details and time of every error that occurs.

Let's take a look at the code for our custom exception class, `AppException`:

```
using System;
using System.Diagnostics;

namespace Wrox.WebModules
{
  /// <summary>
  /// Default exception to be thrown by the website, it will
  /// automatically log the contents of the exception to the
  /// Windows NT/2000 Application Event Log.
  /// </summary>
  public class AppException: System.ApplicationException
  {
    public AppException()
    {
      LogEvent("An unexpected error occurred.");
    }

    public AppException(string message)
    {
      LogEvent(message);
    }
```

In this next overload of the constructor, if an inner (or nested) exception is passed to this exception (this is often called "bubbling", where exceptions throw exceptions with themselves as the inner exception, allowing the exception to "bubble" all the way up to an outer error-handler) then the function will actually log the message of the inner exception as well as the main exception:

```
    public AppException(string message, Exception innerException)
    {
      LogEvent(message);

      if (innerException != null)
      {
        LogEvent(innerException.Message);
      }
    }
```

This next method is the one that actually logs the information to the event log. If there is no event log source called `ThePhile.com` then it will create one. After that, it will proceed to write the exception information to the event log with an entry type of "Error", which appears as a red exclamation point in the Event Viewer on NT/2000/XP.

If you intend to deploy your own version of this code to a web hosting company, you might not have enough permission or access to write directly to the event logs. In this case, you might want to consider rewriting this method to log to a text file somewhere in your private storage area.

```
   private void LogEvent(string message)
   {
      if (!EventLog.SourceExists("ThePhile.COM"))
      {
         EventLog.CreateEventSource("ThePhile.COM", "Application");
      }

      EventLog.WriteEntry("ThePhile.COM", message,
                           EventLogEntryType.Error);
   }
}
}
```

This custom exception is useful in many respects. The first and foremost is that it allows us to log as an event every exception thrown using this class. The other is that it allows other code throughout our application to derive its own custom exceptions from this class – allowing the other modules to inherit the ability to automatically use the event log, as well as perform other custom tasks that those modules might need.

Summary

This chapter has introduced the problem of coming up with the core of the website. After creating an initial design for the website, we went on to create a design for the foundation of our website. This included designing a namespace layout, a preliminary directory tree, and even specifying some coding standards and naming conventions. Then we discussed some of the core concepts of building a data services tier and a business logic tier, and the benefits of splitting functionality into three or more tiers. Finally, we discussed the design concept behind robust error handling and why it is so important to the success of a production website.

After designing the solution to our problem, we went ahead and got into the code, producing the assembly `Wrox.WebModules.Core.DLL`, which can be used by all facets of our website as the initial foundation from which much of the rest of our classes will be built. We even included an alternative `DbObject`, the `ServicedDbObject`, in case we want to make some data services components hosted by COM+ services.

Hopefully you've gained some of the following knowledge after reading this chapter:

❑ The benefits of a strong and cohesive namespace hierarchy

❑ The benefits of separating business logic from pure data services

❑ The benefits and details of robust error handling in a web application

You should also now know how to implement systems that have these benefits.

The classes we developed for the core of our solution can be compiled into the Core DLL at this point. However, as all we've done so far is build the core, we won't actually be putting this code to use until the next chapter, where we will be making use of the foundation code to help build our user interface elements.

Foundations for Style and Navigation

3

Now that we have spent some time discussing many of the issues involved in creating a web application, and have begun building our core foundation, we can move on to creating the foundation of our front end, or **user interface** (**UI**). In this chapter we will first identify the initial problem we need to solve relating to our front end. Then we will move on to designing a solution to this problem. Finally, we'll cover the actual code and implementation of this solution.

This chapter will give you a good look at some of the tasks that are typically considered part of the foundation-building, or setup, phase of website development. These include:

- ❑ Identifying and creating reusable interface components
- ❑ The purpose and implementation of a 'page inheritance hierarchy'
- ❑ The purpose, benefits, and implementation of cascading stylesheets
- ❑ Using XML and XSLT to create content that is quick and easy to maintain

The Problem

At some point we will need a front end (user interface) for our website. It would be fairly easy (especially for those programmers who've already spent a lot of time building classic ASP pages) to just open up a favorite editor and start cranking out page after page of content. I'm sure many of us have been in this situation before, which is why many of us remember the pain and suffering involved when we were told to change the layout, the style, or some other fundamental UI feature after we'd already built dozens of ASP pages from scratch. There's nothing worse than having to go back and rewrite ASP pages because of a color change or something else that should be equally trivial.

To avoid this kind of maintenance nightmare we want the UI to be simple to maintain and modify. In order to achieve this we should build the UI on a *solid foundation*. Without a solid foundation for the user interface, changes are incredibly difficult and painstaking to make, and maintenance of the front end can be a laborious task.

We also want it to be a good UI in terms of user experience. Following good usability and user interface design principles is absolutely essential to the success of your website. If the users are annoyed with the display on their screen when they see your site, they won't come back. Likewise, if they find it too difficult to get what they want from your site because it doesn't flow properly, isn't intuitive, or doesn't have clearly labeled functionality, they will also avoid your site like the plague. One thing to always keep in mind is that, no matter how good your site is, you will always have competition on the Internet.

There are many books on the market today that cover topics such as designing your website to meet the needs of your users, including User-Centered Web Design by John Cato (ISBN 0-201398-60-5). Something else you might want to take into consideration are users with accessibility needs who might have difficulty navigating a website that doesn't make certain interfaces explicitly available to them.

The Problem Statement and Requirements

Our problem has two different facets. The first is, of course, to provide a solid, functional foundation on which to build the rest of our user interface. This is actually the problem statement. The other facet, which we cannot ignore, is the requirement that our design for our UI fundamentals should strive toward the following common goals:

- ❑ Achieve maximum ease-of-use through well-planned UI elements and efficient use of web page 'real estate'. Real estate is the available space on a web page in which you can display meaningful information to a user. Examples of poor use of real estate are pages in which important information occurs in such a position as to force the user to scroll down (or off to the side) in order to see it.

- ❑ Provide maximum flexibility by allowing configuration changes of UI elements to take place with minimal or zero recompilation of code.

- ❑ Keeping in mind that a site's look and feel is almost as important as its functionality, we want to make the website attractive and intuitive to our users.

So far we've created a design and initial implementation for our core middle-tier foundation. The problem that we are attempting to solve in this chapter is to build a solid foundation for our front end too. There are several things we can do to make our front end extremely flexible, to avoid maintenance headaches and to improve usability. In this chapter we'll cover some of the fairly simple things we can do early on in our development process to make maintenance and modification of our application easier.

The Design

Now that we've determined that our problem is the lack of a solid UI foundation, we can go about designing the basics of our user interface, or presentation layer. Anyone with any experience of a full software development life cycle knows that no matter how much effort you put into an initial design, it probably won't cover every scenario. This is why many managers opt for the **Unified Process**, a very common and popular iterative process that makes allowances for changes in specification and design in the middle of a development project. Other managers, especially those producing Microsoft-based solutions, prefer the **Microsoft Solutions Framework** (**MSF**).

You can read more about the Unified Process in the book The Unified Software Development Process by Jacobson, Booch, and Rumbaugh (ISBN 0-201571-69-2). In addition, you can find more information about the Microsoft Solutions Framework at http://www.microsoft.com/msf.

While there are management processes that allow us to make room for changes in our design, specification, and requirements throughout the life cycle of our project, there are some things we can do in terms of code and infrastructure to make the development of those changes easier as well. Some of the common things we can do to make our website code more agile are as follows:

- Use cascading stylesheets to 'classify' different types of UI elements, such as headers, footers, tables used for certain purposes, background colors, and font styles.

- Use an object inheritance hierarchy in our component model to encapsulate functionality, properties, and visual traits common to related groups of pages and UI elements.

- Use reusable controls (server and user) in order to encapsulate common or frequently displayed UI elements that may occur on many or all pages, and to provide a code-enforced uniform look and feel.

We mentioned in the Problem section the desire to create an attractive UI. If you build a website that provides amazing functionality, but the interface is dull, drab, and uninspired, then you're probably not going to be as successful as a competitor who provides fewer services with a nicer-looking website. It is a sad, unfortunate fact. The other thing to keep in mind is that the development process is iterative, and you'll probably go through many iterations of your user interface design before any customer ever sees your website, so don't grow too attached to any one particular idea.

Typically, one of the first steps people take when designing the UI of a website is to create mock-ups or samples of what they think the website might look like during a typical user session. Remember, the purpose here is not to provide any functionality, just a foundation on which to build the UI. We did the same thing when we built this website.

Being a programmer who learned HTML using Emacs on a Unix machine, I still prefer to do my HTML design in Notepad, and so the mock-ups we used to create samples of our user interface were done in simple, static HTML designed in Notepad. However, a lot of people prefer using WYSIWYG editors like FrontPage.

The following is a screenshot of one of the sample mockups that were used in building the 'look and feel' of the website. The black and white format doesn't do it justice, but you should be able to gain some useful information from it:

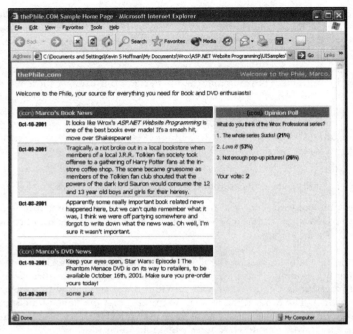

We can see that our page will include various types of content (for example news and opinion polls) and that we'd like to have a welcoming header to make the user feel comfortable with the site. Now that we have some ideas about what we want our website to look like, we can move on to actually working on some of the other issues relating to designing our core navigation and UI for the site.

Cascading Stylesheets

We cannot stress enough the importance of using **cascading stylesheets** (**CSS**). These provide a method by which the site designers can abstract a set of display properties and information. This allows for commonly displayed types of information to inherit certain visual display traits.

For example, if you have a website where you always want to display a product in a table cell, and you want that cell to have a blue background, you could either do it all by hand (and make that cell blue every time you display a product), or you can use a stylesheet. To truly illustrate the benefit of a stylesheet, we will show one in action and then compare it to the 'old' way of doing things. This is, of course, not a chapter intended on teaching you the functionality of stylesheets, so we'll keep the example brief (there is a detailed example of using CSS in the solution section of this chapter). You can judge for yourself which method you'd like to use.

First, here's a fragment of HTML with the display properties embedded:

```
<td style="border:1px; border-style:solid; border-color:#000000;
    border-top:0px; border-left:0px; border-right:0px;"
    bgcolor="#000088">
  <font face="Arial,Helvetica" size="2" color="#ffffff">
  <b><i>This is a Product</b></i>
</td>
```

Looks pretty ugly, doesn't it? Now imagine having to type that in every single time you want to display a product, *anywhere* on your website. Even worse, think about what you'd have to do if your boss came by and said "Actually, how about using a yellow background for all the product names?"

Let's now look at a section of HTML that makes use of a class defined in a stylesheet. All the graphical and display properties that belong to the `Product_Cell` class are stored somewhere else (typically in a `.css` file).

```
<td class="Product_Cell">
    This is a Product
</td>
```

The CSS file contains a definition for the `Product_Cell` style, so we don't have to repeat the details every time we want to use this style, and changes to the style properties need only be made once. Seems pretty straightforward, doesn't it?

So, in order to design our stylesheets, what we need to do is attempt to produce a list of common display types, or classes, that we know we're going to be displaying. We can implement the code for the stylesheet during our actual development phase. The nice thing about the stylesheet functionality is that it's easy to go back later and add new classes.

After looking at our mockup layout for the home page, we can see that we will need quite a few display classes:

- ❑ Site Header – the set of display properties associated with the site header. This applies to the top of the page in our sample home page layout.

- ❑ Poll Header – the style class corresponding to the header information for the poll display. In our sample layout, this is the cell and text within it reading "Opinion Poll".

- ❑ Poll (Generic) – the style class corresponding to any unclassified UI element that belongs in the display of an opinion poll. This would include the results of the poll and list of questions.

- ❑ Book News Header – the style class corresponding to the header of the "Book News" section of the display. In our layout this is a bordered cell with a background and bold, white text.

- ❑ Book News (Generic) – the style class corresponding to any unclassified UI element that belongs in the display of book news.

- ❑ Book News Item (Left Side, Date Field) – the style class corresponding to the items that appear on the left side of the first, third, fifth, etc., row in the display of book news items. In our sample layout this is the text representing the date of the news item for these rows.

- ❑ Book News Item (Right Side, Description Field) – same as above, only this style class applies to the items on the right side of the row, in other words the text representing the news item.

- ❑ Alternating Book News Item (Left Side, Date Field) – same as the Book News Item style class, only this item represents the second, fourth, sixth, etc., rows in the display.

- ❑ Alternating Book News Item (Right Side, Description Field) – same as the above, with the exception that this style class covers the text displayed on the right side of the news item row display.

- ❏ DVD News Header – the style class that represents the header of the DVD News display section.

- ❏ DVD News (Generic) – the style class that represents any unclassified UI element that belongs in the display of DVD News.

- ❏ DVD News Item (Left Side) – just like the style class for Book News Item, only this applies to DVD News.

- ❏ DVD News Item (Right Side) – same as above, only this applies to the right side of the text displayed in the news item row.

- ❏ Alternating DVD News Item (Left Side) – just like the style class for Alternating Book News Item, only this applies to DVD News.

- ❏ Alternating DVD News Item (Right Side) – same as above, only this applies to the right side of the text displayed in the news item row.

- ❏ Site Footer – the style class that applies to any UI element in the site footer.

This list of style classes that we plan on implementing for our website should be sufficient for now. Keep in mind that we will probably discover the need for more UI elements as our development and design progresses and we uncover new and unexpected common UI display classes or types, such as styles for our navigation menus, etc. In more complex implementations of CSS, you will see styles *cascade*, which means that one style inherits visual traits from another style, and that style might inherit traits from another style. For example, you might have a style called "Error", which inherits traits from the "Warning" style, which inherits traits from the "Red" font style, etc.

XSLT

Another way in which we will serve up dynamic content is through the use of **XSLT** (**Extensible Stylesheet Language Transformations**). You might be wondering, then, what is the difference between a cascading stylesheet and XSLT? CSS is designed to, at runtime (or display-time), dynamically configure the visual traits of HTML elements displayed in a browser. XSLT, on the other hand, is far more versatile and has many more uses. One of its many uses is to take raw XML and convert that XML into static HTML elements.

The reason why this is important is that instead of using XSLT to convert XML into an incredibly lengthy set of HTML elements, including font tags, colors, and tables, we can instead use it to convert XML into HTML that utilizes CSS. For example, if we have the following code:

```
<Product Name="A bigger better ball of blue batter" ID="12"/>
```

XSLT can be used to convert it into the following HTML that utilizes stylesheets:

```
<TD><A style="Product" href="product.asp?ID=12">A bigger better ball of blue
batter</a></TD>
```

So, as you can see, XSLT and CSS are both used in helping render user interfaces, but they contribute to the user interface end result in entirely different ways. These can be combined to create an incredibly dynamic and powerful user interface engine. One enormous benefit of using both XSLT and CSS in the generation of UI elements is that, in many cases, you won't have to recompile a single line of code to change any of the display options. You can simply modify the XSLT and CSS files to tweak the user interface as you see fit.

The Page Base Class

In classic ASP, when programmers wanted to indicate that certain pages had functionality in common, they would simply make all of those ASP pages perform a server-side include of the file that contained the common functionality (using `<!--#include ...-->`).

Now that we are developing with the .NET Framework and ASP.NET, we can incorporate the full power of a true class inheritance hierarchy in our ASP.NET web pages. If you are using the code-behind functionality of ASP.NET (which is the default if you're using Visual Studio .NET to build your pages), then you no doubt have noticed that all of these code-behind pages inherit from a single class, `System.Web.UI.Page`. This class provides the basic functionality necessary to drive the most generic ASP.NET web page.

What we'd like to do is create our own class, which inherits from `System.Web.UI.Page`, and which will provide all of our web pages with a common set of functionality related to our application (ThePhile). This is more of a pre-emptive measure than anything else. At the moment, we can't think of too much functionality that *all* of our pages are going to require, but we know that the moment we start developing without this concept of a **page base class**, we'll find something and be unprepared for it. One thing that we expect we will need this page base class for is some common functionality involving user authentication, which we'll be discussing later in the book. We would rather be prepared, with a nearly empty base class, than unprepared, staring at a mountain of rewrites that we need in order to implement common functionality.

Our page class (to start with) will do two things:

❑ Contain a method that is called before the standard `Page_Load` event, allowing us to add functionality to every single page if we need to, simply by modifying this method.

❑ Provide us with a base on which we can add expanded functionality common to all pages, such as identifying and authenticating users.

A Reusable Navigation Control

My hat goes off to any of you who have succeeded in (or even attempted) implementations of a navigation control using classic ASP include files. The maintenance of such a system is typically a nightmare and often results in full-blown rewrites. The reason for this is that often such a system is implemented using server-side include files, which can be extremely difficult to maintain, as every single page must include the file, and must properly call the function (or set up an initial state) in order to properly display the navigation interface.

However, no one can dispute the necessity for users to be able to navigate your website. We discussed in the first chapter of this book that one goal of your website should be to foster the easiest possible communication between user and website. This includes making it straightforward and free of frustration for the user to navigate through the various features of your website.

Just as the high-functionality website could potentially lose visitors with an unpleasant-looking UI, it could also lose visitors if there is no easy and clear way to navigate to all of its features. Typically, websites provide some kind of *toolbar* implementation, where a section of a page is dedicated to a **navigator** of some kind that displays a list of links to the user. Our design calls for this as well.

When designing our navigation control, we are faced with a few questions:

❑   Where is the data going to come from that feeds the control?

❑   How are we going to convert that data into HTML?

❑   How are we going to implement this control?

Remembering that one of our goals is to make it so that we can reconfigure much of our website with little or no recompilation; we decided to use an XML file on disk as the source for the navigation information. This XML file will be placed in a directory somewhere and will contain a list of links that the user can click. The main factor that led us to this decision was reliability. If the database goes down, we should still be able to present the user with a menu that allows them to navigate to the support page where they can e-mail us and complain. If, however, our navigation entries are stored entirely in the database, then we can't very well present a "Contact Us" link if our database is down.

To spruce it up a bit and make the control a bit more flexible, we decided to include categories in our navigation control to make links even easier to find on the control. Each of these categories will also have an icon that will be displayed next to the category name. Having categories will give us more flexibility to organize more complex navigation menus and allow us to create a nice user interface experience with the control.

We will discuss the format of the XML file when we actually get into implementing this control. One other thing we need to decide is how we're going to convert this XML into HTML. The first thing that comes to mind is to use an XSL transformation, especially since we know that the classes provided with the .NET framework provide us with this ability in an easy-to-use `XslTransform` class.

As we did when we first started the design process, we can create a mockup, or a sample user interface, to demonstrate what we'd like our navigation control to look like. Having this on hand when we implement the control will make the coding easier and more straightforward. Here is a screenshot of this sample navigation control:

This should give you a good overview of the general idea. We have two categories, with a font style that is obviously different from that of the links themselves.

Looking at the mockup, it's apparent that in order to make this navigation control as configurable as possible we should create a stylesheet for it. This way, if we want to change the background color of the navigation control, we can simply change the color in the CSS file and not have to worry about re-compiling the control itself.

We can identify the following style elements from the above sample navigation control:

- Main Table – the style class representing the table itself. This will be used to provide the thin black border that surrounds the control.

- Header Cell – the style class representing the header. This is where the text 'ThePhile.COM' appears in the sample.

- Category Cell – the style class representing the category cell. This is where each category is displayed in bold and italics.

- Item Cell – the style class representing the cell for an individual item. This dictates the font and so on for an individual navigation item.

- Item Link – the style class representing the link to an individual item. This dictates behaviors such as the color of the link while the mouse is hovering over it, etc.

Headers and Footers

Two other extremely common user interface elements that we should provide for in our design are **headers** and **footers**. Essentially, a header is some UI element that sits atop every (or nearly every) page served to the client. The footer is a UI element that finishes off nearly every page served to the client. There are quite a few uses for these – we'll discuss a couple of them here and go into more detail about expanding the functionality of the header later in the book, such as in Chapters 5 and 7 on users and advertising.

The most important purpose of the header is for **branding**. Branding is incredibly important to every website, regardless of size, purpose, function, or form. Every page that the user sees should be in some way associated with your brand, which could involve including the company name, logo, or some other identifying mark. If the user forgets who is providing the web page they're currently viewing, then they probably won't remember where to go if they want to come back to that site.

Footers, on the other hand, traditionally have a far more utilitarian purpose. They are typically there to provide copyright and trademark information, as well as a list of links that might not fit in anywhere else on the site. This might include links to a list of available jobs, a tech support page, a contact or feedback page, and other miscellaneous navigation items.

Another purpose for the header that we'll talk about later in the book is for **advertising**. Advertising banners need to be displayed in a prominent place so that users viewing the page will see them. This prominent place is typically right at the top of the page above all other content.

Our design is going to call for a header that displays our branding (logo), as well as a customized greeting that displays a message to the user. This message will greet the user personally if they have logged in. In Chapter 5 we'll expand this header so that it can provide a link to a login form if the user has not yet authenticated.

There are also many other users for header controls. In our particular case, we're not going to make use of as many as we could. For example, if your website provides a search engine that allows users to search through your content, a quick-search type of control could be placed in the header to allow them quick access to your content database. Also, e-commerce sites typically have links in the header to the shopping cart and wish-list features.

Error Handling

When we were building the core foundation of our website, in Chapter 2, we built our own custom exception class, AppException. We did this in order to have an exception class that we could throw that would guarantee the writing of an event log entry. We can also extend this class later to add e-mail functionality to our custom errors without tracking down every single line of code that throws an exception.

As you've been working with ASP.NET you've probably seen the default exception screen. It isn't exactly pretty and our application loses control at that point. What this means is that if we don't trap exceptions properly and they display using ASP.NET's default mechanism, we can't guarantee that any of our code will execute. For this reason, we want to make sure that we're exerting strict control over the exception handling system. For our design, we would like to develop an error trapping system where we control the display of the error information to the users. We aren't quite sure how we're going to accomplish this at this point, but we're certain that we need to implement some form of error trapping system in the core of our presentation tier, especially if errors are going to 'bubble up' from the business tier or data services tier at some point.

The Solution

This chapter has presented a problem – the need for creating a solid foundation for the presentation tier of our web application. After identifying the problem, we went on to discuss the concerns involved in designing a solution to this problem. Now that we have our basic design, and we have a good idea of what we plan on doing to create our presentation-tier foundation, let's get into the code and create some user interface elements.

We are going to be working with three projects, all of them within our main VS.NET Solution:

❑ ThePhile – the solution's default project, containing the site's homepage, and stylesheets. As we develop modules, it will need to reference to the presentation layer of each module. For now it should reference Core, Controls, and PhilePageBase.

❑ Controls – containing site-wide user controls: a header, footer, and navigator.

❑ PhilePageBase – containing a base class for all pages that we create for the site.

Let's look first of all at our stylesheets.

Styles

As we discussed in the design section, we know that we're going to need a stylesheet that provides user interface element templates, or **classes**, for our website. As we discussed earlier, we're going to have one main stylesheet to aid in providing a consistent look and feel, and then we'll create another stylesheet for our navigator control. To recap, the list of elements that we decided would need to be classified in our main stylesheet are as follows:

> Site Header, Poll Header, Poll (Generic), Book News Header, Book News (Generic), Book News Item (Left Side, Date Field), Book News Item (Right Side, Description Field), Alternating Book News Item (Left Side, Date Field), Alternating Book News Item (Right Side, Description Field), DVD News Header, DVD News (Generic), DVD News Item (Left Side), DVD News Item (Right Side), Alternating DVD News Item (Left Side), Alternating DVD News Item (Right Side), and Site Footer.

The true benefit of these classes is that any time we decide to make a change to any of the user interface elements (this includes when sales or marketing decide to make this change, too!) all we have to do is modify the entries in the CSS file, and we don't have to worry about tracking down each and every page that displays the particular UI element we're modifying.

Here is the listing for our main stylesheet source file (ThePhile.css – this file should be created in the Styles directory directly under the main application directory, in other words ThePhile\Styles\ThePhile.css). First we have the style definition for <BODY> elements:

```
BODY {
  background-color: #ffffff;
  font: x-small Verdana, Arial, sans-serif;
  font-size: 10;
}
```

In this next line, we're going to override the default behavior of the <A> element, making the link appear in dark blue instead of whatever the user has set in their browser configuration (to give the site a consistent look and feel):

```
A {
   color: darkblue;
}
```

By providing some style information for the <TD> element, we provide a default font and display size for all information that appears in table cells. This allows us to avoid filling our HTML output with dozens of redundant <font> elements.

```
TD
{
   font: x-small Verdana, Arial, sans-serif;
   font-size: 12;
   line-height: 17px;
}
```

In this next section, we're overriding the hover style of the A class.

Anytime you work with a pre-defined class (A, TD, etc.) they come with their own default styles that are defined by the user's browser options and the browser. The styles that begin A: are used to refine the styling that will be applied to <A> elements when a certain event occurs, such as hovering over such an element with a mouse pointer.

By indicating just the standard blue color here, the effect will be a dark blue link that grows slightly brighter when the mouse hovers over it. It should add a subtle and professional touch to our pages.

```
A:hover {
   color: blue;
}
```

We then have further style definitions that we'll be using later on, including those identified in our design section. To save space we won't show the entire code here, just the list of styles:

```
.Button

.TextBox

.Site_Header

.Poll_Header

.Poll_General

.Book_News_General

.Book_News_Header
```

```
.Book_News_Item_Left

.Book_News_Item_Right

.Book_News_AlternatingItem_Left

.Book_News_AlternatingItem_Right

.DVD_News_General

.DVD_News_Header

.DVD_News_Item_Left

.DVD_News_Item_Right

.DVD_News_AlternatingItem_Left

.DVD_News_AlternatingItem_Right
```

At this point we're pretty sure that we're going to need some administrative functionality added to this website. Each of the modules that we develop in this book is going to have its own administration section, which we'll cover in those modules' respective chapters. However, to provide a consistent look and feel we can include some stylistic templates here that each individual administrative section can adhere to. Again, the full code for each definition is not listed here, but can be seen in the ThePhile.css file in the code download. These are the styles we've included:

```
.Admin_MenuTable

.Admin_MenuRow

A.Admin_MenuItem

A.Admin_MenuItem:hover
```

You will notice that some are sub-styles of a predefined style (for the A tag in this case) but others are style groupings specific to our application, and don't have any foundation in existing HTML.

We know we're going to have errors, so it won't hurt to provide a style that we can use for displaying them. At the moment we're only using red, but at a later date we can always come back and add more style to this class if we want the error messages to really stand out:

```
.ErrorMessage {
  color: red;
}
```

The use of cascading stylesheets should be fairly straightforward. Essentially what we're doing is defining some reusable display properties for all elements that belong to a certain class or category of display type, such as an administrative menu item, or the header for the DVD news section, etc.

Now let's look at the skeleton source for the stylesheet file we're going to use for our navigator control (found in `ThePhile\Styles\Navigator.css`, relative to the root of the website). The full style definitions are not shown here, just the list of styles corresponding to those we identified in the design section:

```
.Navigator_Table

.Navigator_Header_Cell

.Navigator_Category_Cell

.Navigator_Item_Cell

A.Navigator_Item_Link

A.Navigator_Item_Link:Hover
```

The PhilePage Class

As we mentioned in our design, we want a base class from which all pages on our website will either directly or indirectly inherit. This will allow us to either restrict or provide functionality to the entire site with minimal code changes. This kind of functionality might include providing some standard utility methods that we know will be called by many pages, as well as possibly providing some base code for user identification and authentication. At the moment we don't have anything in the base class, but once we set up its core structure, it should be fairly easy to add site-wide functionality to any of our pages.

To create this class, we add a class library project called `PhilePageBase` to our main solution. The default namespace should be `Wrox.ThePhile.Web`, and the class file is called `PhilePage.cs`. Let's take a look at the source code for this class:

```
using System;
using System.Web;
using System.Web.UI;

namespace Wrox.ThePhile.Web
{
  public class PhilePage : System.Web.UI.Page
  {
    protected Wrox.ThePhile.Web.Controls.User.SiteHeader Header;

    public PhilePage()
    {
    }
```

`OnInit` (shown below) is an important method. What we're doing with our override is calling the `OnInit` method in the base class (`System.Web.UI.Page`) and then adding our custom page-load event handler (`PhilePage_Load`) to the `Load` delegate holder:

```
    protected override void OnInit(EventArgs e)
    {
      base.OnInit(e);
      this.Load += new System.EventHandler(this.PhilePage_Load);
```

```
      }

      private void PhilePage_Load(object sender, System.EventArgs e)
      {
        // TODO: Place any code that will take place BEFORE the Page_Load
        // event in the regular page, e.g. cache management, authentication
        // verification, etc.
      }
    }
  }
```

So, once we have created our core `PhilePage` class, we can then create code-behind classes that inherit from this class rather than the default `System.Web.Page`. The following is a quick example of what an empty page class might look like that inherits from `PhilePage`:

```
public class _Default : PhilePage
{
  protected Wrox.ThePhile.Web.Controls.Server.Navigator MenuNav;

  private void Page_Load(object sender, System.EventArgs e)

  // Initialize Page Here.

}
```

This class also contains a protected member declaration for our navigator control, which we're going to discuss next.

The Navigator Control

The navigator control is one of those things that takes only a few lines of code, but is actually quite powerful. We're going to use a *server* control rather than a *user* control, as this will allow us greater influence over the class. It will completely encapsulate the implementation of the navigation system.

To create our navigator, we first need to decide on a format for the XML file from which the information would be loaded. We decided that a standard XML file was appropriate (as opposed to storing a `DataSet` serialization or something similar), but the beauty of encapsulating the functionality into a control is that if we decide to use something other than a file later on, then the change should be easy and straightforward.

Let's take a look at a sample XML file that feeds our navigator. (You can find this file in `ThePhile\Config\NavMenu.xml` relative to the web root).

```xml
<?xml version="1.0"?>
<NavMenu title="ThePhile.COM">
  <Category title="DVDphile" icon="/ThePhile/images/DVDlogo.gif">
    <MenuItem title="Link1" link="/ThePhile/DVD/default.aspx"/>
  </Category>
  <Category title="Bibliophile" icon="/ThePhile/images/Booklogo.gif">
    <MenuItem title="Link2" link="/ThePhile/Books/default.aspx"/>
  </Category>
</NavMenu>
```

We can see that the document element, `<NavMenu>`, has a single attribute, which is the title of the navigation menu. Beneath that we have a list of categories, each indicated by a single `<Category>` node. And finally, at the lowest level in the tree, each of these categories is comprised of `<MenuItem>` nodes. This form of maintaining the list of links for the navigation control is not only incredibly versatile and flexible, but it allows site administrators to make a quick change to a text file and affect possibly hundreds of pages throughout the site without recompiling anything.

Now that we know what data we're going to have in our XML file we can decide how we're going to transform that data into HTML. We discussed earlier that we wanted to use the `XslTransform` class to do our HTML transformation for us. The first thing we need to do in that case is actually build an XSLT file.

Further information on XSLT, including XPath, can be found in several Wrox books, including Professional XML for .NET Developers (ISBN 1-861005-31-8) and XSLT Programmer's Reference 2nd edition (ISBN 1-861005-06-7).

The following is the listing of the XSLT file (found in `ThePhile\Transforms\NavMenu.xslt`, again relative to the web root). You might notice that instead of embedding all kinds of cell formatting, alignment, font sizing, and coloration directly into our XSLT file, we are simply referencing the classes defined in the CSS file we just built. This gives us many advantages. The first and foremost is that if we plan on changing the color scheme for our navigator, we don't have to change our XSLT file as well. Another is that this file is much easier to read and interpret, because all you're looking at is the HTML and associated CSS classes, and you don't have to sift through mountains of `<font>` tags.

```
<?xml version="1.0"?>
<xsl:stylesheet xmlns:xsl="http://www.w3.org/1999/XSL/Transform"
                version="1.0">

<xsl:template match="/NavMenu">
  <table width="150" border="0" cellspacing="0" cellpadding="0"
       class="Navigator_Table">
    <tr>
      <td colspan="2" class="Navigator_Header_Cell">
        <xsl:value-of select="@title"/>
        </td>
    </tr>
```

After we're done displaying the header for the navigator, we then use the `<xsl:for-each>` element to iterate through each `<Category>` element that we find beneath the `<NavMenu>` element. This allows us to create a loop of transformation that is performed on each category:

```
<xsl:for-each select="Category">
<!-- CATEGORY START -->
  <tr>
    <td width="40" align="center">
      <img align="absmiddle">
```

Something that often confuses people is the use of the `<xsl:attribute>` element. This allows you to set the value of a given attribute to a value obtained dynamically through an XPath `select` statement in the `<xsl:value-of>` element. Here, we're using this to dynamically set the `src` attribute of the `<img>` element. Our XPath expression is retrieving the value of the `icon` attribute (@ signifies an attribute):

```
        <xsl:attribute name="src">
          <xsl:value-of select="@icon"/>
        </xsl:attribute>
      </img>
    </td>
    <td width="110" class="Navigator_Category_Cell">
      <xsl:value-of select="@title"/>
    </td>
  </tr>
```

While we're in the master loop (iterating through each `<Category>` element contained within the `<NavMenu>` document element), we will then create a nested loop for each item belonging to each category. This allows us to iterate through the list of items assigned to each category, giving us the ability to transform each item into its own set of HTML elements:

```
    <xsl:for-each select="MenuItem">
    <!-- MENU ITEM START -->
    <tr>
      <td width="40">
        <br/>
      </td>
      <td width="110" class="Navigator_Item_Cell">
        <a class="Navigator_Item_Link">
          <xsl:attribute name="href">
            <xsl:value-of select="@link"/>
          </xsl:attribute>
          <xsl:value-of select="@title"/>
        </a>
      </td>
    </tr>
    <!-- MENU ITEM END -->
    </xsl:for-each>
  <!-- CATEGORY END -->
  </xsl:for-each>
  </table>
</xsl:template>

</xsl:stylesheet>
```

One of the things that many people find they have trouble understanding about XSLT is that it *must produce well-formed XML.* Even though the HTML 4.0 specification looks a lot like XML, it is far more lax in its requirements. For instance, HTML allows you to simply supply a `<br>` tag and be done with it. However, the XML output from an XSLT transformation *must* produce a completed pair of tags, either by producing a `<br>` and a `</br>` or by producing a `<br/>`. This is just something to keep in mind when building your XSLT files. As you can see in the XSLT above, we are producing `<br/>` tags rather than `<br></br>` tag pairs.

Now that we've created not only a sample XML source file, but also a working XSLT transformation file, we're ready to start writing the server control that we're going to use to make the transformation happen. To create this server control, we first create a new project (C# Class Library, called `Controls`) that is part of our main solution that already contains our `Core` project and our `ThePhile` web application project. We then set the default namespace of this project to `Wrox.ThePhile.Web.Controls`, and set the output file to `Wrox.ThePhile.Web.Controls` (Visual Studio .NET will append the DLL to the filename for you, so you don't have to type that). The code for the `Navigator.cs` class begins as follows:

```
using System;
using System.Web;
using System.Web.UI.HtmlControls;
using System.Web.UI;
using System.Xml;
using System.Xml.XPath;
using System.Xml.Xsl;

namespace Wrox.ThePhile.Web.Controls.Server
{
```

In the above code, you'll notice that we're using System.Xml.XPath and System.Xml.Xsl, two namespaces that provide us with basic XSLT functionality. All server controls inherit from System.Web.UI.Control, and our Navigator class is no exception:

```
public class Navigator: System.Web.UI.Control
{
  string transformFilePath;
  string sourceFilePath;
```

The TransformFile and SourceFile properties (shown below) are properties that we can assign within the navigator's server-side ASP.NET tag itself when we place it on our web page. These properties indicate the XML source file path (URL) and the XSLT transformation file path (also a URL).

```
public string TransformFile
{
  get
  {
    return transformFilePath;
  }
  set
  {
    transformFilePath = value;
  }
}

public string SourceFile
{
  get
  {
    return sourceFilePath;
  }
  set
  {
    sourceFilePath = value;
  }
}

protected override void OnInit( EventArgs e )
{
  base.OnInit( e );
}
```

This next method, `Render`, is where the actual work of the control takes place. `Render` is the basic method of a `System.Web.UI.Control` that is responsible for producing the HTML that represents the control. For more information on building ASP.NET controls, see the Wrox book *Professional ASP.NET* (ISBN 1-861004-88-5).

The first thing we do is open the source XML file as an `XPathDocument`. The `XPathDocument` provides phenomenal transformation performance, so we've chosen it over a standard XML document. We use `Context.Server.MapPath` in order to translate the URL into a physical filename (on the local machine) that we can use for the `XPathDocument` constructor. From there, we instantiate an `XslTransform` object and output the results of the transformation to the `HtmlTextWriter` stream.

```
protected override void Render( HtmlTextWriter writer)
{
    XPathDocument xdoc = new XPathDocument(Context.Server.MapPath(
                                            sourceFilePath));
    XslTransform xslt = new XslTransform();
    xslt.Load(Context.Server.MapPath(transformFilePath));
    xslt.Transform(xdoc, null, writer);
}
}
}
```

In the above code, the most important line is the one in which the actual transformation takes place. We call the `Transform` method of the `XslTransform` instance, supplying the XPath document and an `HtmlTextWriter` onto which the results of the transformation will be placed:

```
xslt.Transform(xdoc, null, writer);
```

So, at this point we have a cascading stylesheet that controls the visual appearance of our navigation UI elements, we have an XSLT file that dictates how the source XML file is to be transformed into HTML, and we have the source XML file that actually defines the navigation menu structure. We've seen what the navigator will look like when displayed in the browser, so to see how our XSLT transformation is looking, let's take a look at the HTML generated by this control (you can just do View | Source from any page with the navigator on it to see this):

```
<?xml version="1.0" encoding="utf-8"?>
<table width="150" border="0" cellspacing="0" cellpadding="0"
        class="Navigator_Table">
  <tr>
    <td colspan="2" class="Navigator_Header_Cell">
      ThePhile.COM
    </td>
  </tr>
  <tr>
    <td width="40" align="center">
      <img align="absmiddle" src="/ThePhile/images/DVDlogo.gif"></img>
    </td>
    <td width="110" class="Navigator_Category_Cell">
      DVDphile
    </td>
  </tr>
```

```
<tr>
  <td width="40">
    <br />
  </td>
  <td width="110" class="Navigator_Item_Cell">
    <a class="Navigator_Item_Link"
       href="/ThePhile/DVD/default.aspx">Link1</a>
  </td>
</tr>
<tr>
  <td width="40" align="center">
    <img align="absmiddle" src="/ThePhile/images/Booklogo.gif"></img>
  </td>
  <td width="110" class="Navigator_Category_Cell">
    Bibliophile
  </td>
</tr>
<tr>
  <td width="40">
    <br />
  </td>
  <td width="110" class="Navigator_Item_Cell">
    <a class="Navigator_Item_Link"
       href="/ThePhile/Books/default.aspx">Link2</a>
  </td>
</tr>
</table>
```

If you compare the above output to the output you actually see when you examine the source code for any of the pages using this control, you'll notice that we prettied up the HTML considerably. The transformation we're performing doesn't actually include any whitespace within the elements. Remember that, while whitespace may mean something to the viewer or the reader of the XML or HTML files, whitespace between the end of a parent element and the beginning of a child element is going to be ignored in the resulting output. Thankfully this whitespace removal doesn't have any impact on how the client browser interprets the HTML, it just makes the HTML source a bit painful to read.

The SiteHeader Control

The `SiteHeader` control that we're going to build is a user control. One main difference between a server control and a user control is that while the server control is purely a class inheriting from a control, the user control is actually a mini-ASPX page (with an extension of `.ascx`) and a code-behind class. To build the code for this, we're going to go back to our main web application project (ThePhile), and create a new directory (if you haven't already) called `Controls`.

> *At the time of the public release of Visual Studio .NET, we can't easily define code-behind files that belong to different assemblies other than the target assembly of the website, so we won't cover that method. As such, all of our user controls are actually part of ThePhile. DLL, produced as a website project.*

The following is the code listing for the control 'page' (found in `ThePhile\Controls\SiteHeader.ascx`):

```
<%@ Control Language="c#" AutoEventWireup="false"
          Codebehind="SiteHeader.ascx.cs"
          Inherits="Wrox.ThePhile.Web.Controls.User.SiteHeader"
          TargetSchema="http://schemas.microsoft.com/intellisense/ie5"%>

<link href="/ThePhile/Styles/ThePhile.css" rel="stylesheet">

<table width="100%" border="0" class="Site_Header">
  <tr>
    <td width="50%">
      <a href="/ThePhile/default.aspx">
        <img src="/ThePhile/images/ThePhile.gif" border="0"
            alt="ThePhile.COM">
      </a>
    </td>
    <td align="right" valign="bottom">
      <asp:Label id=Greeting runat="server"></asp:Label>
    </td>
  </tr>
</table>
```

And now for the code-behind class for this header (found in
ThePhile\Controls\SiteHeader.ascx.cs):

```
namespace Wrox.ThePhile.Web.Controls.User
{
  using System;
  using System.Data;
  using System.Drawing;
  using System.Web;
  using System.Web.UI.WebControls;
  using System.Web.UI.HtmlControls;

  /// <summary>
  ///     Summary description for SiteHeader.
  /// </summary>
  public abstract class SiteHeader : System.Web.UI.UserControl
  {
    protected System.Web.UI.WebControls.Label Greeting;
```

Here we're kind of sneaking ahead in the book. We know that we're going to be implementing some
form of authentication system, and we know that the Context.User object is going to house that
information for us. Therefore, we can code our header now to greet the user personally if they've logged
in. Later on in the book, in Chapter 5 on users and authentication, we'll add some more to this page to
provide a link to a login or registration form if the user has not authenticated.

```
    private void Page_Load(object sender, System.EventArgs e)
    {
      // Put user code to initialize the page here
      Greeting.Text = "Welcome, ";
      if (Context.User.Identity.IsAuthenticated)
        Greeting.Text += Context.User.Identity.Name;
      else
        Greeting.Text += "Guest User";
    }
  }
}
```

*For convenience we've removed the web form designer code that ordinarily would be displayed above
after the Page_Load event handler.*

The SiteFooter Control

The `SiteFooter` control is going to have a similar structure to the `SiteHeader` control. Essentially, we're just making a simple user control that we will use to display miscellaneous links, copyright notices, and additional information to the users, and to provide a feeling of closure to the page itself. Without even just a small footer, many users become confused and wonder if a portion of the page might have been broken or is not displaying for some reason. The following is the listing of the user control presentation (found in `ThePhile\Controls\SiteFooter.ascx`). There is no code to speak of in the corresponding code-behind class so we won't bother listing that here.

```
<%@ Control Language="c#" AutoEventWireup="false"
           Codebehind="SiteFooter.ascx.cs"
           Inherits="Wrox.ThePhile.Web.Controls.User.SiteFooter"
           TargetSchema="http://schemas.microsoft.com/intellisense/ie5"%>
  <table width="100%" border="0" cellspacing="0" cellpadding="0">
    <tr>
      <td align="middle">
        <font face="arial" size="1">
          <br><br><br>
          <i>Copyright &copy; 2001-2002 Wrox Press Ltd.</i><br>
          <a href="Contact.aspx">Contact Us</a> | Support | FAQ | Forums |
                            Newsletter | Voting | Your Account
        </font>
      </td>
    </tr>
  </table>
```

Error Handling

After doing some research on how ASP.NET provides for error handling, we've come up with a solution that will allow us to provide a rich, robust solution that is also easy to maintain and extend.

For more information on error handling practices for ASP.NET, consult the MSDN .NET Framework SDK documentation or the aforementioned Professional ASP.NET.

Page classes have the ability to trap events through **event handlers**. One such event is the `Error` event. Pages can provide a custom method that deals with the handling of this error. ASP.NET also provides the ability to define an application-wide event handler for the `Error` event in the case where the page may not have trapped the error.

This works out to be in our favor, because we just finished creating a base class for all of our pages. We developed the base class for cases where we need to add the same functionality to every single page, so that they can inherit it from this base class (theoretically, this should be all of our pages). To allow each and every one of our pages to handle errors in a graceful manner, we're going to provide a local method called `LogEvent`, which functions identically to the `LogEvent` method in our custom `AppException` class. In addition, we're going to provide a default error handler event method that can be overridden, if need be, by inheriting classes.

Let's take a look at the LogEvent method we're adding to our page class (PhilePage.cs):

```
protected void LogEvent(string message, EventLogEntryType entryType)
{
  if (!EventLog.SourceExists("ThePhile.COM"))
  {
    EventLog.CreateEventSource("ThePhile.COM", "Application");
  }
  EventLog.WriteEntry("ThePhile.COM", message, entryType);
}
```

This should look identical to the LogEvent method that we wrote for our custom Exception class. The only difference is that now every single one of our web pages (provided they inherit from PhilePage) has the ability to write to the event log in a standard and uniform way. As we mentioned when discussing event logging for our site's core, you might want to replace the definition of this method with something that logs to a text file rather than the event log, to accommodate restrictions imposed by the deployment environment.

Next, in order to add our custom error handling method to the list of delegates to be invoked in the event of an error, we need to modify our OnInit method. Remember from earlier that we modified this to create a custom 'pre-load' method that we could use in case we needed it. The following is the new version of our OnInit method:

```
protected override void OnInit(EventArgs e)
{
  base.OnInit(e);
  this.Load += new System.EventHandler(this.PhilePage_Load);
  this.Error += new System.EventHandler(this.PhilePage_Error);
}
```

You can see that we've added a new line to the method, which sets up our event handler to be called in the case of a page exception. Now let's take a look at the code that gets launched in response to the error event:

```
protected void PhilePage_Error(object sender, System.EventArgs e)
{
  string errMsg;
  Exception currentError = Server.GetLastError();

  errMsg = "<link rel=\"stylesheet\"
                href=\"/ThePhile/Styles/ThePhile.CSS\">";
  errMsg += "<h1>Page Error</h1><hr/>An unexpected error has occurred on " +
    "this page. The system administrators have been notified. Please feel" +
    " free to contact us with the information surrounding this error.<br/>"+
    "The error occurred in: "+Request.Url.ToString()+"<br/>"+
    "Error Message: <font class=\"ErrorMessage\">"+
    currentError.Message.ToString() + "</font><hr/>"+
    "<b>Stack Trace:</b><br/>"+
    currentError.ToString();

  if ( !(currentError is AppException) )
  {
```

```
        // It is not one of ours, so we cannot guarantee that it has been logged
        // into the event log.
        LogEvent(currentError.ToString(), EventLogEntryType.Error );
    }

    Response.Write(errMsg );
    Server.ClearError();
}
```

Going through the code from beginning to end, we can see that what we're doing is printing out a small HTML page that uses our default stylesheet (to provide for slightly easier-to-read output). However, everything else is extremely simple, pure HTML output; we're not using any server controls, user controls, or anything else. The reason for this is that if there was an error in a control that we were trying to display in our error message, we might end up in an infinite loop of error handling and crash the server.

After we're done displaying the error message to the user, we have the following line of code:

```
    if ( !(currentError is AppException) )
```

This tests to see if the currentError variable can be cast to an AppException. In other words, if currentError is of type AppException, or it is a *descendant* of AppException, this condition will evaluate to true. The reason we're making this test is that if the currentError is one of our own custom exceptions, we know that it has already logged its error information into the event log, so we don't need to do it manually. On the other hand, if the exception came from somewhere else, for example a class in the SqlClient namespace, we need to manually log that error to the event log so that we have a record of it.

To test and make sure that our custom error trapping is working properly, we first need to build our solution to make sure that the precompiled code-behind classes are all up to date, and then we can place some code into our home page that we know is going to cause it to fail. In my case, I placed a line of code in the home page that attempts to open a connection to SQL Server without first having specified the connection string (of course, none of us have ever done this for real, right?). The following is a screenshot of the output I got when attempting to view a page that had this bad code in the Page_Load event:

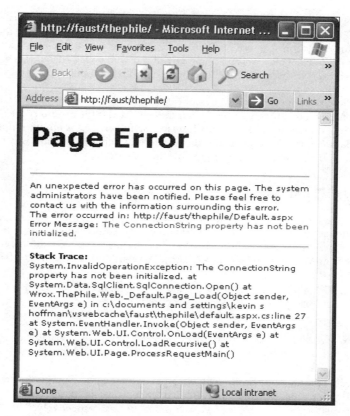

Well, the output is still a little technical, but at least it is now in our control so that if we decide to do something fancier with it at a later date, it is simply a matter of changing a single method in a single class rather than modifying every single web page in our entire application. We're finally starting to see some of the solid benefits of sub-classing in ASP.NET.

Well, we know that at least one part of our code is working. But what about the event log? Let's take a look at the event log to see if the error we generated has appeared in its proper place:

The screenshot above shows that we have an **Error** entry from an application called **ThePhile.COM**. In the particular case it occurred at 10:15 AM. We also know that for exceptions that didn't originate from our code (in this case, from the .NET SQL Provider) we are storing the entire exception text, which includes the stack trace. This way, each time any of our web pages encounters an un-trapped exception it will log the entire stack trace to the event log to aid in troubleshooting.

As our needs, and the complexity of the application, expand, we may want to change the way in which we log errors, for example logging specific numeric event IDs for certain types of subclassed exceptions, as well as sending e-mail to administrators in response to certain (or all) untrapped exceptions. Many pagers these days can receive e-mail, and this would be a remarkably easy way to instantly notify the on-call administrator or programmer of possible application failures.

Home Page Draft

Now that we have laid down a good, solid foundation for our user interface, or presentation tier, let's put all of that together and build the first iteration of our website's home page (found in `ThePhile\default.aspx` and `ThePhile\default.aspx.cs`). We do this by adding a web form to our existing web application project (`ThePhile`). We start with the following lines of code:

```
<%@ Register TagPrefix="WroxUser" TagName="SiteHeader"
             Src="Controls/SiteHeader.ascx" %>
<%@ Register TagPrefix="WroxUser" TagName="SiteFooter"
             Src="Controls/SiteFooter.ascx" %>
<%@ Register TagPrefix="Wrox" Namespace="Wrox.ThePhile.Web.Controls.Server"
             Assembly="Wrox.ThePhile.Web.Controls" %>
```

The three special lines above tell the ASP.NET parser that we're going to be using some controls in our page. The first two elements, which indicate that we're using the `TagPrefix` of `WroxUser`, specify two controls using the `TagName` `SiteHeader` and `SiteFooter` respectively. The `Src` attribute allows us to reference the code in the specified files for the given user controls. Server controls use the `Assembly` attribute to locate the code. The third line above sets up a `TagPrefix` for our navigator server control, indicating that it can be found in the namespace `Wrox.ThePhile.Web.Controls.Server`, in the `Assembly` (which must be in the website's `/bin` directory) `Wrox.ThePhile.Web.Controls.DLL`.

Moving on, we have some fairly standard start-of-page code:

```
<%@ Page language="c#" Codebehind="Default.aspx.cs" AutoEventWireup="false"
         Inherits="Wrox.ThePhile.Web._Default" %>
<!DOCTYPE HTML PUBLIC "-//W3C//DTD HTML 4.0 Transitional//EN" >
<html>
  <head>
    <title>Default</title>
    <meta name="GENERATOR" Content="Microsoft Visual Studio 7.0">
    <meta name="CODE_LANGUAGE" Content="C#">
    <meta name=vs_defaultClientScript content="JavaScript">
    <meta name=vs_targetSchema
          content="http://schemas.microsoft.com/intellisense/ie5">
```

Then, in the next two lines of HTML, we're simply including the two stylesheets that we developed earlier in this chapter; one that is common to all pages throughout the site, and the other that supplies the necessary styles for our navigator:

```html
<link href="Styles/Navigator.css" rel="stylesheet">
<link href="Styles/ThePhile.css" rel="stylesheet">
</head>
<body >

<form id="Default" method="post" runat="server">
```

On this next line we're simply including the SiteHeader user control at the very top of our output:

```html
<WroxUser:SiteHeader id="Header" runat="server"/>
<br/>
<table width="100%" border="0" cellspacing="4" cellpadding="2">
  <tr>
    <td width="100%" valign="top">
      Greetings,<br/>
         <b>ThePhile.COM</b> is an example website
      written by Wrox authors to illustrate the principles of
      design, specification, and implementation of a content-based
      website in ASP.NET. This website is the example that is built
      progressively in the <a href="http://www.wrox.com">Wrox Press
      </a>book, <i>ASP.NET Website Programming</i>. <br/><br/>

      <table width="100%" border="0" style="border:1px;
          border-color:#000000; border-style:solid;">
        <tr>
          <td>
            Dynamic content will more than likely go here...
          </td>
        </tr>
      </table>

    </td>
    <td align="right">
```

Placed in a table cell aligned to the right of the page, we include our Navigator control and indicate the paths (relative URLs) to the source file and the transformation XSLT file:

```html
<Wrox:Navigator id="MenuNav"
                SourceFile="Config/NavMenu.xml"
                TransformFile="Transforms/NavMenu.xslt"
                runat="server"/>
    </td>
  </tr>
</table>

<WroxUser:SiteFooter id="Footer" runat="server"/>

</form>

</body>
</html>
```

When ASP.NET has finished processing our page we receive output that looks something like the following web page. There are a couple of other things that we've done to the system that might not be all that obvious. First, we've placed several images in the /ThePhile/Images directory to contain all of our graphics. Secondly, you'll need to make sure that /ThePhile is a valid IIS application and that you have verified that it has the proper FrontPage extensions (otherwise Visual Studio .NET won't work with it properly). Also, the Core DLL needs to be built as well as the Controls DLL. If you've been using the solution approach in Visual Studio .NET, then it should automatically copy all necessary assemblies to /ThePhile/bin. If you've been doing it manually, you'll need to copy those assemblies yourself.

You can see in the following screenshot that the SiteHeader, Navigator, and SiteFooter controls have all been seamlessly integrated into the web page, with the end user having no knowledge as to the actual control implementations we're using:

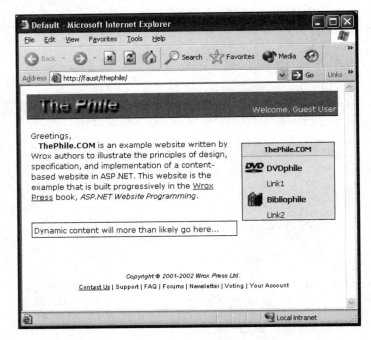

Summary

This chapter began with an introduction to the problem: the need to provide a clear, consistent, solid, and scalable foundation for the presentation tier of our web application. We then worked through the design of this foundation, discussing stylesheets, subclassing the default page class, creating a navigation control, creating headers and footers, and error handling within ASP.NET. After having read this chapter, you should now be familiar with the following concepts:

- ❑ Identifying and creating reusable interface components by creating user and server controls.

- ❑ The purpose and implementation of a page inheritance hierarchy, using a page base class to save time and promote consistency.

- ❑ How to dynamically render HTML using data styled with cascading stylesheets.

- ❑ How to use XSLT to transform XML into HTML and other forms of data, and the difference between XSLT and CSS.

In the next chapter we'll take the core foundation that we've been building and use it as a platform on which to build our first module, a module that allows for administration and maintenance of the site's files remotely via the web.

Maintaining the Site

Any real website is generally made up of a lot of pages, images, XML/XSL files, stylesheets, databases, and other types of document. It's very common to have many hundreds or even thousands of files for a single website. During development of the site these files will usually be modified several times. This will also continue after deployment, since no application is ever really finished – particularly when we can redeploy to all our users at once. As a result, an integral part of any development work is having some kind of maintenance system.

In this chapter we'll explain why it's useful to have an online site management system, and we'll design and build one that allows us to easily maintain the site's files and directories.

Our solution will provide file uploads over HTTP connections, a useful technique that is not limited to site maintenance. For example, web-based e-mail sites use this method to upload attachments, and many community sites use it to upload images for user profiles.

We will also build an online text editor, so that we can edit our ASPX files right in the web browser.

Our tools will really be for administrators or developers to use. But with a simplified, restricted front-end we could use this technique to build a maintenance system for even the most technically inept client!

We will also present an existing third party tool, Microsoft's **Web Data Administrator**. This could save our developers a great deal of time managing the site's SQL Server database, both before and after deployment.

The Problem

During the development of our site, we'll need to add, copy, and move files, change the source code of ASP.NET pages, edit the stylesheets, and generally fix things here and there. Since we're working on a test machine, and as we're all familiar with doing such common operations, this does not pose any problems. Managing the SQL Server database is easy as well, because even if we don't have the program installed on our development machine, through the Enterprise Manager we can do everything we could if we had the SQL Server on our local computer.

After development will come the time to upload everything and to test the website online. We'll almost certainly need to make further changes, upload additions, move files around, and perform other file management operations. The same applies to the database: we'll need to add, edit, or delete records, run and edit stored procedures, and backup the data. If we had an in-house server, we wouldn't expect to encounter any problems here, as we would just need to move everything to the production system. Maintaining the site would be as easy as it was on our development machine. Having an in-house server offers maximum control over the system, and this is important when we need to install additional software, register COM+ components, change the IIS default settings, and so on – in fact, whenever we want to configure things according to *our* needs. However, often we do not require all this power, especially for small and medium sized sites. Also, with ASP.NET, deployment and configuration has been made much easier and flexible (take for example the use of `web.config` to change settings that would previously have required direct access to an IIS snap-in in ASP). Lastly, in-house or dedicated servers are expensive, and not all companies can and/or want to afford them, unless their purpose is very unusual.

Therefore, if we have budget limitations or we simply don't need full control over the system, the common solution for publishing our website is to a rent a shared server from a hosting company. We decided to choose this solution for our website, because we don't really need a deep level of system customization – `web.config` settings are enough for this. Also, we wanted to present an example that would be useful to the majority of readers, and that means using shared hosting.

FTP Versus Online File Management

Now that we've chosen to use a third party hosting service for our site, we should also consider the additional implications that this choice has on the ease of site maintenance. Uploading files is not a problem – we need nothing more than a simple FTP client to upload, download, rename, and perform most of the other necessary operations on the files. There are lots of them on the market, many available for free. On the other hand, using FTP to update every changed file can be slow and boring, especially when you need to upload the same very large file several times for minor changes, perhaps affecting only a single line of code each time. Sometimes FTP can be slow or even inaccessible when the server is busy (remember that we chose to use a *shared* server) or because the FTP server is temporarily down. Imagine another situation: when you're traveling or visiting a client's place without your laptop, you show the project to your client and are asked to make a quick modification. Something simple that should only take a few seconds, but how do you do it if you don't have your ASP.NET source code available, and if you don't have an FTP program to upload your changes? Often company networks have firewalls or proxies that prevent full FTP access.

Some of these issues might not seem important and you may be thinking that we could just ignore them. Admittedly, these situations are not the rule, but they *do* happen, and having a reserve plan can turn out to be a good precaution. So, what is this reserve plan? It is having a web application that serves as a **file manager** for the web site's files and physical structure (that is, the structure of subdirectories). Such a file manager should allow us to do most of the operations that we would normally do through the FTP utility, plus something else that FTP can't provide. That extra something is that, if we have such a tool for our website, we'll be able to explore our files and resources with nothing more than a web browser and an Internet connection. We'll also be able to edit text files (source code) from the web browser itself, so small changes can be made instantly without a download and subsequent upload – useful if you've just uploaded some code, only to realize you missed out one semi-colon!

In short, a file manager tool is pretty handy for site maintenance in some situations.

Database Management

ThePhile.com is a database-driven website that runs against SQL Server 2000. During development we can use the Enterprise Manager to create tables and stored procedures, add/edit/delete records, and set properties on everything. We could do everything with T-SQL scripts written by hand but, to be honest, the Enterprise Manager is so handy that everyone quickly gets used to it and performs most of the required creation and maintenance operations with its help.

However, when we deploy a website and replicate the database to the remote server, we can't always continue to use Enterprise Manager on the shared server. Some hosting plans do not allow webmasters to use Enterprise Manager, due to security reasons. This implies that we should resort to good old T-SQL to do everything, from simple operations such as adding records, to the creation and modification of tables and stored procedures, or the setting of various database options. Although all of this is possible with T-SQL code, it's not as quick as with Enterprise Manager, not to mention that coding long T-SQL statement is more error-prone. This is especially true for those commands that you never use because the Enterprise Manager allows you to just select a checkbox or fill a textbox. Also, you don't see a handy list of all the available tables, columns, stored procedures, and other objects.

So, it seems that there is space for third party tools here! And, in fact, third party tools for general (or SQL-specific) database management are not that difficult to find. There are nice tools made up of a set of pages that allow you to see all the database objects, edit many properties, and in general manage the database in such a way that you won't miss the Enterprise Manager quite as much.

Later in the chapter we'll show how to install and use one of the available tools (called the **Web Data Administrator**), written in ASP.NET and – guess what – kindly provided by Microsoft for free!

The Design

Now that we're aware of the usefulness of having maintenance tools, let's start designing our file manager module by writing down the list of features we want to implement. A typical utility of this type includes the following functionality:

❑ Starting from the web root, the file manager should allow the administrator to see the list of sub directories and files, and to navigate the structure by clicking a directory name to go one level down, or an arrow at the top of the list to go one level up.

❏ It should display information about each file-system item (file or directory) in our application. This will include a predefined icon that describes the item type, size (of all the subdirectories and files if the item is a directory), attributes, creation date, and the date of last modification.

❏ There should be the ability to upload and download files.

❏ It should offer the ability to create, rename, copy, move, and change the attributes of any directories and files.

❏ It should enable us to view and edit the content of text files.

This list includes most of the basic commands that we would expect from any file manager for Windows. We want to reproduce them with a web interface running on a browser, which will allow us to perform common operations without the need for any external tools.

We want this application to respect a couple of basic requirements:

❏ It should be easy to integrate the tool into other existing websites

❏ It should not be possible for an anonymous Internet user to access the file manager; it must have a reliable authentication/authorization system

Let's look at some details to better explain the design choices.

Implementation Design

Most applications are data-driven and have a set of business rules to respect. In this case, as we said in Chapter 2, the first concern for a developer would be to decide how to split the application into several layers: data, business, and user presentation. This application, though, is of a different type – it has no database and the data to be shown is part of the structure of the file system. The components for working with the file system and performing all the required I/O operations are already provided by the huge collection of classes within the .NET Framework, so we don't have to worry about this either. Therefore, what we have to write is only the presentation layer – that is, a set of ASP.NET pages and custom controls.

This is the first *module* we're going to develop for ThePhile.com. By module, we mean a web application that is site-independent, so we should design it in a way that makes it easy to integrate this module with any other site. This is a requirement that all the other modules we'll see in the book should also meet. On the other hand, our designers do want to integrate this module with the rest of the site, so it should have the same color schemes and a similar layout. For this reason we'll make use of the shared stylesheet that we built in Chapter 2 for the entire site, so that if we change the style for an element or a style class, all the pages of our module will automatically change without any further manual intervention. In Chapter 2 we also built header and footer user controls that can be inserted into any page in order to have the same layout without having to manually copy and paste the common HTML code into each page. However, this module does not need the site-wide header and footer controls, since it really is an independent and external tool accessed by administrators only, so we'll avoid using these two shared controls.

The file manager will comprise only two ASP.NET pages: one for navigating the folder structure, uploading, deleting, renaming, copying, and moving files and directories. The other is a simple text editor for creating a new file or editing an existing one.

Security Design

Most sites have an administration section that allows us to update a database or perform other operations that normal users are not allowed to do, and they usually have other parts that are for registered members only. So, securing a website is often a major task that must be taken very seriously during the design phase. ASP.NET offers several types of security, each of which should be used in different situations. You should already know something about this if you've ever developed for the web with .NET, so let's just review them briefly:

❑ Windows authentication: based on IIS authentication and the NTFS file permissions of Windows 2000. After a user is authenticated, they access the protected resources under the context of that account, with its rights and limitations.

❑ Forms-based authentication: the user logs in via a custom ASP.NET page and their credentials are validated against the values stored in the web.config file, a database, an XML file, or some other data source.

❑ Passport authentication: the user is authenticated by an external web service powered by Microsoft at www.passport.com. This service, born in 1999 but not widely used yet, requires a paid subscription.

Each of these types of authentication is best suited to particular situations. Forms-based authentication allows a great deal of customization, and is best suited when you need to add, remove, and manage an unknown number of users quite frequently, and without touching IIS and Windows settings. This type of authentication will be explained in much more detail in the next chapter, where we'll build a users module for the management of the site's members and the administrators of the other modules that we'll present throughout the book.

On the other hand, Windows authentication requires the server administrator to set up a group and a number of users from the Computer Management snap-in, and to associate them with the resources to protect. It offers the opportunity to assign different permissions to different users. It is best suited when we're building a system based on an intranet, or when we know in advance the number of users for which we should create an account. For the file manager module, we have a fixed number of administrators that we want to allow to manage the site's resources, so we can create a few accounts and use Windows authentication. However, with the User Accounts module we build later, you'll see how we could integrate our system with that.

The Solution

Now that we have a clear idea about what we're going to build, we can start creating the project with VS.NET. The files for the presentation layer are part of the main ThePhile project, and sit in the Modules\FileManager folder. Unless otherwise stated, all classes for this module should be part of the Wrox.WebModules.FileManager.Web namespace.

Classes to Work with Files and Directories

In the design section of the chapter we mentioned that the .NET Framework provides quite a lot of classes to easily manipulate and retrieve information about the file system's items. The `System.IO` namespace contains all the classes that have to do with the IO operations for any backing store, and some classes that allow us to do advanced stuff such as monitoring the file system and listening for changes (this was pretty hard to do with the Windows API). Since we'll use some of these classes throughout the chapter, it's worth giving a brief description of the most used IO classes:

Class	Description
Directory	Provides static (shared) methods for enumerating directories and logical drives, creating/deleting/moving directories and files, and retrieving/editing things like the creation date or the last access date.
DirectoryInfo	Used to work with a specified directory and its subdirectories.
File	Provides static methods for working with files: this includes opening or checking the existence of a file, and appending text data to a file.
FileInfo	Used to work with a specific file.
Path	Performs operations such as extracting the root or the file name from the specified path or combining two path strings.
FileSystemWatcher	Monitors the file system and raises events to handle changes.
Stream	Base class used to read from and write a backing store, such as the file system or network.
StreamReader	Used in conjunction with a stream to read characters from a backing store.
StreamWriter	Used in conjunction with a stream to write characters to a backing store.
TextReader	Abstract class used to define methods for reading characters from any source (backing store, string, and so on).
TextWriter	Abstract class used to define methods for writing characters to any source (backing store, string, and so on).
BinaryReader	Used to read primitive types such as string, integer, and boolean from a stream.
BinaryWriter	Used to write primitive types such as string, integer, and boolean to a stream.
FileStream	Used to read and write data in the file system.
MemoryStream	Used to read and write data in a memory buffer.

For a more complete listing of the System.IO namespace's classes and their methods, you can refer to *Professional ASP.NET* (Wrox Press, ISBN 1-861004-88-5) or *Professional C#* (Wrox Press, ISBN 1-861004-99-0). We will look at some of the classes described above in action.

Header and Footer Controls

We start our coding with the module-specific controls – in other words the header and the footer. Create a new user control named Header.ascx, and write the following code in the HTML tab of the IDE:

```
<%@ Control Language="c#" AutoEventWireup="false"
    Codebehind="Header.ascx.cs"
    Inherits="Wrox.WebModules.FileManager.Web.Controls.User.Header"%>
<a name="top">
  <table class="MenuTable" border="0" width="100%">
    <tr>
      <td>
        <b><u>FileManager - Wrox WebModule</u></b>
      </td>
      <td align="right">
        <a href="#bottom">
          <img Alt="Go to the bottom of the page"
              src="./Images/GoDown.gif" border="0" />
        </a>
      </td>
    </tr>
  </table>
```

This is simply HTML code (no need to use ASP.NET controls if we don't need to dynamically program them) that creates a title bar and a hyperlink image. This image links to an anchor placed at the bottom of the page, providing a quick way to scroll the page. Note that we associate the MenuTable style to the HTML table. In Chapter 3 we created a stylesheet, ThePhile.css, and began to define styles for use throughout the site. We have now added several new style definitions that we need for our FileManager module. We won't go into the code here – the modified file is available in code download, and you should refer back to Chapter 3 for an explanation of how cascading styles work. This stylesheet is imported by the page that will use this custom control.

The only modification we need to make in the code-behind is to change the namespace to Wrox.WebModules.FileManager.Web.Controls.User, which follows the conventions we discussed in Chapter 2.

The footer control, similarly, defines a link to jump to the top of the page. It contains an anchor that links from the icon to the header control. Here's the code for Footer.ascx:

```
<%@ Control Language="c#" AutoEventWireup="false"
    Codebehind="Footer.ascx.cs"
    Inherits="Wrox.WebModules.FileManager.Web.Controls.User.Footer"%>
<div align="right" Width="100%">
  <a href="#top">
    <img src="./Images/GoUp.gif"
        Alt="Go to the top of the page" border="0" />
  </a>
</div>
<a name="bottom">
```

Also, modify the namespace in the code-behind for `Footer.ascx` in exactly the same way as we did for the header control. In this particular module the header and footer controls are not really necessary, since we have only two pages, but it's a good practice to build them now, as we might want to add new features (and thus other pages) in the future.

The File Manager's Main Page

Before starting to write the code for this page, which is quite long, let's see how the page will look when it is finished. The screenshot below shows the main page of the finished FileManager while it is browsing the content of the `ThePhile` web directory:

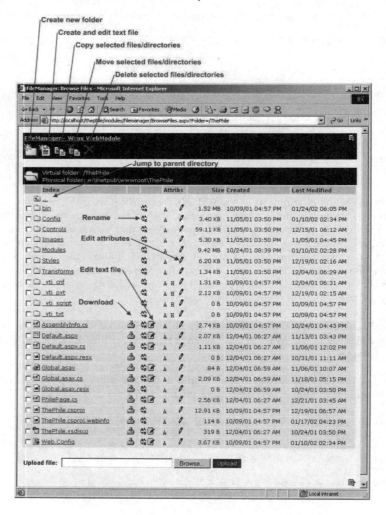

The page lists the directories first and then the files. Clicking the name of an item navigates to that subdirectory or file. For each item the page shows quite a lot of information, aligned by several columns, and some image buttons that allow us to rename the item, edit its attributes, edit a file's content, or download a file. The screenshot describes all the links so you should have no problems understanding how this interface works.

We can now start writing the page that will actually allow the administrator to navigate the site. We'll develop it piece by piece, starting from a simple explorer that just shows the directories and files, and progressively adding more and more information and commands.

First of all, create a new web form called `BrowseFiles.aspx`, and add the following code:

```
<%@ Page language="c#" Codebehind="BrowseFiles.aspx.cs"
    AutoEventWireup="false"
    Inherits="Wrox.WebModules.FileManager.Web.BrowseFiles" %>
<%@ Register TagPrefix="FileManager" TagName="Footer" src="Footer.ascx" %>
<%@ Register TagPrefix="FileManager" TagName="Header" src="Header.ascx" %>
<!DOCTYPE HTML PUBLIC "-//W3C//DTD HTML 4.0 Transitional//EN" >
<html>
  <head>
    <title>FileManager: Browse Files</title>
    <link rel="stylesheet" href="/ThePhile/Styles/ThePhile.css"
        type="text/css">
    <meta name="CODE_LANGUAGE" Content="C#">
  </head>
  <body>
    <form id="BrowseFiles" method="post" runat="server">
      <FileManager:Header ID="Title" runat="server" />
      <br>
      <asp:Table runat="server"
          CssClass="Grid_Header_Thin" Width="100%">
        <asp:TableRow>
          <asp:TableCell Width="36">
            <asp:Image runat="server" Height="32" Width="32"
                ImageUrl="./Images/OpenFolder.gif" />
          </asp:TableCell>
          <asp:TableCell>
            <asp:Label runat="server" ID="FolderDescription"/>
          </asp:TableCell>
        </asp:TableRow>
      </asp:Table>

      <asp:Table ID="FoldersAndFiles" runat="server"
          CssClass="Grid_General" Width="100%">
        <asp:TableRow CssClass="Grid_Header">
          <asp:TableCell Text="Index" />
        </asp:TableRow>
      </asp:Table>

      <br>
      <asp:Label ID="StatusMessage" runat="server"
          CssClass="StatusMessage" Visible="False" Width="100%" />
      <asp:Label ID="FolderStyle" runat="Server"
          Text="Grid_Item" Visible="false" />
      <asp:Label ID="FileStyle" runat="Server"
          Text="Grid_AlternatingItem" Visible="false" />
    </form>
    <FileManager:Footer ID="Footer" runat="server" />
  </body>
</html>
```

At this point the page does not contain many controls. We'll add others along the way, but it's worth describing each of them briefly here:

❑ The table at the top of the page has two columns. The first one shows an icon representing an open folder, while the cell on the right has a label that will be set dynamically to show the virtual and physical path of the folder whose content is currently listed on the page.

❑ The second table, named `FoldersAndFiles`, is the table where we'll actually show the current folder's subdirectories and files. At this point it has just one column for the item name (file or directory). Later in the chapter we'll add more columns for item attributes and command buttons.

❑ The `StatusMessage` label is used to display text representing errors and exceptions.

❑ The `FileStyle` and `FolderStyle` controls are two invisible labels. They are only used to store the name of the style for the rows that will be dynamically created from the code-behind class, to display files or folders respectively. Instead of hard coding such settings in the compiled assembly, we want to leave them in the ASPX page (which can be easily modified without the need to recompile anything) and retrieve them later in the code-behind.

Listing the Contents of a Folder

It's time to write the code that shows the contents of the selected folder in the table. Most of the following code-behind code, `BrowseFile.aspx.cs`, is auto-generated by VS.NET. The procedure we need to focus on is `Page_Load`.

The virtual path of the folder to scan is passed along with the page URL, as a parameter called `Folder`. If not specified, the website root is taken as the default. The procedure gets the parameter value, stores it in a private variable, `folderPath`, and shows the virtual and physical path in the description table at the top of the page.

A second routine, called `FillFoldersAndFilesTable`, is then executed, and that is the one that finally scans the folder. Even though at this point the result just shows the folder and file names, with no additional information, the code for `FillFoldersAndFilesTable` is quite long, so we've left it out for the time being. Here is the remainder of the class:

```
using System;
using System.Collections;
using System.ComponentModel;
using System.Data;
using System.Drawing;
using System.Web;
using System.Web.SessionState;
using System.Web.UI;
using System.Web.UI.WebControls;
using System.Web.UI.HtmlControls;
using System.IO;

namespace Wrox.WebModules.FileManager.Web
{
   public class BrowseFiles : System.Web.UI.Page
   {
      protected System.Web.UI.WebControls.Table FoldersAndFiles;
```

```csharp
    protected System.Web.UI.WebControls.Label FolderDescription;
    protected System.Web.UI.WebControls.Label FolderStyle;
    protected System.Web.UI.WebControls.Label FileStyle;

    protected System.Web.UI.WebControls.Label StatusMessage;
    protected System.Web.UI.WebControls.Table Table1;

    private string folderPath;

    private void Page_Load(object sender, EventArgs e)
    {
      // extract from the querystring the path to scan
      folderPath = Request.Params["Folder"];
      if (folderPath == null || folderPath=="/")
        folderPath = Request.ApplicationPath.ToString();
      // if the folder is not "/" but it ends with "/", remove the last /
      else if (folderPath.EndsWith("/"))
        folderPath = folderPath.Substring(0, folderPath.Length-1);

      // write the physical and virtual path
      FolderDescription.Text = "Virtual folder: " + folderPath +
          "<br>Physical folder: " + Server.MapPath(folderPath);
      // actually scan the specified folder
      FillFoldersAndFilesTable();
    }

    private void FillFoldersAndFilesTable()
    {
      //to be added next...
    }

    public BrowseFiles()
    {
      Page.Init += new System.EventHandler(Page_Init);
    }

    private void Page_Init(object sender, EventArgs e)
    {
      InitializeComponent();
    }

    private void InitializeComponent()
    {
      this.Load += new System.EventHandler(this.Page_Load);
    }
  }
}
```

Let's now fill in the code for the `FillFoldersAndFilesTable` procedure, one part at a time. It begins by retrieving the collection of child files and sub directories for the folder stored in the private `folderPath` variable:

```
private void FillFoldersAndFilesTable()
{
  string location;

  DirectoryInfo parentDir;
  DirectoryInfo[] childDirs;
  FileInfo[] childFiles;
  try
  {
    parentDir = new DirectoryInfo(Server.MapPath(folderPath));
    // get all the child directories and files
    childDirs = parentDir.GetDirectories();
    childFiles = parentDir.GetFiles();
  }
  catch (Exception exc)
  {
    StatusMessage.Text = exc.Message;
    StatusMessage.Visible = true;
    return;
  }
}
```

The code is protected within a `try...catch` block, so in cases where the `folderPath` folder does not exist an error message is shown and the procedure exits gracefully.

Next, the procedure checks whether the current folder is the site root. If it is not, the first row in the table must be a link to the parent folder, whose path is retrieved by removing the part after the last "/" character (remember that we're working with a virtual path here, so we cannot use `Directory.GetParent` as we would do with a physical path):

```
    TableRow rowItem;
    TableCell cellItemLink;
    HyperLink linkItem;

    Style styleFolderRow = new Style();
    styleFolderRow.CssClass = FolderStyle.Text;
    Style styleFileRow = new Style();
    styleFileRow.CssClass = FileStyle.Text;
    Style styleLink = new Style();
    styleLink.CssClass = "GridLink";

    // if the current folder is not the root, add the FolderUp icon and link
    if (folderPath != "/")
    {
      rowItem = new TableRow();
      cellItemLink = new TableCell();
      linkItem = new HyperLink();

      // add the link that points to the parent directory
      linkItem.Text = " ...";
```

```
int lastSlashIndex = folderPath.LastIndexOf("/");
location = folderPath.Substring(0,lastSlashIndex);
if (location.Length==0) location="/";
linkItem.NavigateUrl = "BrowseFiles.aspx?Folder=" + location;
linkItem.ApplyStyle(styleLink);
cellItemLink.Controls.Add(linkItem);

// add the cell to the new row
rowItem.Cells.Add(cellItemLink);

// add the row to the table
rowItem.ApplyStyle(styleFolderRow);
FoldersAndFiles.Rows.Add(rowItem);
}
```

Now we cycle through the `childDirs` collection and add the name of all the child directories. The name text links to `BrowseFiles.aspx`, with the `Folder` parameter set to the `folderPath` plus the name of the `childDirs` collection's current folder:

```
// add all the child directories first
foreach (DirectoryInfo childDir in childDirs)
{

    // create the required cells and controls
    rowItem = new TableRow();
    cellItemLink = new TableCell();
    linkItem = new HyperLink();

    // create the link that points to this sub-directory
    linkItem.Text = childDir.Name;
    location = folderPath;
    if (location.EndsWith("/"))
      location += childDir.Name;
    else
      location += "/" + childDir.Name;
    linkItem.NavigateUrl = "BrowseFiles.aspx?Folder=" + location;
    linkItem.ApplyStyle(styleLink);
    cellItemLink.Controls.Add(linkItem);

    // add the cell to the new row
    rowItem.Cells.Add(cellItemLink);

    // add the new row to the table
    rowItem.ApplyStyle(styleFolderRow);
    FoldersAndFiles.Rows.Add(rowItem);
}
```

Note that, as for the previous piece of code, the dynamically created cell is added to a new row, which is added to the table's `Rows` collection.

The code that cycles through the collection of child files is very similar to the code just shown, except that the link behind the name of each file opens a new window to display the file (letting the web browser select *how* to display it):

```
// now add each child file
foreach (FileInfo childFile in childFiles)
{

  // create the required cells and controls
  rowItem = new TableRow();
  cellItemLink = new TableCell();
  linkItem = new HyperLink();
  int extIndex;

  // create and add the link that points to this file in a new window
  linkItem.Text = childFile.Name;
  location = folderPath;
  if (location.EndsWith("/"))
    location += childFile.Name;
  else
    location += "/" + childFile.Name;
  linkItem.NavigateUrl = location;
  linkItem.Target = "_blank";
  linkItem.ApplyStyle(styleLink);
  cellItemLink.Controls.Add(linkItem);

  // add the cell to the new row
  rowItem.Cells.Add(cellItemLink);

  // add the new row to the table
  rowItem.ApplyStyle(styleFileRow);
  FoldersAndFiles.Rows.Add(rowItem);
  }
}
```

The code that allows the basic navigation functionality is now complete, and we can finally compile the assembly and run the page. If you set `BrowseFiles.aspx` as the Start Page (right click on the file in the Solution Explorer and click the respective command) the project is automatically compiled and the page is run when you press *F5*. Otherwise open Internet Explorer and navigate to http://localhost/ThePhile/Modules/FileManager/BrowseFiles.aspx.

The screenshot below represents what you should see if you use the file manager to navigate to the ThePhile folder:

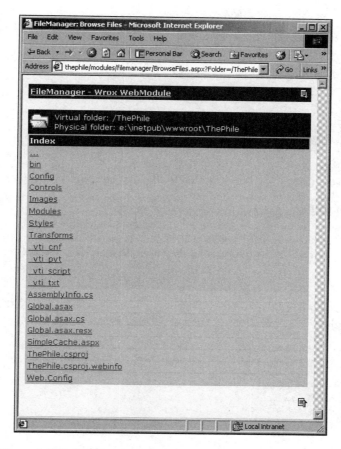

Displaying Additional Attributes

Just displaying the names of the child directories and files is not enough. We want to display much more information: an icon to describe the type of item, the attributes, size, the date of creation, and date of last modification. The first thing to do is to create new columns in the FoldersAndFiles table in BrowseFiles.aspx:

```
<asp:Table ID="FoldersAndFiles" runat="server"
    CssClass="Grid_General" Width="100%">
  <asp:TableRow CssClass="Grid_Header">
    <asp:TableCell Width="36px" />
    <asp:TableCell Text="Index" />
    <asp:TableCell Text="Attribs" Width="50px" />
    <asp:TableCell Text="Size" Width="80px" HorizontalAlign="Right" />
    <asp:TableCell Text="Created" Width="140px" />
    <asp:TableCell Text="Last Modified" Width="140px" />
  </asp:TableRow>
</asp:Table>
```

We also need to declare new cells and controls in the `FillFoldersAndFilesTable` procedure in the code-behind, `BrowseFiles.aspx.cs`:

```
TableRow rowItem;
TableCell cellItemLink;
HyperLink linkItem;
TableCell cellItemIcon;
TableCell cellSize;
TableCell cellAttributes;
TableCell cellCreated;
TableCell cellLastModified;
Label labelAttributes;
System.Web.UI.WebControls.Image imgItemIcon;
```

Now we have to actually create, set, and add these new cells for each directory and file shown in the table. We're going to present the code required for the new columns, one column at a time.

Displaying the Item Icon

Creating the icon for the subdirectories and the link to the parent directory is straightforward, since we use a fixed icon. We just create the `Image` control named `imgItemIcon`, set its `ImageUrl` property, and add it to the first cell. Here's the code for the parent link block, in `BrowseFiles.aspx.cs`:

```
if (folderPath != "/")
{
   rowItem = new TableRow();
   cellItemLink = new TableCell();
   linkItem = new HyperLink();
   cellItemIcon = new TableCell();
   imgItemIcon = new System.Web.UI.WebControls.Image();

   // create the cell with the FolderUp icon
   imgItemIcon.ImageUrl = "./Images/ParentFolder.gif";
   cellItemIcon.Controls.Add(imgItemIcon);
   cellItemIcon.HorizontalAlign = HorizontalAlign.Right;

   // add the link that points to the parent directory
   ...

   // add the cells to the new row
   rowItem.Cells.Add(cellItemIcon);
   rowItem.Cells.Add(cellItemLink);

   // add the row to the table
   rowItem.ApplyStyle(styleFolderRow);
   FoldersAndFiles.Rows.Add(rowItem);
}
```

The code for each child directory is very similar:

```
foreach (DirectoryInfo childDir in childDirs)
{
    // create the required cells and controls
    rowItem = new TableRow();
    cellItemLink = new TableCell();
    linkItem = new HyperLink();
    cellItemIcon = new TableCell();
    imgItemIcon = new System.Web.UI.WebControls.Image();

    // add the icon with the closed folder
    imgItemIcon.ImageUrl = "./Images/ClosedFolder.gif";
    cellItemIcon.Controls.Add(imgItemIcon);
    cellItemIcon.HorizontalAlign = HorizontalAlign.Right;

    // create the link that points to this sub-directory
    ...

    // add the cells to the new row, and add the row to the table
    ...
}
```

So far, so good. Now here's the more interesting part – adding an icon for each file. If we only wanted to differentiate files from folders, we could just associate a fixed icon for all the files (different from the one used for the folders). But we want to do something more. We want to display the icon that is usually shown in Windows Explorer to describe the file *type*. In Windows each file extension is identified by an icon, which is provided by the associated program. This icon is usually stored within a binary EXE or DLL file, and its index is stored in the registry. There are API functions to programmatically retrieve the icon index within a file, and then show the icon through the Windows ListView control, based on the icon's handle.

This is very tricky in ASP.NET, since the src attribute of an <img> tag should point directly to an image file.

> It is possible to extract the icon associated with the file extension from a binary file, save it to disk, and show it with the <img> tag, or even directly send a binary stream to the browser. However, this would require a lot of work, would slow down the execution, and would not bring about any valuable improvements to the application, so we decided not to cover this method here.

We will create a predefined set of fixed images for the most common files used for a website. These images will be assigned to the files based on their extension. If we name such images according to the file extensions (for example, aspx.gif, html.gif, ascx.gif, zip.gif, bmp.gif, gif.gif, etc.) we'll just need to check if there is an image with a name corresponding to the file extension, and if so show it. If there is no image with that name, we'll show a predefined image, unknown.gif. The file icons for many extensions are in the code download, but of course you can add your own.

To speed up the test that verifies the existence of a certain icon, we define an array of extensions for which we've created the appropriate image, and the check is done against this array. Here's how the array is defined, as a private variable for the BrowseFiles class:

```
private string[] extensions = new string[]{".aspx", ".html", ".ascx",
  ".zip", ".bmp", ".gif", ...};
```

The rest of the file extensions have been left out here and you can add any others appropriate to your site's requirements. In the code download you'll find that 52 different extensions are already supported!

Thanks to the `Array.IndexOf` shared method (which returns the index of the element being searched for in the array), checking whether the extension of a file is present within the `extensions` array is a matter of a single line of code. Here is the updated block that adds all the child files to the table:

```
foreach (FileInfo childFile in childFiles)
{

    // create the required cells and controls
    rowItem = new TableRow();
    cellItemLink = new TableCell();
    linkItem = new HyperLink();
    cellItemIcon = new TableCell();
    imgItemIcon = new System.Web.UI.WebControls.Image();
    int extIndex;

    // create and add the link that points to this file in a new window
    ...

    // search for the extension in the array,
    // and if it's found show the respective icon
    // if not found add a general icon for unknown files
    extIndex = Array.IndexOf(extensions, childFile.Extension.ToLower());
    if (extIndex > -1)
      imgItemIcon.ImageUrl = "./Images/" +
        childFile.Extension.Substring(1) + ".gif";
    else
      imgItemIcon.ImageUrl = "./Images/unknown.gif";

    // add the icon to the first cell
    cellItemIcon.Controls.Add(imgItemIcon);
    cellItemIcon.HorizontalAlign = HorizontalAlign.Right;

    // add the cells to the new row
    rowItem.Cells.Add(cellItemIcon);
    rowItem.Cells.Add(cellItemLink);

    // add the new row to the table
    ...
}
```

Displaying the Item Attributes

Let's go ahead with the creation of the third column, the one that displays a list of attributes for the subdirectories and files. The modifications for the block that adds the directories and the block that adds the files are exactly the same. For the first row, which points to the parent directory (if any), we just add an empty cell. This is shown in the following code:

```
if (folderPath != "/")
{
  ...
  // create the cell with the FolderUp icon
  // add the link that points to the parent directory
  ...

  // add the cells to the new row
  rowItem.Cells.Add(cellItemIcon);
  rowItem.Cells.Add(cellItemLink);
  rowItem.Cells.Add(new TableCell());

  // add the row to the table
  ...
}

foreach (DirectoryInfo childDir in childDirs)
{

  // create the required cells and controls
  ...
  cellAttributes = new TableCell();
  labelAttributes = new Label();

  // add the icon with the closed folder
  ...

  // create the link that points to this sub-directory
  ...

  // set the description label to the Attributes cell
  labelAttributes.Text = GetAttributesDescription(childDir.Attributes);
  labelAttributes.Font.Name = "Courier";
  cellAttributes.Controls.Add(labelAttributes);


  // add the cells to the new row and add the row to the table
  rowItem.Cells.Add(cellAttributes);
  ...
}

// now add each child file
foreach (FileInfo childFile in childFiles)
{

  // create the required cells and controls
  ...
  cellAttributes = new TableCell();
  labelAttributes = new Label();

  // create the icon and the link that points to this file
  ...

  // set the description label to the Attributes cell
```

```
labelAttributes.Text = GetAttributesDescription(childFile.Attributes);
labelAttributes.Font.Name = "Courier";
cellAttributes.Controls.Add(labelAttributes);

// add the cells to the new row and add the row to the table
rowItem.Cells.Add(cellAttributes);
...
}
```

As you can see, the string that describes the item's attributes is not built directly in the code above, but is returned by a custom procedure called GetAttributesDescriptions, which receives as input the value of the Attributes property, exposed by both the DirectoryInfo and FileInfo data type. Here is its code:

```
protected string GetAttributesDescription(FileAttributes attribs)
{
  string itemAttribs = "";

  // check if the Archive attribute is set
  if ((attribs & FileAttributes.Archive) == FileAttributes.Archive)
    itemAttribs += "A";
  else
    itemAttribs += " ";

  // check if the ReadOnly attribute is set
  if ((attribs & FileAttributes.ReadOnly) == FileAttributes.ReadOnly)
    itemAttribs += "R";
  else
    itemAttribs += " ";

  // check if the Hidden attribute is set
  if ((attribs & FileAttributes.Hidden) == FileAttributes.Hidden)
    itemAttribs += "H";
  else
    itemAttribs += " ";

  // check if the System attribute is set
  if ((attribs & FileAttributes.System) == FileAttributes.System)
    itemAttribs += "S";
  else
    itemAttribs += " ";

  // return the final result
  return itemAttribs;
}
```

This procedure checks four attributes: Archive, ReadOnly, Hidden, and System. If the attribute being checked is set, the procedure adds its first letter to the description string that will be returned. Otherwise, if the attribute is not set, a space is added. So, for example, the string "A S" means Archive + System, while "ARH " means Archive + ReadOnly + Hidden.

If you look back at the code that calls this procedure, you'll see that the font of the label displaying the attribute description is set to Courier. This is because Courier is a fixed-width font, meaning that, for example, 'i' and 'z' have the same width. Another reason for using Courier is that spaces have the same width as letters, and this allows us to create virtual columns and have all the A letters in the column aligned, and the same for the letters R, H, and S. If an attribute is not set for an item, you see a blank space as large as the letter above it, and then the other attribute letters (if any).

You may also wonder why we created a Label control instead of directly setting the cell's Text property. The reason is that we'll add another control to this column later in the chapter, and it's easier to add two controls to the Controls collection than to set a very long string for the cell's Text property.

Displaying the Item Size

The next column we want to add displays the size of the item. It is easy to get this information for the files, since the FileInfo class exposes a Length property. As the DirectoryInfo class does not have a Length property, we need to calculate the size of a directory by summing the size of all its child files. Here is a procedure that uses recursion to sum the child files of all subdirectories and obtain the overall size of the directory:

```
protected long GetDirectorySize(string path)
{
  long dirSize = 0;
  DirectoryInfo dir = new DirectoryInfo(path);

  // add the size of each file
  foreach (FileInfo file in dir.GetFiles())
    dirSize += file.Length;

    // add the size of each subdirectory, retrieved by
    // recursively calling this same routine
    foreach (DirectoryInfo subdir in dir.GetDirectories())
      dirSize += GetDirectorySize(subdir.FullName);

  return dirSize;
}
```

Now we can easily get the size for both the files and the directories. But the size is returned in bytes, and a series of six or seven figures is not very readable. It would be better to show the size in bytes, kilobytes, or megabytes according to the number of bytes, as follows:

❑   Less than 1024 bytes: show the size in bytes

❑   Between 1024 and 1,048,576 bytes: show the size in KB (for example 2.52 KB, instead of 2,580 bytes)

❑   1,048,576 bytes and above: show the size in MB

The following procedure accepts the size in double format, and returns a string with the size formatted in bytes, KB, or MB by following the rules above:

```
protected string FormatSize(double fileSize)
{
  if (fileSize < 1024)
    return String.Format("{0:N0} B", fileSize);
  else if (fileSize < 1024*1024)
    return String.Format("{0:N2} KB", fileSize/1024);
  else
    return String.Format("{0:N2} MB", fileSize/(1024*1024));
}
```

Now that we can get the size for a directory, and format any size in the proper way, let's add the **Size** column for each item. As we've done for the **Attributes** column, we're going to insert an empty cell for the first row, which links to the parent folder, and a new cell with the size for all files and folders. Here are the necessary updates:

```
if (folderPath != "/")
{
  // create the cell with the FolderUp icon,
  // and add the link that points to the parent directory
  ...

  // add the cells to the new row
  rowItem.Cells.Add(cellItemIcon);
  rowItem.Cells.Add(cellItemLink);
  rowItem.Cells.Add(new TableCell());
  rowItem.Cells.Add(new TableCell());

  // add the row to the table
  ...
}

foreach (DirectoryInfo childDir in childDirs)
{

  // create the required cells and controls
  cellSize = new TableCell();
  ...

  // create the icon, the link that points to this subdirectory
  // and the cell that shows the attributes
  ...

  // set the cell that displays the item's size
  cellSize.Text = FormatSize(GetDirectorySize(childDir.FullName));
  cellSize.HorizontalAlign = HorizontalAlign.Right;

  // add the cells to the new row and add the row to the table
  rowItem.Cells.Add(cellSize);
  ...
}
```

```
// now add each child file
foreach (FileInfo childFile in childFiles)
{

    // create the required cells and controls
    cellSize = new TableCell();
    ...

    // create the icon, the link that points to this file
    // and the cell that shows the attributes
    ...

    // set the cell that displays the item's size
    cellSize.Text = FormatSize(childFile.Length) + " ";
    cellSize.HorizontalAlign = HorizontalAlign.Right;

    // add the cells to the new row and add the row to the table
    rowItem.Cells.Add(cellSize);
    ...
}
```

Displaying the Creation and Last Modification Dates

The last two columns we want to fill are the Created and Last Modified columns. We're lucky here as there's almost nothing to do, since this information is returned by the `CreationTime` and `LastWriteTime` properties exposed by the `DirectoryInfo` and `FileInfo` classes.

Here's the code to add:

```
foreach (DirectoryInfo childDir in childDirs)
{

    // create the required cells and controls
    ...
    cellCreated = new TableCell();
    cellLastModified = new TableCell();

    ...
    // set the created and last modified date
    cellCreated.Text = String.Format("{0:MM/dd/yy hh:mm tt}",
                                            childDir.CreationTime);
    cellLastModified.Text = String.Format("{0:MM/dd/yy hh:mm tt}",
                                            childDir.LastWriteTime);

    // add the cells to the new row
    ...
    rowItem.Cells.Add(cellCreated);
    rowItem.Cells.Add(cellLastModified);

    // add the new row to the table
    ...
}
```

```
foreach (FileInfo childFile in childFiles)
{

  // create the required cells
  ...
  cellCreated = new TableCell();
  cellLastModified = new TableCell();


  ...
  // set the created and last modified date
  cellCreated.Text = String.Format("{0:MM/dd/yy hh:mm tt}", +
                                            childFile.CreationTime);
  cellLastModified.Text = String.Format("{0:MM/dd/yy hh:mm tt}", +
                                            childFile.LastWriteTime);

  // add the cells to the new row
  ...
  rowItem.Cells.Add(cellCreated);
  rowItem.Cells.Add(cellLastModified);

  // add the new row to the table
  ...
}
```

We're finally done with the code for displaying the information about items! If you now recompile the assembly, and refresh the page in the browser, you should see something similar to the screenshot below:

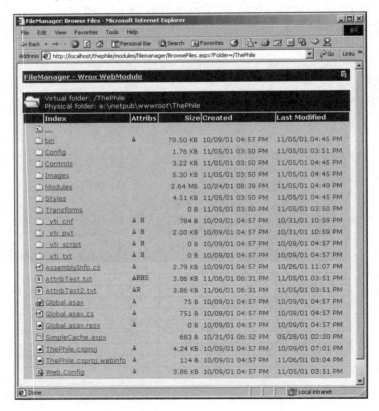

Downloading Files

When you click on an item's link, the file manager opens a new browser window and redirects to that file. If the file is an image or HTML file then you'll see it loaded and displayed by the browser. Instead, if it is a file that the browser is not able to open, such as a ZIP file, it will ask you if you want to download it. However, there are other file types that the browser will neither load nor allow you to download. For example, with `web.config` or `global.asax` you'll get an error page containing the message "This type of page is not served". And other files, particularly ASPX files, are processed on the server – so you'll see the result of the processing, not the source code.

We need to find a way to download a file or view its content without resorting to FTP. We can solve this with streams.

> **Using streams, we can provide a file to the user 'as is' – without the interference of IIS.**

We need a separate ASPX file, called `download.aspx`. This takes a filename as a parameter, and returns the content of that file – unprocessed by the web server. The ASPX file has no user interface – everything is done in the code-behind. Here's the code for `download.aspx.cs` `Page_Load` method:

```
private void Page_Load(object sender, System.EventArgs e)
{
    // retrieve the path of the file to download, and create
    // a FileInfo object to read its properties
    string path = Server.MapPath(Request.Params["File"]);
    System.IO.FileInfo file = new System.IO.FileInfo(path);

    // clear the current output content from the buffer
    Response.Clear();
    // add the header that specifies the default filename for the
    // Download/SaveAs dialog
    Response.AddHeader("Content-Disposition",
                                    "attachment; filename=" + file.Name);
    // add the header that specifies the file size, so that the browser
    // can show the download progress
    Response.AddHeader("Content-Length", file.Length.ToString());
    // specify that the response is a stream that cannot be read by the
    // client and must be downloaded
    Response.ContentType = "application/octet-stream";
    // send the file stream to the client
    Response.WriteFile(file.FullName);
    // stop the execution of this page
    Response.End();
}
```

We now need to add a download button to our `BrowseFiles.aspx` table. The button needs to point to `Download.aspx` with the appropriate parameter:

In the `BrowseFiles.aspx` file we need to add a new column to the `FoldersAndFiles` table:

```
<asp:Table ID="FoldersAndFiles" runat="server"
  CssClass="Grid_General" Width="100%">
  <asp:TableRow CssClass="Grid_Header">
    <asp:TableCell Width="36px" />
    <asp:TableCell Text="Index" />
    <asp:TableCell Width="25px" />
    <asp:TableCell Text="Attribs" Width="50px" />
    <asp:TableCell Text="Size" Width="80px" HorizontalAlign="Right" />
    <asp:TableCell Text="Created" Width="140px" />
    <asp:TableCell Text="Last Modified" Width="140px" />
  </asp:TableRow>
</asp:Table>
```

In `FillFoldersAndFilesTable` in the code-behind we have to create and add an empty cell for the first row, which points to the parent folder, and for all the child directories. We've seen how to do this previously, so we aren't going to repeat the code here. For the file rows we create a new cell and an image that links to `Download.aspx`, with the appropriate parameter:

```
// declare the required cells and controls
...
TableCell cellDownload;
HyperLink linkDownload;
...

// add an empty cell for all the rows that display a directory and to
// the row that points to the parent directory
...refer back to see how to add empty cells to the rows...

foreach (FileInfo childFile in childFiles)
{
  // create the required cells and controls
  ...
  cellDownload = new TableCell();
  linkDownload = new HyperLink();

  // set the other cells and controls
  ...

  // add the link to download the file
  linkDownload.Text = "<img src=\"./Images/Download.gif\" border=\"0\" +
      " height=\"16\" width=\"16\" Alt=\"Download\">";
  linkDownload.NavigateUrl = "Download.aspx?File=" + location;
  cellDownload.Controls.Add(linkDownload);

  // add the cells to the new row
  rowItem.Cells.Add(cellItemIcon);
  rowItem.Cells.Add(cellItemLink);
  rowItem.Cells.Add(cellDownload);
  rowItem.Cells.Add(cellAttributes);
  rowItem.Cells.Add(cellSize);
  rowItem.Cells.Add(cellCreated);
  rowItem.Cells.Add(cellLastModified);
```

```
      // add the new row to the table
      rowItem.ApplyStyle(styleFileRow);
      FoldersAndFiles.Rows.Add(rowItem);
   }
```

Now when we click the download icon, the source file will be downloaded – regardless of the file type.

Uploading Files

In addition to downloading files, we also want to *upload* files. Although we would certainly use FTP if we had to upload lots of files, this tool can be quite handy if you just need to upload a couple of files.

To select the file to upload we can use the standard HTML input control of type `file`. This comprises a textbox and a **Browse** button, which when pressed opens the **Choose File** dialog that allows the user to select a file. This control can be used and accessed in ASP.NET by adding the `runat="server"` attribute.

> In order to accept the submitted file, the form must be declared with the attribute `enctype="multipart/form-data"`.

Let's update our `BrowseFiles.aspx` page by adding this control and a button to submit the file:

```
<form id="BrowseFiles" method="post" runat="server"
    enctype="multipart/form-data">
<!-- other controls as above here -->
...
<asp:Table ID="FoldersAndFiles" runat="server" CssClass="Grid_General"
    Width="100%">
  <asp:TableRow CssClass="Grid_Header">
    <asp:TableCell Width="36px" />
    <asp:TableCell Text="Index" />
    <asp:TableCell Width="25px" />
    <asp:TableCell Text="Attribs" Width="50px" />
    <asp:TableCell Text="Size" Width="80px" HorizontalAlign="Right" />
    <asp:TableCell Text="Created" Width="140px" />
    <asp:TableCell Text="Last Modified" Width="140px" />
  </asp:TableRow>
</asp:Table>
<br>
<asp:Table runat="server">
  <asp:TableRow>
    <asp:TableCell Width="80px" Font-Bold="True" Text="Upload file:" />
    <asp:TableCell>
      <input type="file" ID="UploadedFile" runat="server" size="35">
    </asp:TableCell>
    <asp:TableCell>
      <asp:Button ID="Upload" runat="server" Text="Upload"
          CssClass="Button" OnClick="Upload_Click" />
    </asp:TableCell>
  </asp:TableRow>
</asp:Table>
<!-- other controls as above here -->
...
</form>
```

If we now save the file, VS.NET should add the following declaration to the code-behind:

```
public class BrowseFiles : System.Web.UI.Page
{
   protected System.Web.UI.HtmlControls.HtmlInputFile UploadedFile;


   // other controls below
   ...
```

The following code is for the `Upload_Click` event handler, whose function is to upload the selected file to the current directory, but only if a file has been selected:

```
protected void Upload_Click(object sender, EventArgs e)
{

   // proceed only if a file has been specified
   if (UploadedFile.PostedFile != null &&
     UploadedFile.PostedFile.FileName.Length > 0 )
   {
     string destDir = Server.MapPath(folderPath);

     try
     {

       // save to the current directory
       string fileName = Path.GetFileName(UploadedFile.PostedFile.FileName);
       UploadedFile.PostedFile.SaveAs(Path.Combine(destDir, fileName));

       // refresh the page
       Response.Redirect("BrowseFiles.aspx?Folder=" + folderPath);
     }
     catch (Exception exc)
     {
       StatusMessage.Text = exc.Message;
       StatusMessage.Visible = true;
     }
   }
}
```

The code is straightforward, but you should note one point: after the file is uploaded to the server, we refresh the table by reloading the entire page. This is necessary because in `Page_Load` the table was filled, so if we called `FillFoldersAndFilesTable` again here we would get all the rows twice. Since the redirection is done on the server before any HTML code is sent to the client browser, this does not cause much overhead.

Also note that the code that uploads the file is protected by a `try...catch` block. In case an exception occurs, for example because the current user does not have permission to write on this directory, an error message is shown in the `StatusMessage` label.

> Note that by default the maximum size of the uploaded file is 4MB. If you try to upload a bigger size you'll get an error page. You may want to increase this value, for example because you have ZIP, AVI, or MP3 files bigger than 4MB. To do so, set the **maxRequestLength** attribute of the **<httpRuntime>** setting in the ThePhile's **web.config** file. The size is specified in KB, so **<httpRuntime maxRequestLength="8192" />** sets the maximum file size to 8MB.

It's time to recompile everything and jump to the browser to test the updated file manager. In the screenshot below you can see both the new icons added to the files to download or open them, as well as the file input control and the **Choose file** dialog:

Creating Directories

So far we've seen the features of a typical file explorer (with the addition of a file uploader), but since we're building a file manager, we should also add functionality that will allow us to *change* the content and the structure of the site. We're going to implement many features in this category of commands; the first we'll see is the command to create a new directory.

Our designers want to create a toolbar with a link that, when pressed, pops up a dialog and asks for the name of the directory to create. As you might guess, this is not done by ASP.NET code, but rather by client-side JavaScript code, through the `prompt` function. If the user presses **Cancel**, nothing happens, but if the user types the name of the folder they want to create and presses **OK**, we have to pass this parameter back to the ASP.NET page that will actually create the directory and refresh the table.

The first thought might be to redirect to the current page and add the folder to create as a parameter in the URL. But ASP.NET is great because of its event procedures that handle the postbacks generated by specific controls, so why not use this cool feature? To do so, we need to have a clear understanding about the way the form is posted back when a button or a hyperlink control is pressed.

To demonstrate this we created a test page, which is not part of the final application. In it we placed a HyperLink control, as follows:

```
<asp:LinkButton ID="test" runat="server" Text="Demo" OnClick="Test_Click" />
```

Next, we wrote an empty Test_Click procedure in the code-behind, compiled and then ran the page. This is the HTML code produced:

```
...
<a id="Test" href="javascript:__doPostBack('Test','')">Demo</a>
...
<input type="hidden" name="__EVENTTARGET" value="" />
<input type="hidden" name="__EVENTARGUMENT" value="" />
<script language="javascript">
<!--
   function __doPostBack(eventTarget, eventArgument) {
     var theform = document.BrowseFiles;
     theform.__EVENTTARGET.value = eventTarget;
     theform.__EVENTARGUMENT.value = eventArgument;
     theform.submit();
   }
// -->
</script>
...
```

As you can see, there is nothing magic here. When the link is pressed, instead of redirecting to another page, the __doPostBack JavaScript function is called. The first parameter that the function requires is the name of the control that is going to post back the form and generate the event on the server. The second parameter may contain additional information for the event, but it is empty in this case, and in fact the Click event has no additional information in the standard e parameter.

What the __doPostBack actually does is to set two hidden input controls, with the values passed in the input. Then it submits the form. On the server, the ASP.NET engine extracts the values of those two hidden controls, and calls the server event handler. Again, nothing magic... but very cool!

In conclusion, all the server controls do to post back the form is to call the __doPostBack function, but we can also do this by writing the HTML code by hand.

Back to our original problem: we can create a link that, when clicked, calls a JavaScript function. This function pops up the prompt dialog asking for a name. If the user presses OK, the function can save the specified folder name in a hidden field, and call the __doPostBack function to post back the form. All done then? Almost. Remember that the first parameter of the function is the name of the server control whose Click event (in this case, it might be a different event for other controls) will be raised. This control must actually exist on the page, but we can avoid setting its Text property and so make it invisible, and we add it just to use its associated Click event.

Let's look at the code in the ASP.NET page, `BrowseFiles.aspx`, to better explain how to do this. The code contains the JavaScript that asks for the new directory, the `LinkButton`, and the hidden control declaration:

```
...
<html>
  <head>
    <title>FileManager: Browse Files</title>
    <link rel="stylesheet" HREF="/ThePhile/Styles/ThePhile.css"
        TYPE="text/css" />
    <meta name="CODE_LANGUAGE" Content="C#">
    <script language="javascript">
      function CreateDir()
      {
        dirName = prompt('Type the name of the directory you want to
            create:','');

        if ((dirName) && (dirName!=""))
        {
          document.forms['BrowseFiles'].elements['funcParam'].value =
                                                  dirName;
          __doPostBack('CreateDir', '');
        }
      }
    </script>
  </head>
  <body>
    <form id="BrowseFiles" method="post" runat="server"
        enctype="multipart/form-data">
    <FileManager:Header ID="Title" runat="server" />
    <input type="hidden" id="funcParam" runat="server">
    <table class="MenuTable" border="0" width="100%">
      <tr>
        <td>
          <a href="javascript:CreateDir();">
            <img border="0" src="./Images/NewFolder.gif"
                Alt="Create a new directory" height="28" width="28" />
          </a>
          <asp:LinkButton ID="CreateDir" runat="server"
              OnClick="CreateDir_Click" />
        </td>
      </tr>
    </table>
    <br>
    <asp:Table runat="server" CssClass="Grid_Header_Thin"
        Width="100%" ID="Table1">
      <asp:TableRow>
        <asp:TableCell Width="36">
          <asp:Image runat="server" Height="32"
              Width="32" ImageUrl="./Images/OpenFolder.gif" />
        </asp:TableCell>
```

The rest is unchanged...

105

> You might be wondering why we completely avoided setting the Text property instead of simply setting its Visible property to False. The reason is that we need at least one control recognized by ASP.NET as a control that generates postbacks through a call to __doPostBack. Otherwise ASP.NET detects that there is no need for the __doPostBack function and does not include it in the generated HTML code for the client, which would cause an error when our CreateDir function calls it. A control with the Visible="False" attribute is not created in the HTML, and so neither is __doPostBack. Therefore, we need to declare the control, leaving out the Visible property, so that the JavaScript function is created. Once we have this control, the other similar LinkButton controls we'll use later can be made invisible by the Visible="False" attribute.

In the code-behind we first declare the hidden control used to store the new folder name:

```
protected System.Web.UI.HtmlControls.HtmlInputHidden funcParam;
```

Then we have the Click event handler for the CreateDir ButtonLink:

```
protected void CreateDir_Click(object sender, EventArgs e)
{

  // build the complete path (current path + new dir name)
  string path = folderPath;
  if (path.EndsWith("/"))
    path += funcParam.Value;
  else
    path += "/" + funcParam.Value;

  try
  {

    // create the directory
    Directory.CreateDirectory(Server.MapPath(path));

    // refresh the page
    Response.Redirect("BrowseFiles.aspx?Folder=" + folderPath);
  }
  catch (Exception exc)
  {
    StatusMessage.Text = exc.Message;
    StatusMessage.Visible = true;
  }
}
```

As usual, the possible exception is handled and an error message is shown. If the new directory is created successfully, the page is refreshed and the table re-filled with the updated content.

In this example we've taken advantage of both the client-side script and the ASP.NET event handling mechanism. The following screenshot shows the updated file manager and its dialog to enter the new directory name:

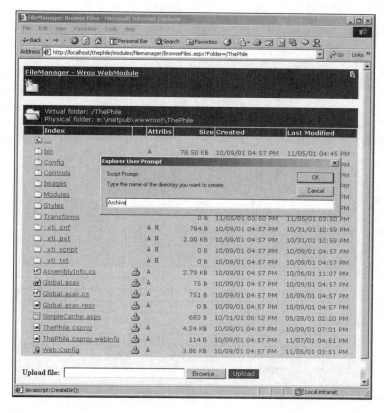

Creating Text Files

If we allow the administrator to create directories, we must also provide the opportunity to create text files (not empty text files of course, but files with some content). The approach is exactly the same as we used to implement the last command: manually calling the __doPostBack function from a JavaScript routine executed by an image link. The new code in the ASPX page is as follows:

```
...
<head>
  <title>FileManager: Browse Files</title>
  <link rel="stylesheet" HREF="/ThePhile/Styles/ThePhile.css"
     TYPE="text/css" />
  <meta name="CODE_LANGUAGE" Content="C#">
  <script language="javascript">

    function CreateDir()
    {
```

```
      ... unchanged from above ...
      }

   function CreateFile()
   {
     fileName = prompt('Type the name of the file you want to create:','');

     if ((fileName) && (fileName!=""))
     {
       document.forms['BrowseFiles'].elements[
         'funcParam'].value = fileName;
       __doPostBack('CreateFile', '');
     }
   }
 </script>
</head>
<body>
 <form id="BrowseFiles" method="post" runat="server"
     enctype="multipart/form-data">
   <FileManager:Header ID="Title" runat="server" />
   <input type="hidden" id="funcParam" runat="server">
     <table class="MenuTable" border="0" width="100%">
       <tr>
         <td>
           <a href="javascript:CreateDir();">
             <img border="0" src="./Images/NewFolder.gif"
               Alt="Create a new directory" height="28" width="28" />
           </a>
           <asp:LinkButton ID="CreateDir" runat="server"
               OnClick="CreateDir_Click" />
           <a href="javascript:CreateFile();">
             <img border="0" src="./Images/NewFile.gif"
                 Alt="Create a new text file" height="28" width="28">
           </a>
           <asp:LinkButton ID="CreateFile" runat="server"
               OnClick="CreateFile_Click" Visible="False"/>
         </td>
       </tr>
     </table>
     ...
```

And here's the addition for the code-behind:

```
protected void CreateFile_Click(object sender, EventArgs e)
{
  string path = folderPath;
  if (path.EndsWith("/"))
    path += funcParam.Value;
  else
    path += "/" + funcParam.Value;

  // if the file already exists, do not go to the text editor
  if (File.Exists(Server.MapPath(path)))
```

```
    {
        StatusMessage.Text = "The file you specified already exists.";
        StatusMessage.Visible = true;
    }
    else
        // redirect to the editor page
        Response.Redirect("EditFile.aspx?File=" + path + "&CreateFile=true");
}
```

The code above first of all checks if the specified file already exists (the whole path is retrieved by combining the current path and the name specified). If so, it just shows an error message – later in the chapter we'll add the possibility to edit an existing file. Otherwise it redirects to EditFile.aspx with the full virtual path of the file to create as a parameter, and another parameter, CreateFile, set to true. We're going to write this new page in the next section.

Building the Text File Editor

We want to build a very simple text editor that allows us to create a new file and also to edit an existing file. The editor will just have a multi-line textbox, a textbox for the destination path, a button to create or update the file, and another button to discard the changes and go back to the file manager.

In VS.NET create a new web form, named EditFile.aspx, and edit its content as follows:

```
<%@ Page language="c#" Codebehind="EditFile.aspx.cs" AutoEventWireup="false"
    Inherits="Wrox.WebModules.FileManager.Web.EditFile" %>
<%@ Register TagPrefix="FileManager" TagName="Header" src="Header.ascx" %>
<%@ Register TagPrefix="FileManager" TagName="Footer" src="Footer.ascx" %>
<!DOCTYPE HTML PUBLIC "-//W3C//DTD HTML 4.0 Transitional//EN" >
<html>
  <head>
    <title>FileManager: text editor</title>
    <link rel="stylesheet" HREF="/ThePhile/Styles/ThePhile.css"
        TYPE="text/css" />
    <meta name="CODE_LANGUAGE" Content="C#">
  </head>
  <body>
    <FileManager:Header ID="Title" runat="server" />
    <form ID="EditFile" method="post" runat="server">
      <asp:Table runat="server" CssClass="Grid_General" Width="100%">
        <asp:TableRow CssClass="Grid_Header">
          <asp:TableCell HorizontalAlign="Center" Text="EDIT TEXT FILE" />
        </asp:TableRow>
        <asp:TableRow>
          <asp:TableCell HorizontalAlign="Center">
            <asp:TextBox runat="server" Width="99%" Rows="20"
              TextMode="MultiLine" ID="FileContent" CssClass="TextBox" />
          </asp:TableCell>
        </asp:TableRow>
        <asp:TableRow>
          <asp:TableCell HorizontalAlign="Right" Text="Save As:">
            <asp:TextBox runat="server" Width="350px"
              ID="SaveAsPath" CssClass="TextBox" />
```

```
                <asp:Button runat="server" Text="Save" ID="Save"
                    CssClass="Button" Width="80px" OnClick="Save_Click"
                    /> 
                <asp:Button runat="server" Text="Back to FileManager" ID="Back"
                    CssClass="Button" Width="150px"
                    OnClick="Back_Click" CausesValidation="False" />
            </asp:TableCell>
        </asp:TableRow>
        <asp:TableRow>
          <asp:TableCell HorizontalAlign="Right">
            <asp:RequiredFieldValidator ID="ValidateSaveAsPath"
                runat="server" ControlToValidate="SaveAsPath"
                Display="dynamic">* The Save As path is required
            </asp:RequiredFieldValidator>
            <asp:Label runat="server" ID="StatusMessage"
                CssClass="StatusMessage" Visible="False" Width="100%" />
          </asp:TableCell>
        </asp:TableRow>
      </asp:Table>
      <br>
    </form>
    <FileManager:Footer ID="Footer" runat="server" />
  </body>
</html>
```

We added a `RequiredFieldValidator` control that ensures that the `SaveAsPath` field is not empty when the form is submitted. Also, when we press the **Back to FileManager** button the form should not be validated, and that's why we set its `CausesValidation` property to `False`.

The Code-behind for EditFile.aspx

The code-behind for this page is not long, and is quite simple, but we'll show it piece by piece, starting from the beginning and including the `Page_Load` procedure:

```
using System;
using System.Collections;
using System.ComponentModel;
using System.Data;
using System.Drawing;
using System.Web;
using System.Web.SessionState;
using System.Web.UI;
using System.Web.UI.WebControls;
using System.Web.UI.HtmlControls;
using System.IO;

namespace Wrox.WebModules.FileManager.Web
{
  public class EditFile : System.Web.UI.Page
  {
    protected System.Web.UI.WebControls.Label StatusMessage;
    protected System.Web.UI.WebControls.TextBox SaveAsPath;
    protected System.Web.UI.WebControls.TextBox FileContent;
```

```
protected System.Web.UI.WebControls.Button Save;
protected System.Web.UI.WebControls.Button Back;

private void Page_Load(object sender, EventArgs e)
{
  if (!IsPostBack)
  {
    string filePath = Request.Params["File"];
    if (filePath != null)
    {
      if (Request.Params["CreateFile"] == null ||
        Request.Params["CreateFile"]=="false")
      {
        // load the content of the specified text file
        try
        {
          StreamReader sr = new StreamReader (File.Open(
                        Server.MapPath(filePath), FileMode.Open) );
          FileContent.Text = sr.ReadToEnd();
          sr.Close();
        }
        catch (Exception exc)
        {
          StatusMessage.Text = exc.Message;
          StatusMessage.Visible = true;
        }
      }
      // set the Save As textbox with the path
      // specified in the QueryString
      SaveAsPath.Text = filePath;
    }
  }
}
```

The Page_Load procedure extracts the path of the file to create or edit from the QueryString. Then it checks if there is a CreateFile parameter set to false, or not present at all. In both these cases it means that the file is already present and the user does not want to create it, but rather to *edit* it. So the procedure opens the file, reads its content, and shows it in a large textbox (this code is protected within a try...catch block as usual).

The next block of code is the procedure called when the **Back to FileManager** button is pressed. Basically, it extracts the parent folder of the file passed in the QueryString, and redirects to BrowseFiles.aspx, pointing to the folder to browse:

```
protected void Back_Click(object sender, EventArgs e)
{
  // redirect to the referrer URL or to the BrowseFiles.aspx page
  // if the referrer is null
  string filePath = Request.Params["File"];
  if (filePath != null && filePath != "/")
  {
    int lastSlashIndex = filePath.LastIndexOf("/");
    string folderPath = filePath.Substring(0, lastSlashIndex+1);
    Response.Redirect("BrowseFiles.aspx?Folder=" + folderPath);
  }
  else
    Response.Redirect("BrowseFiles.aspx");
}
```

Finally, the last procedure is executed when the user presses the **Save** button. The file is created or updated with the new content:

```
protected void Save_Click(object sender, EventArgs e)
{
  // save the text to the specified file
  // (the file is created from scratch even if it already exists)
  try
  {
    string filePath = SaveAsPath.Text;
    if (!filePath.StartsWith("/")) filePath = "/" + filePath;
    StreamWriter sw = File.CreateText(Server.MapPath(filePath));
    sw.Write(FileContent.Text);
    sw.Close();
    StatusMessage.Text = "File successfully saved";
  }
  catch (Exception exc)
  {
    StatusMessage.Text = exc.Message;;
  }
  StatusMessage.Visible = true;
}

// ... other code created by default by VS.NET for the Designer support
  }
}
```

Note that the file is created from scratch in all cases. In other words, if the file already exists it is overwritten by a new file.

At this point we can recompile the assembly with the new page and switch to the browser. Click the **Create a new text file** icon on the toolbar, specify any file name you want (for example `MyTestFile.txt`) and confirm. This displays a page like this:

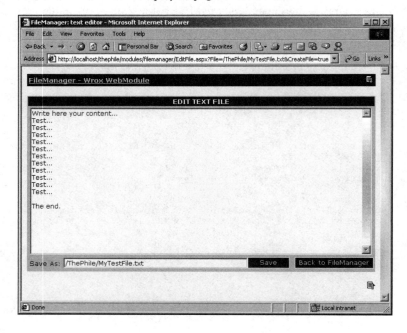

Editing Files

So, we've developed a page that allows the user to create and edit a new text file. We will now go back to the `BrowseFiles.aspx` page and add a new column with a link to the file editor for *all* the text files.

Here's the new column for the `FoldersAndFilesTable` table (this is the last time you need to change it, I promise):

```
<asp:Table ID="FoldersAndFiles" runat="server"
    CssClass="Grid_General" Width="100%">
  <asp:TableRow CssClass="Grid_Header">
    <asp:TableCell Width="36px" />
    <asp:TableCell Text="Index" />
    <asp:TableCell Width="25px" />
    <asp:TableCell Width="45px" />
    <asp:TableCell Text="Attribs" Width="50px" />
    <asp:TableCell Text="Size" Width="80px" HorizontalAlign="Right" />
    <asp:TableCell Text="Created" Width="140px" />
    <asp:TableCell Text="Last Modified" Width="140px" />
  </asp:TableRow>
</asp:Table>
```

Then, in the `FillFoldersAndFilesTable` routine in the code-behind file, add a new empty column (`cellOperations`) for the first row, which links to the parent folder, and for all directory rows. (This is not shown here, look at the code earlier in the chapter to see how to add columns, for example in the *Displaying the Item Attributes* section). We're going to add a link for any text files that are not read-only or system files. We won't add a link for the other files (we can't edit a GIF with a text editor).

The easiest way to decide whether a file is a text file is by looking at its extension. If the extension is `.txt`, `.log`, `.bat`, `.cs`, `.config`, `.aspx`, or some other well-known text file extension, then we should be reasonably sure that the file is a text file. We define an array – private for the entire class – of known extensions, as we did for associating the extensions with an icon:

```
private string[] textExtensions = new string[]{".asa", ".asax",
    ".ascx", ".asmx", ".asp", ".aspx", ".bat", ".config", ".cs",
    ".css", ".disco", ".htm", ".html", ".inc", ".ini", ".log",
    ".sys", ".txt", ".vb", ".vbs", ".vsdisco", ".xls", ".xml"};
```

We could handle the list of text files in other ways, which would integrate with the system of assigning icons to extensions. We would create an XML file that lists the extensions for which we have an icon, where the tag has the name of the extension, and can have a "text" attribute that tells whether the files with that extension are editable through our text editor. Here is an example XML file:

```
<extensions>
    <.aspx text="true"><aspx.gif></.aspx>
    <.bmp><bmp.gif></.bmp>
    <.gif><gif.gif></.gif>
    <.html text="true"><html.gif></.html>
    <.zip><zip.gif></.zip>
    ...
</extensions>
```

This solution would provide the flexibility to add, edit and delete extensions without the need to recompile the assembly. However, working with an XML file is much slower than working with an array in a local private variable, and requires more code and resources. Considering that once you've set up a complete list of extensions you want to support you won't need to update it frequently, employing the XML solution is probably not worth the effort – but it's an option if you want the maximum flexibility and ease of use for the site administrator.

Now, code block that adds the child files to the table, we declare the new cell, and check if the current file's extension is listed in the array and if the file is write-enabled. If both conditions are satisfied the new icon link is added to the column:

```
...
TableCell cellOperations;
...

foreach (FileInfo childFile in childFiles)
{
  // create the required cells and controls
  ...
  cellOperations = new TableCell();
  int extIndex;

  // set the other cells and controls
  ...

  // if this file is a text file and is write-enabled, add an image
  // link that points to EditFile.aspx with its path as the parameter
  extIndex = Array.IndexOf(textExtensions, childFile.Extension.ToLower());
  if (extIndex > -1 &&
    (childFile.Attributes & FileAttributes.ReadOnly) !=
        FileAttributes.ReadOnly &&
    (childFile.Attributes & FileAttributes.System) !=
        FileAttributes.System)
  {
    // create the link and set its properties
    HyperLink linkEditFile = new HyperLink();
    linkEditFile.Text = "<img src=\"./Images/Write.gif\" height=\"16\ +
        " width=\"16\" border=\"0\" alt=\"Edit this file\">";
    linkEditFile.NavigateUrl = "EditFile.aspx?File=" + location;
    cellOperations.Controls.Add(linkEditFile);
  }

  // add the cells to the new row
  rowItem.Cells.Add(cellItemIcon);
  rowItem.Cells.Add(cellItemLink);
  rowItem.Cells.Add(cellDownload);
  rowItem.Cells.Add(cellOperations);
  ...
}
```

Renaming Files and Directories

The next command to implement is one for renaming files or directories. We're going to add a new button to each row in the table, except the first one, if it is the one that points to the parent folder. When pressed, the button will pop up a prompt dialog. If the new name is confirmed then an event will be raised on the server and handled by the proper procedure.

We've already seen how to use JavaScript for postbacks when we showed how to create a new directory or file. What's new here is that we're going to have an unknown number of buttons (one for each row, used to rename the item represented by the row where it is located) that will all raise the same event on the server. This does not make any difference to the actual implementation – we don't need to identify which row was clicked, just the original path name.

The other difference is that we need to submit two pieces of information – the original path name, and the new name. Although we could pack both of these parameters into a single control, adding a new hidden control produces no overhead and makes it simpler to extract the information.

In the ASPX page we just create the new hidden control, the JavaScript function that asks for the new name, and the invisible `LinkButton` control. The links that call this function are dynamically created in the code-behind for each file and directory.

Here's the additional code for `BrowseFiles.aspx`:

```
...
<head>
  <title>FileManager: Browse Files</title>
  <link rel="stylesheet" HREF="/ThePhile/Styles/ThePhile.css"
      TYPE="text/css" />
  <meta name="CODE_LANGUAGE" Content="C#">
  <script language="javascript">

    function CreateDir()
    {
      ...
    }


    function CreateFile()
    {
      ...
    }


    function Rename(path)
    {
      newName = prompt('Type the new name for this file/folder:','');

      if ((newName) && (newName!=""))
      {
        document.forms['BrowseFiles'].elements['funcParam'].value = path;
        document.forms['BrowseFiles'].elements['funcExtraParam'].value =
          newName;
        __doPostBack('Rename', '');
      }
```

```
      }
    </script>
</head>
<body>
    <form id="BrowseFiles" method="post" runat="server"
        enctype="multipart/form-data">
      <FileManager:Header ID="Title" runat="server" />
      <input type="hidden" id="funcParam" runat="server">
      <input type="hidden" id="funcExtraParam" runat="server">
      <table class="MenuTable" border="0" width="100%">
        <tr>
          <td>
            ... other LinkButtons and links for the Toolbar commands
            <asp:LinkButton ID="Rename" runat="server"
                OnClick="Rename_Click" Visible="False" />
          </td>
        </tr>
      </table>
      ...
```

We don't need to add a new column, as we're going to add the new link to the column with the **Edit File** icon. However, in the code-behind we need to create and add this column for the directories too, because the last time we modified it we just added an empty column.

Here are the additions for the code-behind, starting with `FillFoldersAndFilesTable`:

```
...
TableCell cellOperations;
// declare the new HyperLink control
HyperLink linkRename;
...

foreach (DirectoryInfo childDir in childDirs)
{
  ...
  cellOperations = new TableCell();
  // create the new link
  linkRename = new HyperLink();

  // create the other columns and controls
  ...

  // add the Rename link. The 'D' before the file location
  // will be used to determine that the path identifies a directory
  linkRename.Text = "<img src=\"./Images/Rename.gif\" border=\"0\ +
      " height=\"16\" width=\"16\" Alt=\"Rename\">";
  linkRename.NavigateUrl = "javascript:Rename('D" + location + "');";
  cellOperations.Controls.Add(linkRename);

  // add the cells to the new row
  rowItem.Cells.Add(cellItemIcon);
  rowItem.Cells.Add(cellItemLink);
  rowItem.Cells.Add(new TableCell());
```

```
        rowItem.Cells.Add(cellOperations);
        rowItem.Cells.Add(cellAttributes);
        rowItem.Cells.Add(cellSize);
        rowItem.Cells.Add(cellCreated);
        rowItem.Cells.Add(cellLastModified);

        // add the new row to the table
        rowItem.ApplyStyle(styleFolderRow);
        FoldersAndFiles.Rows.Add(rowItem);
    }

    // now add each child file
    foreach (FileInfo childFile in childFiles)
    {
        ...
        cellOperations = new TableCell ();
        // create the new link
        linkRename = new HyperLink();

        // create the other columns and controls
        ...

        // add the Rename link. The 'F' before the file location will be used
        // to determine that the path identifies a file
        linkRename.Text = "<img src=\"./Images/Rename.gif\" border=\"0\ +
            " height=\"16\" width=\"16\" Alt=\"Rename\">";
        linkRename.NavigateUrl = "javascript:Rename('F" + location + "');";
        cellOperations.Controls.Add(linkRename);

        // add the Edit File icon, if the file is write-enabled
        ...

        // add the cells to the new row, and add the row
        ...
    }
```

The only peculiarity in the code above is that a 'D' or 'F' letter is added to the path passed to the JavaScript Rename function. The whole string will then be passed to the server event handler, which will determine if the path identifies a file or a folder by extracting the first letter. This is, of course, necessary because there are two different classes – one for working with folders and one for files.

You can see this in the following procedure:

```
protected void Rename_Click(object sender, EventArgs e)
{
    // the first char of the first param is F if the path identifies a file,
    // D otherwise. Extract the first char to determine this
    bool isFile = funcParam.Value.StartsWith("F");
    // extract the source path
    string sourcePath = Server.MapPath(funcParam.Value.Substring(1));
    string destPath;

    try
```

```
{
  if (isFile)
  {
    FileInfo sourceFile = new FileInfo(sourcePath);
    // create the destination path: source path dir + new name
    destPath = Path.Combine(sourceFile.Directory.FullName, +
        funcExtraParam.Value);
    // move the file = rename
    sourceFile.MoveTo(destPath);
  }
  else
  {
    DirectoryInfo sourceDir = new DirectoryInfo(sourcePath);
    // create the destination path: source path dir + new name
    destPath = Path.Combine(sourceDir.Parent.FullName, +
        funcExtraParam.Value);
    // move the directory = rename
    sourceDir.MoveTo(destPath);
  }
  // refresh the page
  Response.Redirect("BrowseFiles.aspx?Folder=" + folderPath);
}
catch (Exception exc)
{
  StatusMessage.Text = exc.Message;
  StatusMessage.Visible = true;
}
}
```

The item is moved to the current path but with a different name, therefore it is renamed. At the end of the procedure, if no exceptions have been raised, the table is filled with the updated content. The exception handling is very important here: you may have loaded the page with the list of files fifteen minutes ago, and in the meantime another administrator might have deleted or moved some files. But you still see the old content as long as you don't refresh the page, and if you try to rename a file/directory that no longer exists an exception will be generated. In that case it is handled and a message explaining the problem is shown.

Modifying the Attributes of Files and Directories

Earlier in the chapter we added a column to show the attributes of the items, by reading the Attributes property. That property can be read *and* set, so why not add functionality to edit the attributes? Now that we know the trick to pop up a prompt dialog and raise server events, this is a no-brainer problem.

Let's add the new JavaScript to the <script> section, and the respective LinkButton control, in the BrowseFiles.aspx page:

```
...
<script language="javascript">
  function CreateDir()
  { ... }
```

```
function CreateFile()
{ ... }

function Rename(path)
{ ... }

function SetAttributes(path)
{
  attribs = prompt('Type the new attributes for the
      file/folder.\nA=Archive, R=ReadOnly, H=Hidden, S=System:','');

  if ((attribs) && (attribs!=""))
  {
    document.forms['BrowseFiles'].elements['funcParam'].value = path;
    document.forms['BrowseFiles'].elements['funcExtraParam'].value +
        = attribs;
    __doPostBack('SetAttributes', '');
  }
}
</script>
</head>
<body>
...
  <asp:LinkButton ID="SetAttributes" runat="server"
      OnClick="SetAttributes_Click" Visible="False" />
...
```

The `funcParam` hidden control is used to store the path of the item to update, while `funcExtraParam` stores the new attributes. Attributes are specified as a string of characters, where 'A' means Archive, 'R' Read-only, 'H' Hidden, and 'S' System. So, for example, "RS" means Read-only + System.

The column for the attributes is already present in the rows for both directories and files, so the additions for the `FillFoldersAndFilesTable` procedure in the code-behind are limited:

```
// create the required cells and controls
...
TableCell cellAttributes;
Label labelAttributes;
HyperLink linkSetAttribs;
...
foreach (DirectoryInfo childDir in childDirs)
{
  // create the required cells and controls
  ...
  cellAttributes = new TableCell();
  labelAttributes = new Label();
  linkSetAttribs = new HyperLink();

  // set the other columns and controls
  ...

  // set the attributes cell: description label and the icon link
  labelAttributes.Text = GetAttributesDescription(childDir.Attributes);
```

```
    labelAttributes.Font.Name = "Courier";
    linkSetAttribs.Text = "<img src=\"./Images/Edit.gif\" border=\"0\ +
        " height=\"16\" width=\"16\" Alt=\"Edit attributes\">";
    linkSetAttribs.NavigateUrl = "javascript:SetAttributes('" +
        location + "');";
    cellAttributes.Controls.Add(labelAttributes);
    cellAttributes.Controls.Add(linkSetAttribs);

    // add the cells to the new row and the row to the table
    ...
}

// now add each child file
foreach (FileInfo childFile in childFiles)
{
    // create the required cells
    ...
    cellAttributes = new TableCell();
    labelAttributes = new Label();
    linkSetAttribs = new HyperLink();

    // set the other columns and controls
    ...

    // set the attributes cell: description label and the icon link
    labelAttributes.Text = GetAttributesDescription(childFile.Attributes);
    labelAttributes.Font.Name = "Courier";
    linkSetAttribs.Text = "<img src=\"./Images/Edit.gif\" border=\"0\ +
        " height=\"16\" width=\"16\" Alt=\"Edit attributes\">";
    linkSetAttribs.NavigateUrl = "javascript:SetAttributes('" +
        location + "');";
    cellAttributes.Controls.Add(labelAttributes);
    cellAttributes.Controls.Add(linkSetAttribs);

    // add the cells to the new row and the row to the table
    ...
}
```

There is nothing new to explain here, as the code is very similar to the code we added for the **Rename** command. There is a difference in the JavaScript we call and we just pass the plain item path. There is no need to prefix a 'D' or 'F' to identify the path as a directory or a file – we'll see the reason for this in a moment. Look at the code called on the server when the user confirms the new attributes:

```
protected void SetAttributes_Click(object sender, EventArgs e)
{
    string path = Server.MapPath(funcParam.Value);
    string attribs = funcExtraParam.Value.ToUpper();

    FileAttributes fileAttribs = FileAttributes.Normal;
    // search the A (Archive) attribute in the descriptive string
    if (attribs.IndexOf("A") > -1)
        fileAttribs |= FileAttributes.Archive;
    // search the R (ReadOnly) attribute in the descriptive string
```

```
      if (attribs.IndexOf("R") > -1)
        fileAttribs |= FileAttributes.ReadOnly;
      // search the H (Hidden) attribute in the descriptive string
      if (attribs.IndexOf("H") > -1)
        fileAttribs |= FileAttributes.Hidden;
      // search the S (System) attribute in the descriptive string
      if (attribs.IndexOf("S") > -1)
        fileAttribs |= FileAttributes.System;

      try
      {
        // set the new attributes. This works with directories as well
        File.SetAttributes(path, fileAttribs);
        // refresh the page
        Response.Redirect("BrowseFiles.aspx?Folder=" + folderPath);
      }
      catch (Exception exc)
      {
        StatusMessage.Text = exc.Message;
        StatusMessage.Visible = true;
      }
    }
}
```

The procedure checks if the 'A', 'R', 'H', and 'S' letters are present in the user-specified string, and the respective attribute for each occurrence found is added to a variable, of type `FileAttributes`. As a last step the procedure sets the new attributes by calling the `File`'s `SetAttributes` shared method. As you have probably guessed, there was no need to prefix the path with a 'D' or 'F' letter because the `SetAttributes` method works fine with both directories and files, so there is no need to differentiate our code according to the item type.

The following screenshot shows how the file manager looks after these additions. You can see the new icons in the new columns, and the dialog for specifying the new attributes for a file or directory:

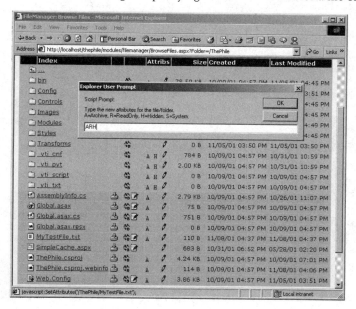

Deleting Files

What we want to implement now is a delete command. We could easily add a further link to the right of each item and associate a server procedure that deletes that item. However, so far we've implemented commands that work on individual files: at the moment we can create *one* file at time, rename *one* file at time, change the attributes of *one* directory at time, etc. Let's say that we want to delete twenty files – it would take twenty reloads to complete the operation, and that would be quite boring. If we take any file manager as a model, we can see that commands like rename work on an individual item, since they are based on the current properties (name, attributes, etc.) of the item. But if we want to delete, copy, or move a set of files, we can select more than one file and delete them in a single step, saving time.

We want to follow the general guidelines of any good file manager, so we will do things that way as well. First problem: allowing the user (administrator) to select the files or directories they want to delete. The solution is to add a checkbox for each item, so that when the user presses the Delete link all the items whose checkboxes are selected are deleted.

In our application this simply translates to dynamically adding a checkbox in the first column (before the item icon) in the `FillFoldersAndFilesTable` procedure in the code-behind. In the `BrowseFiles.aspx` page we add JavaScript that asks the user to confirm the operation, the link on the toolbar, and a new invisible `LinkButton` for the server event handler:

```
<script language="javascript">
  function CreateDir()
  { ... }

  // other javascript functions
  ...

  function Delete()
  {
    if (confirm('Do you want to delete the selected folder(s) ' +
                                      'and/or file(s)?'))
    __doPostBack('Delete','');
  }
</script>
</head>
<body>
  ...
  <table class="MenuTable" border="0" width="100%">
    <tr>
      <td>
        ...
        <a href="javascript:Delete();">
          <img border="0" src="./Images/Delete.gif"
            Alt="Delete the selected files/directories"
            height="28" width="28">
        </a>
        <asp:LinkButton ID="Delete" runat="server"
          OnClick="Delete_Click" Visible="False" />
        ...
      </td>
    </tr>
  </table>
  ...
```

In the `FillFoldersAndFilesTable` procedure in the code-behind, first of all we add the code for creating a checkbox for each item:

```
// create the required cells and controls
...
TableCell cellItemIcon;
CheckBox checkItem;
...
foreach (DirectoryInfo childDir in childDirs)
{
  // create the required cells and controls
  ...
  cellItemIcon = new TableCell();
  checkItem = new CheckBox();

  // set the other columns and controls
  ...

  // add the checkbox, and store path and item type (dir) as attributes
  checkItem.Attributes["Path"] = location;
  checkItem.Attributes["IsFile"] = "false";
  cellItemIcon.Controls.Add(checkItem);
  imgItemIcon.ImageUrl = "./Images/ClosedFolder.gif";
  cellItemIcon.Controls.Add(imgItemIcon);
  cellItemIcon.HorizontalAlign = HorizontalAlign.Right;

  // add the cells to the new row and the row to the table
  ...
}

foreach (FileInfo childFile in childFiles)
{
  // create the required cells and controls
  ...
  cellItemIcon = new TableCell();
  checkItem = new CheckBox();

  // set the other columns and controls
  ...

  // add the checkbox, and store path and item type (file) as attributes
  checkItem.Attributes["Path"] = location;
  checkItem.Attributes["IsFile"] = "true";
  cellItemIcon.Controls.Add(checkItem);
  cellItemIcon.Controls.Add(imgItemIcon);
  cellItemIcon.HorizontalAlign = HorizontalAlign.Right;

  // add the cells to the new row and the row to the table
  ...
}
```

You will notice that the item's path and type (file or directory) are stored as checkbox `Attributes`. The code in the `Delete_Click` procedure will get this information from all the selected checkboxes, and will accordingly use the `Directory` or `File` classes to delete those items. Here's this procedure:

```csharp
protected void Delete_Click(object sender, EventArgs e)
{
  bool redir = true;

  foreach (TableRow tr in FoldersAndFiles.Rows)
  {
    if (tr.Cells[0].Controls.Count==2)
    {
      // get a reference to the checkbox
      CheckBox checkItem = (CheckBox)tr.Cells[0].Controls[0];
      if (checkItem.Checked)
      {
        try
        {
          string path = Server.MapPath(
            checkItem.Attributes["Path"].ToString());
          // is this item a file?
          if (Convert.ToBoolean(checkItem.Attributes["IsFile"])==true)
            File.Delete(path);
          else
            Directory.Delete(path, true);
        }
        catch (Exception exc)
        {
          StatusMessage.Text = exc.Message;
          StatusMessage.Visible = true;
          redir = false;
        }
      }
    }
  }

  // refresh the page
  if (redir) Response.Redirect("BrowseFiles.aspx?Folder=" + folderPath);
}
```

For each row in the table the procedure checks if the first cell has two child controls. If there is only one, it means that this row has only the icon and link to jump to the parent directory. Therefore it does not represent a file system item, and so the code does nothing. If there are two controls, the procedure gets a reference to the checkbox control, and looks to see if the control is checked. If it is checked then it goes ahead, by extracting the path of the item and the attribute specifying if the item is a file or a directory, in order to use the appropriate class to delete the item.

Note that here we don't refresh the page after the operation is performed for just one item, but only when we're finished with *all* the selected items. Therefore we have to redirect just before the end of the procedure, based on the value of the redir variable, which is true when it is declared and set to false if an exception is thrown.

Copying and Moving Files

We're close to completing the features of our file manager, but what's still missing is the ability to copy or move a set of files and folders. We already have the infrastructure for selecting multiple items – what we need to add are the JavaScript function that asks for the destination path, a LinkButton control, and the respective event handler. Copying and moving items are very similar operations, thus we'll handle both of them with the same event handler and the same JavaScript.

As usual, we start by showing the additions to the BrowseFiles.aspx page:

```
<script language="javascript">
  function CreateDir()
  { ... }

  // other javascript functions
  ...

  function CopyMove(op)
  {
    destPath = prompt('Type the destination virtual path:','');

    if ((destPath) && (destPath!=""))
    {
      document.forms['BrowseFiles'].elements['funcParam'].value = destPath;
      document.forms['BrowseFiles'].elements
          ['funcExtraParam'].value = op;
      __doPostBack('CopyMove', '');
    }
  }
</script>
</head>
<body>
  ...
  <table class="MenuTable" border="0" width="100%">
    <tr>
      <td>
        ...
        <a href="javascript:CopyMove('copy');">
          <img border="0" src="./Images/Copy.gif"
              Alt="Copy the selected files/directories"
              height="28" width="28">
        </a>
        <a href="javascript:CopyMove('move');">
          <img border="0" src="./Images/Move.gif"
              Alt="Move the selected files/directories"
              height="28" width="28">
        </a>
        <asp:LinkButton ID="CopyMove" runat="server"
            OnClick="CopyMove_Click" Visible="False" />
        ...
      </td>
    </tr>
  </table>
  ...
```

In the event handler we can find out if the user wants to copy or move the file by looking at the value of the `funcExtraParam` hidden control, which can be "copy" or "move". The other control is used to pass the destination path. Here is the event handler code:

```csharp
protected void CopyMove_Click(object sender, EventArgs e)
{
  bool redir = true;
  // extract the destination directory
  string folder = funcParam.Value;
  // extract the operation to perform: can be "copy" or "move"
  string op = funcExtraParam.Value;

  if (!folder.StartsWith("/"))
  {
    if (folderPath.EndsWith("/"))
      folder = folderPath + folder;
    else
      folder = folderPath + "/" + folder;
  }
  folder = Server.MapPath(folder);

  foreach (TableRow tr in FoldersAndFiles.Rows)
  {
    if (tr.Cells[0].Controls.Count==2)
    {
      // go ahead only if the checkbox is selected
      CheckBox checkItem = (CheckBox)tr.Cells[0].Controls[0];
      if (checkItem.Checked)
      {
        string destPath = Path.Combine(folder,
            ((HyperLink)tr.Cells[1].Controls[0]).Text);
        string path = Server.MapPath(
            checkItem.Attributes["Path"].ToString());
        try
        {
          if (Convert.ToBoolean(checkItem.Attributes["IsFile"])==true)
          {
            // copy or move this file
            if (op=="move")
              File.Move(path, destPath);
            else
              File.Copy(path, destPath, true);
          }
          else
          {
            // copy or move this directory
            if(op=="move")
              Directory.Move(path, destPath);
            else
              CopyDirectory(path, destPath, true);
          }
        }
        catch (Exception exc)
        {
```

```
                StatusMessage.Text = exc.Message;
                StatusMessage.Visible = true;
                redir = false;
            }
        }
    }
}


    // refresh the page
    if (redir) Response.Redirect("BrowseFiles.aspx?Folder=" + folderPath);
}
```

The user can specify a relative or an absolute virtual directory as the destination. If the specified path begins with "/" it means that the path is absolute, so nothing extra needs to be done. Otherwise it is a relative path, and it is added to the current path. Then we get the respective physical path, which is the one we work with.

The other point to note is that both the `File` and `Directory` classes expose the `Move` method, but only the `File` class exposes a `Copy` method. Honestly, I don't know why the `Directory` class does not have a `Copy` method, but this is not a problem that can scare us – we can always write our custom `CopyDirectory` function, right?

No sooner said than done. Here's the code for `CopyDirectory`:

```
private void CopyDirectory(string sourcePath, string destPath,
    bool overwrite)
{
  DirectoryInfo sourceDir = new DirectoryInfo(sourcePath);
  DirectoryInfo destDir = new DirectoryInfo(destPath);

  // the source directory must exist, if not raise an exception
  if (sourceDir.Exists)
  {
    // if destination dir does not exist throw an exception
    if (!destDir.Parent.Exists)
      new AppException("Destination directory does not exist: " +
          destDir.Parent.FullName, new DirectoryNotFoundException());

    if (!destDir.Exists) destDir.Create();

    // copy all the files of the current directory
    foreach (FileInfo file in sourceDir.GetFiles())
    {
      if (overwrite)
        file.CopyTo(Path.Combine(destDir.FullName, file.Name), true);
      else
      {
        // if overwrite = false, copy the file only if it
        // does not exist. This is done to avoid an IOException
        // if a file already exists. This way the other files
        // can be copied anyway...
        if (!File.Exists(Path.Combine(destDir.FullName, file.Name)))
```

```
                file.CopyTo(Path.Combine(destDir.FullName, file.Name), false);
            }
        }

        // recursively call this procedure to copy the subdirectories
        foreach (DirectoryInfo dir in sourceDir.GetDirectories())
            CopyDirectory(dir.FullName, Path.Combine(destDir.FullName,
                dir.Name), overwrite);
    }
    else
        new AppException("Source directory does not exist: " +
            sourceDir.FullName, new DirectoryNotFoundException());
}
```

The procedure accepts the source and destination directories as input, plus a third parameter that specifies whether the files with the same name in the destination directory will be overwritten. The procedure first copies all the child files, and then uses recursion for each subdirectory. If the destination directory does not exist, an exception is thrown through the AppException class, which we built in Chapter 2. In order to use this class we have to add a reference to the Core.dll assembly, or the Core project if it is part of the solution. To add a reference, click the **References** command under the **Project** menu, and select from the list.

Our file manager is finally feature-complete! In the following screenshot you can see the final version, with the checkboxes for all items, the new command links in the toolbar, and the dialog asking for the destination directory for a copy operation:

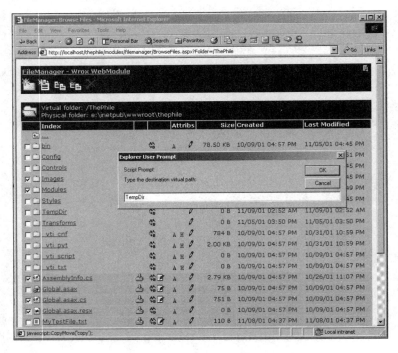

Securing the File Manager Using Windows Security

In the design section of this chapter we explained why security is a fundamental requirement and why we chose to use Windows security. Creating our own forms-based security system will be covered in the next chapter, and later chapters will show how to use it. It would be easy to apply this method to the file manager, and might be the best solution on other sites. But for ThePhile, Windows security is best.

IIS provides security control against IP, user, virtual directory, and NTFS resources. The IP-blocking mechanism allows the administrator to block or process requests coming from a selected range of IP addresses, and is very useful when you know in advance the IPs of the allowed computers, such as when you are working with a intranet, or when you're using a static IP. IIS also allows you to grant or deny read and execute privileges to a virtual directory and all the folders underneath, and to limit the rights of the anonymous user who accesses and browses the site (you typically allow this user to read the pages of a public section, but prevent any writing). Windows NT security is administered through the ACL (Access Control List), a list of permissions for every resource on NTFS partitions (FAT partitions are not supported). In this case we'll be using only the basic Windows NTFS security, but if you have the ability to do so, then you can also set up IP blocking, encryption, and any other available security mechanisms.

First of all we create a new user from the Computer Management console: choose the name, description, and password, and when you're done you'll see the new user added to the list. In our test we have created a user named **ThePhileMaster**, as shown in the list:

Now create a new group, name it ThePhile_FileManagerAdmins, and add the ThePhileMaster user to the list, as illustrated:

Now we have to declare permissions on the website folder and content. To do this, open Windows Explorer, select the physical directory of /localhost/ThePhile (E:\Inetpub\wwwroot\ThePhile on my system) and go to its properties through File | Properties. Switch to the Security tab, and select all the permissions for the ThePhile_FileManagerAdmins group, as follows:

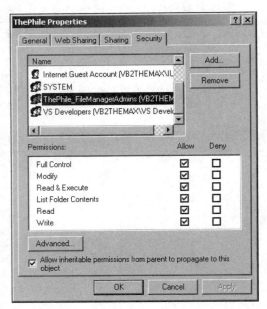

It's worth noting that although we can grant permissions to a specific user and not to the entire group, if we give a group permission to access a resource then we can later add users to that group without having to manually give every single user permissions to the resource. From the same dialog in Windows Explorer we remove the permissions of the IUSR_MACHINENAME user, that is, the Internet anonymous user. Finally, go to the IIS management console, and set the Integrated Windows Security for the **FileManager** folder. Note that the integrated security will only work with Microsoft browsers, unless Basic Authentication or forms authentication is used. This is not a big issue in this case, though, as you can force one of the few administrators to use Internet Explorer. It would be a much more serious problem if we were planning to use this type of security to authenticate/authorize thousands of users that we don't even know.

Now when we try to open the `BrowseFiles.aspx` page from a browser, we get the login dialog asking for our username and password, as shown in the following screenshot:

There's a lot more to Windows security – such as impersonation, anonymous access and other authentication methods, use of certificates, encryption and SSL – but here we just want a working solution for our web module. However, you should seriously consider security and all the available ways to enhance it. There are many Windows security books available. *Windows 2000 Security* (New Riders, ISBN 0-735709-91-2) and *Windows 2000 Security Handbook* (McGraw-Hill, ISBN 0-072124-33-4) are both strong titles.

Remember that Windows security can be set up through the `web.config` file, but we can't have more than one form of authentication/authorization in the same application. In the next chapter we'll be implementing forms-based authentication, so we can't have a different mode for the file manager. Since you need to access the IIS and folder settings only once to enforce Windows security in the traditional way, this is not a big problem. However, should you need to often or dynamically add/edit/remove administrators, then read the next chapter and integrate the accounts/security module to use forms-based authentication here as well.

Database Management Online

At print time, Microsoft's Web Data Administrator had not been updated for .NET 1.0. However, they supply the source code with the download so it should be possible to produce a .NET 1.0 version – check the book's code download or P2P to find out how.

There are several third party tools that allow an administrator to manage a site's databases online. We're going to install a completely free tool (source code included!) – developed by Microsoft – that can be a great help for managing SQL Server databases. This tool is called Web Data Administrator, and can be downloaded from the following URL:

http://msdn.Microsoft.com/code/default.asp?url=/code/sample.asp?url=/msdn-files/026/002/
                                                        458/msdncompositedoc.xml.

Simple database managers, such as the one that might be included in your hosting plan, usually consist of a page with a few textboxes to type in the connection string with your username and password, and the actual SQL commands. Our tool does much more than this; it can dynamically display and interact with many DB objects, such as tables, stored procedures, and so on. This is possible because it uses the SQL-DMO (Distributed Management Interface) library, a COM-based interface that allows us to programmatically manage SQL Server's objects and data. These COM objects are loaded through the .NET interoperability services. To find out more about SQL-DMO, refer to *Professional SQL Server 2000* (Wrox Press, ISBN 1-861004-48-6). Or for more about .NET interoperability services refer to *Professional C#* (Wrox Press, ISBN 1-861004-99-0).

After downloading the `WebdataAdmin.msi` installation package, execute it, specify a virtual folder where you want to install the application, and in a few seconds it will be done. Of course, in some cases the task will be persuading the ISP to install it for you. We installed the tool under /localhost/ThePhile/Modules, but this created a new web application. We don't want a new virtual directory, since we're already working under the domain of the ThePhile application. So, switch to the IIS snap-in, select the DataAdmin virtual directory, go to its properties, and click the Remove button on the right side of the Application Name textbox. Now DataAdmin is a normal subdirectory, and we must move the assemblies from the DataAdmin/bin folder to ThePhile/bin.

The Data Administrator's Help subfolder documents show how to use the tool.

Summary

This chapter presented the design and implementation of a web module, called `FileManager`, which provides functionality to:

- ❑ List and navigate folder contents
- ❑ Create directories
- ❑ Create and edit text files
- ❑ Download files
- ❑ Upload files

❑ Rename files and directories

❑ Modify file/directory attributes

❑ Delete files

❑ Copy and move files

This tool can help you to effectively manage your site files, resources, and directory structure. For all but very major updates, we can now rely on this tool without the need for external FTP clients or other tools.

We also saw how to set up Windows security to protect the `FileManager` module from unauthorized access.

Later in the chapter we installed and explored Microsoft's Web Data Administrator tool, which helps in the online management of SQL Server databases. It's particularly useful when the database serving the website is located on a remote server.

Before concluding, here are a few new features that you could add to enhance the `FileManager`:

❑ Support for multiple file uploads. This would require the addition of other `HtmlInputFile` controls, and the use of the `Request.Files` collection to handle the uploaded files.

❑ A sort facility that allows the user to click on the grid's columns to sort the directories and files by name, size, or creation date.

❑ Logging the most significant operations, such as file or directory deletion, and adding a page to enable certain administrators to easily access this information (the logged events, their details, and the responsible users).

❑ Creating different levels of administrators that each have different permissions. With Windows security you can create users that cannot, for example, write or list files. But we could push this one step further, and show or hide the links for creating, deleting, and editing elements according to the current user and the group they belong to. For some purposes, we might also want to integrate the security for this module with the security system we will develop in the next chapter.

In the next chapter we'll look at building a module that allows administrators to manage the site's users and their roles, granting or denying them access to particular sections and features.

Users and Authentication

One of the most important aspects of a content-based website, or any website for that matter, is *community building*. As we discussed earlier in this book, a website with a strong, enthusiastic community can survive and profit far longer than other websites that might have greater funding, more development staff, or even a bigger advertising or marketing budget.

The first step towards building a thriving community is to give each user an **identity**. Each website has different needs in this area, but a few things are fairly common. The first step is to provide users with an **account** – a password-protected identity that can be used to represent the user on the website. These accounts allow us to add personalization, e-commerce facilities, targeted advertising, direct news delivery, and mailing list participation.

This chapter will first identify some of the issues and problems involved with providing user accounts. Once we've defined the problems, we will produce an initial design for a solution to this problem. Finally we will write the software to implement this solution.

We will also look at how we can secure some of the facilities and pages of our website, and how we can make provisions for administrators and power users.

The Problem

ThePhile.com provides content to users, and also allows users to contribute to the site in several ways, such as forums, which will be covered in Chapter 10. We also want our site to be able to serve different content to different users. All of these features rely on our site being able to identify its users, and determine what features they are allowed to access. In order to do this, the website must **authenticate** the user in some way, to prevent another person from using a particular user's account. For all this to work, **user accounts** will need to be created and maintained, and users will need to be correctly identified by their accounts.

Many features of the site will need to be administered remotely, so we need to allow for administrative users who will be given particular privileges. For example, some users might be able to remove offensive forum postings. However we might not want these users to access every administrative feature on the site – only those features required to moderate the forum. We might want to give another user – the main webmaster, say – access to everything. So this is more complex than simply differentiating between a set of normal users and a set of super users.

Another thing that we feel very strongly about, that should be listed as part of our problem, is the concept of **user-friendliness**. The authentication and authorization system of a content website should be as unobtrusive as possible. The users should barely be aware of the fact that the website has recognized them, and the process of logging into the website should be quick and painless.

> *In many other situations, such as an e-commerce website or a secured intranet application, the authentication system should be very visible, and very, very strong. In our case, however, we want the authentication system to remain in the background to prevent it from slowing down the site and confusing or distracting our users.*

Now that we've described what we are trying to build, we can move on to designing a system that meets these needs.

The Design

With most desktop or intranet applications we can prevent users from accessing the application until they log in. This means that the developer can assume that the user of an application can always be identified. Most websites don't work this way. Many websites don't require the user to supply a password until the very last possible minute. For example, the user is often recognized through a *cookie*, goes shopping for a while, and just after they click the Check Out button, they are prompted for their secure credentials.

Our site will follow the same policy. It will be completely acceptable for an anonymous user, or a user identified with a cookie but not authenticated with a password, to browse the site and use many of its features. If the user is identified with a cookie, some personalization can take place, as long as it doesn't compromise the user's privacy. For those parts of the site where authentication is required, the user will be forced to authenticate, otherwise they will be denied access.

In addition to building several *new* components that will drive our user authentication and security module, we should make sure that our design accounts for changes to the existing code. First of all, we're going to want to provide a link to log in, a page that allows logins, and a customized greeting in the site header that identifies the user by name.

The following UML use case diagram illustrates the process of authenticating a user. As you can see, at all times, any user (anonymous or authenticated) can follow a 'normal', or unsecured, link. This simply loads a new page and the process begins again. However, if the user chooses to authenticate, they can do this by either creating a new user account or by supplying the password information for an existing account. Finally, you can see from the diagram that it is possible to recognize a previously authenticated user without forcing them to manually authenticate. We will do this using the cookie-based system supplied with ASP.NET's forms-based authentication.

Our site will be using forms-based authentication, which is entirely based on cookies. But there are other ways to authenticate website users. For example, in order to truly secure the administrative portions of our application, we are going to use standard NT/2000 domain security (Windows authentication). This has the benefit of adding the requirement of domain membership (or trust) before the user can even attempt to view the page. Securing the administrative directories and only giving access to a particular *group* (as defined by the 'User Administrator for Domains' program), places the burden of only giving access to appropriate users onto the network administrator. We will see more about *how* we are going to implement the security once we've completed our design.

As with the other elements of our website, we'll design a 3-tiered module, with a presentation layer, business layer, and data layer. We'll need a database to store information about our users and the permissions available, and will design stored procedures to assist the interaction between the data layer classes and the database itself. The rest of this design section will walk you through the design decisions we made in creating our `Accounts` module.

> *The reason why we've chosen to call the module* `Accounts` *is that often the 'users' of websites are not individual users at all but are in fact login accounts assigned to companies, groups, or large organizations.*

Designing the Database

Shown overleaf is a diagram representing the database schema for the user accounting module of our sample website, ThePhile.com. It is fairly straightforward – we have three core data structures: users, permissions, and roles. A **role** is a logical grouping of permissions. For example, there might be a role called 'Administrator' that contains a different, more advanced set of permissions than a role entitled 'New User'. Roles can be associated with permissions and users, while permissions are associated with permission categories to allow for visible grouping of related permissions in the user interface. We will prefix every table name with the module name, `Accounts`, so that there is no conflict with other database tables.

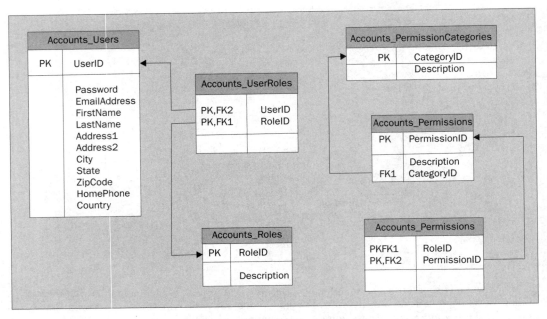

We can't stress enough the importance of a good application design when building your database schema. Because we spent the extra time to make sure that we had thought of as much as possible during the design phase, the creation of the database schema was fairly quick and painless.

The following is a brief description of each of the tables and how they relate to the other tables within the database. As with the other modules in this book, these tables will be added to the main database that we set up in Chapter 2. However, the module will be designed in such a way that, if the need arises, all of its data can come from an entirely separate data source. Full details of the columns, datatypes, keys, and nulls will be given in the solution section later in this chapter.

Table	Description
Accounts_Users	This table is the core table for storing user information. Its primary key is the UserID, which is referenced by the Accounts_UserRoles table. It contains basic user information including password, e-mail address, and home contact information.
Accounts_Roles	This table is the core table for storing roles. RoleID is its primary key, which is referenced by the Accounts_RolePermissions table and the Accounts_UserRoles table.
Accounts_UserRoles	This is a mapping table used for cross-referencing roles and users. It essentially stores user membership within roles. Note that, since the combination of the UserID and RoleID form the primary key, it is possible for a user to be part of more than one role, allowing for some fairly advanced security techniques to be utilized.

Table	Description
Accounts_Permissions	This is the core table that stores verbose descriptions for each of the permissions. Note that when the code checks permissions, it checks them against a **hard-coded enumeration**. This table is used for user-friendly listing and querying of permission names and information. Its primary key is PermissionID, which is referenced by the Accounts_RolePermissions table.
Accounts_RolePermissions	This is another mapping table much like Accounts_UserRoles. It is responsible for mapping membership of permissions within roles. Again, note that, because of the dual primary key, a given permission can be granted to more than one role at a time, allowing for advanced security techniques.

Stored Procedures

Stored procedures are an integral part of the back-end data store for any web application. We could have the software in our data tier access the tables directly. However, it will keep our data tier simpler and easier to maintain, as well as give higher performance, if we include some procedures within the database.

Fortunately for us, we're not doing anything overly complex with our stored procedures. Our procedures essentially mirror the functionality provided by the methods in the data tier components, which we'll look at next. The following is a summarized list of the stored procedures we'll be using in this solution:

Stored Procedure Name	Description
sp_Accounts_CreateRole	Creates a new role in the database
sp_Accounts_DeleteRole	Deletes an existing role, including removing all permissions from the role, and unassigning all users from this role.
sp_Accounts_UpdateRole	Updates the description of a given role.
sp_Accounts_GetRoleDetails	Executes a SELECT, obtaining all pertinent details for a given role.
sp_Accounts_GetAllRoles	Obtains all roles in the entire system.
sp_Accounts_AddPermissionToRole	Adds a given permission to a given role.
sp_Accounts_RemovePermissionFromRole	Removes a given permission from a given role.
sp_Accounts_ClearPermissionsFromRole	Clears all permissions from a given role.

Stored Procedure Name	Description
sp_Accounts_CreateUser	Creates a new user. Accepts only encrypted password arguments.
sp_Accounts_GetStateList	Utility function for obtaining list of all states for populating drop-down list UI control.
sp_Accounts_UpdateUser	Updates pertinent details for a given user.
sp_Accounts_ValidateLogin	Validates a given e-mail address/encrypted password combination. If combination is valid, returns the numeric ID of valid user.
sp_Accounts_TestPassword	Tests a given encrypted password against the encrypted form of the given user ID's password.
sp_Accounts_GetPermissionCategories	Obtains a list of all permission categories in the entire system.
sp_Accounts_GetPermissionCategoryDetails	Obtains all detailed information (currently just a description) of the given category as indicated by the category ID parameter.
sp_Accounts_AddUserToRole	Assigns the given role to the given user.
sp_Accounts_RemoveUserFromRole	Removes the given user from the given role.

The Data Tier

The following is a summary of the design definitions for each of the data tier classes we think we'll need:

User Class Member	Description
Create	Creates a new user in the data store. This method accepts all of the arguments necessary for populating the appropriate database fields.
Retrieve	Retrieves a single user as indicated by the numeric user ID argument passed to the method. Returns a DataRow instance. Also has an overload allowing an e-mail address to be used to retrieve a user.

User Class Member	Description
Update	Commits changes to a given user to the database. All arguments to this method correspond to database fields.
Delete	Removes a specific user from the data store as indicated by the numeric user ID passed to the method.
ValidateLogin	Returns a Boolean indicating whether or not a specific e-mail address and encrypted password is a valid login.
GetUserList	Obtains a completely unfiltered list of all users in the system. This function is intended for administrative purposes and for performance reasons should never be called by any UI function. Returns a DataSet.
GetUserRoles	Returns an ArrayList indicating the list of roles to which the supplied user ID belongs.
GetEffectivePermissionList	Returns an ArrayList indicating the list of all permissions that the user has been granted based on their role membership.
TestPassword	Tests whether a supplied encrypted password is the same encrypted password in the data store for the given user.

Role Class Member	Description
Create	Creates a new role in the data store.
Update	Updates an existing role in the data store.
Delete	Removes an existing role in the data store. Removal of the role also causes all role membership records for this role to be removed, and all role-permission references to be removed.
Retrieve	Retrieves information on a single role in the form of a DataRow.
GetRoleList	Retrieves a list of roles in the system.
AddPermission	Adds a permission to the given role.
RemovePermission	Removes a permission from the given role.
ClearPermissions	Removes all permissions assigned to the role.

Permission Class Member	Description
Retrieve	Retrieves information on a single permission in the form of a DataRow.
GetPermissionList	Retrieves a list of permissions in the system. Returns a DataSet with relations providing a parent/child placing of permissions in categories.
GetPermissionList(role)	Retrieves a DataTable with a list of permissions belonging to a given role.

PermissionCategory Class Member	Description
Retrieve	Retrieves information on a single PermissionCategory in the form of a DataRow.
GetPermissionsInCategory	Retrieves a list of permissions belonging to a given category.
GetCategoryList	Retrieves a list of all permission categories in the system.

The Business Tier

Our business tier contains all the code that encapsulates business logic, workflow, process flow, non-data utility classes, and more. This next section will go through each of the specific things we will be designing for the implementation of the business tier of this module.

We're going to build two main classes as well as two more classes that will allow us to integrate with and extend the existing security system implemented by the ASP.NET core:

❑ The User class – we'll use this class to represent a user of the system.

❑ The Role class – we'll use this class to represent a single role within the system.

❑ PhilePrincipal and PhileIdentity – these two classes, which we will discuss in greater detail later, will be used to integrate our custom security system into the existing security system already in place within ASP.NET.

The User Class

The User class encapsulates a user as they interact with the web application. This class is used specifically for loading information about a specific user, as well as creating, updating, and deleting users.

The User class is not used in authentication schemes – it is used to store general information about the user. We will use this class when users are logging into the system and either creating a new account or updating information on their existing account. We will look at the design for handling authentication schemes in the *Extending .NET Framework User Handling* section later in this chapter.

The following is a detailed description of the features and functionality we have designed into our User class:

User Class Member	Description
UserID	Property indicating the database ID of the given user.
FirstName	Property to set or get the first name of the user.
LastName	Property to set or get the last name of the user.
Address1	Property to set or get the first line of the user's address.

User Class Member	Description
Address2	Property to set or get the second line of the user's address.
City	Property allowing read/write access to the user's city.
State	Property allowing read/write access to the user's state.
ZipCode	Property allowing read/write access to the user's zip code.
Country	Property allowing read/write access to the user's country.
EmailAddress	Property to set or get the e-mail address of the user.
Create()	Method that will translate the set of properties representing a current user by requesting a new user creation from the data tier.
Update()	Method that will update the user's persisted information based on the values of the properties of the current user.
User()	Default constructor.
User(int)	Constructs a new instance of a user based on the numeric database user ID provided as the sole argument.
User(PhilePrincipal)	Creates a new instance of a user based on an instance of the PhilePrincipal class. So User((PhilePrincipal)HttpContext.User) will return information about the currently logged in user.

The Role Class

A content-based website is only as good as its content. In a site such as the one we are building, it is extremely important that we provide new and fresh content. To do this we need to maintain a pool of regular contributors. These contributors are typically responsible for obtaining, arranging for, or creating content.

Many of the site's users need to be able to create content. For example, a website that provides video game reviews needs to allow a team of reviewers to enter in new game reviews. A separate group of people might need to be allowed to upload screenshots of games not yet on the market, and yet another set of site visitors might need the ability to upload game previews or interviews with game publishers and developers. However, in each case we might not want to give all these abilities to all members of staff.

What this all boils down to is the need for roles. A role is a classification of a responsibility, duty, or job. Giving administrators the opportunity to create roles, and assign privileges to these roles, we allow for the type of flexibility we need in order to provide a fully functional content site. This also allows us to support a situation where a single user might have more than one duty. For example, many game review sites have reviewers who also need to post screenshots and interviews. However, there might be others who only need to post screenshots. A flexible system of roles enables this.

So any user can have a number of roles. To encapsulate a role, we will create a `Role` class with the following members:

Role Class Member	**Description**
RoleID	Property containing the numeric database identifier for the given instance of the role.
Description	Property containing the verbose (string) description of the particular instance of a role.
Permissions	Property containing the list/array of permissions granted to the role.
Create()	Creates a new role based on the values of the properties of the current instance.
Delete()	Deletes the current role, removing all associated permissions and unassigning all appropriate users from the role.
Update()	Updates the current role based on the values of the properties of the current instance.
AddPermission(int)	Adds a given numeric permission identifier to the role, effectively granting that permission to all users who belong to the role.
RemovePermission(int)	Removes a given numeric permission identifier from the role, effectively removing that permission from all users who belong to the role.
ClearPermissions()	Removes all permissions from the current instance of a role.
Role()	Default constructor. Used when building a new role for the first time.
Role(int)	Constructor. Creates a new instance of a role based on that role's numeric database identifier.

Extending .NET Framework User Handling

One of the hardest aspects of .NET Framework programming is determining whether the Framework already provides a feature that we need, or whether we need to build it ourselves. If Microsoft already provides features for what we want to do, we should seriously consider using Microsoft's implementation.

The harder decisions appear when Microsoft has implemented something *similar* to what we need. This decision boils down to deciding whether to create our own implementation, or extend the Framework to suit our needs. It is worth spending some time looking for candidates to extend before developing our own solution from scratch.

This is true of our custom security for the website. The built-in user authentication support in ASP.NET is great. It automatically populates a property called `User` in the `Context` object. This property gives us access to all kinds of information, including whether or not the user has been authenticated, the type of authentication used to verify the user, and even the name of the user. Whether we use forms-based or Windows authentication, we can still use the `User` object in the current `HttpContext` instance, represented by the `Context` object.

> The `Context.User` object provided by the .NET Framework is not the same as the `User` class described earlier. `Context.User` is concerned with authentication, while our `User` class is concerned with encapsulating general information about a particular user.

However, Microsoft's implementation doesn't provide a way to obtain permission levels from a database. Microsoft's implementation is designed to use whatever role-based security mechanism is available to it. This means using NT groups when Windows authentication is enabled, etc. But we can extend their system, so that our custom security does everything we need.

Before we spend more time discussing how we plan to extend it, we should talk a little about the existing Framework itself. Security within .NET (not just ASP.NET) is based around the concept of a **principal**. A `principal` object is a representation of the security context of the user on whose behalf the code is running. So, if I am running a program, then the principal is my security context for the duration of that program. One level lower than the principal is the **identity**. The identity represents the user who is executing the code. Therefore, every principal has an identity. This idea of a common principal and identity is used in forms-based authentication, Windows authentication, and is even used to pass credentials to websites and remoting hosts in other aspects of .NET programming. We decided that rather than implement our own security system, we would create our own concept of a principal and identity that snugly snapped into place within Microsoft's existing security framework. To allow programmers to easily adapt the existing security system, Microsoft provided the `IPrincipal` and `IIdentity` interfaces.

The object assigned to `HttpContext.User` must implement the `IPrincipal` interface. One of the properties defined by `IPrincipal` is `Identity`, which must implement the `IIdentity` interface. So if we write our own custom classes that implement these interfaces, we can add any capabilities we need. This is one of the beauties of having an extensive, inheritable framework – once we get familiar with it then we find that a lot of our work is already done.

Creating two classes that implement `IPrincipal` and `IIdentity`, called `PhilePrincipal` and `PhileIdentity`, we can snap our classes into the existing framework. The following table shows the members of the `PhilePrincipal` and `PhileIdentity` classes. Members defined by the standard interfaces have a gray background, while the new ones that we have created have their names in bold:

PhilePrincipal Class Members (available through HttpContext.User)	
Identity	Property that gets the identity of the current principal. Returns an object implementing the IIdentity interface.
IsInRole	Method that returns a Boolean indicating whether or not the current principal belongs to a given role, specified with a string. We will be providing our own custom version of this method that queries our list of custom roles from our database.
Permissions	An array of PermissionIDs that the user has been granted indirectly through membership in various roles.
Roles	An array containing a list of roles to which the current principal belongs. Note that these roles are roles stored in our custom database, and are not to be confused with COM+ roles.
ValidateLogin	A method used to validate a specific set of login credentials, which include an e-mail address and a password.
HasPermission	A method used to query whether or not the principal belongs to a given role, as indicated by the supplied RoleID integer.
EncryptPassword	A method used to encrypt a plain text string representing a password.

The PhilePrincipal class will enable the site to tell what a user is allowed to do. The Identity property will also tell us who the user is. In normal operation, the Framework itself will determine the identity of the user that owns the security context. In our situation, we will manually set the identity of the principal by using forms-based authentication in ASP.NET.

PhileIdentity Class Members (available through HttpContext.User.Identity)	
AuthenticationType	A string property representing the type of authentication used to obtain the current identity.
IsAuthenticated	Boolean value indicating whether or not the current identity is an authenticated user.
Name	A string property representing the name of the current identity.
FirstName	First name of the user identity; used in various UI controls for providing personalized user greetings.
LastName	Last name of the user identity; used in various UI controls for providing personalized user greetings.
EmailAddress	E-mail address of the user identity.
Password	Encrypted, binary form of the user's password.
UserID	Integer representing the database ID of the user identity.
TestPassword(string)	Method that takes a plain text string representing the user's password and compares it against the encrypted form stored in the database. Returns Boolean true if the password matches, false otherwise.

In the solution section (where we get to look at the code implementation of the above security classes and their relationship to the rest of the module), the website itself, and the existing security framework, will become more clear.

Module Configuration

One of the main goals of this book is to illustrate the use and integration of multiple modules that provide different, unique functionality. These modules that we are developing throughout this book are all designed in such a way that they can either use their own database or share a central database. This is accomplished by allowing the modules to be configured through the use of XML configuration files and the `Web.Config` file provided by ASP.NET. These configuration files also allow us to specify module-specific configuration settings in a way that is easy for us to modify and maintain.

Some of this next section may not be all that familiar to you unless you have used XML class **serialization** and **de-serialization** using the .NET Framework. Serialization is the process of converting an instance of a class to a file on disk, or a stream, in the form of XML. De-serialization is converting an XML stream or file into an instance of a class. Every one of the modules we're developing has its own configuration. This configuration is stored in a special XML file for the module itself. In order for the modules to find their own configuration files, they will use the central site configuration file (`Web.Config`). In this central configuration file we will store the location of the module-specific configuration files.

Let's take a look at what a snippet of the `Web.Config` file looks like, with the location of our user module file in it (if you're coding along while reading, you'll want to add the following to your copy of the `Web.Config` file in your `ThePhile` web application):

```
<!-- LOCAL APPLICATION SETTINGS -->
<appSettings>
 <add key="Accounts_SettingsFile" value="/ThePhile/Config/Accounts.Config"/>
</appSettings>
```

This is found at the bottom of our `Web.Config` file, immediately after the `<system.web>` node, but still within the `<configuration>` node.

The essential core of our design is that we're going to create two classes. The first class, `ModuleConfig`, is a helper class that we'll use to save and retrieve (serialize and de-serialize) instances of our `ModuleSettings` class. The `ModuleSettings` class is nothing more than a serializable container of properties that represent **keys** in our custom XML configuration file. These keys are the string keys that are paired with the values in typical name/value pair fashion.

The ModuleConfig Class

As we mentioned above, the `ModuleConfig` class is a helper class that we use to create instances of the `ModuleSettings` class based on our custom XML configuration file, as well as take modified instances of the `ModuleSettings` class and save them back to XML, allowing for programmatic and user-driven changes to the configuration file.

The following is the design definition of our `ModuleConfig` class. As we progress throughout the book, you'll see this concept of the configuration/settings class pair used extensively.

`ModuleConfig` Class Member	Description
`GetSettings()`	Static class method that returns an instance of the `ModuleSettings` class, properly de-serialized according to the values contained in the custom XML configuration file.
`SaveSettings(ModuleSettings)`	Static class method that takes an instance of the `ModuleSettings` class and serializes it into the custom XML configuration file for our module.

The ModuleSettings Class

The `ModuleSettings` class, as we stated above, is simply a class that exposes public, serializable properties. The class *must* be designed so that its state is entirely preserved throughout a serialization and de-serialization. In other words, there can be no 'one-way' (write-only or read-only) properties, or the class will not function properly.

Each `ModuleSettings` class for each module is going to vary in that some modules require more administrative configuration than others (for example, `Forums` and `Advertising`). However, all of the modules are going to require that at least one setting be maintained. That setting is the database connection string used by the data tier in order to communicate with the database.

The following is a sample XML configuration file (`/ThePhile/Config/Accounts.Config`) defining a single serializable property for use by the module, `ConnectionString`. Again, if you're coding along with the chapter, you'll want to create this file now and populate it with the well-formed XML below. Note that this is simply a supporting data file, and there is no need to place this file in Visual Studio .NET:

```xml
<?xml version="1.0"?>
<ModuleSettings xmlns:xsi="http://www.w3.org/2001/XMLSchema-instance"
                xmlns:xsd="http://www.w3.org/2001/XMLSchema">
  <ConnectionString>
    server=(local);database=ThePhile;uid=sa;pwd=;
  </ConnectionString>
</ModuleSettings>
```

We'll show how to configure a class for XML serialization in the solution section of this chapter. The following is the simple definition of our `ModuleSettings` class:

`ModuleSettings` Class	Description
`ConnectionString`	String property to set or get the value of the database connection string for the given module.

You'll have plenty of opportunity to see how the configuration classes are utilized when we cover the source code for this module (and as you examine the source code for virtually any module developed throughout this book).

We've now covered pretty much all of the classes that we plan on building for this particular module, so let's move on to briefly discuss the front-end design.

Administration

There isn't all that much to design in terms of the administration of the `Accounts` module. At a basic level, we will be providing site administrators with the ability to use a set of web pages to create new roles, update existing roles, grant/revoke permissions on roles, and grant/revoke roles on users. For security and confidentiality reasons, we've decided that administrative staff should not have the ability to edit users' personal information. Instead we will allow users to edit their own information on-line.

> *Of course, in a more realistic, real-world situation, the administrative staff of the site should have some kind of back-end tool that allows them to change e-mail addresses for users. Also, most successful large-scale websites include a feature that allows a user to have their password e-mailed to them if they have forgotten it.*

You will see further coverage of how we're planning to administer the security system in the next section, where we will go through the sample source code for the administration pages.

The Solution

We have spent some time looking at our design, and will now start to build the software. To recap, we are implementing a traditional three-tier solution with distinct presentation, business logic, and data services tiers.

We'll start by implementing the database changes, and then work our way up through the data tier and the business tier to the presentation tier.

The Database

We've already looked at the table structure that we'll use for this part of the database. We can choose whether to construct it using visual tools or SQL scripts. In Chapter 6 we'll look at the Enterprise Manager's visual tools, for now we'll present the SQL scripts that can be run in the Query Analyzer. The scripts required are as follows:

```
CREATE TABLE [dbo].[Accounts_PermissionCategories] (
                    [CategoryID] [int] IDENTITY (1, 1) NOT NULL,
                    [Description] [varchar] (50) NOT NULL )
   ON [PRIMARY]
GO

CREATE TABLE [dbo].[Accounts_Permissions] (
                    [PermissionID] [int] NOT NULL,
                    [Description] [varchar] (50) NOT NULL,
                    [CategoryID] [int] NOT NULL )
   ON [PRIMARY]
GO
```

```
CREATE TABLE [dbo].[Accounts_RolePermissions] (
                    [RoleID] [int] NOT NULL,
                    [PermissionID] [int] NOT NULL )
  ON [PRIMARY]
GO

CREATE TABLE [dbo].[Accounts_Roles] (
                    [RoleID] [int] IDENTITY (1, 1) NOT NULL,
                    [Description] [varchar] (50) NOT NULL )
  ON [PRIMARY]
GO

CREATE TABLE [dbo].[Accounts_StateCodes] (
                    [Description] [varchar] (60) NOT NULL,
                    [StateCode] [char] (2) NOT NULL )
  ON [PRIMARY]
GO

CREATE TABLE [dbo].[Accounts_UserRoles] (
                    [RoleID] [int] NOT NULL,
                    [UserID] [int] NOT NULL )
  ON [PRIMARY]
GO

CREATE TABLE [dbo].[Accounts_Users] (
                    [UserID] [int] IDENTITY (1, 1) NOT NULL,
                    [EmailAddress] [varchar] (255) NOT NULL,
                    [FirstName] [varchar] (30) NOT NULL,
                    [LastName] [varchar] (50) NOT NULL,
                    [Address1] [varchar] (80) NOT NULL,
                    [Address2] [varchar] (80) NOT NULL,
                    [City] [varchar] (40) NOT NULL,
                    [State] [char] (2) NOT NULL,
                    [ZipCode] [varchar] (10) NOT NULL,
                    [HomePhone] [varchar] (14) NOT NULL,
                    [Password] [binary] (20) NOT NULL,
                    [Country] [varchar] (50) NOT NULL )
  ON [PRIMARY]
GO
```

Stored Procedures

There are quite a few stored procedures employed in this module. Rather than going through each one, we will look at two representative examples. The full code for all procedures is included in the website's database available in the code download.

The following is the code for creating the sp_Accounts_GetEffectivePermissionList stored procedure. Again, this script can be run in the Query Analyzer. This stored procedure retrieves the list of all permissions granted to a user by virtue of their role membership:

```
CREATE PROCEDURE sp_Accounts_GetEffectivePermissionList @UserID int
AS
  SELECT DISTINCT PermissionID
```

```
        FROM Accounts_RolePermissions
        WHERE RoleID IN
          (SELECT RoleID FROM Accounts_UserRoles WHERE UserID = @UserID)
```

One of the more complex procedures is sp_Accounts_GetPermissionList. This procedure effectively obtains the sum of all permissions granted to a role. It performs a **join** (a way of looking up related data from more than one table) in order to obtain the verbose description of each permission assigned to the given role:

```
CREATE PROCEDURE sp_Accounts_GetPermissionList @RoleID int = NULL
AS
  IF @RoleID IS NULL
    SELECT PermissionID, Description
      FROM Accounts_Permissions
      ORDER BY Description
  ELSE
    SELECT ap.PermissionID, ap.Description
      FROM Accounts_Permissions ap
      INNER JOIN Accounts_RolePermissions apr
      ON ap.PermissionID = apr.PermissionID
      WHERE apr.RoleID = @RoleID
      ORDER BY ap.Description
```

> *Note the use of table name aliases (ap for* Accounts_Permissions *and* apr *for* Accounts_RolePermissions*) to avoid having to type out the full table names each time we use them.*

The Data Tier

Now that we've seen an overview of the database implementation, we will look at the classes residing in our data services tier: User, Role, Permission, PermissionCategory, and a helper class.

User

The User class provides the basic CRUD (Create, Retrieve, Update, Delete) functionality required for any data entity. It does this with methods alone – it has no maintained state – and simply acts as a bridge between the business tier and the database.

The following is the source code listing for the User class. The full code is in the User.cs file from the AccountsData project in the code download. We start by importing namespaces, and declaring that we will extend Wrox.WebModules.Data.DbObject – our data services base class:

```
using System;
using System.Collections;
using System.Data;
using System.Data.SqlClient;

namespace Wrox.WebModules.Accounts.Data
{
  public class User : Wrox.WebModules.Data.DbObject
  {
```

We will use the same constructor logic defined in the base class we developed in Chapter 2. So when the User constructor is called, we simply route the call to the constructor of the base class DbObject:

```
public User(string newConnectionString): base(newConnectionString)
{ }
```

The following method creates a new user record, based on the supplied parameters. Firstly we create an array of SqlParameter objects, and construct each element appropriately. Then we assign them the value given by the corresponding method parameter. We then run the procedure in a try block. If the try fails, we catch the error.

```
public int Create(string emailAddress,
                  byte[] password,
                  string firstName,
                  string lastName,
                  string address1,
                  string address2,
                  string city,
                  string state,
                  string zipCode,
                  string homePhone,
                  string country)
{
  int rowsAffected;
  SqlParameter[]
    parameters = {
             new SqlParameter("@EmailAddress", SqlDbType.VarChar, 255),
             new SqlParameter("@Password", SqlDbType.Binary, 20),
             new SqlParameter("@FirstName", SqlDbType.VarChar, 30),
             new SqlParameter("@LastName", SqlDbType.VarChar, 50),
             new SqlParameter("@Address1", SqlDbType.VarChar, 80),
             new SqlParameter("@Address2", SqlDbType.VarChar, 80),
             new SqlParameter("@City", SqlDbType.VarChar, 40),
             new SqlParameter("@State", SqlDbType.VarChar, 2),
             new SqlParameter("@ZipCode", SqlDbType.VarChar, 10),
             new SqlParameter("@HomePhone", SqlDbType.VarChar, 14),
             new SqlParameter("@Country", SqlDbType.VarChar, 50),
             new SqlParameter("@UserID", SqlDbType.Int, 4) };

  parameters[0].Value = emailAddress;
  parameters[1].Value = password;
  parameters[2].Value = firstName;
  parameters[3].Value = lastName;
  parameters[4].Value = address1;
  parameters[5].Value = address2;
  parameters[6].Value = city;
  parameters[7].Value = state;
  parameters[8].Value = zipCode;
  parameters[9].Value = homePhone;
  parameters[10].Value = country;
  parameters[11].Direction = ParameterDirection.Output;

  try
```

```
            {
        RunProcedure("sp_Accounts_CreateUser", parameters, out rowsAffected);
            }
        catch ( SqlException e )
            {
```

If an error occurred we check the procedure's return value – otherwise we pass the exception up the call stack. If the return value is 2601, it matches our code for "primary key already exists" (in other words we tried to violate a unique index). We return a value from our enumeration – AccountAlreadyOnFile. This allows our user interface to intelligently trap a duplicate user entry failure.

```
            if (e.Number == 2601)
                {
        return (int)Wrox.WebModules.Accounts.ProcResultCodes.AccountAlreadyOnFile;
                }
            else
                {
            throw new
                AppException("An error occurred while executing the
                              Accounts_CreateUser stored procedure", e );
                }
            }

        return (int)parameters[10].Value;
        }
```

The next method retrieves a record from the database, based on a userID:

```
        public DataRow Retrieve(int userID)
        {
        SqlParameter[] parameters =
                        { new SqlParameter("@UserID", SqlDbType.Int, 4) };
        parameters[0].Value = userID;

        using (DataSet users =
                RunProcedure("sp_Accounts_GetUserDetails", parameters, "Users"))
        {
            return users.Tables[0].Rows[0];
        }
        }
```

This illustrates a great C# feature: the using keyword. This allows an entire block of code (enclosed in {} braces) to execute, and when the block of code is complete, any appropriate objects are automatically disposed of. This serves to further ease the task of memory programming in C#. Without this we would need to manually dispose of our information after we made use of it in another tier.

The next method is an overload of `Retrieve` that retrieves details based on an e-mail address instead of a `userID`:

```
public DataRow Retrieve(string emailAddress)
{
  SqlParameter[] parameters =
          { new SqlParameter("@EmailAddress", SqlDbType.VarChar, 255) };
  parameters[0].Value = emailAddress;

  using (DataSet users =
                    RunProcedure("sp_Accounts_GetUserDetailsByEmail",
                    parameters, "Users"))
  {
    if (users.Tables[0].Rows.Count == 0)
    {
      throw new AppException("No user found on file for email:" +
                                                emailAddress);
    }
    else
      return users.Tables[0].Rows[0];
  }
}
```

The `Update` method passes the user's details and updates the database accordingly. The return parameter confirms that the row was updated:

```
public bool Update(int userID,
                   string emailAddress,
                   byte[] password,
                   string firstName,
                   string lastName,
                   string address1,
                   string address2,
                   string city,
                   string state,
                   string zipCode,
                   string homePhone,
                   string country)
{
  int rowsAffected;
  SqlParameter[] parameters = {
              new SqlParameter("@EmailAddress", SqlDbType.VarChar, 255),
              new SqlParameter("@Password", SqlDbType.Binary, 20),
              new SqlParameter("@FirstName", SqlDbType.VarChar, 30),
              new SqlParameter("@LastName", SqlDbType.VarChar, 50),
              new SqlParameter("@Address1", SqlDbType.VarChar, 80),
              new SqlParameter("@Address2", SqlDbType.VarChar, 80),
              new SqlParameter("@City", SqlDbType.VarChar, 40),
              new SqlParameter("@State", SqlDbType.VarChar, 2),
              new SqlParameter("@ZipCode", SqlDbType.VarChar, 10),
              new SqlParameter("@HomePhone", SqlDbType.VarChar, 14),
              new SqlParameter("@Country", SqlDbType.VarChar, 50),
              new SqlParameter("@UserID", SqlDbType.Int, 4) };
```

```
        parameters[0].Value = emailAddress;
        parameters[1].Value = password;
        parameters[2].Value = firstName;
        parameters[3].Value = lastName;
        parameters[4].Value = address1;
        parameters[5].Value = address2;
        parameters[6].Value = city;
        parameters[7].Value = state;
        parameters[8].Value = zipCode;
        parameters[9].Value = homePhone;
        parameters[10].Value = country;
        parameters[11].Value = userID;

        RunProcedure("sp_Accounts_UpdateUser", parameters, out rowsAffected);
        return (rowsAffected == 1);
    }
```

The `Delete` method deletes the specified user, and returns a Boolean indicating whether the operation was useful:

```
    public bool Delete(int userID)
    {
        SqlParameter[] parameters = { new SqlParameter("@UserID",
                                                        SqlDbType.Int, 4) };

        int rowsAffected;

        parameters[0].Value = userID;

        RunProcedure("sp_Accounts_DeleteUser", parameters, out rowsAffected);
        return (rowsAffected == 1);
    }
```

The following method takes an e-mail address and an encrypted password – the password is always encrypted before it's marshaled across tiers. If the user details are valid, it returns the user's ID:

```
    public int ValidateLogin(string emailAddress, byte[] encPassword)
    {
      int rowsAffected;
      SqlParameter[] parameters = {
              new SqlParameter("@EmailAddress", SqlDbType.VarChar, 255),
              new SqlParameter("@EncryptedPassword", SqlDbType.Binary, 20)};

        parameters[0].Value = emailAddress;
        parameters[1].Value = encPassword;

        return RunProcedure("sp_Accounts_ValidateLogin", parameters,
                                                        out rowsAffected);
    }
```

The next method, listed below, takes a specific `userID` (the numeric identity column in SQL Server) and an encrypted password. If the password matches the password belonging to the user as indicated by the database, the method returns a 1, otherwise a 0. This is accomplished by executing the `sp_Accounts_TestPassword` stored procedure.

```
public int TestPassword(int userID, byte[] encPassword)
{
   int rowsAffected;
   SqlParameter[] parameters = {
           new SqlParameter("@UserID", SqlDbType.Int, 4),
           new SqlParameter("@EncryptedPassword", SqlDbType.Binary, 20) };

   parameters[0].Value = userID;
   parameters[1].Value = encPassword;

   return RunProcedure("sp_Accounts_TestPassword", parameters,
                                            out rowsAffected);

}
```

The following method executes the `sp_Accounts_GetUserRoles` stored procedure. It obtains a `SqlDataReader` containing the list of all roles assigned to a given user. This `SqlDataReader` is then converted into an `ArrayList` and returned to the calling tier to be utilized in a property of the `User` class.

```
public ArrayList GetUserRoles( int userID )
{
   ArrayList roles = new ArrayList();
   SqlParameter[] parameters =
                       { new SqlParameter("@UserID", SqlDbType.Int, 4) };
   parameters[0].Value = userID;

   SqlDataReader tmpReader = RunProcedure("sp_Accounts_GetUserRoles",
                                                      parameters);
   while (tmpReader.Read())
   {
     roles.Add( tmpReader.GetString(1) );
   }
   Connection.Close();
   return roles;
}
```

The method listed below calls the `sp_Accounts_GetEffectivePermissionList` stored procedure. This stored procedure returns a `SqlDataReader` indicating all permissions granted to a user by virtue of their role memberships. This `SqlDataReader` is then iterated through, converted into an `ArrayList`, and returned up to the `User` class in the business tier.

```
public ArrayList GetEffectivePermissionList( int userID )
{
   ArrayList permissions = new ArrayList();
   SqlParameter[] parameters =
                       { new SqlParameter("@UserID", SqlDbType.Int, 4) };
```

```
    parameters[0].Value = userID;

    SqlDataReader tmpReader =
        RunProcedure("sp_Accounts_GetEffectivePermissionList", parameters);
    while (tmpReader.Read())
    {
      permissions.Add( tmpReader.GetInt32(0) );
    }
    Connection.Close();
    return permissions;
  }
```

The method below returns a list of all users in the database in the form of a DataSet object:

```
    public DataSet GetUserList()
    {
      return RunProcedure("sp_Accounts_GetUsers",
                                    new IDataParameter[]{}, "Users");
    }
  }
}
```

Role

The Role class in the data services tier is responsible for making all changes to the database relating to roles, as well as retrieving single and multiple roles at a time from the database.

The following is the source code listing for the Role class, which can be found in the Role.cs file from the AccountsData project:

```
using System;
using System.Data;
using System.Data.SqlClient;

namespace Wrox.WebModules.Accounts.Data
{
  public class Role: Wrox.WebModules.Data.DbObject
  {
    public Role(string newConnectionString) : base(newConnectionString)
    { }
```

The method below takes a description of a new role and creates that role in the database. As usual, all database access takes place via stored procedures:

```
    public int Create(string description)
    {
      int rowsAffected;
      SqlParameter[] parameters = {
                  new SqlParameter("@Description", SqlDbType.VarChar, 50) };
      parameters[0].Value = description;
```

```
        return RunProcedure("sp_Accounts_CreateRole", parameters,
                                                out rowsAffected);
}
```

In this next method, a role is deleted by supplying the numeric ID of the role. This is facilitated by the `sp_Accounts_DeleteRole` stored procedure:

```
public bool Delete(int roleId)
{
  int rowsAffected;
  SqlParameter[] parameters = {
                    new SqlParameter("@RoleID", SqlDbType.Int, 4) };
  parameters[0].Value = roleId;
  RunProcedure("sp_Accounts_DeleteRole", parameters, out rowsAffected);
  return (rowsAffected == 1);
}
```

This next method updates an existing role. We supply the existing role's numeric ID and the new description of the role, and the `sp_Accounts_UpdateRole` stored procedure is called to commit the changes to the database:

```
public bool Update(int roleId, string description)
{
  int rowsAffected;
  SqlParameter[] parameters = {
              new SqlParameter("@RoleID", SqlDbType.Int, 4),
              new SqlParameter("@Description", SqlDbType.VarChar, 50) };
  parameters[0].Value = roleId;
  parameters[1].Value = description;
  RunProcedure("sp_Accounts_UpdateRole", parameters, out rowsAffected);
  return (rowsAffected == 1);
}
```

The method below retrieves a single role by requesting it from the database using the role's numeric ID. The data for the role is placed in a single `DataRow` instance.

```
public DataRow Retrieve(int roleId)
{
  SqlParameter[] parameters = {
                    new SqlParameter("@RoleID", SqlDbType.Int, 4) };

  parameters[0].Value = roleId;
  using (DataSet roles = RunProcedure("sp_Accounts_GetRoleDetails",
                                        parameters, "Roles" ))
  {
    return roles.Tables[0].Rows[0];
  }
}
```

This next method returns a `DataSet` populated with a list of all the roles in the database. This list is sorted alphabetically by the `sp_Accounts_GetAllRoles` stored procedure.

```
public DataSet GetRoleList()
{
  using (DataSet roles = RunProcedure("sp_Accounts_GetAllRoles",
                                      new IDataParameter[]{}, "Roles" ))
  {
    return roles;
  }
}
```

This next method adds a permission to an existing role. By supplying the role identifier and the numeric ID for the permission, the `Accounts_RolePermissions` table is modified by calling the `sp_Accounts_AddPermissionToRole` stored procedure. If the permission is already part of the role, the method simply does nothing (the stored procedure exits successfully without making any changes).

```
public void AddPermission(int roleId, int permissionId)
{
  int rowsAffected;
  SqlParameter[] parameters = {
                  new SqlParameter("@RoleID", SqlDbType.Int, 4),
                  new SqlParameter("@PermissionID", SqlDbType.Int, 4) };
  parameters[0].Value = roleId;
  parameters[1].Value = permissionId;
  RunProcedure("sp_Accounts_AddPermissionToRole", parameters,
                                              out rowsAffected);
}
```

This next method is essentially the opposite of the previous. By supplying a role identifier and a permission identifier, we effectively remove the permission from the role. If the permission is not currently part of the role, then the method simply does nothing.

```
public void RemovePermission(int roleId, int permissionId)
{
  int rowsAffected;
  SqlParameter[] parameters = {
                  new SqlParameter("@RoleID", SqlDbType.Int, 4),
                  new SqlParameter("@PermissionID", SqlDbType.Int, 4) };
  parameters[0].Value = roleId;
  parameters[1].Value = permissionId;
  RunProcedure("sp_Accounts_RemovePermissionFromRole", parameters,
                                              out rowsAffected);
}
```

The following method will completely remove all permissions from a given role by calling the sp_Accounts_ClearPermissionsFromRole stored procedure:

```
public void ClearPermissions(int roleId)
{
  int rowsAffected;
  SqlParameter[] parameters = {
                    new SqlParameter("@RoleID", SqlDbType.Int, 4), };
  parameters[0].Value = roleId;
  RunProcedure("sp_Accounts_ClearPermissionsFromRole", parameters,
                                            out rowsAffected);
  }
 }
}
```

Permission

What each permission does is defined by database administrators and programmers of the website. As such, this class cannot change the permissions themselves. It provides an overloaded method called GetPermissionList, which can either obtain an unfiltered list of all permissions in the system, or a list of all permissions belonging to a given role. Both of these methods return a hierarchical DataSet with a parent-child relationship already defined. This means we can traverse it in a data bound control.

The following is the source code listing for the Permission class, found in the Permission.cs file – part of the AccountsData project:

```
using System;
using System.Data;
using System.Data.SqlClient;

namespace Wrox.WebModules.Accounts.Data
{
  /// <summary>
  /// Summary description for Permission.
  /// </summary>
  public class Permission: Wrox.WebModules.Data.DbObject
  {
  public Permission(string newConnectionString) : base(newConnectionString)
  {  }
```

The following method loads a single permission by calling the sp_Accounts_GetPermissionDetails and storing the results in an instance of the DataRow object:

```
public DataRow Retrieve(int permissionId)
{
  SqlParameter[] parameters = {
                    new SqlParameter("@PermissionID", SqlDbType.Int, 4) };

  using (DataSet permissions =
                    RunProcedure("sp_Accounts_GetPermissionDetails",
                    parameters, "Permissions" ))
```

```
  {
    if (permissions.Tables[0].Rows.Count == 0)
    {
      throw new AppException("No such permission found on file (" +
                                              permissionId + ")");
    }
    else
      return permissions.Tables[0].Rows[0];
  }
}
```

The following method loads all permissions in the database into a DataSet instance by calling the sp_Accounts_GetPermissionCategories stored procedure. The categories are then placed into the permissions DataSet. Then, the sp_Accounts_GetPermissions stored procedure is called to obtain all permissions in the database. Once both the permissions and categories are stored in the DataSet, we create a DataRelation to establish a parent/child relationship between permission categories and permissions.

```
public DataSet GetPermissionList()
{
  SqlParameter[] parameters = {
                    new SqlParameter("@RoleID", SqlDbType.VarChar, 4) };
  using (DataSet permissions =
                    RunProcedure("sp_Accounts_GetPermissionCategories",
                    new IDataParameter[]{}, "Categories"))
  {
    RunProcedure("sp_Accounts_GetPermissionList", parameters, permissions,
                                              "Permissions");
    DataRelation permissionCategories = new
              DataRelation("PermissionCategories",
              permissions.Tables["Categories"].Columns["CategoryID"],
              permissions.Tables["Permissions"].Columns["CategoryID"]);
    permissions.Relations.Add( permissionCategories );
    return permissions;
  }
}
```

This next method performs the same task as the previous method, but this time the results are filtered to only include those permissions that belong to a given role:

```
public DataSet GetPermissionList(int roleId)
{
  SqlParameter[] parameters = {
                    new SqlParameter("@RoleID", SqlDbType.VarChar, 4) };
  parameters[0].Value = roleId;
  using (DataSet permissions =
                    RunProcedure("sp_Accounts_GetPermissionCategories",
                    new IDataParameter[]{}, "Categories"))
  {
    RunProcedure("sp_Accounts_GetPermissionList", parameters,
                                      permissions, "Permissions");
```

```
            DataRelation permissionCategories = new
                    DataRelation("PermissionCategories",
                    permissions.Tables["Categories"].Columns["CategoryID"],
                    permissions.Tables["Permissions"].Columns["CategoryID"]);

        permissions.Relations.Add( permissionCategories );
        return permissions;
    }
  }
 }
}
```

PermissionCategory

Just as with permissions, permission categories do not change. Permission categories are in the database only to allow for visible grouping of related permissions by the user interface. Beyond that, the permission categories serve no security-related purpose. The PermissionCategory class provides read access to the list of permission categories in the database.

The following is the source code listing for the PermissionCategory class. This can be found in the PermissionCategory.cs file, also part of the AccountsData project.

```
using System;
using System.Data;
using System.Data.SqlClient;

namespace Wrox.WebModules.Accounts.Data
{
  /// <summary>
  /// Summary description for PermissionCategory.
  /// </summary>
  public class PermissionCategory : Wrox.WebModules.Data.DbObject
  {
    public PermissionCategory(string newConnectionString) : base(
                                                newConnectionString )
    { }
```

The following method retrieves a single permission category from the database and returns it in the form of a DataRow instance:

```
    public DataRow Retrieve(int categoryId)
    {
      SqlParameter[] parameters = {
                      new SqlParameter("@CategoryID", SqlDbType.Int, 4) };
      parameters[0].Value = categoryId;

      using (DataSet categories =
                          RunProcedure("sp_Accounts_GetCategoryDetails",
                          parameters, "Categories"))
      {
        return categories.Tables[0].Rows[0];
      }
    }
```

The following method obtains a list of all permissions that belong to a given category, returning the results in the form of an instance of the DataSet class:

```
public DataSet GetPermissionsInCategory(int categoryId)
{
  SqlParameter[] parameters = {
                new SqlParameter("@CategoryID", SqlDbType.Int, 4) };
  parameters[0].Value = categoryId;
  using (DataSet permissions =
                RunProcedure("sp_Accounts_GetPermissionsInCategory",
                parameters, "Categories"))
  {
    return permissions;
  }
}
```

The following method obtains a list of all of the categories in the database, sorted alphabetically by the sp_Accounts_GetPermissionCategories stored procedure:

```
public DataSet GetCategoryList()
{
  using (DataSet categories =
                RunProcedure("sp_Accounts_GetPermissionCategories",
                new IDataParameter[]{}, "Categories"))
  {
    return categories;
  }
}
```

AccountsTool

Occasionally we need to access a set of data, or some configuration information not directly related to any given model. In these cases, programmers typically employ a tool or helper class. This is the purpose of the AccountsTool class: for handling the miscellaneous tasks that we don't necessarily need a pure object model to handle.

Our AccountsTool class in the business layer will provide the following static methods, all returning datasets:

❏ GetStates – returns a list of states used to populate a drop-down list when the user sets their address.

❏ GetAllPermissions – returns a list of all permissions in the system.

❏ GetRoleList – returns a list of all roles in the database.

The only one of these that does not have its data access needs provided by another data tier class is `GetStates`, so `Accounts.Data.AccountsTool` contains the following method:

```
public DataSet GetStateList()
{
    return RunProcedure("sp_Accounts_GetStateList", new IDataParameter[]{},
                                                          "States");

}
```

This executes a stored procedure in the database, returning all states.

The Business Tier

This next section will take you through the source code for the business tier classes, starting with the implementation of our `PhilePrincipal` and `PhileIdentity` classes.

PhilePrincipal

The `PhilePrincipal` class snaps in to the existing ASP.NET forms-based authentication. This class implements the `System.Security.Principal.IPrincipal` interface, and adds additional functionality to allow pages aware of our customizations to query additional security information. But by obeying the standards in the interface, we ensure that components and pages not aware of our customizations will be able to use our objects.

Here is the source code listing for the `PhilePrincipal` class, from the `PhilePrincipal.cs` file in the `AccountsBusiness` project:

```
using System;
using System.Collections;
using System.Security;
using System.Security.Cryptography;
using System.Text;

using Wrox.WebModules.Accounts;

namespace Wrox.WebModules.Accounts.Business
{
    /// <summary>
    /// Summary description for PhilePrincipal.
    /// </summary>
    public class PhilePrincipal : Wrox.WebModules.Business.BizObject,
                                  System.Security.Principal.IPrincipal
    {
```

Here we create some private member variables to hold our internal data. Referring to the requirements of the `IPrincipal` interface, we know that we must implement an `Identity` property that returns an instance of an `IIdentity` interface. Knowing this, we also put in a member variable to hold the identity for this instance of `IPrincipal`:

```
   protected System.Security.Principal.IIdentity identity;
   protected ArrayList permissionList;
   protected ArrayList roleList;

   // IPrincipal Interface Requirements:
   // property Identity (IIdentity)
   // property IsInRole (boolean)

   public System.Security.Principal.IIdentity Identity
   {
     get
     {
       return identity;
     }
     set
     {
       identity = value;
     }
   }

   public bool IsInRole(string role)
   {
     return roleList.Contains( role );
   }
```

This next method, `HasPermission`, is one of the methods we have added. As long as we typecast properly, we can always have access to this method even though Microsoft's code is handing around pointers to the `IPrincipal` instance:

```
   public bool HasPermission( int permissionID )
   {
     return permissionList.Contains( permissionID );
   }

   public ArrayList Roles
   {
     get
     {
       return roleList;
     }
   }

   public ArrayList Permissions
   {
     get
     {
       return permissionList;
     }
   }
```

The following set of constructors initializes an instance of the `PhilePrincipal` class. There are two ways we can construct this class – by user ID or e-mail address:

```
public PhilePrincipal( int userID )
{
  Configuration.ModuleSettings moduleSettings =
                          Configuration.ModuleConfig.GetSettings();
  Data.User dataUser = new Data.User( moduleSettings.ConnectionString );
  identity = new PhileIdentity( userID );
  permissionList = dataUser.GetEffectivePermissionList( userID );
  roleList = dataUser.GetUserRoles( userID );
}

public PhilePrincipal( string emailAddress )
{
  Configuration.ModuleSettings moduleSettings =
                          Configuration.ModuleConfig.GetSettings();
  Data.User dataUser = new Data.User( moduleSettings.ConnectionString );
  identity = new PhileIdentity( emailAddress );
  permissionList = dataUser.GetEffectivePermissionList(
                          ((Business.PhileIdentity)identity).UserID );
  roleList = dataUser.GetUserRoles(
                          ((Business.PhileIdentity)identity).UserID );
}
```

In this next method, in order to validate the user's plain text ASCII password without transmitting it across a wire in that format, we encrypt it first and then pass it to the data services tier for validation against the encrypted password stored in the database:

```
public static PhilePrincipal ValidateLogin(string emailAddress,
                                            string password)
{
  Configuration.ModuleSettings moduleSettings =
                          Configuration.ModuleConfig.GetSettings();
  int newID;

  byte[] cryptPassword = EncryptPassword( password );

  Data.User dataUser = new Data.User( moduleSettings.ConnectionString );
```

In this next `if` block, we evaluate the result of the `ValidateLogin` method in the data services user component. If the result is greater than -1, then we assume that the result was the numeric identity of the user attempting to log in. If the result was equal to -1, then we assume the login failed and we return `null`, indicating that the login failed.

```
  if ((newID = dataUser.ValidateLogin(emailAddress, cryptPassword)) > -1)
    return new PhilePrincipal( newID );
  else
    return null;
}

public static byte[] EncryptPassword(string password)
```

```
        {
            UnicodeEncoding encoding = new UnicodeEncoding();
            byte[] hashBytes = encoding.GetBytes( password );

            // compute SHA-1 hash.
            SHA1 sha1 = new SHA1CryptoServiceProvider();
            byte[] cryptPassword = sha1.ComputeHash ( hashBytes );

            return cryptPassword;
        }
    }
}
```

PhileIdentity

PhileIdentity implements the System.Security.Principal.IIdentity interface. We use this
interface so that our class can snap in to the existing authentication framework provided by ASP.NET.

The following is the source code listing for the PhileIdentity class, which you can find in the
PhileIdentity.cs file in the AccountsBusiness project:

```
using System;
using System.Data;
using System.Text;
using System.Collections;
using System.Security.Cryptography;

using Wrox.WebModules.Accounts;

namespace Wrox.WebModules.Accounts.Business
{
    /// <summary>
    /// Summary description for PhileIdentity.
    /// </summary>
    public class PhileIdentity:Wrox.WebModules.Business.BizObject,
                                    System.Security.Principal.IIdentity
    {
        private string firstName;
        private string lastName;
        private string emailAddress;
        private byte[] password;
        private int userID;

        // IIdentity interface requirements:
        // property AuthenticationType (string)
        // property IsAuthenticated (bool)
        // property Name (string)

        public string AuthenticationType
        {
            get
            {
                return "Custom Authentication";
```

```
    }
  set
  {
    // do nothing
  }
}

public bool IsAuthenticated
{
  get
  {
    // assumption: all instances of a PhileIdentity have already
    // been authenticated.
    return true;
  }
}

public string Name
{
  get
  {
    return firstName + " " + lastName;
  }
}

// Constructors:
```

Like `PhilePrincipal`, `PhileIdentity` also has two constructors – one for e-mail address and one for user ID:

```
public PhileIdentity(string currentEmailAddress)
{
  Configuration.ModuleSettings moduleSettings =
                         Configuration.ModuleConfig.GetSettings();
  Data.User dataUser = new Data.User(moduleSettings.ConnectionString);
  DataRow userRow = dataUser.Retrieve(currentEmailAddress);

  firstName = (string)userRow["FirstName"];
  lastName = (string)userRow["LastName"];
  emailAddress = currentEmailAddress;
  userID = (int)userRow["UserID"];
  password = (byte[])userRow["Password"];
}

public PhileIdentity(int currentUserID)
{
  Configuration.ModuleSettings moduleSettings =
                         Configuration.ModuleConfig.GetSettings();
  Data.User dataUser = new Data.User(moduleSettings.ConnectionString);
  DataRow userRow = dataUser.Retrieve(currentUserID);

  firstName = (string)userRow["FirstName"];
```

```
        lastName = (string)userRow["LastName"];
        emailAddress = (string)userRow["EmailAddress"];
        userID = currentUserID;
        password = (byte[])userRow["Password"];
    }


    // Properties and methods added on to existing interface implementation.

    public int TestPassword(string password)
    {
        // At some point, we may have a more complex way of encrypting or
        // storing the passwords so by supplying this procedure, we can simply
        // replace its contents to move password comparison to the database (as
        // we've done below) or somewhere else (e.g. another web service, etc).

        Configuration.ModuleSettings moduleSettings =
                                    Configuration.ModuleConfig.GetSettings();
        UnicodeEncoding encoding = new UnicodeEncoding();
        byte[] hashBytes = encoding.GetBytes( password );

        SHA1 sha1 = new SHA1CryptoServiceProvider();
        byte[] cryptPassword = sha1.ComputeHash( hashBytes );

        Data.User dataUser = new Data.User( moduleSettings.ConnectionString );
        return dataUser.TestPassword( userID, cryptPassword );
    }

    public string FirstName
    {
      get
      {
        return firstName;
      }
    }

    public string LastName
    {
      get
      {
        return lastName;
      }
    }
  }
}
```

Again, we've removed a couple of the property definitions from the code listing because it gets a bit redundant when the definitions are merely simple set/get pairs.

169

User

Of course, in a module that provides user authentication and account storage, the User class is going to be the main class in the module. This class provides a model that represents a single user, and can be used to create or update a single user. Do not confuse the User class with either the PhilePrincipal or PhileIdentity classes, as they represent two distinct sets of functionality. The latter two classes are for integrating with ASP.NET security.

The following is a partial source code listing for the User class. The full version is available in User.cs in the AccountsBusiness project:

```
using System;
using System.Data;

namespace Wrox.WebModules.Accounts.Business
{
  /// <summary>
  /// Summary description for User.
  /// </summary>
  public sealed class User : Wrox.WebModules.Business.BizObject
  {
    private Configuration.ModuleSettings moduleSettings;
    private int userID;
    private string firstName;
    private string lastName;
    private string address1;
    private string address2;
    private string city;
    private string state;
    private string zipCode;
    private string homePhone;
    private string emailAddress;
    private byte[] password;
    private string country;

    public User()
    {
      moduleSettings = Configuration.ModuleConfig.GetSettings();
    }

    private void LoadFromID()
    {
      Data.User dataUser = new Data.User(moduleSettings.ConnectionString);
      DataRow userRow = dataUser.Retrieve(userID);

      FirstName = (string)userRow["FirstName"];
      lastName  = (string)userRow["LastName"];
      address1  = (string)userRow["Address1"];
      address2  = (string)userRow["Address2"];
      city      = (string)userRow["City"];
      state     = (string)userRow["State"];
      zipCode   = (string)userRow["ZipCode"];
```

```
      homePhone    = (string)userRow["HomePhone"];
      emailAddress = (string)userRow["EmailAddress"];
      password     = (byte[])userRow["Password"];
      country      = (string)userRow["Country"];
  }

  public User(int existingUserID)
  {
    moduleSettings = Configuration.ModuleConfig.GetSettings();
    userID = existingUserID;
    LoadFromID();
  }
```

The method listed below provides a handy way of converting an existing `Principal` into a `User` object. The usefulness of this might not be immediately obvious, but you will see the source code that utilizes this method later. Essentially, it provides us with an extremely handy shortcut of creating a new instance of a `User` class based on the currently logged-in user account as detected by ASP.NET:

```
  public User(PhilePrincipal existingPrincipal)
  {
    moduleSettings = Configuration.ModuleConfig.GetSettings();
    userID = ((PhileIdentity)existingPrincipal.Identity).UserID;
    LoadFromID();
  }

  public int Create()
  {
    Data.User dataUser = new Data.User(moduleSettings.ConnectionString);
    userID = dataUser.Create(emailAddress, password, firstName, lastName,
                             address1, address2, city, state, zipCode,
                             homePhone, country);

    return userID;
  }

  public bool Update()
  {
    Data.User dataUser = new Data.User(moduleSettings.ConnectionString);
    return dataUser.Update(userID, emailAddress, password, firstName,
                           lastName, address1, address2, city, state,
                           zipCode, homePhone, country);
  }

  // PROPERTIES DEFINED BELOW

  public int UserID
  {
    get
    {
      return userID;
    }
    set
```

```
        {
          userID = value;
        }
      }
    }

// Other properties cut out of code listing for clarity...

    }
  }
```

The code continues to define get/set properties for each private member variable declared above. By now this syntax should be second nature, so we won't include it here. The properties removed from the listing to keep the chapter length manageable are all simple get/set accessors for the first name, last name, address, and so forth.

Role

The `Role` class in the business tier is for administration. All of the information about the permissions and roles granted to a logged-in user is contained in the identity/principal pair. This class is used to create and update roles, as well as grant/revoke permissions on the role.

The following is the source code listing for the `Role` class, which is in `Role.cs`, part of the `AccountsBusiness` project:

```
using System;
using System.Data;
using Wrox.WebModules.Accounts;

namespace Wrox.WebModules.Accounts.Business
{
  /// <summary>
  /// Summary description for Role.
  /// </summary>
  public class Role: Wrox.WebModules.Business.BizObject
  {
    private int roleId;
    private string description;

    public Role()
    { }
```

This next method will instantiate a `Role` object based on the ID of an existing role:

```
    public Role(int currentRoleId)
    {
      Configuration.ModuleSettings moduleSettings =
                            Configuration.ModuleConfig.GetSettings();
      Data.Role dataRole = new Data.Role(moduleSettings.ConnectionString);
      DataRow roleRow;

      roleRow = dataRole.Retrieve(currentRoleId);
      roleId = currentRoleId;
      description = (string)roleRow["Description"];
    }
```

This next method will create a new role and commit the changes to the database by way of the data services tier component:

```
public int Create()
{
  Configuration.ModuleSettings moduleSettings =
                              Configuration.ModuleConfig.GetSettings();
  Data.Role dataRole = new Data.Role(moduleSettings.ConnectionString);

  roleId = dataRole.Create(description);
  return roleId;
}
```

The method shown below will save the current role's state (managed by private member variables exposed as properties) in the database:

```
public bool Update()
{
  Configuration.ModuleSettings moduleSettings =
                              Configuration.ModuleConfig.GetSettings();
  Data.Role dataRole = new Data.Role(moduleSettings.ConnectionString);

  return dataRole.Update(roleId, description);
}
```

This next method will delete the role indicated by the current `RoleID` as stored in the object instance:

```
public bool Delete()
{
  Configuration.ModuleSettings moduleSettings =
                              Configuration.ModuleConfig.GetSettings();
  Data.Role dataRole = new Data.Role(moduleSettings.ConnectionString);

  return dataRole.Delete(roleId);
}
```

This next method adds a given permission to the currently instantiated role:

```
public void AddPermission(int permissionId)
{
  Configuration.ModuleSettings moduleSettings =
                              Configuration.ModuleConfig.GetSettings();
  Data.Role dataRole = new Data.Role(moduleSettings.ConnectionString);

  dataRole.AddPermission(roleId, permissionId);
}
```

This next method removes a given permission from the currently instantiated role:

```
public void RemovePermission(int permissionId)
{
  Configuration.ModuleSettings moduleSettings =
                          Configuration.ModuleConfig.GetSettings();
  Data.Role dataRole = new Data.Role(moduleSettings.ConnectionString);

  dataRole.RemovePermission(roleId, permissionId);
}
```

This next method removes *all* permissions currently associated with the current role instance:

```
public void ClearPermissions()
{
  Configuration.ModuleSettings moduleSettings =
                          Configuration.ModuleConfig.GetSettings();
  Data.Role dataRole = new Data.Role(moduleSettings.ConnectionString);

  dataRole.ClearPermissions(roleId);
}

public int RoleID
{
  get
  {
    return roleId;
  }
}

public string Description
{
  get
  {
    return description;
  }
  set
  {
    description = value;
  }
}
}
}
```

AccountsTool

The following is the source code listing for the AccountsTool class, a utility class that allows us to obtain lists that do not fit into the object model. This class is in the AccountsTool.cs file in the AccountsBusiness project:

```
using System;
using System.Data;
```

```
namespace Wrox.WebModules.Accounts.Business
{
    /// <summary>
    /// Summary description for AccountsTool.
    /// </summary>
    public class AccountsTool: Wrox.WebModules.Business.BizObject
    {
        public static DataSet GetStates()
        {
            Data.AccountsTool tool = new Data.AccountsTool(
                    Configuration.ModuleConfig.GetSettings().ConnectionString);
            return tool.GetStateList();
        }

        public static DataSet GetAllPermissions()
        {
            Data.Permission dataPermission = new Data.Permission(
                    Configuration.ModuleConfig.GetSettings().ConnectionString);
            return dataPermission.GetPermissionList();
        }

        public static DataSet GetRoleList()
        {
            Data.Role dataRole = new Data.Role(
                    Configuration.ModuleConfig.GetSettings().ConnectionString);
            return dataRole.GetRoleList();
        }
    }
}
```

Modifying the UI to Support Authentication

If you remember back to Chapter 3 where we built the core foundation of the user interface, we created several standardized UI elements for use in our ThePhile web application project. Two of these elements were a base class for pages and a user control to display a site header at the top of every page. Both of these were implemented assuming that some kind of authentication would be taking place, but without knowing the exact implementation.

In this section we will change the PhilePage class and the SiteHeader user control in order to take full advantage of our authentication system. These changes are going to make use of the PhileIdentity and PhilePrincipal classes, which we discussed earlier.

Modifying the PhilePage Class

In order to simplify the use of the customized PhileIdentity and PhilePrincipal classes for the rest of the website, including all of the other modules being developed for this book, we decided to make a slight change to the PhilePage class by enhancing its PhilePage_Load method. Here is the new version of that method, in the PhilePage.cs file in the main ThePhile project:

```
private void PhilePage_Load(object sender, System.EventArgs e)
{
```

```
if (Context.User.Identity.IsAuthenticated)
{
  if (!(Context.User is PhilePrincipal))
  {
    // ASP.NET's regular forms authentication picked up our cookie, but we
    // haven't replaced the default context user with our own. Let's do that
    // now. We know that the previous User.Identity.Name is the e-mail
    // address (because we force it to be as such in the login.aspx page)
    PhilePrincipal newUser = new PhilePrincipal(Context.User.Identity.Name );
    Context.User = newUser;
  }
}
}
```

Essentially, this is the "load profile" portion of the user authentication flow diagram that we saw earlier in the chapter. At the very beginning of the load process of the page a check is made to see if the user is authenticated. If the authenticated user *is not* already one of our custom `PhilePrincipal` instances, then we simply create a new instance of the `PhilePrincipal` class based on the current user identity name (we're using the e-mail address as the 'name'). Once the new instance is created, we assign that instance back to the `Context.User` property. This loads a complete user profile into the authentication framework provided by ASP.NET.

Modifying the SiteHeader Control

Another facet of our website that will become a bit more robust with our user authentication solution is our site header control.

One thing we know about user controls is that they each have their own `Page_Load` event, since ASP.NET considers them almost as 'micro pages'. We know that the parent page, if it inherits from `PhilePage`, will have already created an appropriate `PhilePrincipal` in the `Context.User` property. Therefore, to obtain a more user-friendly greeting, all we have to do is modify the site header control (`/ThePhile/Controls/SiteHeader.ascx.cs` file in the `ThePhile` project) in the following way:

```
private void Page_Load(object sender, System.EventArgs e)
{
  // Put user code to initialize the page here
  Greeting.Text = "Welcome, ";
  if (Context.User.Identity.IsAuthenticated)
  {
    // superceded to make more user-friendly since the user's ID is just
    // an e-mail address:
    // Greeting.Text += Context.User.Identity.Name + ".";
    PhileIdentity id = (PhileIdentity)Context.User.Identity;
    Greeting.Text += "<b>" + id.FirstName + " " + id.LastName + "</b>";
    UserLink.Text = "My Account";
    UserLink.NavigateUrl = "/ThePhile/Modules/Users/MyAccount.aspx";
  }
  else
  {
    Greeting.Text += "Guest User.";
    UserLink.Text = "Click to Login";
    UserLink.NavigateUrl = "/ThePhile/Modules/Users/Login.aspx";
  }
}
```

This not only provides a user-friendly greeting, but it intelligently decides which link to display to the user. If they have already logged in, then they are given a link to the "My Account" page, which allows them to make changes to their personal information and preferences. If they have not logged in (no authentication cookie was found), then they are given a link to the login page.

The Login, Registration, and User Details Pages

The following is a screenshot of the new login page, the code for which is available as /ThePhile/Modules/Users/Login.aspx. The top of the page shows the modified SiteHeader control, which has recognized the user and is displaying that user's first and last names. As we just saw, we do this by instantiating a User object from the business tier and obtaining the FirstName and LastName properties.

Finally, let's take a look at a screenshot of the user profile page. This is the page that the user sees when they want to modify their own personal information. A very similar version of this page is displayed when the user is first registering as a new account:

This form is accomplished using some fairly standard and simple ASP.NET data binding techniques. For demonstration purposes, it is sometimes helpful to show how to do things both ways, so in the code for this form (which you can find in /ThePhile/Modules/Users/MyAccount.aspx.cs) we've shown how to manually set the value of the textboxes rather than use data binding. In the administration section (discussed later) we use some more complex data binding to show you the difference in code size and readability.

The following is the Page_Load event for the page displayed above:

```
private void Page_Load(object sender, System.EventArgs e)
{
  {
  // Put user code to initialize the page here
  RoleList.Visible = false;
  SaveMessage.Visible = false;
```

```
if (!Page.IsPostBack)
{
  DataSet states;
  if (Context.User.Identity.IsAuthenticated)
  {
    Wrox.WebModules.Accounts.Business.User currentUser =
          new Wrox.WebModules.Accounts.Business.User(
          (Wrox.WebModules.Accounts.Business.PhilePrincipal)Context.User);

    FirstName.Text = currentUser.FirstName;
    EmailAddress.Text = currentUser.EmailAddress;
    LastName.Text = currentUser.LastName;
    Address1.Text = currentUser.Address1;
    Address2.Text = currentUser.Address2;
    ZipCode.Text = currentUser.ZipCode;
    City.Text = currentUser.City;
    HomePhone.Text = currentUser.HomePhone;
```

The previous few lines of codes set the text property of the page's TextBox controls. The following code block uses data binding to bind a DropDownList control to the list of states available. This list includes a 'blank' state for those people logging in from outside the US:

```
    states = AccountsTool.GetStates();
    StateDropDown.DataSource = states;
    StateDropDown.DataTextField = "Description";
    StateDropDown.DataValueField = "StateCode";
    StateDropDown.DataBind();
    StateDropDown.SelectedIndex =
            StateDropDown.Items.IndexOf(StateDropDown.Items.FindByValue(
            currentUser.State ));

  }
  else
  {
    mainPanel.Visible = false;
  }
}
```

This is another example of where our architecture of expanding on the existing security system is going to pay off. Here, we simply ask the Context.User object if it has any roles assigned to it. If it does, then we will iterate through them, building an HTML unordered list to display those roles.

```
if ( ((PhilePrincipal)Context.User).Roles.Count > 0 )
{
  RoleList.Visible = true;
  ArrayList roles = ((PhilePrincipal)Context.User).Roles;
  RoleList.Text = "You are have been granted the following roles:<ul>";
  for(int i=0; i<roles.Count; i++)
  {
    RoleList.Text += "<li>" + roles[i] + "</li>";
```

```
    }
    RoleList.Text += "</ul>";
  }
}
```

Administering Roles and Accounts

The administration of the roles and accounts system is fairly straightforward. The `Admin` directory of the `User` module has been secured by `NTFS`, which allows us to ensure that nobody without the specific permissions defined on that directory will be able to access those files. If someone attempts to access this directory without the appropriate account, the browser will simply report that it cannot access the files.

> *If you have downloaded the sample code, then more than likely your `Admin` directory will not be secured. For testing purposes, that's fine. However, to secure it, simply right-click it in your file explorer and administer the permissions as you would any other directory. Consult your Windows 2000 or XP manual or reference guide for more information on NTFS permissions.*

The `Accounts` administration module provides a *role editor*. This role editor will allow administrative users to create new roles, as well as edit existing ones. The following screenshot shows a sample of the administration screen that administrative users are greeted with when they first open up the page (they'll have to type in the URL manually, as there are no links to this page):

The following is the listing for the `Page_Load` event from the above page (found in `/ThePhile/Modules/Users/Admin/Roles.aspx.cs`, again, still in our `ThePhile` application):

```
private void Page_Load(object sender, System.EventArgs e)
{
  // Put user code to initialize the page here
  PhilePrincipal currentPrincipal = (PhilePrincipal)Context.User;
  if (!currentPrincipal.HasPermission((int)AccountsPermissions.CreateRoles))
  {
    NewRoleButton.Visible = false;
    NewRoleDescription.Visible = false;
  }
  else
  {
    NewRoleButton.Visible = true;
    NewRoleDescription.Visible = true;
  }
  roles = AccountsTool.GetRoleList();
  RoleList.DataSource = roles.Tables["Roles"];
  RoleList.DataBind();
}
```

As you can see, we are controlling the visibility of the **Create Role** button based on whether or not the currently logged-in user has the `AccountsPermissions.CreateRoles` permission. Beyond that, we simply bind our `DataList` control, `RoleList`, to the `Roles` table returned from the `GetRoleList` method.

As shown in the above screenshot, it is a pretty simple interface. Selecting an existing role presents an interactive screen similar to the one shown below. The core of this particular UI is the side-by-side listboxes. By clicking on a category in the left listbox, the child list of permissions is filled into the listbox on the right. Then, by clicking on the entry for a permission item, the option to remove that permission automatically becomes available. There is also the option to delete the current role:

Let's examine the source code for the code-behind for this page. In order to get all of this to work, the ListBox that contains the permission categories must automatically post back any time an event on it triggers. This allows us to respond to the event on the server-side and obtain more data from the data source to populate the second ListBox for the permissions themselves.

```
public class EditRole : Wrox.ThePhile.Web.PhilePage
{
protected System.Web.UI.WebControls.Label RoleLabel;
protected System.Web.UI.WebControls.ListBox CategoryList;
protected System.Web.UI.WebControls.ListBox PermissionList;
protected Wrox.ThePhile.Web.Controls.Server.Navigator MenuNav;
protected System.Web.UI.WebControls.Button RemovePermissionButton;
protected System.Web.UI.WebControls.Button AddPermissionButton;
protected System.Web.UI.WebControls.DropDownList PermissionDropList;
protected System.Web.UI.WebControls.Button RemoveRoleButton;
protected System.Web.UI.WebControls.LinkButton ManageAssignmentsLink;

private Role currentRole;
```

We knew in advance that there would be several different occasions when we were going to need to configure the data binding properties of this page (each time an event fires that causes a server postback, we need to make sure that our data is returned to the appropriate state after responding to the event). So we placed all of that code into a separate function to be called by any event that needs to. We called this function DoInitialDataBind:

```
private void DoInitialDataBind()
{
  currentRole = new Role(Convert.ToInt32(Request["RoleID"]));
  RoleLabel.Text = "Current Role: " + currentRole.Description;
  PermissionList.Items.Clear();
  RemovePermissionButton.Visible = false;
  CategoryList.DataSource = currentRole.Permissions.Tables["Categories"];
  CategoryList.DataTextField = "Description";
  CategoryList.DataValueField = "CategoryID";
  CategoryList.DataBind();

  DataSet allPermissions = AccountsTool.GetAllPermissions();
  PermissionDropList.DataSource = allPermissions.Tables["Permissions"];
  PermissionDropList.DataTextField = "Description";
  PermissionDropList.DataValueField = "PermissionID";
  PermissionDropList.DataBind();
}
```

Here is the Page_Load event handler. First, we test to see if the user has the right permissions to be viewing this page. If they don't, we simply stop the process and end the Response. Otherwise, we test to see if this is the first time the page has been loaded. If so, then we must perform the initial data binding. If it is a postback, then we know that each control is having its state rebuilt by the ASP.NET server process automatically, so there is no need to rebind:

```
private void Page_Load(object sender, System.EventArgs e)
{
  // Put user code to initialize the page here
  PhilePrincipal currentPrincipal = (PhilePrincipal)Context.User;
  if (!currentPrincipal.HasPermission((int)AccountsPermissions.UpdateRoles))
  {
    Response.Write("You don't have sufficient permission to be using this
                                                       page.");
    Response.End();
  }

  if (!Page.IsPostBack)
  {
    DoInitialDataBind();
  }
}
```

This next method, which was built automatically by the ASP.NET Forms Designer, sets up the event handlers. We are responding to a click on the **Manage Assignments** link, a change in the selected index of the permission category `DropDownList`, a change in the selected index of the permission `DropDownList`, a click on the **Remove Permission** button, a click on the **Add Permission** button, and finally a click on the **Remove Role** button, as well as the standard `Load` event:

```
private void InitializeComponent()
{
  this.ManageAssignmentsLink.Click +=
        new System.EventHandler(this.ManageAssignmentsLink_Click);
  this.CategoryList.SelectedIndexChanged +=
        new System.EventHandler(this.CategoryList_SelectedIndexChanged);
  this.PermissionList.SelectedIndexChanged +=
        new System.EventHandler(this.PermissionList_SelectedIndexChanged);
  this.RemovePermissionButton.Click +=
        new System.EventHandler(this.RemovePermissionButton_Click);
  this.AddPermissionButton.Click +=
        new System.EventHandler(this.AddPermissionButton_Click);
  this.RemoveRoleButton.Click +=
        new System.EventHandler(this.RemoveRoleButton_Click);
  this.Load += new System.EventHandler(this.Page_Load);
}
#endregion
```

In order for our web form to appear as though its state is being properly maintained we need to respond to events. One task we perform over and over again is selecting the category. This method is designed to select a given category as well as populate the permissions `DropDownList` accordingly:

```
private void SelectCategory(int categoryId, bool forceSelection)
{
  if (forceSelection)
  {
    CategoryList.SelectedIndex = CategoryList.Items.IndexOf (
              CategoryList.Items.FindByValue( categoryId.ToString() ));
```

```
      }
      currentRole = new Role(Convert.ToInt32(Request["RoleID"]));
      DataTable categories = currentRole.Permissions.Tables["Categories"];

      DataRow currentCategory = categories.Rows.Find( categoryId );
      if (currentCategory != null)
      {
        DataRow[] permissions =
                        currentCategory.GetChildRows("PermissionCategories");
        PermissionList.Items.Clear();
        foreach (DataRow currentRow in permissions)
        {
          PermissionList.Items.Add(
                          new ListItem( (string)currentRow["Description"],
                          Convert.ToString(currentRow["PermissionID"])) );
        }
      }
    }

    private void CategoryList_SelectedIndexChanged(object sender,
                                                      System.EventArgs e)
    {
      SelectCategory( Convert.ToInt32(CategoryList.SelectedItem.Value), false );
    }
```

We have set up an event to handle the **Remove Permission** button click, for when we want to remove a permission item from our DropDownList of permissions. This works fine, but the category list loses its state – because its state is populated in the initial binding, which we don't need to do in a postback. To account for this, we use the SelectCategory method, forcing a selection of the current category after a permission has been removed:

```
    private void RemovePermissionButton_Click(object sender, System.EventArgs e)
    {
      int currentRole = Convert.ToInt32(Request["RoleID"]);
      Role bizRole = new Role(currentRole);
      bizRole.RemovePermission(
                      Convert.ToInt32(PermissionList.SelectedItem.Value) );
      DoInitialDataBind();
      SelectCategory( Convert.ToInt32(Request["CategoryList"]), true );
    }
```

By default, the **Remove Permission** button is invisible. To reveal the button after a permission is selected in the appropriate ListBox, we respond to the SelectedIndexChanged event by making the **Remove Permission** button visible:

```
    private void PermissionList_SelectedIndexChanged(object sender,
                                                      System.EventArgs e)
    {
      RemovePermissionButton.Visible = true;
    }
```

This next event handler responds to the **Add Permission** button's `Click` event. This will add the currently selected permission to the role currently being edited. While it is physically possible for us to use purely client-side methods to accomplish this same thing visibly, we're going to avoid that. Instead, we're going to use the event model that ASP.NET provides us. The main reason for this is that server-side code is guaranteed to work on all browsers. If we round-trip for this action, we don't care about the client support for JavaScript (ever seen a DHTML page try to run on a WebTV box or a Sega Dreamcast web browser?). By doing all the work on the serverside, we take an initial latency penalty, but since all of the data is already available to the web page to begin with, the performance loss we suffer is negligible and our gains in browser compatibility are well worth it.

```csharp
private void AddPermissionButton_Click(object sender, System.EventArgs e)
{
  int currentRole = Convert.ToInt32(Request["RoleID"]);
  Role bizRole = new Role(currentRole);
  bizRole.AddPermission(
                 Convert.ToInt32(PermissionDropList.SelectedItem.Value) );
  DoInitialDataBind();
  SelectCategory( Convert.ToInt32(Request["CategoryList"]), true);
}
```

This next event handler will delete the current role (the stored procedure will also remove all data dependent on that role) and then transfer control to the `Roles.aspx` page, as the current role will no longer exist.

```csharp
private void RemoveRoleButton_Click(object sender, System.EventArgs e)
{
  int currentRole = Convert.ToInt32(Request["RoleID"]);
  Role bizRole = new Role(currentRole);
  bizRole.Delete();
  Server.Transfer("Roles.aspx");
}

private void ManageAssignmentsLink_Click(object sender, System.EventArgs e)
{
  Server.Transfer("RoleAssignments.aspx?RoleID="+Request["RoleID"]);
}
}
}
```

And finally, as the last part of our user accounting administration section, let's take a look at the source code of the page that manages the user memberships of given roles. Here is a screenshot of this page in action:

This page works in a fairly straightforward manner. The user of the page, who would typically be a system administrator, supplies an e-mail address and can then either click the Assign User to Role button or the Remove User from Role button. If the user is already in the role when being added, no error is displayed. If the user is not in the role when being removed from the role, then no error message is displayed. The reason for not displaying any messages is that if your desired state is *already* the way you intend it, then we shouldn't have to report that the code did nothing to get you to that state. If you want to remove a user who isn't there, why bother telling you we didn't remove a user that wasn't there? Obviously, we could make the administration system more user-friendly by giving more verbose reports, but that's typically something we would work on after the system is fully functional.

Let's take a look at the code-behind for this page
(/ThePhile/Modules/Users/Admin/RoleAssignments.aspx.cs). Instead of listing the entire source code, we'll just include the important method definitions and web form designer code:

```
private void Page_Load(object sender, System.EventArgs e)
{
    // Put user code to initialize the page here
    if (!Page.IsPostBack)
    {
```

```
      Role currentRole = new Role(Convert.ToInt32(Request["RoleID"]));
      CurrentRoleLabel.Text = "Current Role: " + currentRole.Description;
    }
  }

  #region Web Form Designer generated code
  override protected void OnInit(EventArgs e)
  {
    //
    // CODEGEN: This call is required by the ASP.NET Web Form Designer.
    //
    base.OnInit(e);
    InitializeComponent();
  }

  /// <summary>
  /// Required method for Designer support - do not modify
  /// the contents of this method with the code editor.
  /// </summary>
  private void InitializeComponent()
  {
    this.AssignUserButton.Click += new
                      System.EventHandler(this.AssignUserButton_Click);
    this.RemoveUserButton.Click += new
                      System.EventHandler(this.RemoveUserButton_Click);
    this.Load += new System.EventHandler(this.Page_Load);
  }
  #endregion
```

This next event handler is executed in response to clicking the **Assign User to Role** button. First, we obtain a `PhilePrincipal` instance by instantiating the `PhilePrincipal` class with an e-mail address as an argument to the constructor. Then we obtain an instance of a `User` class by passing in the instance of `PhilePrincipal` we just created. Once this is done then we can invoke the `AddToRole` method on that object. Finally, we set the text of a `Label` control to inform the administrative user of what just took place:

```
private void AssignUserButton_Click(object sender, System.EventArgs e)
{
  PhilePrincipal tempPrincipal = new PhilePrincipal( EmailAddress.Text );
  Business.User tempUser = new Business.User( tempPrincipal );
  tempUser.AddToRole( Convert.ToInt32( Request["RoleID"] ) );
  StatusLabel.Text = "User " + EmailAddress.Text + " Granted Role.<br>";
  StatusLabel.Visible = true;
}
```

Just as we did in the last event handler, we obtain an instance of a `PhilePrincipal` class by supplying the e-mail address contained in the form. Once we've accomplished this we can instantiate a `User` object by passing the new `PhilePrincipal` instance to the `User` constructor. Once we have an instance of the `User` class, we can simply call `RemoveRole` on that instance and we're done.

```
private void RemoveUserButton_Click(object sender, System.EventArgs e)
{
```

```
    PhilePrincipal tempPrincipal = new PhilePrincipal( EmailAddress.Text );
    Business.User tempUser = new Business.User( tempPrincipal );
    tempUser.RemoveRole( Convert.ToInt32( Request["RoleID"] ) );
    StatusLabel.Text = "User " + EmailAddress.Text + " Removed from Role.<br>";
    StatusLabel.Visible = true;
}
```

Summary

This chapter started off by presenting a problem that many websites today are faced with: that of identifying, authenticating, remembering, and persisting user accounts. We then went through a design for a solution to this problem. Finally, we looked at the extensive source code for an expandable, powerful implementation.

In this chapter we covered quite a few topics and took a look at a fair amount of code. We covered some important concepts, such as the uses and benefits of role-based security, and the importance of integrating into existing systems rather than creating entirely new infrastructures. We covered a complex system of assigning permissions to roles, and assigning users to those roles, and showed how we can create a fully functioning authentication system around this concept.

Hopefully, you have found this chapter useful, and you will understand the following important concepts that you can use in your own projects and sample applications:

❑   The issues surrounding user identification

❑   Issues involved in user authentication

❑   Issues involved in securing all or some of a web application

❑   Provisions for administrative or 'power' users

Now that we have our Accounts module we can move on and implement other modules that rely on it for user identification and authentication. In the next chapter we'll begin to look at modules relating to the *content* of our site, beginning with one to manage news articles.

6

News Management

The site we're building is basically a content site focused on DVDs and books. Content can be in the form of news, articles, reports of special events, reviews, and so on. In this chapter we're going to point out some of the content-related problems that should be considered for sites of this type. We'll then design and develop an online news manager to enable complete management of our site's content – acquiring news, adding, activating, and removing news, sharing news with others, and so on. While we will focus on managing news, many of these techniques will be relevant when dealing with other types of content.

The Problem

There are several ways to gather information and news for our site's content: we might hunt for news ourselves, get news directly from the users (a great example of this is the **Add Your News** link at www.aspwire.com), or rely upon a company, such as Reuters, whose business it is to gather and organize news and distribute it to third party sites. Another common technique is to keep an eye on other news sites, and scrape articles together from information available on the Internet. Many sites (for example www.wired.com) also provide links to suggested stories elsewhere. It doesn't matter which methods we use, we still need fresh and updated content if our site is to be successful and entice users to return. No user will come regularly to a site if they never, or very seldom, find some new content.

Once we have our news sources, a second problem arises: how to add news and articles to our site. We can immediately rule out manually updating or adding static HTML pages – if we have to add news several times a day, or even just every week, creating and uploading pages and editing all the links is not practical in most cases. In cases where it is practical, we don't need to write a new management system!

For our site, we need a much more flexible system, one that allows the site administrators to easily publish news without requiring special HTML tools or a knowledge of HTML. We want it to have many features, such as enabling us to organize news in categories and show abstracts, and allowing the site users to post their own news. We'll see the complete list of features we're going to implement in the Design section. For now it's sufficient to say that we must be able to manage the content online, without any other tool. Think about what this implies: you can add or edit news as soon as it is available, in a few minutes, even if you're not in your office and even if you don't have access to your own computer; all you need is a connection to the Internet and a browser. And this can work the same way for your news contributors and partners. They won't need to e-mail the news to you and then wait for you to publish it – they can submit and publish content without your intervention (although in our case we will give the administrator the option to approve or edit the content before publication). A good example of this is **www.codeproject.com**, which provides article categories plus an "unedited section" for the user-submitted articles that have not been edited yet.

For small content sites, or for sites where news and articles are not the main business, simply showing news and other resources is sufficient. But others may want to take this one step further, and decide to offer the news they have gathered/written and organized to other sites. Such sites might not want to spend time finding and formatting articles, may not have people who look after a news management system, but might want to fuel their site with some fresh content automatically updated on a regular basis. In many cases, paying a fee for such a service can be relatively cheap and very easy, since the site administrator doesn't have to worry at all about the content, and they'll be able to focus on the site's main business (commerce of goods related to the published news, for example). Therefore the designers of ThePhile.com decided to find a way to offer their news to other companies. They also wanted this data to be available not only for web browsers, but for Windows client applications too.

The last problem is the implementation of security. We want to give full control to one or more administrators, allow a specific group of users to submit news, and allow normal users to just read the news. We could even prevent them from reading the content if they have not registered with the site.

So, to summarize the problem, we need:

❑ A source of news and articles

❑ An online tool for managing news content

❑ A method of allowing other sites to use our content

❑ A system that allows various users different levels of access to the site's content

The Design

In this section we're going to work on the design of our online tool for acquiring, managing, and sharing the news content of our site. Specifically we will:

❑ Provide a full list of the features we want to implement

❑ Design the database tables for this module

❑ Write down a list and a description of the stored procedures that provide access to the database

❑ Describe the object models of the data and business layers

- Describe the user interface services specific to news management, such as the site pages, reusable user controls, and web services

- Explain how we will ensure security for the administration section and for other access-restricted pages

Features to Implement

Let's start our discussion by writing down a list of the features that the news manager module should provide in order to be flexible and powerful, but still easy to use. We might decide to add more features later, but these are the things we definitely need to implement:

- A news item can be added to the database at any time, with the option not to publish it until a specified release date. In addition, the person submitting the news must be able to specify an expiration date, after which the news will be retired. If these dates are not specified then the news should be immediately published and remain active indefinitely.

- News items or articles can have an approved status. If it is the administrator who submits the news item, it should be approved directly. If we allow other people, such as staff or users of the site, to post their own news, then it should be added to the database in a "pending" state. The site administrator will then take care of controlling this content, applying any required modifications, and finally approving the news for publishing once it is considered suitable.

- The system should track *who* originally submitted an article or news item. This is important as it provides information on whether a contributor is active, who is responsible for incorrect content, who to contact for further details if the news is particularly interesting, and so on.

- There should be multiple categories, allowing all news items and articles to be organized in different virtual folders.

- The user should have a page with the available categories as a menu. Each category should be linked to a page that shows a short abstract for each news item. The administrator will use a protected page to define the length of the abstracts. By clicking on the abstract the user can read the whole text.

- We want to expose the news through a web service, so that we can offer content to external sites, and provide a Windows client that downloads the news or links to the respective online pages.

- Above all, the news manager must be integrated with the existing site. In our case this means that the pages must tie in with the current layout, and that we must take advantage of the current authentication/authorization system to protect each section and to identify the author of the submitted content.

Having this list of features is very important when designing the database tables, as we now know what information we need to store, and the information that we should retrieve from existing tables.

Database Design

As we saw in Chapter 2, we are using a single database for all the modules of this site. So, we need to use module-specific prefixes for the tables, stored procedures, and the other objects of our modules. The prefix for the news manager module is News_.

We have only two tables, one for the categories and the other for the actual news content. The following diagram shows how they are linked to each other and to the `Accounts_Users` table that we created in Chapter 5:

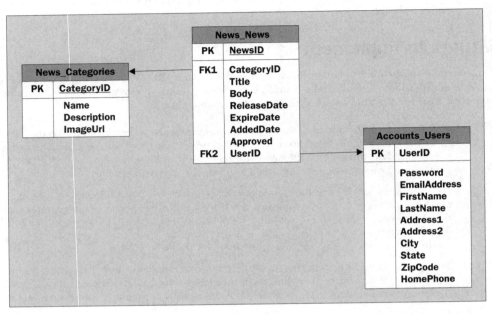

Let's start describing these tables and their relationship in more detail.

The News_Categories Table

Unsurprisingly, the `News_Categories` table stores the name, a description, and an image for each category:

Column Name	Type	Size	Allow Null	Description
CategoryID	int – Identity primary key	4	No	The unique ID for the category.
Name	varchar	50	No	The name of the category.
Description	varchar	250	Yes	The description of the category.
ImageUrl	varchar	100	Yes	The URL of an image that graphically describes the category. It might be used in menus, for example.

This system supports a single level category, meaning that we cannot have subcategories. Enhancing the system to support subcategories is left as an exercise to the reader but, as a suggestion, the DB would only require an additional `ParentCategoryID` column containing the ID of the parent category.

The News_News Table

This table contains the content and all further information for all the news items in all categories. It is structured as follows:

Column Name	Type	Size	Allow Null	Description
NewsID	int – Identity Primary key	4	No	The unique ID for the news item.
CategoryID	int – Foreign key	4	No	The ID of the category to which the news item belongs.
Title	varchar	250	No	The title of the news item.
Body	text		Yes	The body of the news item, in HTML format.
ReleaseDate	datetime	8	No	The date that the news can be released. We use datetime instead of smalldatetime, to provide compatibility with ASP 3.
ExpireDate	datetime	8	No	The date that the news will expire.
AddedDate	datetime	8	No	The date that the news was added.
Approved	bit	1	No	The approved status of the news item. If false, the administrator has to approve the news before it is actually published and available to readers.
UserID	int – Foreign key	4	Yes	The ID of the user who submitted or added this news. It should match an ID in the Accounts_Users table of the Accounts module.

As noted, the `UserID` field refers to a table of the `Accounts` module. Although this would be possible even if the `Accounts_Users` table were in a separate database, having all these tables in the same database allows easier integration between modules.

Stored Procedures

To manage the database we will build a set of stored procedures, which we'll run later in the data layer classes to do everything from the addition of categories and news, to the update of single fields. The stored procedures we need, and their parameters, are listed here (we'll be writing the code later in the chapter in the Solution section):

Stored Procedure	Parameters	Description
sp_News_GetCategories		Returns the entire content of the News_Categories table.
sp_News_GetCategoryDetails	@CategoryID int	Returns the complete row identified by the specified ID.
sp_News_InsertCategory	@Name varchar(50), @Description varchar(250), @ImageUrl varchar(250), @CategoryID int OUTPUT	Inserts a new category. If the specified Name already exists then the output parameter @CategoryID will be set to −1, otherwise it will be set to the new category ID.
sp_News_DeleteCategory	@CategoryID int	Deletes the category identified by CategoryID.
sp_News_UpdateCategory	@CategoryID int, @Name varchar(50), @Description varchar(250), @ImageUrl varchar(100)	Updates all the fields of the category specified by CategoryID.
sp_News_GetNews	@CategoryID int, @CurrentApproved Only bit = 0, @AbstractLength int = −1	Returns all news items for the specified category. If @CurrentApprovedOnly is true it returns only the news items whose Approved field is 1 (true), and for which the current date is between ReleaseDate and ExpireDate. The last parameter is the length for the partial body content that is returned. If @AbstractLength is −1 the whole of the Body is returned.

Stored Procedure	Parameters	Description
sp_News_GetNewsDetails	@NewsID int	Returns the complete row for the specified news item. This also includes the whole Body field content.
sp_News_GetHeadlines	@CategoryID int	Returns only the NewsID, Title, and ReleaseDate for the current and approved news items of the specified category.
sp_News_InsertNews	@CategoryID int, @Title varchar(250), @Body text, @ReleaseDate datetime, @ExpireDate datetime, @Approved bit, @UserID int, @NewsID int OUTPUT	Inserts a news item. If there is already a row with the specified CategoryID, Title, ReleaseDate, and ExpireDate then the output parameter @NewsID is set to −1, and no changes are made. Otherwise it is set to the added news ID.
sp_News_DeleteNews	@NewsID int	Deletes the news item identified by the specified ID.
sp_News_UpdateNews	@NewsID int, @Title varchar(250), @Body text, @ReleaseDate datetime, @ExpireDate datetime, @Approved bit	Updates all the fields of the specified news item.
sp_News_SetNewsApproved	@NewsID int, @Approved bit	Changes the value of the Approved field for the specified news item.

Most of these stored procedures are pretty standard – procedures to insert, update, return, and delete rows. However, it's worth noting some design decisions that will impact on the performance of the site:

❏ The sp_News_GetNews procedure has a parameter that allows us to specify the length of the Body text we want to retrieve. Instead of storing the news abstracts in a separate field, we retrieve an abstract by returning the first @AbstractLength characters of the Body field. The Body field is of type text, thus it can contain very long articles. As we only need to list the available news items, it would be a tremendous waste of time and traffic to retrieve the body text for all the news items. It's therefore a good idea to completely avoid retrieving the body, or, as we did, add a parameter to specify how many characters to retrieve. Also, we included the option to retrieve all the news from the specified table, or only the current and approved news. We'll need to retrieve all the news in cases such as the administration section, where we must be able to see and edit any news. In the pages for the end user we'll only be interested in the active news.

It's worth noting that the method we employ to retrieve the news abstracts assumes that the beginning of each piece of news contains useful information, or at least something that allows the user to understand what the news is about. If we needed to publish long news articles, and couldn't be sure of useful information appearing at the beginning of the text, we could use a separate abstract field instead. This way we can organize the news text any way we like. This chapter does not show how to implement this alternative method, but implementing it would not be difficult.

❏ The sp_News_GetNewsDetails procedure returns all the details (fields) of the specified news item. This includes the whole Body text, and so the procedure is used when we need to display the whole news item in its own dynamically filled page.

❏ The sp_News_GetHeadlines procedure returns only selected information about the current and approved news item, such as the title, ID, and the release date. This information will be useful for a headlines box that we might want to show on the home page, for example. The ID is enough for us to provide a link to the full article.

Designing the Data Layer

Now that we have a clear idea of what the database tables store, and how we retrieve data through the stored procedures, we can design the data services. We will simply create classes with methods that wrap the calls to the stored procedures one by one.

These classes will be part of an assembly of their own, called Wrox.WebModules.NewsManager.Data, and they will all be grouped by this namespace. In Chapter 2 we created a database class in the Wrox.WebModules.Core module. We'll use this DbObject class as the base for all data classes in this module, as DbObject provides methods for creating a connection, and running stored procedures using just a few lines of code. We'll see how easy it is to develop the data classes by inheriting from the DbObject base in the *Solution* section later in the chapter.

Before we look at each of the classes in turn, here is a UML diagram that shows the classes we need in the data layer:

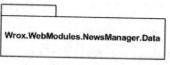

```
Wrox.WebModules.NewsManager.Data
```

```
Wrox.WebModules.NewsManager.Data::Categories

+Categories(in connectionString : string)
+GetCategories() : <unspecified>
+GetDetails() : CategoryDetails
+GetDetailsRow() : <unspecified>
+Add() : int
+Update() : bool
+Delete() : bool
```

```
Wrox.WebModules.NewsManager.Data::CategoryDetails

+CategoryID : int
+Name : string
+Description : string
+ImageUrl : string
```

```
Wrox.WebModules.NewsManager.Data::News

+News(in connectionString : string)
+GetNews() : <unspecified>
+GetHeadlines() : <unspecified>
+GetDetails() : NewsDetails
+GetDetailsRow() : <unspecified>
+Add() : int
+Update() : bool
+SetApproved() : bool
+Delete() : bool
```

```
Wrox.WebModules.NewsManager.Data::NewsDetails

+NewsID : int
+CategoryID : int
+Title : string
+Body : string
+ReleaseDate
+ExpireDate
+AddedDate
+Approved : bool
+UserID : int
+UserName : string
+UserEmail : string
```

The CategoryDetails Class

This class has no methods, just four public properties that map the fields of the News_Categories table. It does nothing by itself – the properties will be set by the calling functions that use this class simply as a data type to return from the Categories class. Doing this will make our business layer simpler.

The Categories Class

This class wraps the calls to the stored procedures that manage the categories. It has only methods, no properties, and it returns an instance of CategoryDetails to return the details of a specific category. Since there are no relationships with other classes (except one method that returns an instance of CategoryDetails), at this point it's easy to provide a list of the methods and their definitions:

Method Name	Description
public Categories(string newConnectionString)	Class constructor taking the connection string as a parameter.
public DataSet GetCategories()	Returns a DataSet containing the names of all the categories.

Method Name	Description
`public CategoryDetails GetDetails(int categoryID)`	Returns an instance of `CategoryDetails` that describes the specified category.
`public DataRow GetDetailsRow(int categoryID)`	Returns the `DataRow` of the category identified by the specified ID.
`public int Add(string name, string description, string imageUrl)`	Adds a new category, and returns the ID of the new record. Returns −1 if the record was already present, and does not change the database.
`public bool Update(int categoryID, string name, string description, string imageUrl)`	Updates all the fields of the specified category.
`public bool Delete(int categoryID)`	Deletes the specified category.

The NewsDetails Class

This class is basically the same as `CategoryDetails` but for the `News_News` table instead of the `News_Categories` table. It has only public properties such as `NewsID`, `CategoryID`, `Title`, and `Body`, which map all the table fields. All are set by external code, this class only serves as the data type for a function we're going to see in a moment.

The News Class

This class wraps the calls to all the stored procedures that manage the news items and their attributes. Like the `Categories` class, this class has a `GetDetails` method that returns an instance of `NewsDetails` containing everything from the specified news record. Here is a complete list of the methods to implement:

Method Name	Description
`public News(string newConnectionString)`	Class constructor taking the connection string as a parameter.
`public DataSet GetNews(int categoryID, bool currentApprovedOnly, int abstractLength)`	Returns the news item for the specified category. The other two parameters are the same as we defined for the `sp_News_GetNews` stored procedure.
`public DataSet GetHeadlines(int categoryID)`	Returns the `NewsID`, `Title`, and `ReleaseDate` for the current and approved news items of the specified category.
`public NewsDetails GetDetails(int newsID)`	Returns an instance of `NewsDetails` that describes the specified news item.

Method Name	Description
`public DataRow GetDetailsRow(int newsID)`	Returns the `DataRow` of the news item identified by the specified ID.
`public int Add(int categoryID, string title, string body, DateTime releaseDate, DateTime expireDate, bool approved, int userID)`	Adds a news item, and returns the ID of the new record. Returns −1 if the record was already present. See the description of `sp_News_InsertNews` for more details.
`public bool Update(int newsID, string title, string body, DateTime releaseDate, DateTime expireDate, bool approved)`	Updates all the fields of the specified news record.
`public bool SetApproved(int newsID, bool approved)`	Changes the `Approved` status of the specified news item.
`public bool Delete(int newsID)`	Deletes the specified news item.

Designing the Business Layer

The data layer is made up of two classes with methods that call the stored procedures, but they don't represent an entity in a real object-oriented way. This is done by the classes of the business layer, which use the data layer classes to access the database, and represents the data as useful objects. These classes will be part of an assembly, `Wrox.WebModules.NewsManager.Business`, and will inherit from the `BizObject` class, as decided in Chapter 2. This means that we can add methods to every business object in the application in one go, by modifying `BizObject`. We'll look at each of our classes in turn. But first, here is the UML diagram that describes the classes. To save space, some method overloads are not included:

Wrox.WebModules.NewsManager.Business

Wrox.WebModules.NewsManager.Business::Category
+CategoryID : int
+Name : string
+Description : string
+ImageUrl : string
+Category()
+Category(in existingCategoryID : int)
+Category(in existingCategory : Category)
-LoadFromID()
-ResetProperties()
+LoadFromID(in existingCategoryID : int) : int
+Create() : int
+Update() : bool
+Delete() : bool
+GetNews() : <unspecified>
+AddNews() : News
+GetHeadlines() : <unspecified>
+GetCategories() : <unspecified>

Wrox.WebModules.NewsManager.Business::News
+CategoryID : int
+Category : Category
+NewsID : int
+Title : string
+Body : string
+ReleaseDate
+ExpireDate
+AddedDate
+Approved : bool
+UserID : int
+UserName : string
+UserEmail : string
+News()
+News(in existingNewsID : int)
+News(in existingNews : News)
-LoadFromID()
-ResetProperties()
+LoadFromID(in existingNewsID : int) : int
+Create() : int
+Update() : bool
+Delete() : bool

The Category Class

This class has properties that fully describe a news category, with methods to create, update, or delete one category, or add news child items. The following table shows the declaration and description of each member:

Member Name	Description
`public int ID`	Read-only property: the category's ID.
`public string Name`	Gets/sets the name of the category.
`public string Description`	Gets/sets the description of the category.
`public string ImageUrl`	Gets/sets the image URL of the category.
`public Category()`	Class constructor with no parameters. Resets property values.
`public Category(int existingCategoryID)`	Class constructor that sets the properties to the category identified by the input ID.
`public Category(Category existingCategory)`	Class constructor that sets the properties to describe the category identified by an existing `Category` object.
`private void LoadFromID()`	Loads the properties of the category identified by a private ID variable. This method is called by the constructors or when the data has to be refreshed.
`private void ResetProperties()`	Resets the properties.
`public int LoadFromID(int existingCategoryID)`	Loads all the properties of the category identified by the input ID. This method allows us to load a different category after the object has been created, or to load the properties if we created an object but didn't specify an ID for the constructor.
`public int Create(string categoryName, string categoryDescription, string categoryImageUrl)`	Creates a new category, and sets the properties of the object to represent the new record.
`public bool Update()`	Updates the current category with the new values of the public properties.
`public bool Delete()`	Deletes the category.
`public static DataSet GetCategories()`	Static method that returns all the categories.

Member Name	Description
`public DataSet GetNews()`	Returns all the child news items.
`public DataSet GetNews(bool currentApprovedOnly)`	Overloaded method that can return only the approved child news items.
`public DataSet GetHeadlines()`	Returns the `NewsID`, `Title`, and `ReleaseDate` for the current and approved news items in the category, plus the full URL of the whole news page.
`public News AddNews(string newsTitle, string newsBody, DateTime newsReleaseDate, DateTime newsExpireDate, bool newsApproved, int newsUserID)`	Adds a child news item.

You might be wondering why the `Create` method requires all the properties for the new category as input, instead of retrieving them from the public variables. This is because in other classes we might require values that are exposed as read-only properties, so we would need to get them through input parameters. So for consistency with future classes, we require all the values as parameters, and then set the properties accordingly. Also note that the `AddNews` method returns an object of type `News`, which is described in the next section.

The most notable method here is `GetHeadlines`. It not only calls the homonymous method of the data layer, but it also adds a column to the table of the returned `DataSet`. The value of this column is the complete URL of the page where the user can read the whole news, and not just its abstract. The complete path is made up of a base path of the ASPX page, plus the `NewsID` attribute as a parameter. For example, say that the page is `ShowNews.aspx`, and that the base path is localhost/ThePhile/Modules/NewsManager/ShowNews.aspx, then the URL for a news item would be something like localhost/ThePhile/Modules/NewsManager/ShowNews.aspx?NewsID=4.

Adding this column is really important for providing the ability to share headlines with external sites and to browse the news with programs other than a web browser. What we're going to do later in the chapter, in fact, is to build a Windows application that shows the current headlines, and that opens a browser and loads the whole news item when a headline is clicked. The client application does not have to do anything to find the URL to which it must redirect, as it is given along with the other data in the table, and the client developer is not required to know the path of the `ShowNews.aspx` page in advance. In addition to being easier for the client developer, this also means that if the webmaster moves the page or changes its name, the client application will continue to work fine as soon as it downloads an updated `DataSet`, without requiring any modification to the code.

We could have returned only the `NewsID` from the business layer, and had the presentation layer objects construct a URL link themselves. This would be a more pure way of building an n-tier system, but would require slightly more code. So in this case it's best to compromise our n-tier architecture a little.

The News Class

This class describes and manipulates a news record, using the following properties and methods:

Member Name	Description
`public int ID`	Read-only property that returns the ID of the news item represented by the object.
`public int CategoryID`	Read-only property that returns the ID of the parent category.
`public Business.Category Category`	Returns the parent category.
`public string Title`	Gets/sets the title of the news item.
`public string Body`	Gets/sets the body of the news item.
`public bool Approved`	Gets/sets the Approved status.
`public DateTime ReleaseDate`	Gets/sets the release date.
`public DateTime ExpireDate`	Gets/sets the expiry date.
`public DateTime AddedDate`	Read-only property that returns the date when the news item was added to the database.
`public int UserID`	Read-only property that returns the ID of the user who submitted the news item.
`public string UserName`	Read-only property that returns the name of the user who submitted the news.
`public string UserEmail`	Read-only property that returns the e-mail address of the user who submitted the news.
`public News()`	Class constructor with no parameters. It only resets the properties.
`public News(int existingNewsID)`	Class constructor that sets the properties to describe the news item identified by the input ID.
`public News(News existingNews)`	Class constructor that sets the properties to describe the news item identified by an existing news object.

Member Name	Description
`private void LoadFromID()`	Loads the properties of the news item identified by a private ID variable. This method is called by the constructors, or when the data has to be refreshed.
`private void ResetProperties()`	Resets the properties.
`public int LoadFromID(int existingNewsID)`	Loads all the properties of the news item identified by the input ID. This method allows us to load a different news item after the object has been created, or to load the properties if we created an object but didn't specify an ID for the constructor.

`public int Create(int newsCategoryID, string newsTitle, string newsBody,`
 	
`DateTime newsReleaseDate, DateTime newsExpireDate, bool newsApproved, int newsUserID)`
	Creates a news item, and sets the properties of the object to represent the new record.

`public bool Update()`	Updates the current news item with the new values of the public properties.
`public bool Delete()`	Deletes the news item.

It's worth noting that here the `Create` method requires input values such as the parent category and the user ID. These values are exposed by read-only variables, so we need to pass them as parameters. As mentioned above, we decided to pass all the necessary parameters to the `Create` method of other classes as well, to avoid confusion.

Storing and Retrieving Settings

In addition to categories and news, our module also has some settings to store, such as the database connection string. In the previous chapter we discussed the advantages of storing the settings as an XML file produced by serializing a class. We've seen how to de-serialize the content of that same file to create a class instance with the state it had in the previous session. With this module we're going to use exactly the same method. We have a `Wrox.WebModules.NewsManager.Configuration.dll` assembly and a namespace with the same name. It will include two classes. `ModuleConfig` gets and sets the settings, by de-serializing the file to an object or serializing an object to a file. `ModuleSettings` exposes the settings as public properties, and whose state will be serialized or de-serialized. The `ModuleSettings` class has three properties:

❑ `ConnectionString`: the connection string that all the data classes use to access the database.

❑ `NewsUrl`: the URL of the `ShowNews.aspx` page, necessary to build the full links from the headlines to the whole news.

❑ `AbstractLength`: the number of characters that make up an abstract by truncating the news item's `Body`.

Here is the UML diagram that represents this component:

Designing the Presentation Layer

The design of the ASP.NET pages is nothing really special, so there's not much to discuss. We have a set of pages, some for the administrators and some for the end-users, which allow us to manage news, and navigate through categories and read news, respectively.

The main consideration is that we must integrate these module-specific pages into the rest of the site, but this is easily possible by adding the site-wide header and footer controls to our pages, and by using a common CSS file.

Let's focus on some of the more news-specific needs: plugging headlines into other parts of the site, and providing headlines as a Web service.

Plug-in Headlines

The first new issue here is that we need a way to quickly add the headlines to any page we want. It's not enough to just have entirely new pages – we want to plug the headlines into *existing* pages. A user control is the best solution in this case, because it will allow us to add news and customize appearance with a single line in an ASPX page.

Our headlines control must expose properties that select the headlines we want to show, and define the style and size of the control on the page. We could add many more graphical properties, but these are enough for a fully working and useful control.

The control will connect to the database with a connection string that is automatically retrieved. The webmaster will only need to know the appearance they want to assign to the control, and the ID of news category they want to display. This way, we can insert the control into a page with just a couple of lines of code, and without knowledge of the underlying object model.

The Headlines Web Service

We said earlier that we want to allow other sites to use our headlines, and also build non-browser applications (such as a Windows client) to show the headlines. If we were planning to distribute the whole of the news item, we would probably want to make some money from it, but we will take a different approach. Instead of giving away the whole news item, we will share only the headlines. Any external site and program can get them for free, with a link to our own site for the full story. This page with the full news text is only available on our site. What this means is that if we allow everybody to insert our headlines into their sites, and if a lot of sites take up this opportunity, we're going to have lots of advertising and new traffic *for free*! Whenever a user clicks on a title they will be redirected to ThePhile.com, and they will probably end up generating page views (which can lead to revenue if we're selling advertisement space). They may visit some other sections of the site, or buy something if we're selling products or services. And, if nothing else, our site will gain a better reputation and a larger audience.

Later, if this service is successful, we could push things further and offer an extended service that allows external sites to insert the whole news item into their own pages. But this time for a fee!

However, for this book's scope the first type of service is enough, so let's go ahead and see what it should provide. This web service only needs a couple of methods for what we plan to do:

Method Name	Description
DataSet GetCategories()	Returns all the available categories.
DataSet GetHeadlines(int categoryID)	Returns ID, title, and URL for all published news from the specified category.

Providing such a service is really easy in VS.NET (and also with the .NET Framework without the help of the VS.NET's wizards): a web service takes care of all the details, and plumbing code deals with the communication protocols and SOAP messages. Thus, designing a simple web service is very simple and similar to designing a class. There are many differences between web services and classes, of course, such as the fact that they can be called remotely, and they are stateless, but essentially a web service is still a class that exposes some public methods.

We remember that the data classes accept the connection string as input in the constructor method, and then use it in all the other methods. Here we can't do this, due to the fact that the web service is stateless and can't store the connection string with a private variable. The easy solution is to get the connection string every time a method is called. We have only two methods, so there isn't much work, and the connection string is cached (we'll show how to do this in the implementation of the Settings assembly), so there is no overhead.

The Need for Security

The news manager module divides into two basic parts:

- ❑ The administration section, which allows the webmaster or someone else to add, delete, or edit the categories, publish news, and change the module's settings

- ❑ The end-user section, which has pages to navigate through the categories and read the news, or see the headlines on the homepage

The division is made more complex because of the page where users can post their own news. The administrator can decide to allow any user to access this page, or select a group of trusted people and block access to everybody else. So this page could be for end-users, or for administrators.

In the previous chapter we developed a very flexible module that allows us to administer the registered users, read or edit their profile, and dynamically assign permissions for certain operations. For the news manager we'll have a NewsManagerPermissions enumeration, with the following three permissions that we can assign to users:

❑ AdministerNews: the user has full power over the news system. They can add, edit, or delete categories, approve and publish news items, and change the settings. Only one person (or at least very few people) should have this permission.

❑ SubmitNews: the user can submit their own news items, but these won't be published until the administrator approves them. We could give this permission to any user, if we want to gather as much news as possible, or a selected group of people otherwise.

❑ PublishNews: the user can submit their own news items, and these will be immediately published. There is no need for any intervention by the administrator. Only a selected group of trusted people should have this permission, because everything they send will be available straight away. You must be pretty sure that they won't send incorrect content and that what they write won't require any editing.

Enforcing these security rules is a simple task with the help of the Users module, which also provides a GUI tool for changing the permissions of users. We can integrate it in the solution and then allow the general administrator to choose trusted people and give them the appropriate rights.

The Solution

We've discussed just about every aspect of the design, and we are now ready to produce the solution. We'll follow the same pattern as in the *Design* section: from the creation of database tables and stored procedures to the implementation of security, passing through the data access and user interface services coding.

Working on the Database

Creating the database tables is straightforward, using the Enterprise Manager, so we won't cover it here. The best way to set up the database is to use the backed up version in the code download.

Now let's look at how to create the relationships between the tables and write some stored procedures, although these already exist in the backup.

Relationships Between the Tables

We create a new diagram in the Enterprise Manager, and by following the wizard we add the News_Categories, News_News, and Accounts_Users tables. As soon as the three tables are added to the underlying window, the Enterprise Manager should recognize a relationship between News_Categories and News_News and automatically add a connection with the correct properties. However, if it does not, click on the News_News table's CategoryID field and drag and drop the icon that appears over the News_Categories table. Once you release the button, a dialog with the relationship's properties appears. You should set the options as shown in the screenshot below:

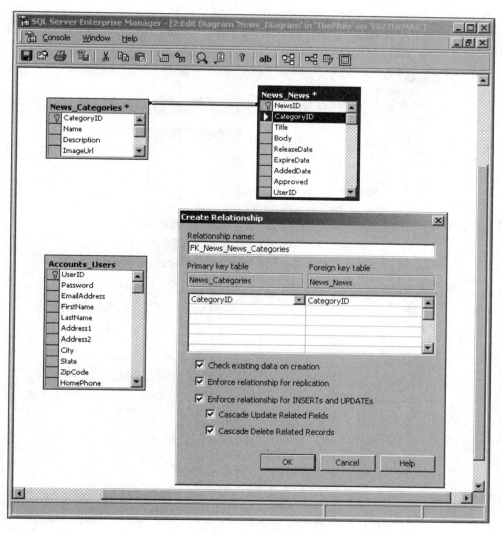

The **Cascade Update Related Fields** option ensures that if we change the `CategoryID` primary key in the `News_Categories` table, this change is propagated to the foreign keys in the `News_News` table.

> *The primary key should never be changed, since it is used for identification. The administration pages won't allow us to change it, but it's a good idea to select this option anyway.*

The **Cascade Delete Related Records** option ensures that if we delete a category, all the related news items are deleted as well. This option is very important and must be checked, because otherwise we'll end up with a database filled with unreachable news (since the parent category will no longer exist).

Now we have to create a relationship between News_News and Accounts_Users, based on the UserID field of both tables. As before, click the News_News table's UserID field, drag and drop the icon over the Accounts_Users table, and complete the **Properties** dialog as follows:

Things are a bit tricky with this relationship and, as you might have noticed, the settings are different from before: we don't select the **Enforce relationship for INSERTs and UPDATEs** option. In the first relationship we built, we wanted all dependent news items to be deleted whenever a category was deleted. Here, when we delete a user we don't want to delete all their news items too. That user might be a former employee of our company, or they might have unregistered from the site, but we want to keep their news in the database.

> *If we select the* **Enforce relationship for INSERTs and UPDATEs** *option but not the* **Cascade Delete Related Records** *option, if we try to delete a user then we'll get an error. This is because we would have a constraint that ensures that the foreign key can't point to a non-existent row in the referenced table. If we don't select the former option we still have the foreign key, but we can also delete a user without automatically deleting the respective news.*

We're not finished yet. We can't leave a foreign key to a row that no longer exists, because if we change another user's ID or add a new user with the same ID as the deleted user, the news will end up referencing not a non-existent user, but the wrong user. We simply need to "reset" (set to null) the UserID field in the News_News table for the news whose author has been deleted from the Accounts_Users table. This issue can be easily resolved with a **trigger**, which we're going to see in the next section.

A Trigger for the UserID Foreign Key

To create the trigger that sets the UserID foreign key to null when a user is deleted, go back to the Enterprise Manager main window (save the diagram before closing the designer), right-click the Accounts_Users table, and click **All Tasks | Manage Triggers**. A dialog pops up with the textbox for the trigger text, which is as follows:

```
CREATE TRIGGER SetNewsAuthorToNull ON [dbo].[Accounts_Users]
FOR DELETE
AS


UPDATE News_News
  SET UserID = NULL
  WHERE UserID = (SELECT UserID FROM Deleted)
```

This code creates a trigger named SetNewsAuthorToNull, which is raised when a record in the Accounts_Users table is deleted. It sets the rows in News_News that were linked to the deleted row to null.

Creating the Stored Procedures

In this section we'll show the code for some of the stored procedures. We won't cover all of them, since the code is actually very similar regardless of whether we are adding, editing, or deleting a category or a news item. The stored procedures that work with the news items are more elaborate than the respective procedures that manage the categories, because they have to join two tables and usually have more parameters, so these are the ones we'll look at.

sp_News_GetNews

Here's the code to create the procedure that returns the news item:

```
CREATE PROCEDURE sp_News_GetNews
@CategoryID              int,
@CurrentApprovedOnly     bit,
@AbstractLength          int
AS


-- if @AbstractLength is not -1 return the first @AbstractLength
-- chars of the Body field, otherwise return the whole news body
IF @AbstractLength <> -1
  BEGIN
  IF @CurrentApprovedOnly = 1
    BEGIN
    SELECT NewsID, Title,
```

```
            LEFT(CAST(Body AS varchar(1000)), @AbstractLength)  +
                '...' AS Abstract,
            ReleaseDate, ExpireDate, AddedDate, Approved,
            News_News.UserID, (FirstName + ' ' + LastName) AS UserName,
            EmailAddress AS UserEmail
        FROM News_News LEFT JOIN Accounts_Users
            ON News_News.UserID = Accounts_Users.UserID
        WHERE CategoryID = @CategoryID AND Approved = 1 AND
            ReleaseDate <= GETDATE() AND ExpireDate >= GETDATE()
      END
    ELSE
      BEGIN
        SELECT NewsID, Title,
            LEFT(CAST(Body AS varchar(1000)), @AbstractLength)  +
                '...' AS Abstract,
            ReleaseDate, ExpireDate, AddedDate, Approved,
            News_News.UserID, (FirstName + ' ' + LastName) AS UserName,
            EmailAddress AS UserEmail
        FROM News_News LEFT JOIN Accounts_Users
            ON News_News.UserID = Accounts_Users.UserID
        WHERE CategoryID = @CategoryID
      END
    END
  ELSE
    BEGIN
    IF @CurrentApprovedOnly = 1
      BEGIN
        SELECT NewsID, Title, Body AS Abstract, ReleaseDate, ExpireDate,
            AddedDate, Approved, News_News.UserID,
            (FirstName + ' ' + LastName) AS UserName,
            EmailAddress AS UserEmail
        FROM News_News LEFT JOIN Accounts_Users
            ON News_News.UserID = Accounts_Users.UserID
        WHERE CategoryID = @CategoryID AND Approved = 1 AND
            ReleaseDate <= GETDATE() AND ExpireDate >= GETDATE()
      END
    ELSE
      BEGIN
        SELECT NewsID, Title, Body AS Abstract, ReleaseDate, ExpireDate,
            AddedDate, Approved, News_News.UserID,
            (FirstName + ' ' + LastName) AS UserName,
            EmailAddress AS UserEmail
        FROM News_News LEFT JOIN Accounts_Users
            ON News_News.UserID = Accounts_Users.UserID
        WHERE CategoryID = @CategoryID
      END
    END
  END
GO
```

Although the procedure is quite long, it is really very simple. It executes different SELECT queries according to the passed parameters. If we want to retrieve only the current and approved news items then one query is run, if we want all the news items then a less restrictive query is run instead. And the same applies for the abstract length: if it is not −1 we must truncate the Body field after the specified characters, otherwise we simply return the whole content (aliased as Abstract).

sp_News_GetNewsDetails

This procedure is simpler, since it has no parameters except for the NewsID, and it returns the whole row:

```
CREATE PROCEDURE sp_News_GetNewsDetails
@NewsID int
AS

SELECT NewsID, CategoryID, Title, Body, ReleaseDate, ExpireDate, AddedDate,
    Approved, News_News.UserID,
    (FirstName + ' ' + LastName) AS UserName, EmailAddress AS UserEmail
  FROM News_News LEFT JOIN Accounts_Users
      ON News_News.UserID = Accounts_Users.UserID
  WHERE NewsID = @NewsID
GO
```

sp_News_GetHeadlines

This procedure returns a few fields for the active news only, so this is very short and easily understandable:

```
CREATE PROCEDURE sp_News_GetHeadlines
@CategoryID     int
AS

SELECT NewsID, Title, ReleaseDate
  FROM News_News
  WHERE CategoryID = @CategoryID AND Approved = 1 AND
      ReleaseDate <= GETDATE() AND ExpireDate >= GETDATE()
  ORDER BY ReleaseDate DESC
GO
```

sp_News_InsertNews

The following code inserts a new row in the News_News table, and returns the ID of the added row as the output parameter. If a news record with that ID exist, the procedure does nothing:

```
CREATE PROCEDURE sp_News_InsertNews
@CategoryID     int,
@Title          varchar(250),
@Body           text,
@ReleaseDate    datetime,
@ExpireDate     datetime,
@Approved       bit,
@UserID         int,
@NewsID         int OUTPUT
AS

DECLARE @CurrID int

-- see if the news already exists
SELECT @CurrID = NewsID
  FROM News_News
```

```
     WHERE CategoryID = @CategoryID AND Title = @Title AND
         ReleaseDate = @ReleaseDate AND ExpireDate = @ExpireDate

-- if not, add it
IF @CurrID IS NULL
  BEGIN

  INSERT INTO News_News
      (CategoryID, Title, Body, ReleaseDate, ExpireDate,
      AddedDate, Approved, UserID)
    VALUES (@CategoryID, @Title, @Body, @ReleaseDate, @ExpireDate,
        GETDATE(), @Approved, @UserID)

  SET @NewsID = @@IDENTITY

  IF @@ERROR > 0
    BEGIN
    RAISERROR ('Insert of News failed', 16, 1)
    RETURN 99
    END
  END
ELSE
  BEGIN
  SET @NewsID = -1
  END
GO
```

sp_News_UpdateNews

This procedure updates all the fields of a row, except for the ID of course. It runs within a **transaction**, so that the changes can be rolled back if an error occurs:

```
CREATE PROCEDURE sp_News_UpdateNews
@NewsID         int,
@Title          varchar(250),
@Body           text,
@ReleaseDate    datetime,
@ExpireDate     datetime,
@Approved       bit
AS

BEGIN TRANSACTION UpdateNews

UPDATE News_News
  SET
    Title = @Title,
    Body = @Body,
    ReleaseDate = @ReleaseDate,
    ExpireDate = @ExpireDate,
    Approved = @Approved
  WHERE NewsID = @NewsID

IF @@ERROR > 0
```

```
     BEGIN
     RAISERROR ('Update of News failed', 16, 1)
     ROLLBACK TRANSACTION UpdateNews
     RETURN 99
     END

COMMIT TRANSACTION UpdateNews
GO
```

Running the SQL commands within a transaction ensures that the data is updated correctly, and that **atomicity** is maintained. A transaction is atomic if all statements must complete, or all fail. Say that we need to execute three UPDATEs, and that the last one generates an error and does not complete correctly. If you run all the three statements within a transaction you'll be able to rollback the transaction, returning the data to its original state. If all statements run fine, we can commit the transaction to persist the changes.

Transactions are a complex topic, beyond the scope of this book. To find out more about this subject, you can refer to *Professional SQL Server 2000* (ISBN 1-861004-48-6).

sp_News_SetNewsApproved

This procedure works in a similar way to the procedure above, but with the difference that only the Approved field is updated. This is useful when the administrator only needs to approve a currently inactive news item, or to disapprove a news item already published, without having to supply the current values for all the other fields to the procedure, as was the case above:

```
CREATE PROCEDURE sp_News_SetNewsApproved
@NewsID int,
@Approved   bit
AS

BEGIN TRANSACTION UpdateNews

-- update the news item's approved state
UPDATE News_News
  SET Approved = @Approved
  WHERE NewsID = @NewsID

IF @@ERROR > 0
  BEGIN
  RAISERROR ('Update of News failed', 16, 1)
  ROLLBACK TRANSACTION UpdateNews
  RETURN 99
  END

COMMIT TRANSACTION UpdateNews
GO
```

sp_News_DeleteNews

This is the easiest procedure. It deletes the row with the specified ID:

```
CREATE PROCEDURE sp_News_DeleteNews
@NewsID int
AS

DELETE FROM News_News
  WHERE NewsID = @NewsID
GO
```

Implementing the Data Access Assembly

Now that the database is complete, let's go ahead and start writing the .NET code for the data access component. We create a Class Library project within the ThePhile solution, with the assembly name and the default namespace `Wrox.WebModules.NewsManager.Data`. The `AssemblyInfo.cs` file needs editing as follows:

```
using System.Reflection;
using System.Runtime.CompilerServices;

[assembly: AssemblyTitle("NewsManager Module - Data component")]
[assembly: AssemblyDescription("NewsManager Module - Data component")]
[assembly: AssemblyConfiguration("")]
[assembly: AssemblyCompany("Wrox Press Ltd")]
[assembly: AssemblyProduct("Wrox.WebModules")]
[assembly: AssemblyCopyright("(C) 2001 Wrox Press Ltd")]
[assembly: AssemblyTrademark("")]
[assembly: AssemblyCulture("")]
[assembly: AssemblyVersion("1.0.0.0")]
[assembly: AssemblyDelaySign(false)]
[assembly: AssemblyKeyFile(@"\Wrox\Keys\ThePhile.snk")]
[assembly: AssemblyKeyName("")]
```

We need a reference to the assembly of the Core project, and to the `System.Data.Dll` assembly, in order to use the `DBObject` base class developed in Chapter 2, and the ADO.NET classes, respectively.

The project consists of two class files, `Categories.cs` and `News.cs`. We will only look at `News.cs` here, because `Categories.cs` is very similar – there's no point in going over both. It's easy to complete the code for the other class, and the complete code is available in the code download.

The News Class

This simple class provides methods that closely map all the available stored procedures that manage news. We'll look at each method in turn. The class's file name is `News.cs` and the namespace must be `Wrox.WebModules.NewsManager.Data`. The name should already be correct if the default namespace is set in the project properties.

We need a using directive in order to use the types in the System.Data and SystemData.SqlClient namespaces without having to specify the namespaces. We're going to be using classes and enumerations of these namespaces very often in the code for this class, and it's quicker to write only the class name and not the full namespace as the prefix.

The News class must inherit from the DbObject class of the Core assembly, and the constructor method must the base constructor. So a skeleton of our class would be:

```
using System;
using System.Data;
using System.Data.SqlClient;

namespace Wrox.WebModules.NewsManager.Data
{
  public class News : Wrox.WebModules.Data.DbObject
  {
    public News(string newConnectionString) : base(newConnectionString)
    {  }
  }
}
```

Now let's take a look at the methods.

The GetNews Method

This method wraps the call to the stored procedure sp_News_GetNews. It accepts as input exactly the same parameters as the stored procedure. It creates an array of SqlParameter objects (one for each input parameter), calls the RunProcedure function to execute the stored procedure, and returns the resulting DataSet:

```
public DataSet GetNews(int categoryID, bool currentApprovedOnly,
    int abstractLength)
{
  // create the parameters
  SqlParameter[] parameters = {
    new SqlParameter("@CategoryID", SqlDbType.Int, 4),
    new SqlParameter("@CurrentApprovedOnly", SqlDbType.Bit, 1),
    new SqlParameter("@AbstractLength", SqlDbType.Int, 4)
  };

  // set the values
  parameters[0].Value = categoryID;
  parameters[1].Value = currentApprovedOnly;
  parameters[2].Value = abstractLength;

  return RunProcedure("sp_News_GetNews", parameters, "News");
}
```

The DbObject class is very useful, and spares us having to manually create and use a SqlDataAdapter. The RunProcedure function also uses the SqlConnection it has instantiated in the base constructor, so we don't need to create and store our own instance. All of this allows us to speed up the code development for methods like this and the following ones, and the resulting code is also more readable.

The GetHeadlines Method

This method simply retrieves all the headlines (ID, ReleaseDate, and Title of the active news) by calling the sp_News_GetHeadlines stored procedure:

```
public DataSet GetHeadlines(int categoryID)
{
    // create the parameter
    SqlParameter[] parameters = {
        new SqlParameter("@CategoryID", SqlDbType.Int, 4)
    };
    parameters[0].Value = categoryID;

    return RunProcedure("sp_News_GetHeadlines", parameters, "Headlines");
}
```

The GetDetails Method

This method retrieves only the row for the specified ID, and returns an instance of a custom NewsDetails class. As previously said, this class only exposes a set of public fields, and is used as a return type. Here is the class, which is located in the same file, just below the namespace declaration and before we declare the News class:

```
public class NewsDetails
{
    public int NewsID;
    public int CategoryID;
    public string Title;
    public string Body;
    public DateTime ReleaseDate;
    public DateTime ExpireDate;
    public DateTime AddedDate;
    public bool Approved;
    public int UserID;
    public string UserName;
    public string UserEmail;
}
```

We could have used public properties here, but we don't need any processing or checks of validity before modifying state, so public fields are sufficient in this case.

Here is the code that gets the specified news record, creates an instance of NewsDetails, and returns it:

```
public NewsDetails GetDetails(int newsID)
{
    // create the parameter
    SqlParameter[] parameters = {
        new SqlParameter("@NewsID", SqlDbType.Int, 4)
    };
    parameters[0].Value = newsID;
```

```
      using(DataSet news = RunProcedure("sp_News_GetNewsDetails",
        parameters, "News"))
    {
      NewsDetails details = new NewsDetails();
      // if the record was found, set the properties of the class instance
      if (news.Tables[0].Rows.Count > 0)
      {
        DataRow rowNews = news.Tables[0].Rows[0];
        details.NewsID = (int)rowNews["NewsID"];
        details.CategoryID = (int)rowNews["CategoryID"];
        details.Title = rowNews["Title"].ToString();
        details.Body = rowNews["Body"].ToString();
        details.ReleaseDate = Convert.ToDateTime(rowNews["ReleaseDate"]);
        details.ExpireDate = Convert.ToDateTime(rowNews["ExpireDate"]);
        details.AddedDate = Convert.ToDateTime(rowNews["AddedDate"]);
        details.Approved = Convert.ToBoolean(rowNews["Approved"]);
        details.UserID = (rowNews["UserID"]==DBNull.Value ? -1 :
            (int)rowNews["UserID"]);
        details.UserName = rowNews["UserName"].ToString();
        details.UserEmail = rowNews["UserEmail"].ToString();
      }
      else
        details.NewsID = -1;

      return details;
    }
  }
```

You can see that the DataSet returned by RunProcedure is defined within the scope of a using statement. This way the DataSet variable will be disposed of as soon as the using's scope ends. The code then creates an instance of NewsDetails, but sets its fields only if the DataSet variable contains a row. Otherwise it means that there is no news with the specified ID and so we set the NewsID field to -1, as an indication for the code that called the method. Each DataRow field is converted to the type of the respective NewsDetails field.

We remember that the UserID field may be null (if the user has been deleted) and if it is null it can't be converted to an int value. We must check if the field is null and in that case we set the NewsDetails field to -1. We write a single line to set the field in both cases, by taking advantage of the ?: operator.

The GetDetailsRow Method

This method is a simpler version of the previous method. It obtains the details of the specified news item, without any processing, by returning the respective DataRow:

```
public DataRow GetDetailsRow(int newsID)
{
  // create the parameter
  SqlParameter[] parameters = {
      new SqlParameter("@NewsID", SqlDbType.Int, 4)
  };
  parameters[0].Value = newsID;
```

```
using(DataSet news = RunProcedure("sp_News_GetNewsDetails",
    parameters, "News"))
{
  return news.Tables[0].Rows[0];
}
}
```

Although not used in this module, this method will be useful if we want to add this row to a custom table. Later, in Chapter 8, we'll see why and how to use a method like this in an effective way.

The Add Method

This method passes all the input parameters to the sp_News_InsertNews stored procedure, and returns the ID of the added news item. This value is returned by the last parameter, which is declared as an output parameter by setting its Direction property to ParameterDirection.Output:

```
public int Add(int categoryID, string title, string body,
    DateTime releaseDate, DateTime expireDate, bool approved, int userID)
{
  int numAffected;

  // create the parameters
  SqlParameter[] parameters = {
      new SqlParameter("@CategoryID", SqlDbType.Int, 4),
      new SqlParameter("@Title", SqlDbType.VarChar, 50),
      new SqlParameter("@Body", SqlDbType.Text),
      new SqlParameter("@ReleaseDate", SqlDbType.DateTime),
      new SqlParameter("@ExpireDate", SqlDbType.DateTime),
      new SqlParameter("@Approved", SqlDbType.Bit, 1),
      new SqlParameter("@UserID", SqlDbType.Int, 4),
      new SqlParameter("@NewsID", SqlDbType.Int, 4)
  };

  // set the values
  parameters[0].Value = categoryID;
  parameters[1].Value = title.Trim();
  parameters[2].Value = body.Trim();
  parameters[3].Value = releaseDate;
  parameters[4].Value = expireDate;
  parameters[5].Value = approved;
  parameters[6].Value = userID;
  parameters[7].Direction = ParameterDirection.Output;

  RunProcedure("sp_News_InsertNews", parameters, out numAffected);

  return (int)parameters[7].Value;
}
```

It's worth noting that although we use RunProcedure as before, this is actually an overloaded version that executes a non-query command (a command that does not return a set of rows). The last parameter, numAffected, is an output parameter that we can use to determine the number of rows affected by the command. In this method the value is not used, because we always add one at a time. It will be in the next method, as we'll see in a moment.

The Update Method

The code of this method is very similar to the code above, except that here we also specify the ID of the news item to update, and the method returns a Boolean value to indicate whether the command was successfully executed. This will be true when at least one record is affected by the query:

```
public bool Update(int newsID, string title, string body,
    DateTime releaseDate, DateTime expireDate, bool approved)
{
  int numAffected;

  // create the parameters
  SqlParameter[] parameters = {
      new SqlParameter("@NewsID", SqlDbType.Int, 4),
      new SqlParameter("@Title", SqlDbType.VarChar, 50),
      new SqlParameter("@Body", SqlDbType.Text),
      new SqlParameter("@ReleaseDate", SqlDbType.DateTime),
      new SqlParameter("@ExpireDate", SqlDbType.DateTime),
      new SqlParameter("@Approved", SqlDbType.Bit, 1)
  };

  // set the values
  parameters[0].Value = newsID;
  parameters[1].Value = title.Trim();
  parameters[2].Value = body.Trim();
  parameters[3].Value = releaseDate;
  parameters[4].Value = expireDate;
  parameters[5].Value = approved;

  RunProcedure("sp_News_UpdateNews", parameters, out numAffected);

  return (numAffected == 1);
}
```

The SetApproved Method

This is basically a wrapper procedure for the sp_News_SetNewsApproved stored procedure, and has nothing in particular that needs further explanation. Here is the code:

```
public bool SetApproved(int newsID, bool approved)
{
  int numAffected;

  // create the parameters
  SqlParameter[] parameters = {
      new SqlParameter("@NewsID", SqlDbType.Int, 4),
      new SqlParameter("@Approved", SqlDbType.Bit, 1)
  };

  // set the values
  parameters[0].Value = newsID;
  parameters[1].Value = approved;
```

```
        RunProcedure("sp_News_SetNewsApproved", parameters, out numAffected);

        return (numAffected == 1);
    }
```

The Delete Method

Similar to the method above, this just wraps a call to sp_News_DeleteNews:

```
public bool Delete(int newsID)
{
    int numAffected;

    // create the parameter
    SqlParameter[] parameters = {
        new SqlParameter("@NewsID", SqlDbType.Int, 4)
    };
    parameters[0].Value = newsID;

    RunProcedure("sp_News_DeleteNews", parameters, out numAffected);

    return (numAffected == 1);
}
```

This is all we need to do for the News and NewsDetails classes. Category and CategoryDetails are very similar to this, so we won't go over them here – they can be found in the code download.

The Configuration Assembly

The next step in the development of the news manager module should be the implementation of its business layer. However, the business layer needs a configuration component to retrieve the connection string and the other settings (we want the business classes to get the required settings by themselves, instead of passing them as parameters when the object is created), so we'll examine the configuration assembly first. We've already seen how to create this assembly for another module in Chapter 5, so we will be fairly brief here. For the ModuleConfig class the code is almost the same, while the ModuleSetting class will contain new properties specific to this module.

We use a new Class Library project, with the namespace and assembly name Wrox.WebModules.NewsManager.Configuration. The AssemblyInfo.cs file is the same as for the data assembly. Now let's look at the code.

The ModuleSettings Class

In the design section we've already discussed what settings we're going to store and use for this module. They are ConnectionString, AbstractLength, and the ShowNews.aspx path. We give these properties the XmlElement attribute, so that they are serialized to XML elements. Here is the class:

```
public class ModuleSettings
{
    private string connectionString;
```

```
        private string newsUrl;
        private int abstractLength;

        [XmlElement]
        public string ConnectionString
        {
          get { return connectionString; }
          set { connectionString = value; }
        }

        [XmlElement]
        public string NewsUrl
        {
          get { return newsUrl; }
          set { newsUrl = value; }
        }

        [XmlElement]
        public int AbstractLength
        {
          get { return abstractLength; }
          set { abstractLength = value; }
        }
      }
    }
```

The ModuleConfig Class

As we said earlier, this class is very similar to the ModuleConfig class in the previous chapter. What's different here is the name of the settings file, and the entry name used to store a ModuleSettings instance in the cache. The following code highlights the lines that differ:

```
public class ModuleConfig
{
  public static ModuleSettings GetSettings()
  {
    HttpContext context = HttpContext.Current;

    ModuleSettings data = (ModuleSettings)context.Cache[
        "NewsManager_Settings"];

    if (data == null)
    {
      XmlSerializer serializer = new XmlSerializer(typeof(ModuleSettings));
      try
      {
        string fileName = HttpContext.Current.Server.MapPath(
            GetSettingsFile());
        FileStream fs = new FileStream(fileName, FileMode.Open);
        data = (ModuleSettings)serializer.Deserialize(fs);
        fs.Close();

        context.Cache.Insert("NewsManager_Settings",
```

223

```
                data, new CacheDependency(fileName));
        }
        catch (System.IO.FileNotFoundException)
        {
            data = new ModuleSettings();
        }
    }
    return data;
}


public static void SaveSettings(ModuleSettings data)
{
    string fileName = HttpContext.Current.Server.MapPath(GetSettingsFile());
    XmlSerializer serializer = new XmlSerializer (typeof(ModuleSettings));

    FileStream fs = new FileStream(fileName, FileMode.Create);
    serializer.Serialize(fs, data);
    fs.Close();
}

private static string GetSettingsFile()
{
    HttpContext context = HttpContext.Current;
    string filePath = (string)context.Cache["NewsManager_SettingsFile"];
    if (filePath == null)
    {
        filePath=ConfigurationSettings.AppSettings[
            "NewsManager_SettingsFile"];
        context.Cache["NewsManager_SettingsFile"] = filePath;
    }
    return filePath;
}
}
```

The Settings File

If the settings file is not present then the module automatically builds it. However, since the connection string is needed to access the database and it is stored in the settings file, we must have it before testing the pages we'll be building. Here is a typical example – the connection string and server name (in NewsUrl) will be different on some machines:

```xml
<?xml version="1.0"?>
<ModuleSettings xmlns:xsi="http://www.w3.org/2001/XMLSchema-instance"
    xmlns:xsd="http://www.w3.org/2001/XMLSchema">
  <ConnectionString>
    server=(local);database=ThePhile;uid=sa;pwd=;
  </ConnectionString>
  <NewsUrl>
    http://localhost/thephile/modules/newsmanager/shownews.aspx
  </NewsUrl>
  <AbstractLength>100</AbstractLength>
</ModuleSettings>
```

This file is called `NewsManager.Config` under `/ThePhile/Config`. We can store this file anywhere we like, provided we specify it in `Web.Config` as follows:

```xml
<?xml version="1.0" encoding="utf-8" ?>
<configuration>
  <appSettings>
    <add key="NewsManager_SettingsFile"
        value="/ThePhile/Config/NewsManager.Config" />
  </appSettings>
  ...
</configuration>
```

Implementing the Business Classes

In this section we'll be building the Business classes for this module. These will get data from the data layer we've just looked at and give it to the presentation layer in an object-oriented, business-centered way. Again we have a **Class Library** project within our ThePhile solution, with all the usual settings and modifications to the `AssemblyInfo.cs` file. We need to reference `Core`, `NewsManager.Data`, and `NewsManager.Configuration` projects. The `News` and `Categories` business layers are similar – we will focus on `News` again.

The `News` class is located in the `News.cs` file, while `Category` is in `Category.cs`. We also have a class named `News` in a file called `News.cs` in the data access project. This is not a problem because the files are placed in different folders and have different namespaces.

The News Class

To start off, we declare the `News` class and define its private, and public read/write or read-only properties. There's no point in looking at all of them – here are a few representative declarations:

```csharp
using System;
using System.Data;
using System.Data.SqlClient;

namespace Wrox.WebModules.NewsManager.Business
{
  public sealed class News : Wrox.WebModules.Business.BizObject
  {
    private Configuration.ModuleSettings settings;
    private int newsID;
    private int categoryID;
    private string title;
    public News()
    {
      // we'll fill this in in a moment...
    }

    public int CategoryID
    {
      get { return categoryID; }
    }
```

```
    public Business.Category Category
    {
      get { return new Category(categoryID); }
    }

    public int ID
    {
      get { return newsID; }
    }

    // Other property declarations

  }
}
```

It's worth noting that the class is defined as `sealed`, meaning it can't be inherited. We can do this since we know we won't need to create derived classes.

The Constructors

We have three different constructors for this class: one with no parameters that just resets the properties to their default values, one that takes the news ID as input and loads the corresponding news item, and one that takes an existing `News` object and initializes itself based on the passed news item's ID. Here's the code:

```
public News()
{
  settings = Configuration.ModuleConfig.GetSettings();
  ResetProperties();
}

public News(int existingNewsID)
{
  settings = Configuration.ModuleConfig.GetSettings();
  newsID = existingNewsID;
  LoadFromID();
}

public News(News existingNews)
{
  settings = Configuration.ModuleConfig.GetSettings();
  newsID = existingNews.ID;
  LoadFromID();
}
```

Each one of these constructors retrieves the settings through the `Configuration` assembly, and saves the `ModuleSettings` instance to the private variable.

Loading and Resetting the Properties

The constructors also set the object properties with the attributes of the specified news item or, in the case of the parameter-less constructor, reset them. Here's the code of the `LoadFromID` and `ResetProperties` private methods:

```
private void LoadFromID()
{
  Data.News news = new Data.News(settings.ConnectionString);
  Data.NewsDetails details = news.GetDetails(newsID);

  newsID = details.NewsID;
  categoryID = details.CategoryID;
  title = details.Title;
  body = details.Body;
  releaseDate = details.ReleaseDate;
  expireDate = details.ExpireDate;
  addedDate = details.AddedDate;
  approved = details.Approved;
  userID = details.UserID;
  userName = details.UserName;
  userEmail = details.UserEmail;
}

private void ResetProperties()
{
  newsID = -1;
  categoryID = -1;
  title = "";
  body = "";
  releaseDate = new DateTime();
  expireDate = new DateTime();
  addedDate = new DateTime();
  approved = false;
  // -1 means "no valid record"... it does not affect
  // the primary key in the database
  userID = -1;
  userName = "";
  userEmail = "";
}
```

It's worth noting that the LoadFromID method also reads the NewsID field of the NewsDetails object returned by Data.News.GetDetails, and stores the value in the private newsID variable. Why is this required? We already had the newsID, in fact we used it to retrieve all the other properties! The reason is that the ID passed to the class constructor might not be present in the database (because the news has been deleted, or simply because the caller specified an invalid ID value). In this case, we don't want to have all the properties reset, and the NewsID property returns a wrong ID. Thus, we also reset the newsID variable: if a record was found, its value remains valid, otherwise it is set to -1.

We also have a public LoadFromID method that takes as input the ID of the news item we want to load, and which can be used instead of the constructor to specify the ID:

```
public int LoadFromID(int existingNewsID)
{
  newsID = existingNewsID;
  LoadFromID();
  return newsID;
}
```

Create, Update, and Delete a News Item

Finally, we have three methods to manipulate the news. Firstly the `Create` method:

```
public int Create(int newsCategoryID, string newsTitle, string newsBody,
    DateTime newsReleaseDate, DateTime newsExpireDate,
    bool newsApproved, int newsUserID)
{
  Data.News news = new Data.News(settings.ConnectionString);
  newsID = news.Add(newsCategoryID, newsTitle, newsBody,
      newsReleaseDate, newsExpireDate, newsApproved, newsUserID);
  LoadFromID();
  return newsID;
}
```

This method calls the `Data.News.Add` method to create the new record, and then calls `LoadFromID` to refresh the properties and refresh the news item just created. If for some reason the news item is not added, for example because it is duplicated, the `Add` method returns `-1`, and the properties are reset.

The `Update` method simply takes the current values of the object properties, and passes them to `Data.News.Update`:

```
public bool Update()
{
  Data.News news = new Data.News(settings.ConnectionString);
  return news.Update(newsID, title, body, releaseDate, expireDate,
      approved);
}
```

The `Delete` method works in the same way:

```
public bool Delete()
{
  Data.News news = new Data.News(settings.ConnectionString);
  bool ret = news.Delete(newsID);
  ResetProperties();
  return ret;
}
```

The Category Class

This class (saved in `Category.cs`) has methods for loading, creating, updating, and deleting a category, just like the `News` class. But it also has some other methods to create a child news item, return all the child headlines or news items, and return all the available categories. We'll briefly look at these new methods here.

The GetCategories Method

There's nothing special about this method expect that it is declared as `static`. This is because it applies to all categories (the entire category class, not a category object):

```
public static DataSet GetCategories()
{
  Configuration.ModuleSettings settings =
      Configuration.ModuleConfig.GetSettings();
  Data.Categories categories = new Data.Categories(
      settings.ConnectionString);
  return categories.GetCategories();
}
```

It's worth noting that since this is a static method, the settings are not retrieved in the class constructor when it is called, so we must get them from inside this function.

Adding and Returning Child News Items

To return the child news items, we use the `Data.News.GetNews` method. Below we see the small amount of code required, and also an overloaded version of the function. This passes `false` as the default parameter to the first version, meaning that we want to retrieve all the news, and not just the current and active news:

```
public DataSet GetNews(bool currentApprovedOnly)
{
  Data.News news = new Data.News(settings.ConnectionString);
  return news.GetNews(categoryID, currentApprovedOnly,
      settings.AbstractLength);
}

public DataSet GetNews()
{
  return GetNews(false);
}
```

To add a child news item we don't have to directly access the data layer. We create a new `Business.News` instance and use its `Create` method:

```
public News AddNews(string newsTitle, string newsBody,
    DateTime newsReleaseDate, DateTime newsExpireDate,
    bool newsApproved, int newsUserID)
{
  Business.News news = new Business.News();
  news.Create(categoryID, newsTitle, newsBody, newsReleaseDate,
      newsExpireDate, newsApproved, newsUserID);
  return news;
}
```

The GetHeadlines Method

This method calls the `GetHeadlines` method of the data layer, but it also adds a new custom field to the table – the full URL of the page showing the whole news story. The field value is made up of the base page URL retrieved from the settings, plus the `NewsID` as a parameter appended to this URL:

```
public DataSet GetHeadlines()
{
  Data.News news = new Data.News(settings.ConnectionString);
  DataSet headlines = news.GetHeadlines(categoryID);
  // add the NewsUrl column that is a link to the page that
  // shows the entire news body
  headlines.Tables[0].Columns.Add("NewsUrl",
      System.Type.GetType("System.String"),
      "'" + settings.NewsUrl + "?NewsID=' + newsID");
  return headlines;
}
```

It's worth noting that the new column is named `NewsUrl`, and the pages or programs that will call this method will use the value of this column to show the whole news item in a web browser when the headline's title is clicked.

The User Interface

The database, data access, business, and configuration classes are complete, and so much of the work is done. We'll now look at the user interface, which will sit on top of our business layer, and complete the application.

Administration

We'll start by looking at the administration system. Then we can use it to populate the database with some stories, and look at how we display that to readers. But before looking at the ASP.NET and C# code for the pages, let's see a small part of the result we want to achieve:

The page shown above is part of the administration console, and allows the administrator to see the available categories, create, delete, or edit a category, and jump to other pages in the application.

The table displays all the categories that it gets from the database, shows their properties, and gives the opportunity to sort them by their ID, Name, or Description. The icons on the left and right of the grid are hyperlinks to other pages to do something else related to the category of that row. Specifically, the icon on the far left representing a pencil puts the grid into edit mode (we'll see what this means shortly), the recycle bin deletes a record, and the group of sheets on the far right is used to jump directly to the page to manage the news for the category. The grid, the menu bar, and the other controls are plugged into the site layout, with the title bar at the top and the menu box on the right.

Let's look at the code now. In the main ThePhile project, we create a new folder under /ThePhile/Modules/ called NewsManager. We need to add a reference to NewsManager.Business, and NewsManager.Configuration. We don't need to reference NewsManager.Data, since the presentation layer never directly accesses the data layer.

Creating the Header and Footer User Controls

In the previous chapters we've already talked about the advantages of having reusable user controls for the interface, so we won't do it again here. With regard to a shared site-wide layout, in Chapter 2 we saw our site-wide header and footer user controls. These can be inserted into any page in order to have the same layout without having to manually copy and paste the common HTML code onto each page. This module follows exactly the same design pattern, and additionally has its own two private controls. The trick to easily plug the module into the existing layout is to insert the site-wide header at the top of the module-specific header, and the site-wide footer at the bottom of the module-specific footer. The following picture illustrates the various pieces that form the final page:

This way, with a few lines we'll get our module to fit into the existing website structure. If the site layout changes later, we won't need to do anything to the module, as it will just continue to load the updated site header and footer.

For this module, we want to have different header and footer controls for the administration section and for the end-user section, because we want the administration section's header to show the menu bar with links to the protected pages.

Admin Header

Let's start with the administration section's header: add a new User Control to the NewsManager project and name it AdminHeader.ascx. This control renders the site-wide title bar at the very top of the page, and then the module's title and menu. Let's look at the complete HTML code first, and then we'll discuss it:

```
<%@ Control Language="c#" AutoEventWireup="false"
    Codebehind="AdminHeader.ascx.cs"
    Inherits="Wrox.WebModules.NewsManager.Web.Controls.User.AdminHeader"%>
<%@ Register TagPrefix="WroxUser" TagName="SiteHeader"
    Src="/ThePhile/Controls/SiteHeader.ascx" %>
<WroxUser:SiteHeader id="Header" runat="server" />
<br>
<table width="100%" border="0" cellspacing="4" cellpadding="2">
  <tr>
    <td width="100%" valign="top">
      <script language="JavaScript1.2">
        function SetStatusBarText(text)
        {
          StatusBar.innerHTML = text;
        }
      </script>

<a name="top" />
  <table class="MenuTable" border="0" width="100%">
    <tr>
      <td>
        <table class="MenuTable" border="0" width="100%">
          <tr>
            <td>
              <b><u>NewsManager - Wrox WebModule</u></b>
            </td>
            <td align="right">
              <a href="#bottom"><img Alt="Go to the bottom of the page"
                  src="./Images/GoDown.gif" border="0" /></a>
            </td>
          </tr>
        </table>
      </td>
    </tr>
    <tr>
      <td>
        <table border="0" width="100%">
          <tr>
            <td>
              <a class="MenuItem"
                  onMouseOver="SetStatusBarText('Manage the categories');"
                  onMouseOut="SetStatusBarText('');" href="Categories.aspx">
                Categories
              </a>
            </td>
```

Similar table entries follow, providing links to `News.aspx` and `Settings.aspx`. There's no point in repeating them here. Here's the final section:

```
            </tr>
          </table>
        </td>
      </tr>
      <tr>
        <td width="100%">
          <div align="left" id="StatusBar">
        </td>
        <td>
           
        </td>
      </tr>
    </table>
```

This is just plain HTML (except for the site-wide header at the beginning). There is no need to use ASP.NET controls if we want to produce static and non-programmable content, and plain HTML is faster to process. The code is pretty simple and shouldn't require much explanation. We create a table – the first row shows the title, the second row contains a further table with columns for each menu item and separator. The last row has a container (an HTML `<div>` element). Each hyperlink of the menu points to another ASPX page, and calls the `SetStatusBarText` method when the mouse enters or leaves its area. `SetStatusBarText` sets the content of our HTML `<div>` element to the specified string.

Admin Footer

The footer user control is called `AdminFooter.ascx` (a new **Web User Control** in VS.NET) and is composed of only a few lines of code:

```
<%@ Control Language="c#" AutoEventWireup="false"
    Codebehind="AdminFooter.ascx.cs"
    Inherits="Wrox.WebModules.NewsManager.Web.Controls.User.AdminFooter"%>
<%@ Register TagPrefix="Wrox" Namespace="Wrox.ThePhile.Web.Controls.Server"
    Assembly="Wrox.ThePhile.Web.Controls" %>
<%@ Register TagPrefix="WroxUser" TagName="SiteFooter"
    Src="/ThePhile/Controls/SiteFooter.ascx" %>

<br>
<div align="right" Width="100%">
  <a href="#top"><img src="./Images/GoUp.gif" Alt="Go to the top of the
    page" border="0">
  </a>
</div>
<a name="bottom"></a>
</td>
<td align="right" valign="top">
  <Wrox:Navigator id="MenuNav" SourceFile="/ThePhile/Config/NavMenu.xml"
      TransformFile="/ThePhile/Transforms/NavMenu.xslt" runat="server" />
</td>
</tr></table>
<WroxUser:SiteFooter id="Footer" runat="server" />
```

Here we add a new column to the table opened in the header to create the page layout, insert the site menu, and finally close that table and insert the site-wide footer.

We change the namespace to `Wrox.WebModules.NewsManager.Web.Controls.User`, according to our conventions from Chapter 2.

The Categories Manager Page

The previous screenshot shows how the categories management page appears when it is loaded. The display changes, however, according to the action we want to perform. For example, this is what you get when you press the pencil icon at the far left to edit a category:

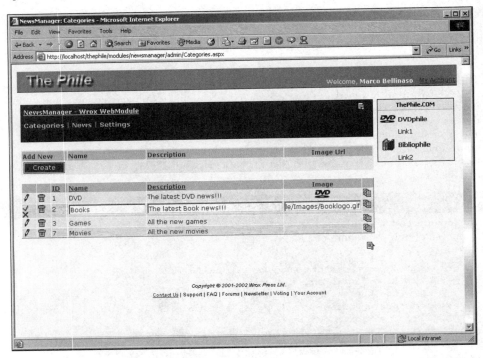

The current Name, Description, and ImageUrl of the category are displayed inside three textboxes. The administrator can change these values and click the green tick icon to update the values in the database, or click the X to abort the operation. The ID column is not editable, because the ID is a counter column whose value cannot be changed. By default the categories are sorted by ID. Sorting is done by clicking on the header of the column you want to sort by.

To add a new category the administrator clicks the **Create** button at the top-left of the main page, and this is the result:

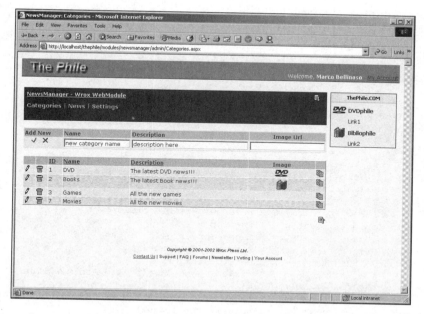

Three empty textboxes are shown, and the administrator fills them with the name, description, and path of an image for the category to be created. The action can be confirmed or canceled by clicking on one of the two icons on the left side. In both cases, and this is true for editing too, the textboxes are hidden and the display returns to how it was. While this effect is done almost automatically when we click the icon to edit a new row, we need to handle the events of the controls and show or hide the textboxes by ourselves when adding a new row. However, this process is much simpler than it might seem at first glance – only a few lines of code are needed, which we'll see in just a minute.

The Categories.aspx Page

This is the ASP.NET page where the user interface is defined. The source code of the page is too long to be shown all at once, so we'll look at it piece by piece.

The page starts with the declaration of the code-behind file and the `<head>` section. There's nothing new here, so let's go in at the `<body>` element:

```
<body>
  <form method="post" runat="server" ID="Categories">
    <!-- Insert the menu user control -->
    <NewsManager:AdminHeader ID="Menu" runat="server" />
```

First we open a new form, and add our `AdminHeader` control. Moving on, we reach a table with four columns and a **Create** button. When this button is pressed, two textboxes and the icons for confirming or canceling the operation appear, as shown previously, while the rest of the display remains the same. All these controls are defined in the page, but only the button is visible at the beginning – the rest have `Visible` set to `false`:

235

```
<asp:Table id="TableNewCategory" runat="server" CssClass="Grid_General"
    Width="100%">
  <asp:TableRow CssClass="Grid_Header">
    <asp:TableCell Width="85px" Text="Add New" />
    <asp:TableCell Width="150px" Text="Name" />
    <asp:TableCell Text="Description" />
    <asp:TableCell Width="170px" Text="Image Url" />
  </asp:TableRow>
  <asp:TableRow ID="CreateNewRow">
    <asp:TableCell HorizontalAlign="Center">
      <asp:Button runat="server" Text="Create" ID="Create"
          CssClass="Button" OnClick="Create_Click" Width="80px" />
    </asp:TableCell>
    <asp:TableCell ID="AddNewResultCell" ColumnSpan="3">
      <asp:Label runat="server" CssClass="Error" ID="AddNewError"
          Text="This item was already present" Visible="false" />
    </asp:TableCell>
  </asp:TableRow>
  <asp:TableRow ID="AddNewControlsRow" Visible="false">
    <asp:TableCell VerticalAlign="Top">
      <asp:Image ImageURL="./Images/Spacer.gif" Width="15px"
          Height="1px" runat="server" ID="Image1" />
      <asp:LinkButton ID="AddNew" runat="server"
          Text="<img border=0 src=./Images/OK.gif Alt='Add new list'>"
          OnClick="AddNew_Click" />
      <asp:Image ImageURL="./Images/Spacer.gif" Width="15px"
          Height="1px" runat="server" ID="Image2" />
      <asp:LinkButton ID="CancelAddNew" runat="server"
          CausesValidation="false"
          Text="<img border=0 src=./Images/Cancel.gif Alt='Cancel
          editing mode'>" OnClick="CancelAddNew_Click" />
    </asp:TableCell>
    <asp:TableCell VerticalAlign="Top">
      <asp:TextBox runat="server" CssClass="TextBox"
          ID="NewCatName" Width="150px" />
      <asp:RequiredFieldValidator Id="ValidateNewName" runat="server"
          ControlToValidate="NewCatName" Display="dynamic">
        <br>* Name is required
      </asp:RequiredFieldValidator>
    </asp:TableCell>
    <asp:TableCell VerticalAlign="Top">
      <asp:TextBox runat="server" CssClass="TextBox"
          ID="NewCatDescr" Width="100%" />
    </asp:TableCell>
    <asp:TableCell VerticalAlign="Top">
      <asp:TextBox runat="server" CssClass="TextBox"
          ID="NewCatImageUrl" Width="100%" />
    </asp:TableCell>
  </asp:TableRow>
</asp:Table>
```

Note that all the server controls that will need to be accessed programmatically have an ID attribute, and that all the code is placed within a server-side form. Also note that the name of the category is required when a new category is created, and this is ensured by a `RequiredFieldValidator` control. The meaning of the `ControlToValidate` property is clear, and the `Display` property, set to dynamic, specifies that the space to show the error message will be created dynamically.

We use a `DataGrid` control to display the categories. This is one of the most useful ASP.NET controls. If you haven't used it before then it's well worth investigating – see the .NET Framework documentation, or *Professional ASP.NET 1.0* from Wrox (ISBN 1-861007-03-5) for more information.

Here is the declaration for the `DataGrid` in our page:

```
<asp:DataGrid id="CatGrid" runat="server"
    Width="100%"
    CssClass="Grid_General"
    HeaderStyle-CssClass="Grid_Header"
    ItemStyle-CssClass="Grid_Item"
    AlternatingItemStyle-CssClass="Grid_AlternatingItem"
    AllowSorting="True"
    AutoGenerateColumns="False"
    DataKeyField="CategoryID"
    OnEditCommand="CatGrid_Edit"
    OnCancelCommand="CatGrid_CancelEdit"
    OnUpdateCommand="CatGrid_Update"
    OnDeleteCommand="CatGrid_Delete"
    OnSortCommand="CatGrid_Sort">
```

The `DataGrid` does a lot of the work for us. After setting its appearance, we set `AllowSorting` to True. That's all we need to do to let the user sort the table any way they like – a big job in ASP 3!

To enable `DataGrid` editing, we need to specify the primary key of the data in the grid – that way the `DataGrid` can communicate which row to edit/update back to the server. We use the `DataKeyField` property for this. The last lines define the event procedures that are called to handle the operations of the grid. We'll see how to write these event procedures shortly, when looking at the code-behind class.

Back to our ASPX – we need to manually declare how each column has to be rendered. We need the following columns:

❑   A clickable image to edit the row

❑   A clickable image to delete the row

❑   A column to display the category's name

❑   A column to display the category's description

❑   A column to display the category's image when the grid is in normal display mode, or the URL of the image during editing

❑   A clickable image to jump to the page that shows the news items for the category of the current row

Here's the code needed for the first two columns:

```
<Columns>
  <asp:EditCommandColumn
      ItemStyle-Width="25px"
      EditText="<img border=0 Alt='Edit' src=./Images/Edit.gif>"
      CancelText="<img border=0 src=./Images/Cancel.gif>"
      UpdateText="<img border=0 src=./Images/OK.gif>"
  />
  <asp:ButtonColumn
      ItemStyle-Width="25px"
      Text="<img border=0 Alt='Delete' src=./Images/Delete.gif>"
      CommandName="delete"
  />
```

The `EditCommandColumn` is a specific column with a link to begin the editing, while `ButtonColumn` creates normal buttons or links whose `Click` event must be handled to perform any operation you need. Note that we render the graphical buttons by including an `<img>` tag in the `Text` property of the column. If we write a normal string instead of the HTML, we get a standard button with that string as its caption.

Here is the code for the columns that display the list's ID, name, description, and image:

```
<asp:BoundColumn HeaderText="ID"
    ItemStyle-Width="30px" DataField="CategoryID"
    ReadOnly="True" SortExpression="CategoryID"
/>
<asp:TemplateColumn HeaderText="Name"
    SortExpression="Name" ItemStyle-Width="150px">
  <ItemTemplate>
    <asp:Label runat="server"
        Text='<%# DataBinder.Eval(Container.DataItem, "Name") %>'
    />
  </ItemTemplate>
  <EditItemTemplate>
    <asp:TextBox ID="EditCatName" runat="server"
        Text='<%# DataBinder.Eval(Container.DataItem, "Name") %>'
        CssClass="TextBox" Width="150px"
    />
    <asp:RequiredFieldValidator Id="ValidateEditName"
        runat="server" ControlToValidate="EditCatName"
        Display="dynamic">* Name is required
    </asp:RequiredFieldValidator>
  </EditItemTemplate>
</asp:TemplateColumn>
<asp:TemplateColumn HeaderText="Description"
    SortExpression="Description">
  <ItemTemplate>
    <asp:Label runat="server" Text='<%#
        DataBinder.Eval(Container.DataItem, "Description") %>'
    />
  </ItemTemplate>
  <EditItemTemplate>
```

```
            <asp:TextBox ID="EditCatDescr" runat="server" Text='<%#
                DataBinder.Eval(Container.DataItem, "Description") %>'
                CssClass="TextBox" Width="100%"
            />
        </EditItemTemplate>
    </asp:TemplateColumn>
    <asp:TemplateColumn HeaderText="Image"
        ItemStyle-Width="150px" ItemStyle-HorizontalAlign="Center">
        <ItemTemplate>
            <asp:Label runat="server" Text='<%# GetImage(
                DataBinder.Eval(Container.DataItem, "ImageUrl")) %>'
            />
        </ItemTemplate>
        <EditItemTemplate>
            <asp:TextBox ID="EditCatImageUrl" runat="server" Text='<%#
                DataBinder.Eval(Container.DataItem, "ImageUrl") %>'
                CssClass="TextBox" Width="100%"
            />
        </EditItemTemplate>
    </asp:TemplateColumn>
```

The first column is defined as a normal, non-editable column and there isn't much to say about it. The other three are more interesting because they show how to create a templated column that uses a label to show the value, or a textbox to edit it. The proper view is automatically set when we enter or exit the editing mode for a row. Note that the text of the label and textboxes is handled by the `DataBinder.Eval` method, which returns the value of a column for the row being read, and that the list's name is required, as shown earlier in the table to add a new category.

Of even more interest is the final column, which shows an image when in normal mode, and its path in a textbox when in editing mode. Since the `ImageUrl` can be `null`, we call the external function `GetImage`. This accepts the field value and returns an empty string or a complete `<img>` tag, depending on whether the field is `null` or not.

The last column on the far right shows the icon to jump to the details page:

```
    <asp:HyperLinkColumn ItemStyle-Width="20px"
        DataNavigateUrlField="CategoryID"
        DataNavigateUrlFormatString="News.aspx?CategoryID={0}"
        DataTextFormatString="<img border=0 Alt='Show news'
            src=./Images/Group.gif>"
    DataTextField="CategoryID"
    />
</Columns>
```

It is a non-editable hyperlink rendered as an image, and the URL which it points to is built with a string template defined in the `DataNavigateUrlFormatString`: the ID of each row will replace the {0} marker.

The page ends with the closing tag for the DataGrid control, the footer control, and the closing tag for the form:

```
    </asp:DataGrid>
    <!-- Insert the footer -->
    <NewsManager:AdminFooter ID="Footer" runat="server" />
  </form>
  </body>
</html>
```

The Code-behind for Categories.aspx

Finally we can start looking at the code that handles the execution of the page. The code-behind file (Categories.aspx.cs) was automatically created by VS.NET together with the page itself. Again, we'll examine it one section at a time.

After the namespace declaration (which we change to Wrox.WebModules.NewsManager.Web and the controls declaration, we come to where the page functionality is implemented. Here is the handler that it runs when the page is loaded:

```
protected void Page_Load(object sender, EventArgs e)
{
  if (!Page.IsPostBack)
  {
    // bind the page's controls
    BindGrid();
  }
}
```

Then there is the BindGrid method, called by the above routine, which fills the grid with the categories:

```
protected void BindGrid()
{
  // get all the categories
  DataView myDV = Business.Category.GetCategories().Tables[0].DefaultView;

  // sort the data according to the SortExpression value
  if (CatGrid.Attributes["SortExpression"] != null)
    myDV.Sort = CatGrid.Attributes["SortExpression"];

  CatGrid.DataSource = myDV;
  CatGrid.DataBind();
}
```

The function is only called if the page's IsPostBack property is false: when the page is loaded for the first time or manually refreshed by the user with the browser's Refresh/Reload command. It is not called when the page is reloaded because the user posted some data to the form. In fact, when that page is posted back, the state of the controls is stored in a hidden HTML control (named __VIEWSTATE) and then automatically restored, avoiding the need for re-executing a query on the database. The content of this hidden field is passed back and forth between the client to the server, which can cause a significant overhead in case of big grids or lots of controls that must maintain their state.

BindGrid is the core function of this page, because it gets the data from the database and displays the records through the DataGrid. The first line gets a DataView with all the available categories, by calling the GetCategories static method of Business.Category. The DataView is then sorted according to a DataGrid attribute, which is a custom attribute set by our code later: the first time the function is called this attribute is null and the DataView is not sorted. The last two lines associate the DataView to the DataSource property, and call the DataBind method to display the rows.

Talking about data binding, we remember that a column in the DataGrid calls a GetImage method to create an <img> tag and show the category's image, if the ImageUrl field is not null. The code is really simple – the only important point is that the function must be declared as public:

```
public string GetImage(object imageUrl)
{
  if (imageUrl.ToString().Length > 0)
    return "<img border=\"0\" src=\"" + imageUrl.ToString() + "\">";
  else
    return "";
}
```

Sorting the Categories

When a column header is clicked, the CatGrid_Sort function is called on the server, which looks like this:

```
protected void CatGrid_Sort(Object sender, DataGridSortCommandEventArgs e)
{
  AddNewError.Visible = false;
  ShowAddNewControls(false);
  CatGrid.EditItemIndex = -1;
  // set the SortExpression attribute that will be used to actually sort
  // the data in the BindGrid method
  CatGrid.Attributes["SortExpression"] = e.SortExpression.ToString();
  BindGrid();
}
```

The function first of all hides the controls for adding a new category, or displaying an error message. Then it disables the editing mode of a row, if enabled. Finally it gets from the input parameter the sort expression to use to actually sort the data, and refreshes the DataGrid's content by calling BindGrid.

Editing and Updating Categories

Now we will implement the methods that deal with the editing and updating of rows. The first puts the relevant row in edit mode, the second cancels the current edit:

```
protected void CatGrid_Edit(object sender, DataGridCommandEventArgs e)
{
  AddNewError.Visible = false;
  ShowAddNewControls(false);
  // start editing
  CatGrid.EditItemIndex = (int)e.Item.ItemIndex;
  BindGrid();
}
```

```
protected void CatGrid_CancelEdit(object sender, DataGridCommandEventArgs e)
{
  CatGrid.EditItemIndex = -1;
  BindGrid();
}
```

CatGrid_Edit hides the controls for adding a row, and sets the EditItemIndex property to the index of the row to edit: this value is retrieved from the Item object which is exposed as a property of the object e passed as a parameter to the function. Finally, BindGrid is called again to bind the data for that row to the three textboxes. When the X icon is pressed, the EditItemIndex is simply set to −1 and the grid is refreshed.

Now let's look at CatGrid_Update, which does most of the work:

```
protected void CatGrid_Update(object sender, DataGridCommandEventArgs e)
{
  if (Page.IsValid)
  {
    // get the new values from the textboxes
    string catName = ((TextBox)e.Item.FindControl("EditCatName")).Text;
    string catDescr = ((TextBox)e.Item.FindControl("EditCatDescr")).Text;
    string catImageUrl = ((TextBox)e.Item.FindControl(
        "EditCatImageUrl")).Text;
    int categoryID = (int)CatGrid.DataKeys[e.Item.ItemIndex];

    // update the values
    Business.Category category = new Business.Category(categoryID);
    category.Name = catName;
    category.Description = catDescr;
    category.ImageUrl = catImageUrl;
    category.Update();

    CatGrid.EditItemIndex = -1;
    BindGrid();
  }
}
```

Firstly, note that the code is executed only if the page is valid, that is when the rules of the validator controls are observed. In this case the Name textbox must be filled with a valid (not null) name. If this check succeeds, the execution goes ahead and gets the current values of the three textboxes. The reference to each textbox control is returned by the FindControl method of Item, and then the content is read from the Text property. Note that that the generic Control object returned by FindControl does not have a Text property, so we need to manually cast the returned object to a TextBox. The last parameter we need is the ID of the row to update, which is very easy to get because this column was set as the primary key for the DataGrid, so our work is reduced to reading in a property value. Finally, we create a Business.Category object for the selected category, set its properties, and call the Update method to persist the changes to the database. As a last step we refresh the DataGrid to reflect the changes.

Deleting a Category

The procedure for the CatGrid_Delete event follows exactly the same structure as the previous ones, although it is simpler. We create a Business.Category object for the category identified by the category ID returned by the DataKeys enumerator property, and then call its Delete method:

```
protected void CatGrid_Delete(object sender, DataGridCommandEventArgs e)
{
    AddNewError.Visible = false;
    ShowAddNewControls(false);
    CatGrid.EditItemIndex = -1;
    // get the ID of this record and delete it
    Business.Category category = new Business.Category(
        (int)CatGrid.DataKeys[e.Item.ItemIndex]);
    category.Delete();
    // re-bind
    BindGrid();
}
```

Creating a Category

The last task is adding a new row. When the **Create** button is pressed, three textboxes and the respective icons for confirming or canceling the operation are shown, while the **Create** button is made invisible. The DataGrid's EditItemIndex property is also set to -1, to stop any editing operation from taking place. Here is the code for this event, and for the function that shows or hides the controls according to the passed Boolean parameter:

```
protected void Create_Click(object sender, EventArgs e)
{
    // show the textboxes and buttons for adding a new record
    AddNewError.Visible = false;
    ShowAddNewControls(true);
    CatGrid.EditItemIndex = -1;
    BindGrid();
}

protected void ShowAddNewControls(bool ShowControls)
{
    // show/hide the controls for adding a new record
    NewCatName.Text="";
    NewCatDescr.Text="";
    NewCatImageUrl.Text="";

    AddNewControlsRow.Visible = ShowControls;
    CreateNewRow.Visible = !ShowControls;
}
```

The method is called when the user confirms the new row, by clicking the tick icon:

```
protected void AddNew_Click(object sender, EventArgs e)
{
  if (Page.IsValid)
  {
    Business.Category category = new Business.Category();
    // add the new record
    if (category.Create(NewCatName.Text, NewCatDescr.Text,
        NewCatImageUrl.Text) < 0)
    {
      // if Add returned -1, the category was already present
      AddNewError.Visible = true;
    }
    ShowAddNewControls(false);
    BindGrid();
  }
}
```

If the data is valid (it obeys the rules enforced by the validators declared in the Categories.aspx page), the code gets the content of the three textboxes and passes these strings to the Create method of a Business.Category object. In this case the code is simpler because we can directly reference the two textboxes, since they are uniquely identified by name. If the Category.Create method returns –1 it means that a category with the same name was already present in the database and it can't be added twice. Therefore we show the AddNewError label on Categories.aspx, with the Text property set to an error message that explains the problem.

The icon for canceling the addition is a ButtonLink control, which when clicked restores the grid to the default display. Here's the code for its Click event:

```
protected void CancelAddNew_Click(object sender, EventArgs e)
{
  ShowAddNewControls(false);
}
```

There is one important point to note here. When a button is pressed it causes the page to be posted back. The control for the category's name is validated when a page is posted back, which would cause the posting to be stopped if the new category's name were missing. Since we are canceling, and don't care what the user has typed, we set the button's CausesValidation property to false.

The code for the categories management page is now complete. This page particularly shows how much better ASP.NET is than classic ASP – to build a grid like this in ASP 3 would take hundreds, perhaps thousands, of lines of code.

Managing the News

The page for managing the news in each category has a very similar structure to the page just analyzed, but it also has some additions that we're going to highlight. The image below shows the page while adding a news item. The administrator has attempted to add a news item but has specified an invalid release date in the From textbox, so the validator controls tell the user why the form can't be submitted and the news added:

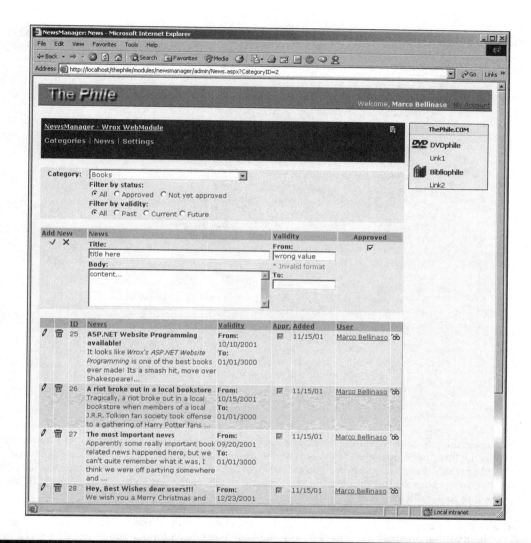

The News.aspx Page

The above screenshot shows how this page differs from the previous one. We have a different number of columns and grid content, a drop down list where we can select a category to view its news, and radio button controls so that the administrator can filter the news.

The ASPX is fairly similar to Categories.aspx. We will only look at the notable differences. The first major differences are the DropDownList control for the categories, and the set of controls to filter the grid rows:

```
<asp:table Width="100%" ID="TableNews" runat="server"
    CssClass="Grid_General">
  <asp:TableRow>
```

```
        <asp:TableCell Width="85px" HorizontalAlign="Center"
            VerticalAlign="Top" Font-Bold="True" Text="Category:" />
      <asp:TableCell>
        <asp:DropDownList runat="server" ID="CatDropDown" Width="300px"
            DataTextField="Name" DataValueField="CategoryID"
            CssClass="TextBox" AutoPostBack="True"
            OnSelectedIndexChanged="CatDropDown_IndexChanged"
        />
        <br>
        <b>Filter by status:</b><br>
        <asp:RadioButton runat="server" ID="ShowAll"
            GroupName="ShowByStatus" Text="All"
            Checked="True" AutoPostBack="True"
            OnCheckedChanged="ShowNews_CheckedChanged"
        /> 
        <asp:RadioButton runat="server" ID="ShowApproved"
            GroupName="ShowByStatus" Text="Approved"
            Checked="False" AutoPostBack="True"
            OnCheckedChanged="ShowNews_CheckedChanged"
        /> 
        <asp:RadioButton runat="server" ID="ShowPending"
            GroupName="ShowByStatus" Text="Not yet approved"
            Checked="False" AutoPostBack="True"
            OnCheckedChanged="ShowNews_CheckedChanged"
        />
        <br>
        <b>Filter by validity:</b><br>
        ...the other RadioButtons go here...
      </asp:TableCell>
    </asp:TableRow>
  </asp:table>
```

The main thing to note is that the dropdown list has the `AutoPostBack` property set to `true`, which causes the form to be posted back every time the user changes the selected item. This event raises the `OnSelectedIndexChanged` event and so calls the `CatDropDown_IndexChanged` procedure. Also, the `RadioButtons` set this property to `true`, and they all use the same `ShowNews_CheckedChanged` procedure to handle the event.

The rest of the page is similar to what we have seen before, but the `DataGrid`'s columns are used more fully than for the previous page. Let's look at the extra or updated lines of the `DataGrid` declaration:

```
<asp:DataGrid ID="NewsGrid" runat="server"
    DataKeyField="NewsID"
    OnEditCommand="NewsGrid_Edit"
    OnCancelCommand="NewsGrid_CancelEdit"
    OnUpdateCommand="NewsGrid_Update"
    OnDeleteCommand="NewsGrid_Delete"
    OnSortCommand="NewsGrid_Sort"
    AllowPaging="True"
    PageSize="20"
    PagerStyle-HorizontalAlign="Right"
    PagerStyle-PageButtonCount="20"
```

```
        PagerStyle-Mode="NumericPages"
        OnPageIndexChanged="NewsGrid_PageChanged"
        OnSelectedIndexChanged="NewsGrid_SelectionChanged"
        SelectedItemStyle-CssClass="Grid_SelectedItem"
```

The new lines say that the data will be displayed in pages of twenty rows each, and that the user will be able to navigate the pages through the page numbers on the bottom right side. An event procedure to handle the page changing is defined. The last two lines define an event handler and the style for the selected item. We're going to add an icon on the far right side of the grid that, when clicked, will highlight the row and show the whole news text in a label at the bottom of the page.

Let's also look at the declaration of some of the columns, as there are a few new bits. The following code adds the column for the news title and abstract:

```
<asp:TemplateColumn HeaderText="News" SortExpression="Title">
  <ItemTemplate>
    <asp:Label runat="server"
        Text='<%# DataBinder.Eval(Container.DataItem, "Title") %>'
        Font-Bold="True" />
    <br>
    <asp:Label runat="server"
        Text='<%# DataBinder.Eval(Container.DataItem, "Abstract") %>' />
  </ItemTemplate>
  <EditItemTemplate>
    <b>Title:</b>
    <br>
    <asp:TextBox runat="server" CssClass="TextBox"
        Text='<%# DataBinder.Eval(Container.DataItem, "Title") %>'
        ID="EditTitle" Width="100%" />
    <asp:RequiredFieldValidator runat="server"
        ControlToValidate="EditTitle" Display="dynamic">
        * Title is required
    </asp:RequiredFieldValidator>
    <br>
    <b>Body:</b>
    <br>
    <asp:TextBox runat="server" CssClass="TextBox"
        TextMode="MultiLine" Rows="5" Text='<%#
        GetNewsText(int.Parse(DataBinder.Eval(
            Container.DataItem, "NewsID").ToString())) %>'
        ID="EditBody" Width="100%" />
  </EditItemTemplate>
</asp:TemplateColumn>
```

The first thing we note is that we can add all the controls to the same column, but this is not a special feature. The important point here is that in normal display mode the column shows the news abstract by binding to the Abstract field (which is, as you might remember, dynamically created by the stored procedures by truncating the Body field), whereas in editing mode we use a custom GetNewsText function to retrieve the whole news text. We've already said that we get the whole text only when it is strictly necessary, while that field is not returned by the standard procedure because it would be slow.

Next, we add the columns for the release and expiry dates:

```
<asp:TemplateColumn HeaderText="Validity"
    SortExpression="ReleaseDate" ItemStyle-Width="100px">
  <ItemTemplate>
    <b>From:</b>
    <br>
    <asp:Label runat="server" Text='<%# DataBinder.Eval(
        Container.DataItem, "ReleaseDate", "{0:MM/dd/yyyy}") %>' />
    <br>
    <b>To:</b>
    <br>
    <asp:Label runat="server" Text='<%# DataBinder.Eval(
        Container.DataItem, "ExpireDate", "{0:MM/dd/yyyy}") %>' />
  </ItemTemplate>
  <EditItemTemplate>
    <b>From:</b>
    <br>
    <asp:TextBox runat="server" CssClass="TextBox" Text='<%#
        DataBinder.Eval(Container.DataItem, "ReleaseDate",
        "{0:MM/dd/yyyy}") %>' ID="EditReleaseDate" Width="100%" />
    <asp:CompareValidator runat="server"
        ControlToValidate="EditReleaseDate" Type="Date"
        Operator="DataTypeCheck" Display="dynamic">
        * Invalid format
    </asp:CompareValidator>
    <asp:CompareValidator runat="server" ControlToValidate="EditReleaseDate"
        ControlToCompare="EditExpireDate" Type="Date"
        Operator="LessThanEqual" Display="dynamic">
        * Invalid value
    </asp:CompareValidator>
    <br>
    <b>To:</b>
    <br>
    <asp:TextBox runat="server" CssClass="TextBox" Text='<%#
        DataBinder.Eval(Container.DataItem, "ExpireDate",
        "{0:MM/dd/yyyy}") %>' ID="EditExpireDate" Width="100%" />
    <asp:CompareValidator runat="server"
        ControlToValidate="EditExpireDate" Type="Date"
        Operator="DataTypeCheck" Display="dynamic">
        * Invalid format
    </asp:CompareValidator>
  </EditItemTemplate>
</asp:TemplateColumn>
```

This column's code isn't of particular interest except for the validator controls that ensure the dates are in a valid format, and that the expire date is after the release date. The dates aren't required, and if not specified we'll insert default values; if they are supplied they can't contain invalid characters.

Now we have the column that shows and allows editing of the `Approved` field. This is a bit special because it uses a read-only `CheckBox` in normal display mode, and a writeable `CheckBox` in edit mode:

```
<asp:TemplateColumn HeaderText="Appr." SortExpression="Approved"
    ItemStyle-Width="30px" HeaderStyle-HorizontalAlign="Center"
    ItemStyle-HorizontalAlign="Center">
  <ItemTemplate>
    <asp:CheckBox runat="server" Enabled="false"
        Checked='<%# Convert.ToBoolean(
        DataBinder.Eval(Container.DataItem, "Approved")) %>'
    />
  </ItemTemplate>
  <EditItemTemplate>
    <asp:CheckBox ID="EditApproved" runat="server"
        Checked='<%# Convert.ToBoolean(
            DataBinder.Eval(Container.DataItem, "Approved")) %>'
    />
  </EditItemTemplate>
</asp:TemplateColumn>
```

To determine whether the control has to be checked, we convert the field value to a Boolean value by using the `ToBoolean` shared method of the `Convert` class.

We'll skip the **Added** column as it really has nothing new to be shown. Let's move straight to the **User** column, which shows a hyperlink that opens the default program to send an e-mail to the writer's e-mail address. Here is its declaration:

```
<asp:TemplateColumn HeaderText="User"
    SortExpression="UserName" ItemStyle-Width="100px">
  <ItemTemplate>
    <asp:HyperLink runat="server" NavigateUrl='<%#
        "mailto:" + DataBinder.Eval(Container.DataItem, "UserEmail") %>'
        Text='<%# DataBinder.Eval(Container.DataItem, "UserName") %>'
        CssClass="GridLink"
    />
  </ItemTemplate>
</asp:TemplateColumn>
```

The code above creates a `HyperLink` control and sets its `NavigateUrl` and `Text` properties to the user's e-mail address and user's full name, respectively.

Lastly, we have the column that, when clicked, highlights the row and shows the whole news text at the bottom:

```
<asp:ButtonColumn CommandName="Select" ItemStyle-Width="20px"
    Text="<img border=0 Alt='View news' src=./Images/View.gif>"
/>
```

Its `CommandName` property is set to `Select`, and this means that when it is clicked it raises the `OnSelectedIndexChanged` event.

The Codebehind for News.aspx

The structure of the codebehind for the News page is the same as for the Categories page. There are a few more lines of code to handle the new controls added. Here's the code that executes when the page loads:

```
protected void Page_Load(object sender, EventArgs e)
{
  // get the CategoryID from the QueryString
  string categoryID = Request.Params["CategoryID"];
  NewsGrid.Attributes["CategoryID"] = categoryID;

  if (!Page.IsPostBack)
  {
    // load all the available lists in the DropDown control
    DataView myDV = Business.Category.GetCategories().Tables[0].DefaultView;
    CatDropDown.DataSource = myDV;
    CatDropDown.DataBind();

    if (categoryID!=null)
    {
      // select the DropDown element according to the CategoryID
      CatDropDown.SelectedIndex = CatDropDown.Items.IndexOf(
          CatDropDown.Items.FindByValue(categoryID));
    }

    // (re)bind the page's controls
    BindGrid();
  }
}
```

On the Categories.aspx page, the right side of each grid's row contained a button that passed the user to the News.aspx page to see the news for that category. To do this, the button pointed to the News.aspx page and added the category's ID as a parameter in the query string. This value is retrieved from the query string and saved as an attribute of the DataGrid control, because it is used to create a Business.Category object, needed to get its child news items.

In addition to the usual BindGrid call, this time there is also a drop-down list to fill with the available categories. This is done directly within Page_Load by calling the GetCategories static method of the Business.Category class and assigning the resulting table to the DataSource for the drop-down. Then we use the ID in the page's querystring to select the correct item in the drop-down.

The BindGrid method for this page has code to read the category's ID for which we want to retrieve the news, and also filters the results as specified by the RadioButtons at the top of the page:

```
protected void BindGrid()
{
  int categoryID;

  // get the CategoryID value from the Grid's attributes
  if ( NewsGrid.Attributes["CategoryID"] != null )
    categoryID = int.Parse(NewsGrid.Attributes["CategoryID"]);
```

```
  else
    categoryID = int.Parse(CatDropDown.SelectedItem.Value);

  // get all the news in this category
  DataView myDV = new Business.Category(
      categoryID).GetNews(false).Tables[0].DefaultView;

  // sort the records according to the SortExpression
  // value in the Grid's attributes
  if ( NewsGrid.Attributes["SortExpression"]!="" )
    myDV.Sort = NewsGrid.Attributes["SortExpression"];

  // show only the approved/pending news, as specified in the options
  if (ShowApproved.Checked)
    myDV.RowFilter = "Approved = 1";
  else if (ShowPending.Checked)
    myDV.RowFilter = "Approved = 0";
  else
    myDV.RowFilter = "1 = 1";
  // show only the past/current/future news, if specified in the options
  if (ShowPast.Checked)
    myDV.RowFilter += " AND ExpireDate < '" + DateTime.Today + "'";
  else if (ShowCurrent.Checked)
    myDV.RowFilter += " AND ReleaseDate <= '" + DateTime.Today + "' AND
        ExpireDate >= '" + DateTime.Today + "'";
  else if (ShowFuture.Checked)
    myDV.RowFilter += " AND ReleaseDate > '" + DateTime.Today + "'";

  NewsGrid.DataSource = myDV;
  NewsGrid.DataBind();

}
```

The records are filtered as specified by the user, by appending conditional expressions to the RowFilter property of the DataView. The BindGrid function is called every time a RadioButton is selected, so that the records are immediately filtered accordingly:

```
protected void ShowNews_CheckedChanged(object sender, EventArgs e)
{
  UnselectGridItem();
  BindGrid();
}
```

The following function handles the selection of an item in the drop-down list:

```
protected void CatDropDown_IndexChanged(object sender, EventArgs e)
{
  Response.Redirect("News.aspx?CategoryID=" +
      CatDropDown.SelectedItem.Value);
}
```

251

This redirects the browser to the same page, but with the ID of the selected item, in order to load the correct subscribers the next time `BindGrid` is called.

When the user navigates to another of the grid's pages, we need to cancel editing mode – which means that before rebinding the grid we have to hide the controls for adding a new row, and hide the error message that would be shown when the news we want to add is already present in the category. And of course we have to set the `CurrentPageIndex` property to the new value to actually change the current page:

```
protected void NewsGrid_PageChanged(Object sender,
  DataGridPageChangedEventArgs e)
{
  UnselectGridItem();
  AddNewError.Visible = false;
  ShowAddNewControls(false);
  // change the current page
  NewsGrid.CurrentPageIndex = e.NewPageIndex;
  BindGrid();
}
```

Next we have the procedure that executes when we select an item:

```
protected void NewsGrid_SelectionChanged(object sender, EventArgs e)
{
  ShowAddNewControls(false);

  // get the ID of the selected row
  int newsID = int.Parse(
      NewsGrid.DataKeys[NewsGrid.SelectedIndex].ToString());

  // show the Body text in the Preview label
  NewsPreview.Text = new Business.News(newsID).Body;
  NewsPreview.Visible = true;

  NewsGrid.EditItemIndex = -1;
  BindGrid();
}
```

This gets the ID of the clicked row, retrieves the whole body of the news, and shows it in a label. If the news body is in HTML format, it will be shown in HTML format, so there is no limitation to what we can store and show. By the way, the `GetNewsText` method does almost the same thing, but it is used in the ASP.NET page to show the full text for editing mode. Here we see a highlighted row, with the corresponding label at the bottom of the page:

The methods for deleting, updating, and adding a row are very similar to the ones we've seen earlier for the `Categories.aspx` page. However, there are some additions, especially to the method for adding news items, which we'll look at now:

```
protected void AddNew_Click(object sender, EventArgs e)
{
  if (Page.IsValid)
  {
    int categoryID = int.Parse(CatDropDown.SelectedItem.Value);
    string title = NewTitle.Text;
    string body = NewBody.Text;
    bool approved = NewApproved.Checked;

    // set predefined release/expire dates, in case they are not specified
    DateTime releaseDate = DateTime.Today;
    DateTime expireDate = new DateTime(3000,1,1);

    // if dates are supplied, take them, otherwise keep the predefined ones
    if (NewReleaseDate.Text.Trim().Length > 0)
      releaseDate = DateTime.Parse(NewReleaseDate.Text);
    if (NewExpireDate.Text.Trim().Length > 0)
      expireDate = DateTime.Parse(NewExpireDate.Text);

    // add the news
    Business.Category category = new Business.Category(categoryID);
```

```
    SiteIdentity currUser = (SiteIdentity)Context.User.Identity;
    if (category.AddNews(title, body, releaseDate, expireDate, approved,
       currUser.UserID).ID < 0)
    {
      // if the call to the Add method returned -1, it means that this news
      // was already present, so show the label that tells this
      AddNewError.Visible = true;
    }

    // hide the controls for adding a news
    ShowAddNewControls(false);
    BindGrid();
  }
}
```

You may remember that the release and expiry date are not required when adding a news item, but they are required in the database. If we don't specify a release date, we want to have the current date as the default. If we don't specify an expiry date then we'll take 1/1/3000 as the default, which practically means forever. We set the variables to these default values first, and then replace them if the dates are supplied.

The other very important point is that the last parameter of the AddNews method is the ID of the user currently logged in. We don't need to retrieve a name or e-mail address, only the ID, as the other information is already present in the Accounts_Users table. Retrieving the current user's ID is a simple task, thanks to the Business component of the Accounts module we developed in the previous chapter. To use it, we have to add a reference to that project, and we also reference the namespace at the top of the file, with the following line of code:

```
using Wrox.WebModules.Accounts.Business;
```

At this point we can cast the Context.User.Identity object to the SiteIdentity type, and save a reference to it, as follows:

```
SiteIdentity currUser = (SiteIdentity)Context.User.Identity;
```

The value currUser.UserID is the ID we were looking for, and we can pass it to the AddNews method.

Modifying the Settings Online

So far we've used some of the values stored in the NewsManager.Config XML file as we set them when we created the file. But if the administrator wants to change some values, then a web page is needed to enable the online modification of these settings, to avoid having to sit down at the web server and manually update the file. The page is represented below:

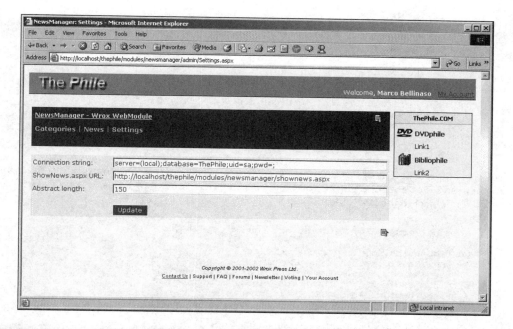

The Settings.aspx Page

The ASP.NET page is formed by a set of controls that show and allow the editing of the respective settings contained in the XML file. The values are not directly bound in a declarative method in the ASPX page, as they were in the previous pages. Here we have three textboxes identified by unique names, and we can easily set their Text property from the code-behind in the Page_Load event. There's very little that's new in the ASPX file, except the validator we use on the Abstract Length field:

```
<asp:TextBox runat="server" Width="100%"
    ID="AbstractLength" CssClass="TextBox" />
<asp:CompareValidator runat="server"
    ControlToValidate="AbstractLength" Type="Integer"
    Operator="DataTypeCheck" Display="dynamic">
  <br>* Invalid format</asp:CompareValidator>
```

Here we ensure that the value supplied is a number. If other characters are inserted we allow the form to be submitted. We used this same control in the News.aspx page to validate the dates, the difference here is that the Type property is set to Integer.

Now let's move straight onto the codebehind.

The Codebehind for Settings.aspx

The codebehind for Settings.aspx is composed of two procedures: Page_Load and Update_Click.

Page_Load retrieves the settings from the XML file (or from the cache if this is not the first time we have requested them) using the ModuleConfig and ModuleSettings classes in the Configuration assembly. Let's start by looking at the code that sets the textboxes to the current values when the page loads:

```
protected void Page_Load(object sender, EventArgs e)
{
  if (!IsPostBack)
  {
    // load all the settings
    Configuration.ModuleSettings settings =
        Configuration.ModuleConfig.GetSettings();
    ConnectionString.Text = settings.ConnectionString;
    NewsURL.Text = settings.NewsUrl;
    AbstractLength.Text = settings.AbstractLength.ToString();
  }
}
```

The second procedure is Update_Click. It gets the new settings from the controls, sets the properties of a new ModuleSettings object, and finally calls ModuleConfig.SaveSettings to serialize the settings object to the XML file:

```
protected void Update_Click(object sender, EventArgs e)
{
  Configuration.ModuleSettings settings =
      new Configuration.ModuleSettings();
  // set the new properties values and update everything
  settings.ConnectionString = ConnectionString.Text.Trim();
  settings.NewsUrl = NewsURL.Text.Trim();
  // if no abstract length is specified (textbox empty),
  // set to -1 (whole news body)
  if (AbstractLength.Text.Trim().Length > 0)
    settings.AbstractLength = int.Parse(AbstractLength.Text);
  else
  {
    AbstractLength.Text = "-1";
    settings.AbstractLength = -1;
  }
  // save the new settings
  Configuration.ModuleConfig.SaveSettings(settings);
}
```

As explained in the comments, if the AbstractLength is not supplied it is set to -1, and -1 is also shown in the textbox (remember that we didn't create a validator control that requires us to specify this setting).

Summary of the Administration Console

The administration section is complete and fully functional. We now have facilities to:

❑ View, add, delete, and edit categories of news. The data is shown through a grid that also shows the category's image when in view mode, or its path during editing. The grid also has a link for each row, allowing the administrator to jump directly to the page showing the news items for the selected category.

❑ View, add, delete, and edit the news articles. The user can filter the articles on whether they are released, and whether they have been approved. In addition to the news item's title, the grid shows the abstract for each news item, made up from the specified number of characters from the article.

❑ Change the application's settings, such as the DB connection string. Using this page, the administrator need not manually edit the configuration file and re-upload it to the server.

Now let's look at how we display the news to users.

Showing News to the User

We can now add news content to the database, but now we need a way for the users to read it. In this section we're going to build a small set of pages that will allow the user to navigate through the available categories, and read abstracts or entire news articles. Later we'll also see how to build a user control to plug the headlines into any page we want.

These pages use another set of header/footer controls, named Header.ascx and Footer.ascx: their content is the same as the admin controls, except that here the header does not show the menu bar. We want to keep them separate so that future changes to the admin header or footer do not affect the user end of the site. We won't show the code here, because they are so similar to the admin controls.

Showing the Categories

First of all we write the page that lists the categories, called ShowCategories.aspx. The interface is made up of a single control: a DataList that shows the categories in two columns, together with their image and description. Here's the ASPX code for the datalist:

```
<asp:DataList id="CategoriesList" runat="server">
  <ItemTemplate>
    <table cellpadding="2" width="100%">
      <tr>
        <td valign="top" width="20px">
          <asp:Label runat="server" Text='<%# GetImage(
              DataBinder.Eval(Container.DataItem, "ImageUrl")) %>'
          />
        </td>
        <td valign="top">
          <asp:HyperLink runat="server" Text='<%#
              DataBinder.Eval(Container.DataItem, "Name") %>'
              NavigateUrl='<%# "ShowAbstracts.aspx?CategoryID=" +
              DataBinder.Eval(Container.DataItem, "CategoryID") %>'
              Font-Bold="True" Font-Size="12" CssClass="GridLink"
          />
          <br>
          <asp:Label runat="server" Text='<%# DataBinder.Eval(
              Container.DataItem, "Description") %>' />
        </td>
      </tr>
    </table>
  </ItemTemplate>
</asp:DataList>
```

As in the DataGrid, the ItemTemplate section gets repeated for each record in the bound table. The difference is that here it's up to us to create all the HTML code, whereas the strength of the DataGrid is that it creates all of the HTML required for the grid structure.

The codebehind for this page only binds the categories returned by the GetCategories static method of the Business.Category class to the DataList. It's nothing new, so we won't show it here – you can find the full code listings in the download.

Here are the results you should get if you run this new page:

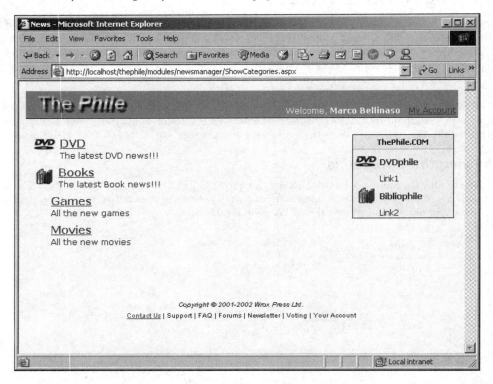

There is something to consider, though. The content of this page won't change frequently, new categories are rarely added, so why query the database every time if we know that we'll likely get the same results every time? We could create a static HTML page, but this would make the admin systems useless. The Premier and Enterprise Architect versions of ASP.NET offer a new feature called **dynamic output caching** that allows us to store a page in the cache for a certain amount of time, if certain conditions are met (such as the client browser or URL of the page being the same, for example). This means that the first time the page is requested we access the database and create the HTML to send to the client. This HTML is then stored in the server cache, and sent as a response to subsequent requests, saving processing time and cycles.

Of course, this feature is applicable when we know that the content for the page does not change for some time, which is exactly the case for this page. To add this feature to our existing page, just add the following line at the top of the page:

```
<%@ OutputCache Duration="600" VaryByParam="none" %>
```

Setting the Duration parameter to 600 specifies that the page will be cached for ten minutes. Setting VaryByParam to none means that the cached page does not depend on the URL's parameters (in cases like this one, where any parameters provided are ignored).

> If you'd like to show a box with the news categories in more than one page, or maybe plug a box directly into the shared site layout, you could move the code of this page to a custom control. The code that binds the data to the **DataList**, and the **DataList** declaration, would be exactly the same.

Showing the Abstracts

We now write the ShowAbstracts.aspx page, called by ShowCategories.aspx when the user clicks a category name. This page is as simple as the previous one; let's look at the main code:

```
<%@ OutputCache Duration="600" VaryByParam="*" %>
```

The opening tags for the page, such as <html>, <head>, <body>, <form>, and the header control go here – we have seen them many times, so let's jump straight to the datagrid:

```
<asp:DataGrid ID="NewsGrid" runat="server"
    BorderWidth="0" Width="100%" PagerStyle-CssClass="Grid_Item"
    PageSize="20" AllowPaging="True" PagerStyle-HorizontalAlign="Right"
    PagerStyle-PageButtonCount="20" PagerStyle-Mode="NumericPages"
    AutoGenerateColumns="False" OnPageIndexChanged="NewsGrid_PageChanged">
  <Columns>
    <asp:TemplateColumn>
      <ItemTemplate>
        <br>
        <asp:HyperLink runat="server" Text='<%#
            DataBinder.Eval(Container.DataItem, "Title") %>'
            NavigateUrl='<%# "ShowNews.aspx?NewsID=" +
            DataBinder.Eval(Container.DataItem, "NewsID") %>'
            CssClass="GridLink"
        />
        <asp:Label runat="server" Text='<%#
            DataBinder.Eval(Container.DataItem, "ReleaseDate",
            "{0:MM/dd/yy}") %>' ForeColor="DarkBlue" Font-Size="8" />
        <br>
        <asp:Label runat="server" Text='<%#
            DataBinder.Eval(Container.DataItem, "Abstract") %>' />
        <br>
        <hr>
      </ItemTemplate>
    </asp:TemplateColumn>
  </Columns>
</asp:DataGrid>
// Add footer control and close the page here.
```

The abstracts are shown in a read-only DataGrid, with links that point to the ShowNews.aspx page – the same way that ShowCategories.aspx links to ShowAbstract.aspx.

The `VaryByParam` parameter of the `@ OutputCache` is now set to `'*'`. This means that the page is processed if a parameter in the URL changes. This is what we want, because we need to get the abstracts directly from the database if the `CategoryID` parameter is not the same as the value in a previous call to the page. The ASP.NET cache feature is smart enough to detect when the parameters on the URL change, and hold a different cache entry for different parameters.

The HTML output is cached on the server, which could lead to a memory overhead that can impact on the server's performance. This can happen when:

❑ We try to cache hundreds of different ASP.NET pages

❑ We cache a few ASP.NET pages, but that can each have many different parameter values. Each different value is like having a completely different page, and the full HTML text is cached.

In our case we have a few pages, with one or no parameters at all, so it's not a big issue. It's just a question of balancing the cost of hitting the database more often with the cost of occupying more memory. The right decision will vary from site to site.

In the following screenshot you can see the result you should get in your browser when you click a category name. The current and approved news items are displayed from the newest to the oldest:

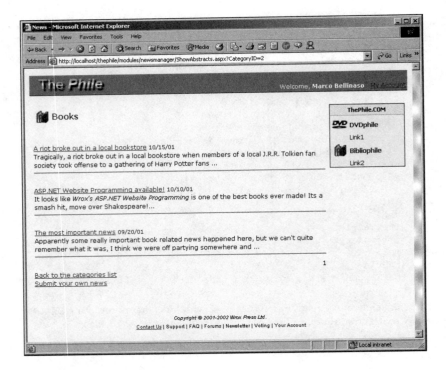

Showing the Whole News Item

The ShowNews.aspx page shows the whole text of the specified news item, and of course the title and release date. It is probably the simplest page we've built so far. Let's just look at the code for the body:

```
<asp:Label runat="server" ID="Title" ForeColor="Navy"
    Font-Bold="True" Font-Size="15" />
<asp:Label runat="server" ID="ReleaseDate"
    ForeColor="DarkBlue" Font-Size="8" />
<br>
<asp:Label runat="server" ID="Body" Width="100%" />
<br>
<a href="javascript:history.back();">Go back</a>
```

In the code-behind we create an instance of Business.News by passing to the constructor the ID specified, along with the URL, and we set the labels to the respective values. Here is the finished page:

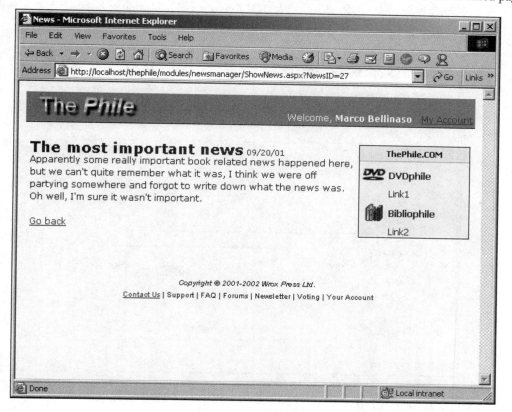

User-Submitted News

We've already discussed why we might want to allow the users (or maybe our external contributors who have no access to the administration section) to post their own news. We need to build a form for users to submit news to the server.

This page, called `SubmitNews.aspx`, does almost the same as the administration `News.aspx` but is only for adding new articles. It also hides the `Approved` value passed to the `AddNews` method of the `Business.Category` class. If the current user has permission to publish a news item, it will be added to the database with the `Approved` status set to `true`, otherwise it will be `false`. We'll come back and show how to do this shortly, while discussing the implementation of security. But the rest of the code is exactly the same so we won't show it here (it is available in the code download). You can see the result in the following screenshot:

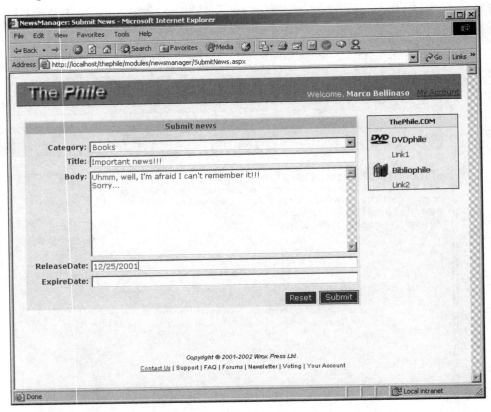

The Headlines User Control

The administration section is complete, and the users can browse the news in each category. Now what? Well, currently the news items are only shown in their own page. We also want a user control that will allow us to easily plug a headlines grid into any page we want with just a couple of lines of code. It seems that we've got something new to do, finally!

Although user controls are a powerful feature of ASP.NET, they are as easy to develop as ASP.NET pages. There's not much difference between a control and a page, except that they use a @Control directive instead of @Page, and they should almost never contain a web form or the <body> tag, because these are present in the page that hosts the control.

Headlines.ascx, part of the NewsManager project, has the following code:

```
<%@ OutputCache Duration="300" VaryByParam="none" %>
<asp:Label ID="HeadlinesHeader" runat="server" />
<asp:DataGrid ID="HeadlinesGrid" runat="server"
    ShowHeader="False" AutoGenerateColumns="False">
  <Columns>
    <asp:TemplateColumn ItemStyle-Width="100px">
      <ItemTemplate>
        <asp:Label runat="server" Font-Bold="True" Text='<%#
          DataBinder.Eval(Container.DataItem,
          "ReleaseDate", "{0:MM/dd/yy}") %>'
        />
      </ItemTemplate>
    </asp:TemplateColumn>
    <asp:TemplateColumn>
      <ItemTemplate>
        <asp:HyperLink runat="server" NavigateUrl='<%#
          DataBinder.Eval(Container.DataItem, "NewsUrl") %>'
          Text='<%# DataBinder.Eval(Container.DataItem, "Title") %>'
        />
      </ItemTemplate>
    </asp:TemplateColumn>
  </Columns>
</asp:DataGrid>
```

There is really nothing new to explain here. There is a DataGrid that displays the release date and title of the news article, and when clicked it redirects to the page with the whole article.

Let's look at the codebehind file. This class should be in the Wrox.WebModules.NewsManager.Web.Controls.User namespace:

```
public abstract class NewsHeadlines : System.Web.UI.UserControl
{
  protected System.Web.UI.WebControls.DataGrid HeadlinesGrid;
  protected System.Web.UI.WebControls.Label HeadlinesHeader;

  private int categoryID;
```

There are several properties exposed here. They simply provide access to member variables, or properties of HeadlinesGrid. Let's move on to the methods:

```
private void Page_Load(object sender, System.EventArgs e)
{
  if (!IsPostBack)
    DataBind();
```

```
  }

  public override void DataBind()
  {
    // get the row describing this category
    Business.Category category = new Business.Category(categoryID);
    // set the image and the category name
    HeadlinesHeader.Text = new Categories().GetImage(category.ImageUrl);
    HeadlinesHeader.Text += category.Name;
    // show all the headlines of this category
    DataView myDV = category.GetHeadlines().Tables[0].DefaultView;
    HeadlinesGrid.DataSource = myDV;
    HeadlinesGrid.DataBind();
  }

  // ...auto generated code...
}
```

The core procedure is DataBind, which overrides the implementation of the base class and binds the headlines table to the grid. There is also the Page_Load event that calls DataBind if the page that hosts the control is not posted back. We could avoid implementing the Page_Load event, and leave the host page with the task of calling the control's BindData method, as we've done for controls in the previous pages. However, this is a special control because it gets the records and sets the DataGrid's properties on its own, so it makes sense that it also binds the data to the grid without any external intervention.

Testing the Control

To test the control we create a ShowHeadlines.aspx file with an external text editor. We don't want to create a new page in VS.NET because it would be added to the project and its code-behind compiled into the assembly, which is not what we want since this is just a test page and not a class to compile and reuse. Here is the content for the page:

```
<%@ Page Inherits="Wrox.ThePhile.Web.PhilePage" %>
<%@ Register TagPrefix="NewsManager" TagName="Headlines"
    src="Headlines.ascx" %>
<%@ Register TagPrefix="NewsManager" TagName="Header" src="Header.ascx" %>
<%@ Register TagPrefix="NewsManager" TagName="Footer" src="Footer.ascx" %>

<html>
<head>
  <title>NewsManager: NewsHeadlines</title>
  <link rel="stylesheet" HREF="/ThePhile/Styles/ThePhile.css" />
  <link href="/ThePhile/Styles/Navigator.css" rel="stylesheet">
  <meta name="CODE_LANGUAGE" Content="C#">
</head>

<body>
  <!-- Insert the menu user control -->
  <NewsManager:Header ID="Menu" runat="server" />

  <!-- Insert the headlines boxes -->
```

```
<NewsManager:Headlines
    ID="DVD"
    runat="server"
    CssClass="DVD_News_General"
    HeaderStyle="DVD_News_Header"
    ItemStyle="DVD_News_Item"
    AlternatingItemStyle="DVD_News_AlternatingItem"
    Width="100%"
    CategoryID="1"
/>
<br><br>
<NewsManager:Headlines
    ID="Books"
    runat="server"
    CssClass="Book_News_General"
    HeaderStyle="Book_News_Header"
    ItemStyle="Book_News_Item"
    AlternatingItemStyle="Book_News_AlternatingItem"
    Width="500px"
    CategoryID="2"
/>

<!-- Insert the footer -->
<NewsManager:Footer ID="Footer" runat="server" />

</body>
</html>
```

We declare two `Headlines` controls, set the properties for the style (the two controls have different header and item styles, and a different width), and select a different category for each. Here is the result:

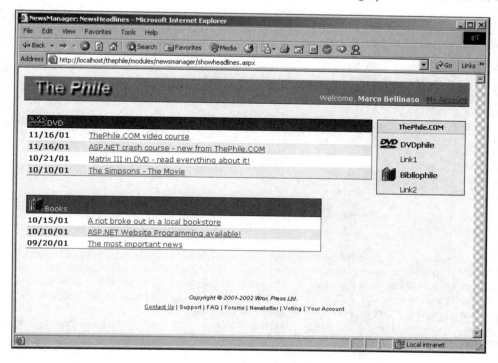

The user interface section is now functionally complete – we just need to develop the security system. After that, we will look at how to provide our news content to other sites and applications.

Securing the Module

Now that the administration console and the user side of things are complete, but before going ahead with the web service and the Windows client, we should think about the implementation of security. In the design section we discussed the three permissions we need, so now we only have to define the enumeration that contains them, and perform the proper checks when the pages are loaded. We need to add these to the Enums.cs file of the Core module, as we did for the Accounts permissions in Chapter 5:

```
namespace Wrox.WebModules.NewsManager
{
  public enum NewsManagerPermissions
  {
    AdministerNews = 200,
    PublishNews = 201,
    SubmitNews = 202
  };
}
```

Now, when any administration page loads, we must ensure that the current user has the AdministerNews permission. To do this, add the following code to the Page_Load event of those pages (Categories.aspx, News.aspx, and Settings.aspx):

```
protected void Page_Load(object sender, EventArgs e)
{
  // check if the current user is allowed to administer the news
  if (!Context.User.Identity.IsAuthenticated ||
    !((SitePrincipal)Context.User).HasPermission(
      (int)NewsManagerPermissions.AdministerNews))
  {
    // if not, redirect to the Login page
    Response.Redirect(
        "/ThePhile/Modules/Users/Login.aspx?ShowError=true", true);
  }

  if (!Page.IsPostBack)
  {
    ...
  }
}
```

We cast the Context.User object to SitePrincipal, which exposes the HasPermission method. This code uses the short-circuiting feature of C# to check if the current user has the right permission only if the first condition is met, namely if the current user is authenticated. This is necessary because if we tried to access the page before logging in, the page would generate an exception, because it could not cast Context.User object to SitePrincipal. If either condition of the if block returns false, the user is redirected to the login page, where an error message will inform them that they don't have permission to view the page.

The code above has to be pasted into all of the administration pages. For the `SubmitNews.aspx` page we instead want to grant access to anyone who has any of the three possible permissions:

```
SitePrincipal currentPrincipal = (SitePrincipal)Context.User;
if (
!currentPrincipal.HasPermission((int)NewsManagerPermissions.AdministerNews) &&
!currentPrincipal.HasPermission((int)NewsManagerPermissions.PublishNews)
&& !currentPrincipal.HasPermission((int)NewsManagerPermissions.SubmitNews))
{
    Response.Redirect(
        "/ThePhile/Modules/Users/Login.aspx?ShowError=true", true);
}
```

Then, when the news is added to the database, if the user has the `AdministerNews` or `PublishNews` permissions the news will be approved immediately, otherwise it will be added in the pending state, with `Approved = false`:

```
SitePrincipal currPrincipal = (SitePrincipal)Context.User;
SiteIdentity currUser = (SiteIdentity)Context.User.Identity;
// add the news
Business.Category category = new
    Business.Category(int.Parse(CatDropDown.SelectedItem.Value));
if (category.AddNews(NewTitle.Text, NewBody.Text, releaseDate, expireDate,
    (currPrincipal.HasPermission((int)NewsManagerPermissions.PublishNews) ||
    currPrincipal.HasPermission((int)NewsManagerPermissions.AdministerNews)),
    currUser.UserID).ID < 0)
    StatusMessage.Text = "Your news was not added, because already present";
else
    StatusMessage.Text = "Thank you for submitting your news!";
```

And that's all! Pretty simple, isn't it? Now you can test the module with different users, or try removing and adding permissions to your user account through the `Accounts` administration module developed in the previous chapter. (Remember that you have to manually add the new permissions to the database first.)

The Headlines Web Service

The last thing we have to implement for this module is the web service that will allow us to share the headlines with any other website or program that can send and receive XML/SOAP packages.

We have a new web service called `Headlines.asmx`. There is nothing in the ASMX file, just the declaration of the codebehind file, whose incredibly short content is listed here in its entirety:

```
using System;
using System.Data;
using System.Data.SqlClient;
using System.Web.Services;

namespace Wrox.WebModules.NewsManager.Web.Services
{
```

```
public class Headlines: WebService
{
   [WebMethod(Description="Returns the headlines for the current
       and approved News of the specified category")]
   public DataSet GetHeadlines(int categoryID)
   {
      return new Business.Category(categoryID).GetHeadlines();
   }

   [WebMethod(Description="Returns all the categories")]
   public DataSet GetCategories()
   {
      return Business.Category.GetCategories();
   }

   }
}
```

We've changed the namespace to `Wrox.WebModules.NewsManager.Web.Services`, following the guidelines given in Chapter 2. The `Headlines` class inherits from `System.Web.Services.WebService`, and although it has the same name as the class for the `Headlines` user control, the two classes don't clash because they are located in different namespaces. The web service exposes two methods, `GetHeadlines` and `GetCategories`, which simply return the result of the calls to the methods in the `Business.Category` class. The small detail that turns two normal methods into web accessible methods is the `[WebMethod]` attribute, which also has a parameter to specify a description.

Testing the Web Service

It's easy to test web services. Just jump to the `Headlines.asmx` file with your browser, you'll get the following:

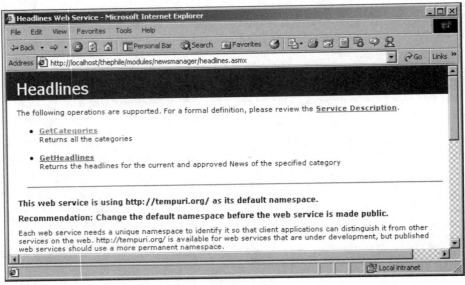

You can see the two web methods listed on the page, together with their description. Click on a link to test that method. For example, click the GetHeadlines link and you'll get this page:

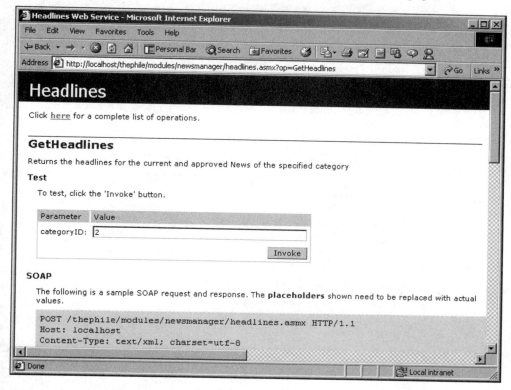

The method is detected to require a parameter, so the page provides a textbox where you can enter the ID of a category. Press Invoke and you'll finally execute the method. This is the result produced for a categoryID of 2:

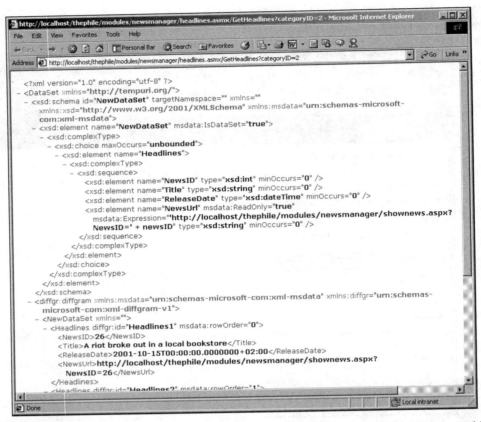

We get a page with XML/SOAP output that represents a `DataSet`. The `DataSet` includes one table containing the headlines. The web service seems to work very well, so we can now go ahead and build the client.

The News Ticker Application

We can build different types of clients that consume the web service, such as a web page or a desktop program. To show how to access web services, we'll build a small Windows application for browsing the headlines by category, and opening a browser window with the whole news body by double-clicking on a headline. We could offer this program to our site's visitors, so that they can check if there are new headlines without typing the URL in the browser and manually refreshing the page.

We add a new C# Windows Forms project to the solution (we could create this application anywhere we wanted, it's just convenient to keep all our code together).

We then add a reference to the web service using the Project | Add Web Reference... menu option. We specify the full URL of the web service file, and clicking Add Reference VS.NET automatically creates a proxy class to access the web service. Note that in the Solution Explorer a new entry has been added under Web References, called localhost, and underneath it you can see the WSDL and the discovery files created. We renamed localhost to ThePhile, but it isn't really important, it is just the name we'll use to access the proxy class.

The form contains a `DropDownList` for listing the categories, a `DataGrid` to show the headlines, a button to refresh the headlines, and a timer to automatically refresh the headlines after a certain amount of time. You should place the controls as shown in the following screenshot:

Explaining how to create Windows Forms in detail is beyond the scope of this book, but we'll quickly look at the code piece by piece:

```
public class Viewer : System.Windows.Forms.Form
{
  // ...controls declaration here...

  private DataSet dsHeadlines;
  private DataSet dsCategories;
  private bool categoriesLoaded;

  // ...other auto generated code here...

  private void Viewer_Load(object sender, System.EventArgs e)
  {

    // get the categories and the headlines for the first category
    ThePhile.Headlines headlines = new ThePhile.Headlines();
    dsCategories = headlines.GetCategories();
```

```
        // bind dsCategories to the ComboBox, display the Name and
        // keep the CategoryID as value for each item
        Categories.DataSource = dsCategories.Tables[0].DefaultView;
        Categories.DisplayMember = "Name";
        Categories.ValueMember = "CategoryID";
        categoriesLoaded = true;

        // fill the grid with the headlines
        FillHeadlinesGrid();
    }
```

In the Viewer_Load event (which corresponds to Page_Load in ASP.NET pages) we retrieve the categories and save them to a private DataSet variable. We then bind them to the DropDownList, and call another routine to get the headlines and fill the grid:

```
    private void FillHeadlinesGrid()
    {
      // if the categories have not been loaded yet,
      // or if there is no category in the ComboBox --> exit now
      if (!categoriesLoaded || Categories.Items.Count == 0) return;

      // get the headlines for the selected category
      ThePhile.Headlines headlines = new ThePhile.Headlines();
      dsHeadlines = headlines.GetHeadlines((int)Categories.SelectedValue);

      // remove the current grid columns (if any)
      Headlines.TableStyles.Clear();

      // bind dsHeadlines to the Grid, and show the ReleaseDate and
      // Headline titles in two custom columns
      Headlines.SetDataBinding(dsHeadlines, "Headlines");
      DataGridTableStyle ts = new DataGridTableStyle();
      ts.MappingName = "Headlines";
      ts.AlternatingBackColor = Color.LightGray;

      // Add the ReleaseDate column
      DataGridColumnStyle TextCol = new DataGridTextBoxColumn();
      TextCol.MappingName = "ReleaseDate";
      TextCol.HeaderText = "Release Date";
      TextCol.Width = 80;
      ts.GridColumnStyles.Add(TextCol);

      // Add the headline's title column
      DataGridColumnStyle TitleCol = new DataGridTextBoxColumn();
      TitleCol.MappingName = "Title";
      TitleCol.HeaderText = "Headline";
      TitleCol.Width = 400;
      ts.GridColumnStyles.Add(TitleCol);

      // Add the (hidden) NewsUrl column
      DataGridColumnStyle UrlCol = new DataGridTextBoxColumn();
      UrlCol.MappingName = "NewsUrl";
```

```
     UrlCol.Width = 0;
     ts.GridColumnStyles.Add(UrlCol);

     // finally add the table to the grid
     Headlines.TableStyles.Add(ts);
 }
```

The code above creates a new column for each column of the data table, and binds these columns to the respective fields. When the user clicks a row header of the grid, we want to open the default browser and redirect to the page that shows the whole news story. The URL of the news item is one of the columns in the data table, and opening the default browser is done with a single line, thanks to the System.Diagnostic.Process class. The following code checks if the user double-clicks on a row header and in that case loads the news page within the browser:

```
private void NewsGrid_DoubleClick(object sender, System.EventArgs e)
{
    // get the current cursor position relative to the Headlines
    Point pt = Headlines.PointToClient(Cursor.Position);
    // navigate to the link only if the user clicked on the row header
    //if (navigateLink)
    if (Headlines.HitTest(pt.X, pt.Y).Type ==
        DataGrid.HitTestType.RowHeader)
    {
        BindingManagerBase bmGrid;
        bmGrid = BindingContext[dsHeadlines, "Headlines"];
        // open the default browser and navigate to the Url
        // of the currently selected row
        System.Diagnostics.Process.Start(
            ((DataRowView)bmGrid.Current)["NewsUrl"].ToString()
        );
    }
}
```

The last three procedures are called, respectively, at the timer's interval, when the user selects another category, or when the user presses the **Refresh** button. All of them simply call the FillHeadlinesGrid procedure to refresh the grid:

```
private void RefreshTimer_Tick(object sender, System.EventArgs e)
{
    FillHeadlinesGrid();
}

private void Categories_SelectedIndexChanged(object sender,
    System.EventArgs e)
{
    FillHeadlinesGrid();
}

private void RefreshButton_Click(object sender, System.EventArgs e)
{
    FillHeadlinesGrid();
}
```

All the code is finally complete, and if you run the application you'll get the following form:

You might also want to test this application in detail, by adding some news through the NewsManager administration section, and then waiting a few minutes to see if the grid is automatically refreshed (or manually refill it by clicking Refresh).

> If you want to know more about Windows Forms programming in C#, you can refer to
> *Professional C#*, ISBN 1-861004-99-0, or *Professional Windows Forms*,
> ISBN 1-861005-54-7, both from Wrox Press. For more about web services, try
> *Professional ASP.NET Web Services*, ISBN 1-861005-45-8, or *Professional C# Web
> Services*, ISBN 1-861004-39-7, also from Wrox Press.

Summary

In this long chapter we have seen how to build a complex and feature-rich module to completely manage the site's news and articles. We've provided numerous features through the chapter:

❑ A tool for managing the database.

❑ Pages for browsing the published content.

❑ Integration with the Accounts module to secure the module and track the authors of the news items.

❑ A user control for showing the headlines on the homepage or in any other page.

❑ A web service that can share the headlines with any site or program that can use and understand XML/SOAP messages.

❑ A Windows client program that uses the web service to show the headlines of all the available categories, and that opens a browser and shows the whole news item when a title is clicked.

This system should be flexible enough to be successfully plugged into many real world applications. When customized to fit a particular site's needs, it could become very powerful.

7

Advertising

No matter how wonderful the website, how amazing the look, how talented the programmers, or how useful the service – a site will not last long without a consistent source of funding. Some sites are maintained by volunteers who donate their own time and money, and others get subscription fees from readers. Many of these sites try to supplement their revenue with advertising, and other sites rely on it entirely.

Many sites use banner advertisement-style features even when they don't sell advertising space. For example, some sites exchange links with other sites. Others (for example www.play.com) use banner advertising to provide links to areas of their product catalogue that the viewer would not necessarily go looking for.

In this chapter we will present an overview of the problems involved with advertising and some common design patterns in overcoming those problems. We'll develop a reusable advertising module that we'll plug into our website and that we can easily adapt to our future needs.

The Problem

There are two main concepts you need to be familiar with to provide advertising on a website: impressions and hits.

Impressions

An **impression** occurs when a particular advertisement is displayed on a web page to a single user. Website owners, administrators, and marketing managers should consider impressions a commodity – chips to bargain with when obtaining lucrative advertising contracts.

Consider this scenario: a popular content website receives over a million impressions a day. For the sake of example, imagine that it is a fan club website dedicated to a popular video game. Its audience consists of a wide range of browsers from older adults to young teenagers and pre-teens. An impression on this site would be considered an extremely valuable commodity to a video game manufacturer. However, a manufacturer of a popular brand of craft glue would probably not find those impressions particularly valuable.

Impressions are *yours* to sell, and you should look for a buyer for your impressions that would be most interested in your target audience. Therefore, you *must* know the audience of your website in order to market your impressions to the right audience.

Typically, impressions are sold in bulk. A typical advertising contract will consist of the advertising buyer paying for a mathematical or statistical guarantee that a certain number of impressions of a given ad will be displayed in a given time period (usually measured in weeks or months).

Hits

While impressions are yours to sell, **hits** are to be considered rewards or prizes. An impression occurs and an advertisement appears on the user's page. If the user is particularly interested in what the advertisement has to offer, then the user will click the advertisement. This is called a hit. Just to confuse things more, virtually every dotcom company has a different term for hits, including clicks, click-throughs, scores, buy-ins, and more. No matter what term is used, it all boils down to the simple act of the user clicking on the advertisement.

This is where advertising gets more profitable. Hits are worth more than impressions. Advertising contracts typically pay percentages of sales resulting from banner advertisement hits, or they pay a flat rate per hit.

When designing an advertising system we need to keep track of the following:

❑   Impression counts

❑   Hit counts

❑   Community demographics – *who* is using your web site, what they do and don't have in common, their interests, etc.

Earlier in the book we discussed community building and mentioned that opinion polls provide a fun way for users to interact with your site. They also provide an easy way for you to obtain valuable demographics that you might be able to use to land that advertising contract you might not have otherwise been able to get. For example, if you put up a poll asking users what their favorite DVD is, and 75% of them say that their favorite DVD is *Star Wars: Episode I*, then chances are you could use that information to strike a pretty lucrative advertising deal with a DVD on-line retailer.

Requirements

There are many things that we need to cover in the design of our advertising module. We want to make sure that it takes care of all of our needs and solves our problem – which is that we need to generate revenue, so we need impression/hit data to attract advertisers, and a way of putting adverts in our pages. In addition, we want to make it flexible and scalable enough so that if our advertising needs increase in the future, it should be easy enough to create more code and functionality to deal with this.

In short, our design is going to need to take care of the following issues for us:

❑ **Database design** – we need to make sure that we have a database that can track all necessary information, and provide the reporting capabilities we know we're going to need.

❑ **Layout and display** – we need to make sure that we have a good place to put our advertisement and a layout in mind that won't intrude on or interfere with the existing interface.

❑ **Auditing** – we need to track as much information as possible about the advertisements, and make that information available in such a way that we can obtain useful reports whenever we need them.

❑ **Administration** – our website administrators, who may not necessarily be located in the office, need to be able to log in to some administration console to make changes and additions to the advertising data.

Administrative users should be able to perform the following tasks:

❑ Create new advertisements

❑ Edit/view existing advertisements

❑ Add details of new advertising companies

❑ View all current advertisements

❑ Generate reports to show advertising activity

Design

Now that we have specified the broad requirements of our advertising system, let's lay down a design for it. Once again ASP.NET provides a component that almost does what we want – the AdRotator. So before we look at the components we are going to build, let's look at how the AdRotator works and what impact using it will have on the rest of our design.

Using the AdRotator

The AdRotator handles a lot of the work associated with displaying an advert. It will save us time overall if we use it, but it has its own foibles that we need to overcome.

We would like to store all data for our application in the database, but AdRotator only supports an XML file. So we will need to find a way to work around this. Information required by the AdRotator will go in the XML file, while related data will go in the database. We will need a way to tell which entry in the database relates to which entry in the XML file.

Another limitation is that the AdRotator doesn't come with the ability to record hits or impressions. It doesn't expose a click event that we could use ourselves to record hits, so we'll have to implement this functionality ourselves. However, it does fire an event every time an ad is displayed – so we can use this to record an impression.

The XML file for an `AdRotator` stores the following details:

Property	Description
ImageUrl	Absolute or relative URL to an image to be displayed as the banner advertisement.
NavigateUrl	The URL of the page to go to if a user clicks the ad.
AlternateText	Text to display in the images ALT attribute.
Keyword	An optional keyword for the advertisement, to allow filtering. We won't be using this feature here, consult the MSDN documentation for more information on this property.
Impressions	This number indicates the *relative* importance of this advertisement with respect to all other ads in the rotators XML file. The larger this number, the more frequently the ad will be displayed. This number will typically be adjusted based on how much the advertiser is paying.

So, we will store this information in the XML file, and anything else in the database. Heres an example of a single ad in the XML file. Note that the properties listed above have all been serialized as XML elements.

```
<Advertisements>
  <Ad>
    <ImageUrl>http://localhost/thephile/images/wroxbanner.jpg</ImageUrl>
    <NavigateUrl>/ThePhile/Modules/AdsManager/PassThrough.aspx?AD=9
    </NavigateUrl>
    <AlternateText>Wrox Press</AlternateText>
    <Keyword>wrox</Keyword>
    <Impressions>1</Impressions>
  </Ad>
  <!-- more advertisements here, each with the Ad element. -->
</Advertisements>
```

For more information on the `AdRotator` control, consult the MSDN .NET Framework SDK Developer's Guide entry for AdRotator. Its available at http://msdn.microsoft.com/library/default.asp?url=/library/en-us/cpgenref/html/cpconadrotatorwebcontrol.asp.

The Database

One of the first steps in any database design, from the smallest to the largest, is an **entity list**. Before figuring out what kind of columns we need, what data types we need, etc., we need to know the basic list of the *things* we need to keep track of. The following is a list of the entities that we need in order to maintain an effective advertising database:

❏ Advertisements

❏ Companies

❏ Impressions

❏ Hits

We need to store some basic descriptive information about the advertisement in the database. Because we know a little bit about how ASP.NET's AdRotator control works, we know we're not going to need to store things like image file names and relative importance in the database.

As for other modules in this book, all tables will be given a unique prefix (AdsManager_). The database will use the following schema:

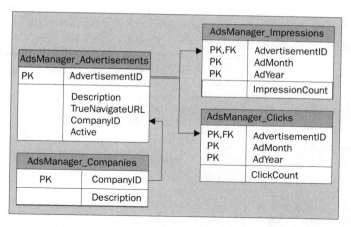

The AdsManager_Advertisements table is pretty straightforward. It has AdvertisementID as the main primary key/identity field. From there we get to the AdsManager_Impressions and AdsManager_Clicks tables. Each of these uses as a primary key the combination of the AdvertisementID, the AdMonth, and the AdYear fields. The AdYear and AdMonth fields are simple number fields that contain the month and year during which the click count or impression count was accumulated. This allows monthly summaries to be generated without bogging the database down with slow and complex date calculations.

The interesting thing about this design is that we are doing a little bit of warehousing in the way we are storing our data. It would be inefficient to add a row to the database every time someone sees or clicks a banner ad. So we have taken inspiration from data warehousing, and we just store *summary* information. Data warehousing is basically the storage of summary (or otherwise calculated) data separately from the live (also called transactional) data. We store monthly totals of both clicks and impressions for a given advertisement. As opposed to storing each click in its own row with a pinpoint time/date stamp, like this:

2/02/2002 05:34 1
2/02/2002 05:36 2

we instead store the total sum of all the clicks for February 2002 as follows:

02   2002   85

This way, to retrieve all clicks for February, we retrieve one row, without calculation, saving us an immense amount of effort. Because each advertisement belongs to a single company, it becomes very easy to obtain reports of monthly activity for all the advertisements for the same company or group of companies.

In addition to the database tables, our database will also contain several stored procedures. These will make the system slightly more efficient, and simplify our data layer.

Stored Procedure	Description
sp_AdsManager_CreateAdvertisement	Creates a new advertisement in the database. This only creates the in-database portion of the advertisement. The XML stored in the AdRotators config file is handled by the data services component itself.
sp_AdsManager_CreateCompany	Creates a new company profile in the database. Currently we only store the company's name, but the module can be adapted to store more information.
sp_AdsManager_GetAdList	Retrieves a full list of all advertisements in the database. Used for administration.
sp_AdsManager_GetAdvertDetails	Obtains all of the available details concerning a given advertisement.
sp_AdsManager_GetCompanyList	Obtains an alphabetically sorted list of all companies in the database.
sp_AdsManager_GetCompanyReport	Data is formatted and retrieved to provide a company with all the relevant information as to the progress and history of their advertising campaigns. Can be used to support a billing process by being fed into a reporting tool such as Crystal Reports.
sp_AdsManager_RecordClick	Records the event in which a user *clicks* on an ad banner.
sp_AdsManager_RecordImpression	Records the event in which a user *sees* an ad banner.
sp_AdsManager_UpdateAdvertisement	Updates the pertinent information about a given advertisement.

The Data Services Layer

As with other modules, our data services layer will consist of stateless classes that provide access to the data source. However, because we are using the AdRotator, we have two data stores – the database and the XML file. We want to keep this complication hidden from the business layer, so our data services objects will need to aggregate the information from the different sources.

We will use two classes in the data layer:

❑ AdMaster – deals with data requests that do not refer to a single advert: manipulating companies, or returning a list of all ads in the database.

❑ Advertisement – deals with data requests referring to a particular advert: creating, updating, and retrieving ads, and recording click-throughs and impressions.

The Business Layer

With a solid data layer, the business layer can safely ignore the complication of having two data sources.

The AdMaster class in the business tier will simply call methods in the data tier, which in turn call stored procedures in the database. Like the AdMaster data class, it is stateless.

The Advertisement class in the business tier provides an abstraction of a single advert. When we instantiate it, we can provide an ID to identify a given advert. We then have methods and properties to manipulate that advert. This class does maintain state during the lifetime of its instantiation.

Alternatively we can instantiate a new advert and save it. The data layer will create a new database record and XML entry.

The Presentation Layer

We now have all the data and logic that we need to make the advertisement system work, and can move on to looking at the presentation layer. The presentation layer needs to do two things:

❑ Display the advertisement and record an impression

❑ Handle a hit (click) – record it, and pass the user to the appropriate site

We will display the advert using the AdRotator, which will automatically select an advert based on a weighting. However, the AdRotator does not record impressions. To do that, we can catch the AdCreated event, and use that to record the impression.

The AdRotator control simply provides a link – it does not expose a click event. So if we link directly to the target site, we will not know when a user has clicked the advert. To record hits, we will use a **pass-through page**. This is a page on our own site that uses the business components to record which advertisement was clicked, and then forwards the browser on to the eventual target. The AdRotator link points to the pass-through page, not the target site.

Advertising Administration

Also in the presentation layer is our administration system. Our design is fairly straightforward. We will provide administrators with a web interface for administering the banner ads and their related properties. We also want to have a stored procedure for feeding a reporting tool, such as Crystal Reports, for supplying data to advertisers in a professional, easy-to-read format.

Configuration

As with the previous modules described in this book, there are two configuration classes used to abstract access to and from a configuration file: `ModuleConfig` and `ModuleSettings`. `ModuleConfig` is a utility class designed to de-serialize an instance of `ModuleSettings` from the appropriate file and serialize that same class back into the file if changes are necessary.

The Solution

As with any project, we hope that by the time we are ready to code we have created a good, solid, effective design. In our design we covered the data services and business layer classes that we would need to create. We also discussed the fact that we would be using the `AdRotator` control.

This is actually a very simple control to use, and is the core of our advertising solution. You just put the `AdRotator` control onto your ASP.NET page and indicate where it can find the advertisement files – it then handles everything else. In this section we'll show you how we use this control to record impressions and hits, two things that it doesn't have built-in support for recording. We'll also show you how we have implemented the rest of our design to support the advertising solution.

The Database Tables

Before building our database, we need to decide on the details of the tables. Here is a fuller schema, which we will use to build the database.

AdsManager_Advertisements Table

Column Name	Data Type	Description
AdvertisementID	int – Identity primary key	Unique ID for the advertisement.
Description	varchar	Description of the advertisement.
CompanyID	int foreign key	ID of company owning the advertisement.
Active	bit	Boolean flag indicating whether the advertisement is active.
TrueNavigateUrl	varchar	URL where the user will be redirected from the pass-through page.

AdsManager_Companies Table

Column Name	Data Type	Description
CompanyID	int – Identity primary key	Unique ID for the company.
Description	varchar	Description of the company.

AdsManager_Impressions Table

Column Name	Data Type	Description
AdvertisementID	int	Advertisement ID for the given impression count.
AdMonth	int	Month for the given impression count.
AdYear	int	Year for the given impression count.
ImpressionCount	int	Actual impression count for an ad/year/month.

AdsManager_Clicks Table

Column Name	Data Type	Description
AdvertisementID	int	Advertisement ID for the given click count.
AdMonth	int	Month for the given click count.
AdYear	int	Year for the given click count.
ClickCount	int	Actual click count for a given month/year/ad ID.

Stored Procedures

The scripting source for all the stored procedures is in the code download. We don't have the space to list the source code for all of the stored procedures, so we've selected a few samples that represent some of the most frequently performed tasks.

sp_AdsManager_CreateAdvertisement

The sp_AdsManager_CreateAdvertisement stored procedure takes a few simple arguments and returns as an output parameter the ID of the created advertisement:

```
CREATE PROCEDURE sp_AdsManager_CreateAdvertisement
            @CompanyID int,
            @Description varchar(255),
            @TrueNavigateUrl varchar(255),
            @AdvertisementID int output
AS
  INSERT INTO AdsManager_Advertisements(CompanyID, Description,
                                                     TrueNavigateUrl)
    VALUES(@CompanyID, @Description, @TrueNavigateUrl)

  SET @AdvertisementID = @@IDENTITY
GO
```

sp_AdsManager_GetAdList

The sp_AdsManager_GetAdList stored procedure obtains a list of all advertisements in the database. It uses an inner join to combine details of the ad with details of the company:

```
CREATE PROCEDURE sp_AdsManager_GetAdList
AS
SELECT ad.AdvertisementID,
       ad.Description,
       ad.CompanyID,
       cp.Description as CompanyName
  FROM AdsManager_Advertisements ad
  INNER JOIN AdsManager_Companies cp ON ad.CompanyID = cp.CompanyID
  ORDER BY CompanyName ASC, ad.Description ASC
GO
```

sp_AdsManager_GetCompanyReport

The sp_AdsManager_GetCompanyReport stored procedure queries the database to provide a history of all of the advertising campaigns for a given company during a certain time period. Clicks and impressions are stored as a month-by-month count, rather than by creating a new record for each click or impression:

```
CREATE PROCEDURE sp_AdsManager_GetCompanyReport
                 @CompanyID int,
                 @StartMonth int,
                 @StartYear int,
                 @EndMonth int,
                 @EndYear int
AS
  SELECT adimp.AdvertisementID, adimp.ImpressionCount, adimp.AdMonth,
         adimp.AdYear, adclick.ClickCount, ad.Description
    FROM AdsManager_Impressions adimp
    INNER JOIN AdsManager_Advertisements ad
      ON adimp.AdvertisementID = ad.AdvertisementID
    LEFT JOIN AdsManager_Clicks adclick
      ON adimp.AdvertisementID = adclick.AdvertisementID
    WHERE ad.CompanyID = @CompanyID AND
      (adclick.AdYear >= @StartYear AND
      adclick.AdYear <= @EndYear AND
      adimp.AdYear >= @StartYear AND
      adimp.AdYear <= @EndYear) AND
      (adclick.AdMonth >= @StartMonth AND
      adclick.AdMonth <= @EndMonth AND
      adimp.AdMonth >= @StartMonth AND
      adimp.AdMonth <= @EndMonth)

    ORDER BY adimp.adYear ASC, adimp.adMonth ASC
GO
```

This stored procedure facilitates reporting but we have not implemented a user interface for it. This user interface can easily be implemented in a reporting tool such as Crystal Reports or by a program written for an advertising manager. The following is the output summarizing a brand new company's ad campaign history:

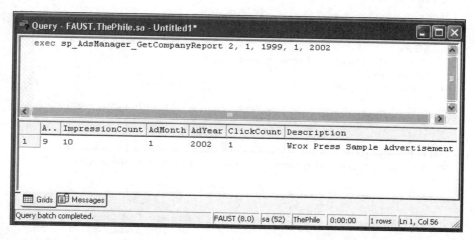

The data shows each company's advertising campaigns. Each campaign will have a single row for each month during the time specified by the stored procedure. This makes it incredibly easy to create a grouping in a reporting tool that allows sub-reports and other interactive features, or in an ASP.NET web page. As you can see, the above ad campaign had ten impressions and one click during January 2002. If this campaign had been created during December 2001, there would be another row for that month, also summarizing that month's activity.

The Data Services Layer

Now that we've taken a look at the format of our data in SQL Server and we've seen what stored procedures we're going to be working with, it will be fairly easy to turn that into a set of methods that the data services layer requires.

Let's take a look at the source code for each of the required classes. We'll also examine some of the decisions that went into choosing a particular code style or algorithm. To get started, we'll create a new Class Library project (in C#) and call it AdsManagerData. We'll make sure that the default namespace for this project is Wrox.WebModules.AdsManager.Data, as well as making sure that the output filename is Wrox.WebModules.AdsManager.Data. One last thing before we start looking at the source code for the classes is to add a reference to the Core project.

The AdMaster Class

The AdMaster class is pretty straightforward. It provides a front-end to the stored procedures in the database for performing operations that don't belong to the Advertisement class. As with all the other data services classes in this book, this class inherits from Wrox.WebModules.Data.DbObject, which we looked at in Chapter 2:

```
using System;
using System.Data;
using System.Data.SqlClient;
using Wrox.WebModules.Data;

namespace Wrox.WebModules.AdsManager.Data
{
  /// <summary>
  /// Summary description for AdMaster.
  /// </summary>
  public class AdMaster : Wrox.WebModules.Data.DbObject
  {
    public AdMaster(string newConnectionString): base(newConnectionString)
    { }
```

The method below will retrieve a list of companies from the database by using the
sp_AdsManager_GetCompanyList stored procedure, and will store the results in a DataSet:

```
    public DataSet GetCompanyList()
    {
      DataSet companies = RunProcedure("sp_AdsManager_GetCompanyList",
                                        new SqlParameter[]{}, "Users");
      return companies;
    }
```

This next method retrieves the master list of all advertisements in the database into a DataSet:

```
    public DataSet GetAdList()
    {
      DataSet ads = RunProcedure( "sp_AdsManager_GetAdList",
                                   new SqlParameter[]{}, "Advertisements" );
      return ads;
    }
```

The following method uses a stored procedure to create a new company in the database given the name
of the company as an argument:

```
    public void CreateCompany(string companyName)
    {
      int rowsAffected;

      SqlParameter[] parameters =
                { new SqlParameter("@CompanyName", SqlDbType.VarChar, 255) };
      parameters[0].Value = companyName;
      RunProcedure("sp_AdsManager_CreateCompany", parameters,
                                                   out rowsAffected);

    }
  }
}
```

The Advertisement Class

Now we add a class called `Advertisement` to the `AdsManagerData` project we created earlier. This class has a bit more functionality than the previous class. It is responsible for loading the details for a single advertisement, updating the details for an advertisement, creating a new advertisement, and recording clicks and impressions for an existing advertisement. The tricky part of this class comes in completely abstracting the source of the data. As you'll see, the data for a single "advertisement" entity is split between both a database and an XML file. The business layer above, however, has no idea that this split exists. This allows us flexibility in upgrading the class to obtain more information from more sources. In pure OOP terms, this concept is called **information aggregation** or **information hiding**.

> *Note that the `Retrieve` method in the business object accesses the XML file directly. Strictly speaking, if we wanted to be true to the tier separation model, even though we're only accessing a text file, we should still do all data access (regardless of the storage medium) in the data services tier. So the data layer `Retrieve` method could integrate data from the XML file, and we could add columns to the row that the data object returns programmatically, so it will appear to the business tier that it all came from one database. We won't take this approach here but bear in mind that it is an option.*

The `Advertisement` class has no properties and provides the following methods:

- ❑ **Create** – creates a new advertisement in the database, as well as populating the `AdRotator` XML file with the appropriate data. Invokes the `sp_AdsManager_CreateAdvertisement` procedure.

- ❑ **RecordClick** – records in the summary tables that a click occurred on a given advertisement. Invokes the procedure `sp_AdsManager_RecordClick`.

- ❑ **RecordImpression** – records in the summary tables that an impression occurred on a given advertisement. Invokes the procedure `sp_AdsManager_RecordImpression`.

- ❑ **RetrieveAd** – obtains all the relevant details for a given advertisement. Pulls information from the database via the `sp_AdsManager_GetAdvertDetails` stored procedure.

- ❑ **Update** – saves changes to an existing advertisement by calling the `sp_AdsManager_UpdateAdvertisement` stored procedure and by modifying the XML configuration file.

Let's take a look at the source for `Advertisement.cs` (found in the project for the `Wrox.WebModules.AdsManager.Data` namespace, which is in the `AdsManagerData` class library we've been working with up to this point):

```
using System;
using System.Data;
using System.Data.SqlClient;
using Wrox.WebModules.Data;
using Wrox.WebModules.AdsManager;
using System.Xml;

namespace Wrox.WebModules.AdsManager.Data
{
    /// <summary>
```

```
/// Summary description for Advertisement.
/// </summary>
public class Advertisement: Wrox.WebModules.Data.DbObject
{
public Advertisement(string newConnectionString):base(newConnectionString)
{ }

public DataRow RetrieveAd(int advertisementId)
{
  SqlParameter[] parameters = { new SqlParameter("@AdvertisementID",
                                                 SqlDbType.Int, 4) };
  parameters[0].Value = advertisementId;

  using (DataSet ads = RunProcedure("sp_AdsManager_GetAdvertDetails",
                                    parameters, "Advertisements"))
  {
    return ads.Tables[0].Rows[0];
  }
}

/// <summary>
/// Records an impression for a given advertisement. An impression is a
/// single display of an advertisement to a viewer's browser.
/// </summary>
/// <param name="advertisementId">advertisementId for which to record the
/// Impression.</param>
public void RecordImpression(int advertisementId)
{
  int rowsAffected;
  SqlParameter[] parameters =
                { new SqlParameter("@AdvertisementID", SqlDbType.Int, 4) };
  parameters[0].Value = advertisementId;

  RunProcedure("sp_AdsManager_RecordImpression", parameters,
                                                 out rowsAffected);
}

public void RecordClick(int advertisementId)
{
  int rowsAffected;
  SqlParameter[] parameters =
                { new SqlParameter("@AdvertisementId", SqlDbType.Int, 4) };
  parameters[0].Value = advertisementId;

  RunProcedure("sp_AdsManager_RecordClick", parameters, out rowsAffected);
}

public void Create(string imageUrl, string trueNavigateUrl,
                   string alternateText, string keyword, int companyId,
                   string description, string rotatorFile)

{
  int rowsAffected;
  SqlParameter[] parameters =
```

```
            { new SqlParameter("@CompanyID", SqlDbType.Int, 4),
          new SqlParameter("@Description", SqlDbType.VarChar, 255),
          new SqlParameter("@TrueNavigateUrl", SqlDbType.VarChar, 255),
          new SqlParameter("@AdvertisementID", SqlDbType.Int, 4)};
    parameters[0].Value = companyId;
    parameters[1].Value = description;
    parameters[2].Value = trueNavigateUrl;
    parameters[3].Direction = ParameterDirection.Output;
    RunProcedure("sp_AdsManager_CreateAdvertisement", parameters,
                                              out rowsAffected);
```

This next section of code is where things get a bit fancy. We have seen that the AdRotator gets its data from an XML file. We want to keep this, as much as possible, secret from the business layer. So, when the business layer issues a call to create an advert, we need to synchronize entries between the database and the XML file.

We also want the link taken when the user clicks an ad to be to the pass-through page. There we need to retrieve the true destination, and forward the user to it. These are issues for the presentation layer, but it does mean that when we create an ad entry we need to enter the link to the pass-through, and not the true target, into the AdRotator's XML file. The link to the pass-through needs to provide all the information we need to record the click and pass the user on to the correct site.

So the link we use as NavigateUrl in the XML file will include the ad ID as a parameter, which the pass-through page can use to obtain full details from the database.

Below, we're going to use some standard XML code to create the appropriate elements and save them in the AdRotator's XML file. The location of this XML file is stored in our config file (AdsManager.Config) and retrieved using the standard configuration classes. When we add the advert to the database, the stored procedure returns the new ad's ID. We use that in the XML file's NavigateUrl:

```
    // now that the new ad is in the DB, put the rest of the
    // details in the Rotator's XML file.
    Configuration.ModuleSettings settings =
                            Configuration.ModuleConfig.GetSettings();

    XmlDocument rotatorDom = new XmlDocument();
    rotatorDom.Load(rotatorFile);
    XmlElement temp;
    XmlElement newAd = rotatorDom.CreateElement("Ad");

    temp = rotatorDom.CreateElement("ImageUrl");
    temp.InnerText = imageUrl;
    newAd.AppendChild( temp );

    temp = rotatorDom.CreateElement("NavigateUrl");
    temp.InnerText = settings.PassThroughPage + "?AD=" +
                            parameters[3].Value.ToString();
    newAd.AppendChild( temp );
```

```
            temp = rotatorDom.CreateElement("AlternateText");
            temp.InnerText = alternateText;
            newAd.AppendChild( temp );

            temp = rotatorDom.CreateElement("Keyword");
            temp.InnerText = keyword;
            newAd.AppendChild( temp );

            temp = rotatorDom.CreateElement("Impressions");
            temp.InnerText = "1";
            newAd.AppendChild( temp );

            rotatorDom.DocumentElement.AppendChild( newAd );
            rotatorDom.Save( rotatorFile );
    }

    public void Update(int advertisementId, string imageUrl,
                       string trueNavigateUrl, string alternateText,
                       string keyword, string description, int impressions,
                       bool active, string rotatorFile)
    {
        int rowsAffected;
        SqlParameter[] parameters =
                { new SqlParameter("@AdvertisementID", SqlDbType.Int, 4),
                  new SqlParameter("@TrueNavigateUrl", SqlDbType.VarChar, 255),
                  new SqlParameter("@Description", SqlDbType.VarChar, 255),
                  new SqlParameter("@Active", SqlDbType.Bit) };

        parameters[0].Value = advertisementId;
        parameters[1].Value = trueNavigateUrl;
        parameters[2].Value = description;
        parameters[3].Value = active;

        RunProcedure("sp_AdsManager_UpdateAdvertisement", parameters,
                                                 out rowsAffected);

        Configuration.ModuleSettings settings =
                        Configuration.ModuleConfig.GetSettings();
```

In this next section of this method, we update the information contained in the AdRotator's XML file. This is a bit trickier than creating the original <Ad> element in the Create method. In order to update a single element in a database or file, we need to *locate* the item we're updating. In an RDBMS we do this by supplying a key, or some information about the row that is entirely unique to that row only.

The AdRotator XML file doesn't contain any support for numeric identifiers. We didn't want to modify the format of the AdRotator XML file – that would negate the purpose of reusing an existing control. However, we do know that the database ID of an advertisement is stored in the NavigateUrl element. Therefore, we're going to use the NavigateUrl element as our unique key and we'll use a little XPath to find the appropriate element:

```
        XmlDocument rotatorDom = new XmlDocument();
        rotatorDom.Load(rotatorFile);
```

```
    string xPathFind = "//Ad[NavigateUrl=\"" + settings.PassThroughPage +
                          "?AD=" + advertisementId.ToString() +"\"]";

    XmlElement currentAd =
        (XmlElement)rotatorDom.DocumentElement.SelectSingleNode(xPathFind);
    XmlElement temp;
    temp = (XmlElement)currentAd.SelectSingleNode("ImageUrl");
    temp.InnerText = imageUrl;

    temp = (XmlElement)currentAd.SelectSingleNode("AlternateText");
    temp.InnerText = alternateText;

    temp = (XmlElement)currentAd.SelectSingleNode("Keyword");
    temp.InnerText = keyword;

    temp = (XmlElement)currentAd.SelectSingleNode("Impressions");
    temp.InnerText = impressions.ToString();

    rotatorDom.Save(rotatorFile);
  }
}
}
```

The Business Layer

The advertising module only deals with keeping track of advertisements, and as such shouldn't have an overly complex object model. Our business tier is also a small one, consisting of only two main classes: `AdMaster` and `Advertisement`. The following sections give a detailed description and source listing of each of the classes in our business layer. But before we get into the source code for the classes in this project, let's actually create the project. To do this, we create a new Class Library and add it to the current solution (ThePhile). Then, we set the default namespace and output file to `Wrox.WebModules.AdsManager.Business`.

The AdMaster Class

The `AdMaster` class in the business layer is a layer of abstraction on top of the `AdMaster` class in the data services tier. It implements four methods:

- ❑ Default constructor.

- ❑ **GetCompanyList** – this method obtains a list of all companies in the system. It is sorted alphabetically. It is a simple forwarded call to the data tier to populate a `DataSet`.

- ❑ **GetAdList** – this method obtains a list of all advertisements in the system. It is a forwarded call to the data tier to populate a `DataSet`.

- ❑ **CreateCompany** – a method with no return value that creates a new company in the database by forwarding the call to the data tier.

```
using System;
using System.Data;
using Wrox.WebModules.AdsManager;

namespace Wrox.WebModules.AdsManager.Business
{
  /// <summary>
  /// Summary description for AdMaster.
  /// </summary>
  public class AdMaster
  {
    public AdMaster()
    { }

    public DataSet GetCompanyList()
    {
      AdsManager.Data.AdMaster admaster = new AdsManager.Data.AdMaster(
                Configuration.ModuleConfig.GetSettings().ConnectionString);
      return admaster.GetCompanyList();
    }

    public DataSet GetAdList()
    {
      AdsManager.Data.AdMaster admaster = new AdsManager.Data.AdMaster(
                Configuration.ModuleConfig.GetSettings().ConnectionString);
      return admaster.GetAdList();
    }

    public void CreateCompany( string companyName )
    {
      AdsManager.Data.AdMaster admaster = new AdsManager.Data.AdMaster(
                Configuration.ModuleConfig.GetSettings().ConnectionString);
      admaster.CreateCompany( companyName );
    }
  }
}
```

The Advertisement Class

The Advertisement class is the core component in our business tier. It is added as a new class in our
AdsManagerBusiness project. It is responsible for handling all of the activities that can take place
with regard to an advertisement, such as creation, deletion, updating, and recording clicks and
impressions. Most calls are forwards to the data tier, though some logic often takes place before the call
to the data services component:

```
using System;
using System.Web;
using System.Data;
using System.Xml;
using Wrox.WebModules.Business;

namespace Wrox.WebModules.AdsManager.Business
{
```

```
public class Advertisement: Wrox.WebModules.Business.BizObject
{
  private string imageUrl;
  private string navigateUrl;
  private string alternateText;
  private string keyword;
  private int impressions;
  private string trueNavigateUrl;
  private int advertisementId;
  private int companyId;
  private bool isActive;
  private string description;

  public Advertisement()
  {
    // constructor used when creating an empty instance.
  }

  public Advertisement(int advertId)
  {
    HttpContext context = HttpContext.Current;
    Configuration.ModuleSettings settings =
                              Configuration.ModuleConfig.GetSettings();
    string xPathFind = "//Ad[NavigateUrl=\"" +
            settings.PassThroughPage + "?AD=" + advertId.ToString() +"\"]";

    Data.Advertisement ad =
                       new Data.Advertisement(settings.ConnectionString);
    DataRow advertData = ad.RetrieveAd(advertId);

    advertisementId = advertId;
    description = (string)advertData["Description"];
    trueNavigateUrl = (string)advertData["TrueNavigateUrl"];
    isActive = (bool)advertData["Active"];
    companyId = (int)advertData["CompanyID"];
```

As we saw in our previous discussion of the data services component, the data is split between the database and the XML file. The following code will use the XPath method to search for a unique NavigateUrl element in the XML document and then retrieve the appropriate information into private members used to populate properties:

```
    // now fill up the rest of the properties with information from the
    // XML file.
    XmlDocument adDom = new XmlDocument();
    adDom.Load(context.Server.MapPath(settings.RotatorXmlFile));
    XmlElement adCurrent =
            (XmlElement)adDom.DocumentElement.SelectSingleNode(xPathFind);
    if (adCurrent == null)
      throw new InvalidOperationException("Advertisement Selected Does not
                                   Exist in Rotator XML Source");

    imageUrl = adCurrent.SelectSingleNode("ImageUrl").InnerText;
    navigateUrl = adCurrent.SelectSingleNode("NavigateUrl").InnerText;
```

```
      alternateText = adCurrent.SelectSingleNode("AlternateText").InnerText;
      keyword = adCurrent.SelectSingleNode("Keyword").InnerText;
      impressions =
         Convert.ToInt32(adCurrent.SelectSingleNode("Impressions").InnerText);
   }

   public void RecordImpression()
   {
      Configuration.ModuleSettings settings =
                              Configuration.ModuleConfig.GetSettings();
      Data.Advertisement currentAd =
                        new Data.Advertisement(settings.ConnectionString);
      currentAd.RecordImpression(advertisementId);
   }

   public void RecordClick()
   {
      Configuration.ModuleSettings settings =
                              Configuration.ModuleConfig.GetSettings();
      Data.Advertisement currentAd =
                        new Data.Advertisement(settings.ConnectionString);
      currentAd.RecordClick(advertisementId);
   }

   public void Create()
   {
      HttpContext context = HttpContext.Current;
      Configuration.ModuleSettings settings =
                              Configuration.ModuleConfig.GetSettings();
      Data.Advertisement newAd =
                        new Data.Advertisement(settings.ConnectionString);
      newAd.Create(imageUrl, trueNavigateUrl, alternateText,
                    keyword, companyId, description,
                    context.Server.MapPath(settings.RotatorXmlFile));
   }

   public void Update()
   {
      HttpContext context = HttpContext.Current;
      Configuration.ModuleSettings settings =
                              Configuration.ModuleConfig.GetSettings();
      Data.Advertisement currentAd =
                        new Data.Advertisement(settings.ConnectionString);
      currentAd.Update(advertisementId, imageUrl, trueNavigateUrl,
                    alternateText, keyword, description,
                    impressions, isActive,
                    context.Server.MapPath( settings.RotatorXmlFile));
   }
```

In this next section we've used the #region meta-command to indicate a collapsible **region** of code. Regions are used to logically differentiate large blocks of code from each other to make viewing the source code in Visual Studio .NET easier. It significantly reduces time wasted trying to locate a block of code when you can collapse the regions of code you don't need to look at. We've also cut out most of the properties, since displaying the code for all of the properties would be a waste of space.

```
#region Publicly Exposed Properties

  public int Impressions
  {
    get
    {
      return impressions;
    }
    set
    {
      impressions = value;
    }
  }

#endregion
  }
}
```

The Presentation Layer

Our presentation layer consists of several ASP pages and the code-behind classes that support them. Keep in mind that all our changes and additions to the presentation tier take place in the original "ThePhile" web application project that is part of our main solution. In addition, we've made some changes to the SiteFooter control in order to facilitate the display of our banner ads. The following is a list of the elements that comprise our presentation tier:

❑ Admin.aspx [.cs] – main page of the advertising administration system. Displays the list of advertisements in a data grid and contains links for creating ads and entries for companies.

❑ AdDetail.aspx [.cs] – web page and related code-behind class to display and edit the details of a given advertisement.

❑ NewAd.aspx [.cs] – web form for creating a new advertisement.

❑ NewCompany.aspx [.cs] – web form for creating a new entry for a company.

❑ Passthrough.aspx [.cs] – pass-through page (discussed next) facilitating proper auditing of hits on banner advertisements.

The Pass-through Page

Despite the fact that this page has absolutely no user interface, it is the most important part of the entire advertising module. Without this page the advertising module cannot function at all.

The purpose of this page is to accept an incoming request that contains a single URL parameter, called AD. This parameter contains the numeric ID of a particular advertisement that has been clicked. The page then looks up the advertisement in the database to find out the *actual* destination intended for the advertisement. Once this information has been obtained, the page records a click on the advertisement in the database and redirects the user to the appropriate advertiser's product or home page.

To see how this works, take a look at the Page_Load event of the `Passthrough.aspx.cs` file:

```
private void Page_Load(object sender, System.EventArgs e)
{
  AdsBusiness.Advertisement currentAd =
              new AdsBusiness.Advertisement(Convert.ToInt32(Request["AD"]));
  currentAd.RecordClick();
  Response.Redirect(currentAd.TrueNavigateUrl);
}
```

The New SiteFooter Control

In order to get the advertisements to appear all over our site without having to rewrite too much of our existing code, we're going to modify the `SiteFooter` control. Because we built all of the pages to use the footer control to begin with, only a few changes are required in order to display our `AdRotator` control.

Take a look at the new code for the `SiteFooter` control (`SiteFooter.ascx`), which replaces the original:

```
<%@ Control Language="c#" AutoEventWireup="false"
            Codebehind="SiteFooter.ascx.cs"
            Inherits="Wrox.ThePhile.Web.Controls.User.SiteFooter"
            TargetSchema="http://schemas.microsoft.com/intellisense/ie5" %>
<table width="100%" border="0" cellspacing="0" cellpadding="0">
<tr>
  <td align="middle">
    <font face="arial" size="1">
      <br><br>
      <asp:AdRotator ID=Rotator Runat=server
                     AdvertisementFile="/ThePhile/Config/AdRotator.xml"/>
      <br>
      <i>Copyright &copy; 2001-2002 Wrox Press Ltd.</i><br>
      <a href="Contact.aspx">Contact Us</a> | Support | FAQ | Forums |
                            Newsletter | Voting | Your Account
    </font>
  </td>
</tr>
</table>
```

We've added an `<asp:AdRotator>` control, given it a name (ID), and pointed it to the appropriate XML file. This XML file is also indicated by the `AdsManager` configuration object.

Putting the `AdRotator` in the page as we've shown above gives us the ability to track clicks and display the ad, but it isn't quite complete if we need to track impressions (displays). In order to do that, we need to provide a handler for the `AdCreated` event, which is listed below (found in the code-behind class in `SiteFooter.ascx.cs`):

```
private void Rotator_AdCreated(object sender,
                       System.Web.UI.WebControls.AdCreatedEventArgs e)
{
  int advertId;
string adnumber;
  int eqPos;
```

```
eqPos = e.NavigateUrl.IndexOf("=");
adnumber = e.NavigateUrl.Substring(eqPos+1,
                                    e.NavigateUrl.Length- eqPos-1);
advertId = Convert.ToInt32(adnumber);
AdsBusiness.Advertisement currentAd =
                              new AdsBusiness.Advertisement(advertId);
currentAd.RecordImpression();
}
```

In the code above, we need to determine *which* advertisement has been displayed. As we said earlier, the default implementation of the AdRotator control doesn't support numbering or keying of individual advertisements. Therefore, to find the database ID of the advertisement that was displayed we need to extrapolate it from other information. For the duration of this event, we have access to the standard information about the advertisement, such as the NavigateUrl property. We know that this property contains the AD parameter to send to the pass-through page. The above code extracts that value from the URL and uses it to create a new instance of the advertisement class in order to record the impression.

You may have noticed by now that the RecordImpression and RecordClick methods both eventually call the database. This means that every time the SiteFooter control is displayed on the bottom of a page, a call to the stored procedure is made to record an impression. This is a little on the inefficient side. As an exercise, you might want to consider ways to speed up this process and make it more efficient for recording clicks and impressions. One option might be to maintain an in-memory cache of clicks and impressions, and periodically flush that cache to the database rather than make a database call every single time an impression or a click takes place.

Administering Advertisements

There are two things we can do with advertisements: display them and administer them. We've already seen how to display the advertisements, and we've seen the business and data components that enable the administration. Now let's take a look at implementing the administration system.

Admin.aspx

This page should be treated as the default page for the administration section of the advertising module. It displays a list of all of the advertisements in the database in a DataGrid that is coded to support data paging. It also allows us to click a link in that DataGrid to drill down into a detailed view page. There are links to create companies and advertisements from here. Here is a screenshot of the advertisement administration main page:

You can see from the above screenshot that there is a single advertisement currently in the database. This particular advertisement is one that links back to the Wrox Press home page. You can see the advertisement indicated by the DataGrid displayed at the bottom of the page in the SiteFooter control.

Let's take a look at the HTML code in the ASPX page that creates the DataGrid:

```
<asp:DataGrid id=dgAdvertisements
              runat="server"
              AutoGenerateColumns="False"
              BorderColor="Tan"
              BorderWidth="1px"
              BackColor="LightGoldenrodYellow"
              CellPadding="2"
              GridLines="None"
              AllowPaging="True"
              PageSize="15"
              ForeColor="Black">

  <SelectedItemStyle
    ForeColor="GhostWhite"
    BackColor="DarkSlateBlue">
```

```
      </SelectedItemStyle>

      <AlternatingItemStyle
        BackColor="PaleGoldenrod">
      </AlternatingItemStyle>

      <HeaderStyle
        Font-Bold="True"
        BackColor="Tan">
      </HeaderStyle>

      <FooterStyle
        BackColor="Tan">
      </FooterStyle>

      <Columns>
        <asp:ButtonColumn Text="Details"
          HeaderText="Details"
          CommandName="Details">
        </asp:ButtonColumn>

        <asp:BoundColumn
          DataField="CompanyName"
          HeaderText="Company">
        </asp:BoundColumn>
        <asp:BoundColumn
          DataField="Description"
          HeaderText="Advertisement">
        </asp:BoundColumn>
        <asp:BoundColumn
          Visible="False"
          DataField="AdvertisementID">
        </asp:BoundColumn>
      </Columns>

      <PagerStyle
        HorizontalAlign="Center"
        ForeColor="DarkSlateBlue"
        BackColor="DarkKhaki"
        Mode="NumericPages">
      </PagerStyle>
    </asp:DataGrid>
```

The DataGrid uses a ButtonColumn, has defined a PagerStyle, and has enabled the AllowPaging flag.

The ButtonColumn is a custom templated column that allows programmers to place a button in a DataGrid column and give the button access to the information contained within the DataGrid. In our case, the ButtonColumn redirects the user to the AdDetail.aspx page, allowing the user to edit an existing advertisement. It does this by providing a handler for the ItemCommand event in the DataGrid, which is triggered when a command button is clicked on a row. Here is the method that handles the ItemCommand event in Admin.aspx.cs:

```
private void dgAdvertisements_ItemCommand(object source,
                    System.Web.UI.WebControls.DataGridCommandEventArgs e)
{
  if (e.CommandName == "Details")
  {
    string Id = e.Item.Cells[3].Text;
    Response.Redirect("AdDetail.aspx?AD=" + Id);
  }
}
```

Only one ItemCommand event handler is used for the entire DataGrid, regardless of how many ButtonColumns are used. The items differentiate themselves by providing a CommandName property. Therefore, we check if the CommandName property of the command was "Details". If so, then we can continue. The first thing we do is to obtain the ID of the advertisement clicked. This is accomplished by getting the value of the last bound column in the row. This particular column is hidden, allowing us to make the ID easily available without cluttering up our display with information the end user might find useless or confusing.

Next we need to support paging across a large result set. The stored procedure for obtaining the list of advertisements pulls the entire set, so it is possible that the UI would get cluttered extremely fast without providing support for paging. Just simply enabling the AllowPaging property on the DataGrid isn't quite enough to support paging. We need to provide a handler for the PageIndexChanged event, which is listed below:

```
private void dgAdvertisements_PageIndexChanged(object source,
                    System.Web.UI.WebControls.DataGridPageChangedEventArgs e)
{
  dgAdvertisements.CurrentPageIndex = e.NewPageIndex;

  DoDataBind();
}
```

First we obtain the new page index, and then we bind the DataGrid accordingly, having set its current page index to the new page. This allows the grid to move to the right page within the data set. The following is a listing for the DoDataBind method in Admin.aspx.cs, which binds the data to the DataGrid:

```
private void DoDataBind()
{
  AdsBusiness.AdMaster admaster = new AdsBusiness.AdMaster();
  DataSet Advertisements;
  Advertisements = admaster.GetAdList();
  dgAdvertisements.DataSource = Advertisements.Tables[0];
  dgAdvertisements.DataBind();
}
```

AdDetail.aspx

We've seen how the main page, which displays a list of advertisements and allows us to drill down to edit an existing one, was made. Now let's take a look at the AdDetail.aspx page. After clicking the Details link on the DataGrid, the user is presented with a pre-populated web form like this:

It looks like a pretty standard input form. It presents the user with all the fields they can edit (as well as displaying a read-only company dropdown, an example of the UI enforcing a business rule) and then presents the user with Save and Cancel buttons. The Cancel button takes the user back to the Admin page, while the Save button will commit the changes both to the database and to the rotator XML file. The UI makes no visible distinction as to which data is stored in the XML file and which data is stored in the database. That boundary is completely invisible to the presentation layer.

Let's take a look at the code that sets up the pre-population for the form:

```
private void DoDataBind()
{
  AdsBusiness.Advertisement currentAd =
            new AdsBusiness.Advertisement(Convert.ToInt32(Request["AD"]));
  AdsBusiness.AdMaster admaster= new AdsBusiness.AdMaster();
  DataSet companies = admaster.GetCompanyList();

  lbCompanies.DataSource = companies.Tables[0];
  lbCompanies.DataTextField = "Description";
  lbCompanies.DataValueField = "CompanyID";
  lbCompanies.DataBind();
  lbCompanies.SelectedIndex =
          lbCompanies.Items.IndexOf(
          lbCompanies.Items.FindByValue(currentAd.CompanyID.ToString() ));
  Description.Text = currentAd.Description;
  ImageUrl.Text = currentAd.ImageUrl;
```

```
      TrueNavigateUrl.Text = currentAd.TrueNavigateUrl;
      Keyword.Text = currentAd.KeyWord;
      Impressions.Text = currentAd.Impressions.ToString();
      AlternateText.Text = currentAd.AlternateText;
      Active.Checked = currentAd.IsActive;
   }
```

The method is called `DoDataBind` more out of convention than anything else – not much binding is going on. The `Text` property of the input controls is being manually set to the data retrieved from the instance of the advertisement. The only binding happening is the binding of the company dropdown list to the list of companies retrieved by the `AdMaster` object. Because we are editing a single record, and will only ever save or cancel, the 'pre-populate' approach is better.

When editing an advertisement, the company dropdown listbox is disabled. This establishes a business rule preventing the company ownership of an advertisement campaign.

When the user has finished making changes, they click the **Save** button and trigger the following event (`SaveChanges_Click`, a button click handler):

```
   private void SaveChanges_Click(object sender, System.EventArgs e)
   {
      // save the input of the current form as changes to an existing
      // advertisement
      int advertId = Convert.ToInt32(Request["AD"]);
      AdsBusiness.Advertisement currentAd =
                                     new AdsBusiness.Advertisement(advertId);

      currentAd.AlternateText = AlternateText.Text;
      currentAd.Description = Description.Text;
      currentAd.ImageUrl = ImageUrl.Text;
      currentAd.Impressions = Convert.ToInt32(Impressions.Text);
      currentAd.IsActive = Active.Checked;
      currentAd.KeyWord = Keyword.Text;
      currentAd.TrueNavigateUrl = TrueNavigateUrl.Text;
      currentAd.Update();
      Response.Redirect("Admin.aspx");
   }
```

NewAd.aspx

This page works much like the `AdDetail.aspx` page. However, it doesn't allow you to set the value of the `Impressions` property (that is set to 1 for all newly created advertisements). It also doesn't allow you to choose the `Active` checkbox because a newly created advertisement is considered active by default. The following is a screenshot of the "New Advertisement" web form:

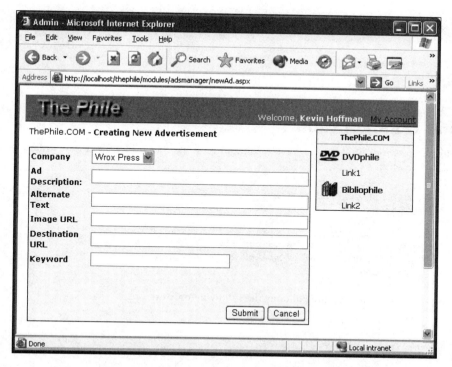

Again, the only binding we're going to use on this form is going to be for the dropdown list. This is done in our `DoInitialDataBind` method, shown below (from `NewAd.aspx.cs`):

```
private void DoInitialDataBind()
{
  Wrox.WebModules.AdsManager.Business.AdMaster adMaster =
                       new Wrox.WebModules.AdsManager.Business.AdMaster();
  Companies = adMaster.GetCompanyList();
  lbCompanies.DataSource = Companies.Tables[0];
  lbCompanies.DataTextField = "Description";
  lbCompanies.DataValueField = "CompanyID";
  lbCompanies.DataBind();
}
```

When the user has completed the form and is ready to create the new advertisement, this code handles the `Click` event of the **Submit** button:

```
private void OKButton_Click(object sender, System.EventArgs e)
{
  Ads.Business.Advertisement newAd = new Ads.Business.Advertisement();
  newAd.ImageUrl = ImageUrl.Text;
  newAd.Description = Description.Text;
  newAd.TrueNavigateUrl = NavigateUrl.Text;
  newAd.KeyWord = Keyword.Text;
```

```
    newAd.AlternateText = AlternateText.Text;
    newAd.CompanyID =
         Convert.ToInt32(lbCompanies.Items[lbCompanies.SelectedIndex].Value);
    newAd.Create();
    Response.Redirect("Admin.aspx");
}
```

Module Configuration

As with the previous modules we have a configuration file that is identified in the main `Web.Config` in the following way:

```
<!-- LOCAL APPLICATION SETTINGS -->
   <appSettings>
     <add key="Accounts_SettingsFile"
          value="/ThePhile/Config/Accounts.Config"/>
     <add key="AdsManager_SettingsFile"
          value="/ThePhile/Config/AdsManager.Config"/>
   </appSettings>
```

The `AdsManager.Config` file contains the following entries:

```
<?xml version="1.0"?>
<ModuleSettings xmlns:xsi="http://www.w3.org/2001/XMLSchema-instance"
                xmlns:xsd="http://www.w3.org/2001/XMLSchema">
  <ConnectionString>server=(local);database=ThePhile;uid=sa;pwd=;
  </ConnectionString>
  <RotatorXmlFile>/ThePhile/Config/AdRotator.Xml</RotatorXmlFile>
  <PassThroughPage>/ThePhile/Modules/AdsManager/PassThrough.aspx
  </PassThroughPage>
</ModuleSettings>
```

As you can see, it contains its own database connection string to allow for maximum flexibility. If, for some reason, an administrator wanted the advertising database to be separate from all the others, then the only requirement would be to change the connection string in this config file. There are definitions for the rotator XML file (which we have already covered in detail) and for the pass-through page.

The source code for the module configuration class files has been covered already in this book and by now you should be able to determine what the property definitions for the `ModuleSettings` class might look like for the above XML file.

Summary

Advertising is an interesting and exciting facet of doing business on the web. Many websites pay their bills by offering advertising. Website owners and administrators can track the demographics of their audience and use that information to convince advertisers that paying for impressions on their site is a worthwhile investment. Those same administrators can also keep track of how many impressions and clicks a particular advertisement receives and use that information to bill the client (advertiser).

After reading this chapter, you should have a solid understanding of:

❑ Storing information on advertisements by aggregating both XML and RDBMS data in the data layer, hiding the distinction from the business layer.

❑ Keeping audit trails of clicks and impressions by trapping events in the `AdRotator` control and doing some data warehousing in the database.

❑ Providing sufficient information to advertisers to prove ad effectiveness (or lack of) by providing a stored procedure designed to pull reporting information from the data warehouse.

So far we've looked at several ways of providing our site visitors with information. In the next chapter we'll show how to find out what our readers think, by implementing an opinion polls module.

8

Polls

In this chapter we'll discuss polls – which comprise a question with a set of optional responses that the user can select from and vote for. First we'll recap why polls are useful and important for different websites. We'll then demonstrate how to design and implement an easily pluggable and maintainable voting module for our ThePhile.com site. We'll also show how to make it accessible to external clients, such as other sites or Windows programs, via a web service.

The Problem

We briefly discussed the benefits of polls in Chapter 1. To recap, sites that provide a poll usually do so because they are interested in what people think. They use polls as a form of user-to-site communication because they want views on the products they sell or review, or opinions about the market in general, or they want to know who the users are, their age, their occupation, and other demographic information. Good polls always contain targeted questions that can help the site's managers to know who their users are and what they want to find on their site. This information can be used to identify which parts of the site to improve.

Polls are valuable for e-commerce sites too, because they can indicate which products have higher interest and demand. Armed with this information, e-commerce businesses can highlight those products, provide more detailed descriptions or case studies, or offer discounts to convince users to buy from their site.

Another use for the information is to attract advertising revenue. If you look on any middle to large site the chances are that you'll see an "Advertise with us" link, or something similar. On that page you'll probably find information about the age of the typical users, the regions or countries they live in, and sometimes also their average income. This information is often gathered by direct or indirect polls. The more details you provide about your typical audience, the more chance you have of finding a sponsor to advertise on your site.

Another benefit is user-to-user communication. Users generally like to know what their peers think about a product or a subject of interest to them, and maybe even how much they earn! I must admit that I'm usually curious when I see a poll on a website. Even if I don't have a very clear opinion about the question being asked, I vote, often because I want to know which is the most popular response! This explains why polls are usually well accepted, and why users generally vote quite willingly.

> *Another reason why users might be willing to vote is that they may feel that their choice has some significance for the people behind the scenes. And the votes actually are important; as we've seen, the results can drive the future content of the site and other decisions.*

We want the benefits of a poll facility for ThePhile.com, and therefore want to implement some form of poll on the website. Now we should consider some further details about web polls, namely the problems that we must address to successfully run a polling system.

First of all, as for the news and other content, the same poll shouldn't remain active for too long. If we leave the same poll on the page for, say, two months, we might gather some more votes, but we risk losing the interest of users who voted early on. Neither can we keep a poll up for just a couple of days, at least not if we want to achieve significant results. The right duration depends mostly on the average number of visitors we have and how often they come back to visit the site. As a rough guide, if we know that several thousands of users regularly come to visit the site each week, then that is a good duration for the active poll. Otherwise, if we have less visitors, we can leave the poll for two or more weeks, but probably never longer than a month.

> *In case you're wondering how to get the information you need to make this decision, there are several services that allow you to easily retrieve statistics for your site, such as the frequency and the number of visitors, and much more. Some of these services are commercial, but you can also find some good ones for free: examples are www.extremetracking.com, www.sitemeter.com, and www.fastcounter.com, but there are others. Most of these services give you some information for free, while other statistics (such as visitors by search engine and search word, client browser information, traffic forecast, etc.) are subscription-based. Of course you could implement your own hit counter – it would be pretty easy to track visitors and generate some basic statistics, but to reproduce all the advanced features sold by specialized services would involve quite a lot of work, and it would probably be cheaper to subscribe to the professional/advanced plan of one of the services mentioned above.*

When you change the active poll, a new question arises – what to do with the old questions and their results. Should we throw them away? Certainly not! They might be very interesting for new users who didn't take part in the vote, and the information will probably remain valid for some time, so we should keep them available for viewing. They can even be considered as part of the content of our site, and we should probably build an archive of past polls.

If we allow a user to vote however many times they want to, we'll end up with incorrect results. The vote will be biased towards that user's personal opinion. Having false results is just as useless as having no results at all, since we can't base any serious decisions on them. Therefore, in general we will want to prevent the user from voting more than once for the same question.

However, there are occasions when we might want to allow the user to vote several times. For example, during the development and testing stage, we may need to post many votes to see if the module works well. The administrator could just manually add some votes through the Enterprise Manager's table viewer, or by directly calling the appropriate stored procedure. But using the polling user interface that we'll build is a much more convenient method, that more thoroughly tests the module, so we want to leave this door open.

There are reasons for wanting to allow multiple votes after deployment too. Imagine that we are running a competition to select the best resource on any selected topic, and the list of these resources (external sites, our site's sections, downloads, etc.) is updated weekly, and the competition lasts one month. If we prevented multiple votes we would have to create a new poll for each of the four weeks, and after one month we would need to add together the results of the four distinct polls to get the final winner. There wouldn't be much extra work to do, but it's not very elegant. A better and quicker solution would be to have only one poll for the entire month, but allow the user to re-vote, with the limitation of one vote per week. This way, at the end of the month we will have the final results without doing anything else.

In this discussion we're talking about polls that only allow a single option to be selected (those poll boxes with a series of radio buttons). However, there is also another type of poll that allows the user to vote for multiple options in a single step (the options are listed with checkboxes, and you can select more than one). This might be useful if you wanted to ask a question like "What do you usually buy online?" and you wanted to allow the user to answer "books, DVDs, games, etc." through multiple separate options. However, this type of poll is quite rare. The design of this type of poll would complicate our module, so we decided to leave it out. But be aware that they exist, and you may want to use them in situations like the one mentioned above.

So in summary our problem definition is that we want to implement a poll facility on our site to gauge the opinions of our users and to generate a sense of community. We don't want users to lose interest but we want the results to be significant, so we will need to add new questions and change the current poll sufficiently often. We also want to generate content for our site, so we'd like to make all the results available for viewing. Finally, we want to control the voting so the results are as unbiased and accurate as possible.

In the next section we're going to discuss the design in more detail, and consider how we will solve these problems.

The Design

As usual, in this section we're going to work on the design of the solution. We'll be looking at how we can provide voting functionality for our site. This module – like most of the others presented in the previous chapters – stores the data (questions, answers, votes, etc.) in the database shared by all modules of this book. To easily access the database we'll need a set of stored procedures and a data access layer, and a business layer to keep the presentation layer separate from the database and the details of its structure. Of course there will be some sort of user interface that allows the administrators to view and manage the data through their favorite browser.

To start with we'll list the features we want to implement, then we'll begin to design any database tables, stored procedures, data and business layers, user interface services, and security that we need for this module.

Features to Implement

Let's start our discussion by writing down a list of features that the polls module should provide:

❏   In order to easily change the current poll and add or remove questions, the administrator will need an access-protected administration console. It should allow multiple questions, and their options, to be added, edited, or removed. The ability to have multiple questions is important, because we might want to have different polls in different sections of our site. The administration pages should also show the current results for each option, and the total number of votes for each question.

❏   A user control that builds the poll box that can be inserted into any page. The poll box should display the question text and the available options (usually rendered as radio buttons to allow only one choice). Each question will be identified by a unique ID, which should be specified as a custom property for the user control, so that the web master can easily change the currently displayed question by setting the value for that property.

❏   We should prevent the user from voting multiple times for the same poll. Or, even better, we should be able to dynamically decide if we want to allow the user to vote more than once, and specify the period for which they will be prevented from voting again. We'll further discuss why we might want to do this in the next section.

❏   We can have only one poll (question) declared as current. When we set a question as being current, the question that was previously the current one should change its state. The current poll will be displayed unless we specify another question ID for the poll box. Any non-archived poll can be displayed. Of course we can have different polls on the site at the same time depending on the section (one for DVDs and one for books, for example), but setting the default question is useful because we'll be able to add a poll box without specifying the ID of the question to display (through the custom property mentioned above). We'll also be able to change the question through the administration console, without manually changing the page and re-uploading it.

❏   A poll should be archived when we decide that we no longer want to use it. Once archived, a question cannot be displayed even if we explicitly declare its ID for the poll box.

❏   A page that displays all the archived polls and their results. We don't need a page for the results of the current poll, since we want to show them in the poll box – instead of the list of options – when we detect that the user has already voted. This way, the users are forced to express their opinion if they want to see the current poll's results. (Once the poll expires it will be archived and anyone can see the results even if they haven't voted.) You can bet this will bring in more votes than if the current results were freely available to users that have not voted.

Shortly we'll see the database tables for this module, and the respective stored procedures. The administration pages don't require further discussion here. The ASP.NET pages of this section are merely a handy user interface for managing the database records through the stored procedures.

As for the user control that creates the poll box, it will be discussed in more detail a bit later, after describing the database tables and stored procedures. What we need to discuss at this point, before starting to think about the database design, is how to handle multiple votes.

Handling Multiple Votes

We discussed above that we want to be able to control whether users can cast multiple votes, and allow them to vote again after a specified period. It would be pretty cool to do this, and we like to implement cool things, so we decided to do it!

So, we want to give the administrator the ability to prevent multiple votes, or to allow multiple votes but with a specified lock duration (one week in the example above). We still have to find a way to ensure that the user does not vote more times than is allowed. The simplest solution is to write a **cookie** to the client that stores the ID of the question for which the user has voted. Then, when the poll box loads, it will first try to find a cookie matching the question. If a cookie is not found the poll box will display the options and the user can vote. Otherwise, the poll box will show the latest results and not allow the user to vote again. To allow multiple votes, the cookie must have an expiration date. If we set it to the current date plus seven days, it means that in seven days time the user will be allowed to re-vote.

Writing and checking cookies is really straightforward, and in most cases it is sufficient. In *most cases*, unfortunately not all cases. The drawback of this method is that the user can easily turn off cookies through a browser option, or delete the cookies from their machine, and then be allowed to vote however many times they want to. (Only a very small percentage of users keep cookies turned off– except for company users where security is a major concern – since they are used on many sites and are sometimes actually required.)

However, there is an alternative method for preventing multiple votes: **IP locking**. When the user votes, their computer's IP address can be retrieved and stored in the database together with the other vote details. Later, when the poll box loads or when the user tries to vote again, we can run a query that returns the records matching both the current computer's IP address and the question ID. If a record is found, the user has already voted and we can prevent further voting. The expiration date can be saved as an additional field in the database table.

There is yet another option. We could track the logged users through their ID, instead of their computer's IP address. However, this will only work if the user is registered. We don't want to limit the vote to registered users only, and will not cover this last method in practice in this chapter. It is an additional option you could add in future if required.

In our module we'll provide the option to employ both the cookie and IP locking methods, only one of them, or neither. Employing neither of them means that we will allow multiple votes with no limitations, and this should only be used during the testing stage. In a real scenario we might need to disable one method. Say that we run the application on an intranet, and that the computers that access the pages with the poll are in a lab. Several users share each computer (students for example, who don't have their own PC). Each user has his own account, so the cookies are not shared, but the IP is static. This means that if we employ IP checking, only the first user to access the application with that computer can vote. IP locking is usually fine when employed on a LAN where you can be reasonably sure that any user has their own computer. However, this will not prevent people from using multiple machines to vote multiple times if they really want to do so. Another issue about IP locking is that if the user gets a dynamic IP from their ISP, every time they disconnect and reconnect, they will get a new IP, so this locking strategy won't have any effect. Yet another case where IP locking causes problems is when someone is surfing with a group through a proxy, because they would always echo the IP of the proxy, regardless of the machine that they were surfing on. IP locking is fine on an intranet but on the Internet can be awkward for this reason. That is why we decided to let the administrator decide which methods should be employed, according to the particular situation.

In conclusion, the polls module will have the following options:

- ❏ Multiple votes can be allowed

- ❏ Multiple votes can be prevented with client cookies or IP locking or a combination of the two methods

- ❏ Limited multiple votes can be allowed, in which case the administrator can specify a lock duration for either method

This way, the polls module will be flexible and can be used with the options that best suit the particular situation.

Designing the Database Tables

Having a precise list of features to implement is fundamental to designing tables from scratch (although this might be impossible with large systems that grow over time). Basically, we need to store questions, options, and votes. At first we might think that two tables would be enough: one for the questions and another for the options, with a column for the number of votes, incremented every time a user votes for that option. However, we've said that we want to store information about the user that voted, such as the IP address and the date, and of course this additional data can't be stored together with the options – we must have a separate table that contains all the details of any vote. So we need at least three tables. You may also suggest a further **linking table** (also known as an associate table) in order to create a many-to-many relationship between the questions and the options tables. This could be useful if we wanted to use the same options, such as simple "yes" and "no" answers, for multiple questions. However, this would make it more difficult to store and retrieve the votes, because it would no longer be possible to identify an option by its ID, but it would be necessary to use the option's ID plus the question's ID, since the same option could be shared by several questions. Furthermore, short and general answers such as "yes" and "no" are not as useful as having more specific options. For these reasons, we decided to avoid the many-to-many relationship between the questions and options, and opted for a simpler one-to-many relationship. In conclusion, we need just three tables: one for the questions, one for the options for each question, and one for the votes. We have a good idea of the information we need to store in the database, now we're ready to design it.

As mentioned in previous chapters, we need a prefix for our module-specific tables, because we have only one SQL Server database, shared by the tables of all the modules in this project. The prefix for this module is `Polls_`. Let's see the diagram that shows the tables and their relationships, before describing them in more detail:

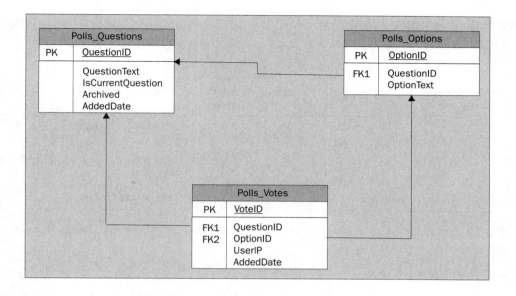

The Polls_Questions Table

The `Polls_Questions` table contains all the questions for the polls, and their attributes, such as whether they are the default question, and the archived status:

Column Name	Type	Size	Allow Null	Description
QuestionID	int - Identity primary key	4	No	The unique ID for the question.
QuestionText	varchar	150	No	The text of the question.
IsCurrentQuestion	bit	1	No	If true (1) this question is the default for the poll box, and is used when no other question ID is specified.
Archived	bit	1	No	If true (1) the question can no longer be used in the poll box but its results are still made accessible through an Archive page.
AddedDate	datetime	8	No	When the question was added.

The Polls_Options Table

The Polls_Options table contains the options (possible answers) for all the questions in the Polls_Questions table:

Column Name	Type	Size	Allow Null	Description
OptionID	int – Identity primary key	4	No	The unique ID for the option.
QuestionID	int foreign key	4	No	The ID of the question to which the option belongs.
OptionText	varchar	150	No	The text of the option.

This is a simple table that has a many-to-one relationship with the Polls_Questions table, through the QuestionID foreign key.

The Polls_Votes Table

The Polls_Votes table stores all the votes for each option, and some details that will be used to prevent multiple votes by the same user:

Column Name	Type	Size	Allow Null	Description
VoteID	int - Identity primary key	4	No	The unique ID for the vote.
QuestionID	int foreign key	4	No	The ID of the question for which the user has voted.
OptionID	int foreign key	4	No	The ID of the option to which the user has given their vote.
UserIP	varchar	15	No	The IP address of the user's computer.
AddedDate	datetime	8	No	When the vote was added.

We keep track of both the question and the specific option that the user has voted for. Both pieces of information are useful for counting how many votes there have been, for a question and for each option. You might think that retrieving the number of votes for each option by counting all the individual records with the specified OptionID is slower than incrementing a number in a field in the Polls_Options table (and the same for the total number of votes in the Polls_Questions table). However, our method makes the insertion of a new vote a bit faster, because we don't need to update other fields, and we also avoid the problems of potential concurrent updates – we actually add a new record for each new vote. Later in the chapter we'll also see how to avoid having to requery the database every time we display the results in the poll box, in order to save the time that would be required to recount the votes.

In addition, storing the ID of the question allows us to quickly count the total number of votes for a given question, and easily check if the user has already voted for it. Although we could find this out by looking at the OptionID they have voted for and matching this to a QuestionID, adding the extra ID directly to the Options_Votes table makes queries much faster. The user is identified by the IP address of their computer.

Finally, we store the date when the vote was added, and not the IP lock expiration date. This is more flexible, because we can dynamically change the lock duration and have the new duration applied not only to the future votes, but also to the current votes. In practice, the expiration date is calculated from the AddedDate column and a lock duration value supplied later in the code.

The Stored Procedures that Manage the Database

To manage the database we will build a set of stored procedures. We'll run these later in the data layer classes to do everything from the addition or deletion of questions, options, and votes, to the update of single fields. Here is the complete list of the stored procedures we'll build later, with their parameters:

Stored Procedure	Description
sp_Polls_GetQuestions	Returns all the questions or just the archived questions, according to the @ArchivedOnly parameter. The questions are sorted by date, in descending order (from the newest to the oldest).
sp_Polls_GetQuestionDetails	Returns the complete row for the specified question.
sp_Polls_GetCurrentQuestionID	Returns the ID of the current question, which is used as the default for the poll box when no other ID is explicitly set.
sp_Polls_SetCurrentQuestionID	Changes the ID of the current question. This means setting the IsCurrentQuestion field of the specified question to 1, and the field for all the other questions to 0.

Table continued on following page

Stored Procedure	Description
sp_Polls_InsertQuestion	Inserts a new question. If a question already exists with the same text, and it is not archived, the new question is not added and the output parameter is set to -1. Otherwise @QuestionID will be set to the new question's ID.
sp_Polls_UpdateQuestion	Updates all the fields of the question identified by the specified ID.
sp_Polls_SetQuestionArchived	Updates only the Archived field of the specified question.
sp_Polls_DeleteQuestion	Deletes the specified question.
sp_Polls_GetOptions	Returns all the options for the specified question.
sp_Polls_GetOptionDetails	Returns the complete row for the specified option.
sp_Polls_InsertOption	Inserts a new option for the specified question. If the question already has an option with the same text, the option is not added and @OptionID is set to -1, otherwise it is set to the added option's ID.
sp_Polls_UpdateOption	Updates all the fields of the specified option.
sp_Polls_DeleteOption	Deletes the specified option.
sp_Polls_GetVotes	Returns all the votes for the specified question.
sp_Polls_GetVoteDetails	Returns the complete row for the specified vote.
sp_Polls_GetUserVoteID	Sets the output parameter to the ID of the vote for the specified question, posted by the user identified by the IP address. If @VoteID is set to -1, it means that the user has not yet voted for that question.
sp_Polls_InsertVote	Inserts a new vote for the specified question, and also stores the ID of the option selected by the user.

Most of these stored procedures are simple ones that return, insert, delete, or update records in the various tables. The descriptions in the table above are sufficient for most of them, but there are a few points that are worth a better explanation here before proceeding:

❑ `sp_Polls_GetQuestions`, `sp_Polls_GetOptions`, and the two procedures that return only a single row, are a bit more complex than a plain SELECT query. They all add a dynamically calculated column, `TotalVotes`, which contains the number of votes for the questions and the options, respectively. Later, in the implementation section, we'll see how to do this.

❑ `sp_Polls_GetOptions` and `sp_Polls_GetOptionDetails` return a calculated data column, in addition to the `TotalVotes` column. The column is called `Percentage`, and it contains the votes for each option as a percentage of the total votes for the question.

❑ `sp_Polls_InsertVote` inserts the vote for the specified question and option. It does not check if the user has already voted. In fact, we might have chosen to allow multiple votes. Multiple votes are prevented, if necessary, by the business component that we'll see later.

Designing the Data Layer

Now that we have a clear picture of what the database tables store, and how we retrieve data through the stored procedures, we can design the data services. These are nothing but a set of classes that wrap calls to the stored procedures. In fact, you'll see that the methods of the classes have exactly the same parameters as the respective stored procedures.

These classes will be part of an assembly called `Wrox.WebModules.Polls.Data`, all under the `Wrox.WebModules.Polls.Data` namespace. As we've done in previous chapters, we inherit the data classes from `DbObject`, the base class from the `Core` assembly that we built in Chapter 2.

The QuestionDetails Class

This class has no methods – it just exposes six public fields that map the values of the five physical fields of the `Polls_Questions` table, plus the calculated column, `TotalVotes`. This class is used as a return type for a `GetDetails` method that, instead of returning a `DataRow` type, returns an instance of an object that exposes the values in an immediately accessible way.

The Questions Class

This class wraps calls to the stored procedures that manage the questions. Contrary to the class above, this one has only methods, whose return values are the values of the output parameters of the respective stored procedures, or a Boolean indicating whether the query succeeded. One method returns an instance of `QuestionDetails`.

Method Name	Description
`public Questions(string newConnectionString)`	Class constructor taking the connection string as a parameter.
`public DataSet GetQuestions()`	Returns a `DataSet` containing all the questions.

Table continued on following page

Method Name	Description
`public DataSet GetQuestions(bool archivedOnly)`	The same as above, but here we have the opportunity to specify if we only want the archived questions.
`public QuestionDetails GetDetails(int questionID)`	Returns an instance of `QuestionDetails` that describes the specified question.
`public DataRow GetDetailsRow(int questionID)`	Returns the `DataRow` of the question identified by the specified ID.
`public int GetCurrentID()`	Returns the ID of the current/default question, or -1 if there is no current question.
`public int Add(string questionText, bool isCurrentQuestion, bool archived)`	Adds a new question, and returns its ID, or -1 if the same question was already present.
`public bool Update(int questionID, string questionText, bool isCurrentQuestion, bool archived)`	Updates all the fields of the specified question.
`public bool SetArchived(int questionID, bool archived)`	Changes the `Archived` state of the specified question.
`public bool Delete(int questionID)`	Deletes the specified question.

Another way to retrieve all the polls or only those archived would have been to define two public methods with different names, such as `GetAllQuestions` and `GetArchivedQuestions` that, in turn, call a helper private method called `GetQuestions(bool bArchivedOnly)`. However, if we later wanted to allow retrieval of polls archived in a certain interval of time, or with other properties, we would need to add further methods in addition to the new overloaded methods. More code would be needed, but without bringing significant advantages, since it should be already clear to the client what the overloaded methods do with different parameters.

The OptionDetails Class

This class is basically the same as `QuestionDetails` but for the `Polls_Options` table instead. It has only public fields that map the physical fields of the table, plus the `TotalVotes` and `Percentage` fields that are calculated values returned by the `sp_Polls_GetOptionDetails` stored procedure.

The Options Class

This class wraps the calls to all the stored procedures that manage the options, in the same way as the `Questions` class does for the questions. Here is a complete list of the methods to implement:

Method Name	Description
`public Options(string newConnectionString)`	Class constructor taking the connection string as a parameter.
`public DataSet GetOptions(int questionID)`	Returns the options for the specified question.
`public OptionDetails GetDetails(int optionID)`	Returns an instance of `OptionDetails` that describes the specified option.
`public DataRow GetDetailsRow(int optionID)`	Returns the `DataRow` of the option identified by the specified ID.
`public int Add(int questionID, string optionText)`	Adds an option and returns the ID of the added record, or -1 if an option with the same text was already present for the specified question.
`public bool Update(int optionID, string optionText)`	Updates all the fields of the specified option.
`public bool Delete(int optionID)`	Deletes the specified option.

The VoteDetails Class

This class is similar to the two `xxxDetails` classes above, with the following public fields: `VoteID`, `QuestionID`, `OptionID`, `UserIP`, and `AddedDate`.

The Votes Class

This class is similar to `Questions` and `Options`, but a bit simpler because here we don't need methods that update and delete votes. If this functionality is really necessary, for example during the testing stage, you should resort to the Enterprise Manager or some other database manager, like the one we discussed in Chapter 4, which allows the administrator to work online. Here are the methods for this last data access class:

Method Name	Description
`public Votes(string newConnectionString)`	Class constructor taking the connection string as a parameter.
`public DataSet GetVotes(int questionID)`	Returns all the votes for the specified question.
`public VoteDetails GetDetails(int voteID)`	Returns an instance of `VoteDetails` that describes the specified vote.

Method Name	Description
`public DataRow GetDetailsRow(int voteID)`	Returns the `DataRow` of the specified vote.
`public int GetUserVoteID(int questionID, string userIP)`	Returns the ID for the vote for the specified question posted by the user whose computer's IP is `userIP`. Returns `-1` if no record is found.
`public int Add(int questionID, int optionID, string userIP)`	Adds a vote for the specified question and option, and returns the ID of the added record. The record is always added; multiple votes, when not allowed, are prevented by a business class.

Storing and Retrieving Settings

Before showing the design of the business layer we'd better spend a moment thinking about the settings we want to offer, because they will be important for the logic of some of the business methods. The most obvious setting is the connection string for the database, but there are others relating to the methods to be employed to avoid unwanted multiple votes.

In the previous chapters we've already extensively discussed how to store and retrieve settings: we decided to use an XML file, written and read by a separate module-specific assembly with two classes. The assembly for this module should be named `Wrox.WebModules.Polls.Configuration.dll` and there should be a corresponding namespace for the classes. The first class is `ModuleConfig`, and this takes care of persisting and retrieving the settings to and from the XML file. The other class is `ModuleSettings`, which has public properties that expose the settings, and that is used as source and destination for the serialization and de-serialization of the settings. This is achieved thanks to a great ASP.NET class, `XmlSerializer`, which we've already seen in action earlier.

The properties we need for `ModuleSettings` are as follows:

❑ `ConnectionString`: the connection string that all the data classes use to access the database.

❑ `LockByCookie`: Boolean property that, if `true`, means that we want to use cookies to prevent multiple votes.

❑ `LockByIP`: Boolean property that, if `true`, means that we want to use IP locking to prevent multiple votes.

❑ `LockDuration`: integer property that specifies the duration of the lock, during which the user is not allowed to vote more than once. The period is specified in days. If `-1`, it means that the lock never expires.

Designing the Business Layer

The data access classes are sufficient for administering the database, since there are no particular rules to respect when adding, editing, or deleting records. Simple rules, such as preventing the addition of a record that is already present, are applied within the stored procedures. However, we have more complex business rules to take care of, for example preventing the user from voting multiple times if the administrator has decided that this should not be possible, or writing and retrieving cookies when the user votes. In addition, we want to access the data in a more object-oriented way; the data layer basically provides a mere set of functions, without properties that describe the object and relationships between child and parent objects. Therefore we must create another couple of classes to do this, and so separate the business logic from the data layer. This is needed because a lower layer is not supposed to access information available to another layer – if you need such information it is supposed to be passed as a method parameter. The business layer is based on top of the data layer, and has classes that provide a completely object-oriented description of the entities (questions and options), as well as methods to manipulate them. It hides the details of the data layer, and prevents direct access to protected records, such as the votes.

We'll put the business classes in a new assembly, `Wrox.WebModules.Polls.Business`, whose classes will inherit from `BizObject` in the `Core` assembly.

The Question Class

This class fully describes a question, and is based on the data layer's `Questions`, `Options`, and `Votes` classes. It also provides methods that check if the current user is allowed to vote, add their vote, and add or return the possible options for a question:

Method Name	Description
`public int ID`	Read-only property that returns the ID of the question represented by the object.
`public string Text`	Gets/sets the question text.
`public bool IsCurrent`	Gets/sets the `IsCurrentQuestion` status of the question.
`public bool Archived`	Gets/sets the `Archived` status of the question.
`public int TotalVotes`	Read-only property that returns the number of votes for all the child options.
`public DateTime AddedDate`	Read-only property that returns the date when the question was added to the database.
`public bool AllowVote`	Read-only property that, based on the current settings, returns a value indicating whether the current user can vote for this question.

Table continued on following page

Method Name	Description
`public Question()`	Class constructor with no parameters. It just resets the public properties to a default value. For example, the `ID` property is set to `-1`, indicating that no record is represented by the object, `TotalVotes` is 0, `Text` is an empty string, etc.
`public Question(int existingQuestionID)`	Class constructor that sets the properties to describe the question identified by the input ID.
`public Question(Question existingQuestion)`	Class constructor that sets the properties to describe the question identified by an existing `Question` object.
`private void LoadFromID()`	Loads the properties of the question identified by a private ID variable. This method is called by the constructors, or when the data has to be refreshed.
`private void ResetProperties()`	Resets the properties.
`public int LoadFromID(int existingQuestionID)`	Loads all the properties of the question identified by the input ID. This method allows a different question to be loaded after the object has been created, or the properties to be loaded if we created an object but didn't specify an ID for the constructor.
`public int LoadCurrent()`	Loads the question marked as current, and sets the properties accordingly.
`public int Create(string questionText, bool isCurrentQuestion, bool questionArchived)`	Creates a new question, and sets the properties of the object to represent the new record.
`public bool Update()`	Updates the current question with the new values of the public properties.
`public bool Delete()`	Deletes the question.
`public static DataSet GetQuestions(bool archivedOnly)`	Static method that returns all the questions or only the archived ones.
`public static DataSet GetQuestions()`	Overloaded version of the method above that returns all the questions.
`public static int GetCurrentID()`	Returns the ID of the question defined as the current/default question.

Method Name	Description
`public static DataSet GetCurrent()`	Returns a `DataSet` with two tables: the first has a row that identifies the current/default question, and the second has all the child options.
`public DataSet GetOptions()`	Returns all the child options.
`public Option AddOption(string optionText)`	Adds a child option.
`public bool Vote(int optionID)`	Votes for the child option identified by the specified ID.
`public bool Vote(Option option)`	Votes for the option specified in the input. This overloaded version accepts an `Option` object instead of its ID, and is actually based upon the previous version.

Here we have quite a few interesting methods and properties, such as `AllowVote`, `Vote`, and `GetCurrent`. `AllowVote` determines whether the user is allowed to vote for the question according to the options set by the administrator and exposed by the configuration component explained above. It checks for the presence of a cookie on the client's system, and checks against the IP address to see if they have already voted. We'll be using this property from inside the `Vote` method to find out if the current user has already voted, and therefore whether we should show the list of options and radio buttons for the question, or whether we should show the results.

The other interesting method is `GetCurrent`, but we'll describe it in more detail shortly, when discussing the design of the presentation layer, and specifically the design of the web service.

The Option Class

This is a simple class that describes a particular option and allows us to update, delete, or create a new one. Below is the list of methods and properties we'll be implementing:

Method Name	Description
`public int ID`	Read-only property that returns the ID of the option represented by the object.
`public int QuestionID`	Read-only property that returns the ID of the parent question.
`public Business.Question Question`	Returns the parent question.
`public string Text`	Gets/sets the text of the option.

Table continued on following page

Method Name	Description
`public int TotalVotes`	Read-only property that returns the number of votes this option received.
`public float Percentage`	Read-only property that returns the percentage of votes this option received, in relation to all the options of the parent question.
`public Option()`	Class constructor with no parameters. It just resets the properties.
`public Option(int existingOptionID)`	Class constructor that sets the properties to describe the option identified by the input ID.
`public Option(Option existingOption)`	Class constructor that sets the properties to describe the option identified by an existing `Option` object.
`private void LoadFromID()`	Loads the properties of the option identified by a private ID variable.
`private void ResetProperties()`	Resets the properties.
`public int LoadFromID(int existingOptionID)`	Loads all the properties of the option identified by the input ID. This method allows a different option to be loaded after the object has been created, or the properties to be loaded if we created an object but didn't specify an ID for the constructor.
`public int Create(int optionQuestionID, string optionText)`	Creates a new option, and sets the properties of the object to represent the new record.
`public bool Update()`	Updates the current option with the new values of the public properties.
`public bool Delete()`	Deletes the option.

Designing the User Interface Services

In this section we'll discuss the user control that will allow us to insert the poll box into any page we want, with just a couple of lines of code. In addition, we'll also see the design of a web service that makes the current poll's question and results available to any client that can send and understand XML/SOAP messages (for example, another site, or a Windows or Linux application).

The Poll User Control

This control has two functions:

❑ If we detect that the user has not voted for the question yet, the control presents a list of radio buttons with the various options, and a Vote button.

❑ If we detect that the current user has already voted, instead of the radio buttons we have to show the results. We will show the percentage of votes for each option, as a number and also graphically as a colored bar.

In both cases the control can optionally show header text, and a link at the bottom that points to the Archive page. Some polls that you may have found around the web are simpler, they always show the options, and tell you that you can't vote again only when you try to do so. The results are displayed through a pop-up window when you vote, or with an explicit link. Our method is much better, as it doesn't need any additional window and it intelligently hides the radio buttons if the user can't vote. Why show the options and the Vote button if the user will get an error message when it is pressed?

Let's think a bit about the actual voting system: how do we handle the option posted by the user? We have two possibilities, both with advantages and disadvantages:

❑ We can use the ASP.NET postback events, and thus have all the required code in the codebehind of the user control. The advantage is that it is easy to implement, and similar to the normal ASP.NET pages we've already developed so far: just a RadioButtonList, a button, and its server-side Click event. The drawback is that the user control must be declared inside a server-side form to be able to handle postback events. This is not a problem when we want to insert the poll box in single pages that we know about in advance, but say that we want to insert the poll box in the site layout, the header or footer of the site, in order to show the box from every page. We'll have to be sure that the header/footer controls are declared inside the server form, and often this isn't the case. (It is not necessary when we are showing static HTML, only if we have to show server controls.)

❑ The other possibility is to work as in traditional ASP: we create a normal HTML <form> tag and post the selected option to a different ASP.NET page. The advantage of this solution is that we can easily insert the poll box outside a server form and into the site layout, maybe in a column that is always visible. The drawback is that to ensure that the form will correctly post the data it must be declared outside the server form, in case it exists. This is OK if we want to insert the box into an external column of the layout, but it is a problem if we want to insert the control into a particular page, with other controls that are declared in a server-side form. There are other drawbacks, such as the need to manually build the list of options (we can't use a RadioButtonList bound to a data source from outside a server form), and we need to have a separate page for processing the selected option being posted. In practice we lose all the advantages of ASP.NET.

As you can see, there isn't a perfect solution for every case, but the pure ASP.NET solution has many more advantages than the latter, and the drawback is limited, especially if we are aware of it! For these reasons we decided to build a real ASP.NET user control that posts back the form and handles the events on the server.

Having decided how to solve the most compelling issue, handling the vote posting, we can now complete the discussion of the user control with the list of properties we want to implement:

Property Name	Description
public int QuestionID	The ID of the question to ask within the poll box. If no ID is specified, the question with the IsCurrentQuestion field set to 1 will be used (if any).
public bool ArchiveLinkVisible	If true, shows a link at the bottom of the control, pointing to the Archive page.
public string HeaderText	The text for the control's header bar.
public Unit Width	The width, in pixels or percentage, of the poll box.
public HorizontalAlign HorizontalAlign	The alignment of the text inside the box.
public string CssClass	The CSS class for the box content. (CSS styles were discussed in Chapter 3.)
public string QuestionStyle	The CSS class for the question. If not specified then CssClass is used for the question as well.
public string HeaderStyle	The CSS class for the header bar. If not specified the CssClass is used for the header as well.
public string ButtonStyle	The CSS class for the Vote button.
public string LinkStyle	The CSS class for the link to the Archive page.
public string ResultsStyle	The CSS class for the result percentages (in numbers).
public string BarStyle	The CSS class for the results percentage bar.

We could add more properties for the graphical aspect, but these should be enough for a complete and functional example. The data will actually be shown in the control through a call to an overridden DataBind method.

The Poll Web Service

The site staff can discover the results of the current poll either by adding their own vote, or by accessing the administration section. However, instead of having to refresh the page from time to time to requery the database and see the latest results, it would be cool if they could check the result with a small Windows client that connects to the site, downloads all the results from the polls, and shows them through different types of graph. Or it could simply be something more appealing to show to a client!

For our example we're going to keep things simple: we'll just show the results for the current question, using a grid displaying the numerical percentages. Explaining a more complex Windows application is beyond the scope of the book, but it wouldn't be that much more difficult. The web service would still be structured in a very similar way.

The web service is a small piece of software that will allow our future Windows client to query the database on the server. We want to show the current poll, so we must retrieve the row describing the current question and the corresponding options. We could simply use two methods to do this. However, we've chosen to return a DataSet, because this will be disconnected from the physical data on the database, and the cursor can be moved through the records in any direction. Remember that a DataSet is basically a container for any number of tables (it can also include constraints and relationships among tables, but let's keep it simple for now) so we can return both the question and the options in a single step. We can get a DataSet with the options, and then add a table for the row of the parent question. This would also work fine if we wanted to return all the questions, not just the current one, as we would just add more rows to this table.

So, the web service will have only one method, defined as follows:

❑   public DataSet GetCurrent: returns a DataSet with a table called Questions containing the current question, and a table named Options containing all the options (and the results) for the current question. This method is based upon the static GetCurrent method of the Business.Question class that we mentioned earlier.

Of course we'll need to use the [WebMethod] attribute to make the method remotely accessible, while retrieving the required data will be straightforward through the use of the data access component.

It's worth highlighting again that this method returns the question's details every time we call it. This is a little wasteful because, unlike the options, the question does not change between consecutive calls. Therefore there is no need to retrieve it again every time, we could just get it the first time and then only download the updated results. However, this is not a big issue in our case because we've decided to retrieve just the *current* question and its options/results, and we don't need to retrieve the questions very often as we only have a few administrators who need to access this information (we want to make the web service available to the site staff only). If, on the other hand, we were designing the web service to return any archived polls (maybe hundreds), and for a large number of clients, then the time required to retrieve the questions from the database and to send them to the client every time would be much more significant. In that case it would be better to have a method that returns all the questions, and have a separate method that returns the options/results for a particular question. This way the questions could be downloaded only when the client starts, and the options could be downloaded when the user changes the selected question. This is very similar to what we've done in Chapter 6, for the news manager's web service. If you think you need better performance for the polls web service, refer back to that chapter to see how to change the implementation presented in this chapter.

The Need for Security

The Polls module is basically split in two parts:

❑   The administration section that allows the web master (or someone else) to add, delete, or edit the questions and their options, and change the module's settings.

❑   The poll box control, the respective ASP.NET page that handles its data posted to the server to add the vote to the database, and the page that shows the archived polls' results.

The second part is freely accessible to the user, but we must protect access to the administration pages. Only one person, or a selected set of people, should be allowed to enter this section. In the previous chapters, especially in Chapters 6 and 7, we saw how to enforce security in a similar situation by using the `Accounts` module developed in Chapter 5.

We will follow exactly the same strategy here. We'll place the administration pages under an `Admin` directory, and allow only the users who have `AdministerPolls` permission to enter. If they do not have that permission, they will be redirected to the default login page.

The Solution

Now that we have a thorough design for the module, we can start the hands-on part – the implementation of the solution. We'll follow the same order as we did in the design section: starting with the implementation of the database tables, we'll move on to the data, configuration, and business assemblies, and finally we'll look at the presentation layer. This comprises the administration section, the poll user control, the web service, and the Windows web service consumer.

Working on the Database

With the help of the Enterprise Manager, creating the tables for our SQL Server database is such a simple task that it is not necessary to describe it in detail here. Earlier in this chapter we presented the complete lists of the columns for each table, along with the most significant properties, so you should have no problems creating them. (Alternatively, script files to create the tables are available in the code download, as is a complete backup of the database.)

You can create the new tables (or even a new database if you need to) right within Visual Studio .NET, without opening SQL Server. On the far left of the IDE, near the Toolbox, you find another tab called **Server Explorer**. This window allows the developer to explore the server components such as SQL Server databases, events logs, message queues, etc., through an easy-to-browse tree control. Under the SQL Server leaf are listed all the available databases. If you select and expand one you can see its tables, stored procedures, views, diagrams, and functions. You can edit or delete existing objects, or create new ones, by clicking the respective commands of the popup menu that appears by right-clicking on a tree item. The following screenshot shows the IDE while displaying the data of the `Polls_Options` table:

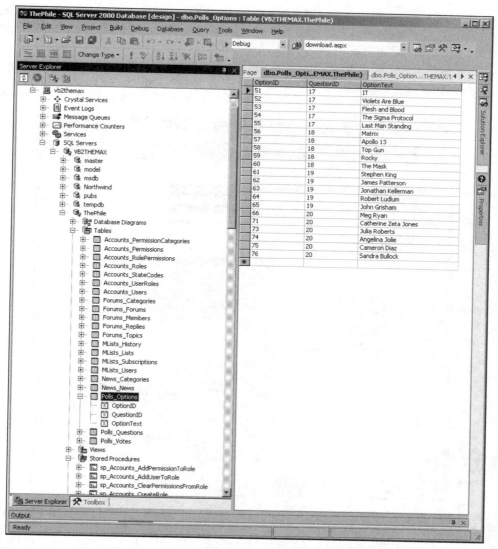

The data is displayed and edited with an interface very similar to the Enterprise Manager's editors, and the same is true for the table designers. What's even cooler is that you can drag and drop a table/view or a stored procedure over a form or control (Windows or Web, it doesn't matter), and Visual Studio .NET will auto-generate the code for the respective `DataAdapter`, `SqlConnection`, and `SqlCommand` objects. Honestly, I don't use this feature very much because Visual Studio .NET generates code for any constructor parameter and for most properties – even if not required – and I prefer to write tighter code. But it's actually great if you just want to quickly test a stored procedure or fill a grid on the page, for example.

In the next sections we'll see the relationships we need to create between the tables, and the code for some of the stored procedures.

Creating the Relationships

After creating the tables, we have to create the relationships between them, as shown in the diagram in the design section. As we saw in Chapter 6, with the Enterprise Manager (or with the Visual Studio .NET's Server Explorer) this is also a simple matter, so we won't go into details here. We need three relationships:

❑   A relationship between the question and the possible options that can be selected. This relationship, FK_Polls_Options_Questions, is between the QuestionID column of the Polls_Options table and the Polls_Questions table. The other settings are as shown:

We select the **Cascade Update** and **Cascade Delete** options, so that if a question ID is changed (which shouldn't happen, since the QuestionID is an identity field) the QuestionID foreign key in the Polls_Options table will change accordingly, and if a question is deleted all the child options will be deleted as well.

❑   A relationship between the votes and the question. FK_Polls_Votes_Questions links the QuestionID column of the Polls_Votes table with the Polls_Questions table, and has the same settings as seen above.

❑   A relationship between the votes and the options. FK_Polls_Votes_Options links the OptionID column of the Polls_Votes table with the Polls_Options table, and again has the same settings.

All three relationships are many-to-one, since many options belong to the same question, and many votes refer to the same question and option.

Creating the Stored Procedures

The code for inserting, deleting, or updating a record is very similar for all three tables, and is similar to the respective procedures already seen in previous chapters, so here we'll only show the few procedures that differ somehow. You can easily derive the code for the other procedures, or use the scripts in the code download to create all the procedures.

sp_Polls_GetQuestions

Here's the code for the sp_Polls_GetQuestions procedure that returns the archived questions only, or all the questions, according to the input parameter:

```
CREATE PROCEDURE sp_Polls_GetQuestions
                 @ArchivedOnly   bit = 0
AS

DECLARE @QuestionID int

IF @ArchivedOnly = 1
  BEGIN
  SELECT QuestionID, QuestionText, IsCurrentQuestion, Archived, AddedDate,
    (SELECT COUNT(*) FROM Polls_Votes WHERE QuestionID = Q.QuestionID)
     AS TotalVotes
   FROM Polls_Questions Q
   WHERE Archived = 1
  END
ELSE
  BEGIN
  SELECT QuestionID, QuestionText, IsCurrentQuestion, Archived, AddedDate,
    (SELECT COUNT(*) FROM Polls_Votes WHERE QuestionID = Q.QuestionID)
     AS TotalVotes
   FROM Polls_Questions Q
  END
GO
```

There are two distinct SELECT statements – which one is run depends on whether we are retrieving *archived* questions or *all* questions. The most important point to note is how we declare and calculate the new TotalVotes column. This contains the total number of votes for the row's question. Basically, we run a sub query that counts the votes where the QuestionID field is equal to the QuestionID of the current row in the Polls_Questions table being queried, and the result is kept in a new column named TotalVotes.

sp_Polls_GetCurrentQuestionID

The sp_Polls_GetCurrentQuestionID procedure runs a simple SELECT to get the ID of the row that contains the current (non-archived) question. If no current question is found, the procedure returns –1, as an indication for the caller code:

```
CREATE PROCEDURE sp_Polls_GetCurrentQuestionID
                @QuestionID int OUTPUT
AS

SELECT @QuestionID = QuestionID
  FROM Polls_Questions
  WHERE IsCurrentQuestion = 1 AND Archived = 0

IF @QuestionID IS NULL
  SET @QuestionID = -1
GO
```

sp_Polls_SetCurrentQuestionID

The sp_Polls_SetCurrentQuestionID procedure is used to assign the current question. It can't just update the IsCurrentQuestion field of the selected question, it must also ensure that only one question is marked as current. So it first sets to 0 the IsCurrentQuestion field of all the rows, and then sets to 1 the field of the specified question:

```
CREATE PROCEDURE sp_Polls_SetCurrentQuestionID
                @QuestionID int
AS

-- first set IsCurrentQuestion = 0 for all questions
UPDATE Polls_Questions
  SET IsCurrentQuestion = 0

-- set the current question
UPDATE Polls_Questions
  SET IsCurrentQuestion = 1
  WHERE QuestionID = @QuestionID
GO
```

sp_Polls_InsertQuestion

The following code, sp_Polls_InsertQuestion, inserts a new row in the Polls_Questions table, and returns the ID of the added row through the output parameter. If the question already exists and it is not archived, it is not added again:

```
CREATE PROCEDURE sp_Polls_InsertQuestion
                @QuestionText varchar(150),
                @IsCurrentQuestion int,
                @Archived int,
                @QuestionID int OUTPUT
AS

DECLARE @CurrID int

-- see if the question already exists
-- (check only the non-archived questions)
SELECT @CurrID = QuestionID
  FROM Polls_Questions
  WHERE QuestionText = @QuestionText AND Archived = 0
```

```
    -- if not, add it
IF @CurrID IS NULL
  BEGIN

  INSERT INTO Polls_Questions
      (QuestionText, IsCurrentQuestion, Archived, AddedDate)
      VALUES (@QuestionText, @IsCurrentQuestion, @Archived, GETDATE())

  SET @QuestionID = @@IDENTITY

  IF @@ERROR > 0
    BEGIN
    RAISERROR ('Insert of Question failed', 16, 1)
    RETURN 99
    END

  -- if @CurrentQuestion is 1, set this question as the active one.
  -- This could not be done in the Insert statement because we need to
  -- set CurrentQuestion = 0 for the other questions first
  IF @IsCurrentQuestion = 1
    EXEC sp_Polls_SetCurrentQuestionID @QuestionID

  END
ELSE
  BEGIN
  SET @QuestionID = -1
  END
GO
```

In the INSERT statement we specify the input value for the IsCurrentQuestion field. If the parameter is 0, we're done. If it is 1, we must ensure that the new row is the only one that has IsCurrentQuestion set to 1, and so we must call the sp_Polls_SetCurrentQuestionID procedure that does this, as we've seen earlier.

sp_Polls_UpdateQuestion

The sp_Polls_UpdateQuestion procedure updates all the fields of the specified question, except for the ID of course. If @IsCurrentQuestion is 1 then we must call sp_Polls_SetCurrentQuestionID, for the reason explained above:

```
CREATE PROCEDURE sp_Polls_UpdateQuestion
              @QuestionID int,
              @QuestionText varchar(150),
              @IsCurrentQuestion bit,
              @Archived bit
AS

BEGIN TRANSACTION UpdateQuestion

UPDATE Polls_Questions
  SET QuestionText = @QuestionText, IsCurrentQuestion = @IsCurrentQuestion,
      Archived = @Archived
  WHERE QuestionID = @QuestionID
```

```
-- if @CurrentQuestion = 1, call the sproc that unchecks the value
-- for all the other questions, and check this
-- if @CurrentQuestion = 0, it has already been updated by the command above
IF @IsCurrentQuestion = 1
  EXEC sp_Polls_SetCurrentQuestionID @QuestionID

IF @@ERROR > 0
  BEGIN
  RAISERROR ('Update of Question failed', 16, 1)
  ROLLBACK TRANSACTION UpdateQuestion
  RETURN 99
  END

COMMIT TRANSACTION UpdateQuestion
GO
```

sp_Polls_GetOptions

This procedure returns the options for the specified question, and the total number of votes. It also creates a new column that shows the votes for each option as a percentage of the votes for all the options of this question. Here's the code:

```
CREATE PROCEDURE sp_Polls_GetOptions
               @QuestionID int
AS

DECLARE @QuestionTotalVotes int

-- get the total of number votes for this question
SELECT @QuestionTotalVotes = COUNT(*) FROM Polls_Votes
  WHERE QuestionID = @QuestionID

IF @QuestionTotalVotes = 0
  SET @QuestionTotalVotes = 1

-- get the OptionID and OptionText
-- + count the total number of votes for each options
-- + calc the percentage for each option
SELECT OptionID, OptionText,
     (SELECT COUNT(*) FROM Polls_Votes WHERE OptionID = O.OptionID)
         AS TotalVotes,
     (CAST((SELECT COUNT(*) FROM Polls_Votes WHERE OptionID = O.OptionID)
         AS Decimal) * 100 / @QuestionTotalVotes)
         AS Percentage
  FROM Polls_Options O
  WHERE QuestionID = @QuestionID
GO
```

It first gets the total number of votes for all the options of this question, and saves this value in a variable. If no votes are found, it sets the variable to 1, because otherwise the forthcoming division would produce an error. Finally it executes the SELECT query and adds the Percentage column, with the following code:

```
(CAST((SELECT COUNT(*) FROM Polls_Votes WHERE OptionID = O.OptionID)
    AS Decimal) * 100 / @QuestionTotalVotes)
    AS Percentage
```

The number of votes for an option are multiplied by 100 and then divided by the total number of votes for the question. It's worth noting that the expression is CAST to Decimal, in order to achieve more accuracy than an integer percentage would provide.

The code of the sp_Polls_GetOptionDetails procedure is almost identical to this code, with two exceptions. It is restricted to a single record, and the question's ID is not provided as a parameter, but must be retrieved with a simple SELECT query to select the QuestionID field of the specified option.

Implementing the Data Access Assembly

Now that the database is complete, let's go ahead and look at the .NET code for the data access component. In Visual Studio .NET we add a new Class Library project called Polls.Data to our ThePhile solution, and using its **Properties** dialog set both the assembly name and the default namespace to Wrox.WebModules.Polls.Data. Then we edit the automatically created AssemblyInfo.cs file with the assembly's description, version, and other information, as we've already seen in previous chapters.

At this point you should rename the default Class1.cs file to Questions.cs, and we also need two other classes, for the options and the votes. These classes are simply wrappers for the stored procedures, as mentioned earlier, and their code is very similar to the code of the data access classes described in Chapter 6. Therefore, to avoid useless repetition of code we will not show the code here, but of course you can download the finished assembly from the Wrox site.

The Configuration Assembly

In previous chapters, we've already seen (more than once) the implementation of the configuration assembly, so we won't repeat all the details again here. Briefly, we create a new **Class Library** project, change the project's properties (the namespace and assembly name are both Wrox.WebModules.Polls.Configuration), and edit the AssemblyInfo.cs file as we did for the data assembly. We are then ready to write the classes.

The ModuleSettings Class

In the design section we listed the settings we need to store, and here you'll find the necessary code for the class:

```
public class ModuleSettings
{
  private string connectionString;
  private bool lockByIP;
```

```
    private bool lockByCookie;
    private int lockDuration;

    [XmlElement]
    public string ConnectionString
    {
      get { return connectionString; }
      set { connectionString = value; }
    }

    [XmlElement]
    public bool LockByIP
    {
      get { return lockByIP; }
      set { lockByIP = value; }
    }

    [XmlElement]
    public bool LockByCookie
    {
      get { return lockByCookie; }
      set { lockByCookie = value; }
    }

    [XmlElement]
    public int LockDuration
    {
      get { return lockDuration; }
      set { lockDuration = value; }
    }
  }
```

As you can see, it is a simple class – the key point is the use of [XmlElement]. This tells the serializer that the property state has to be serialized and de-serialized to and from the chosen settings file.

The ModuleConfig Class

This class differs from the implementations of the previous chapters in just a few lines, basically the name of the key in the site-wide web.config file – Polls_SettingsFile – and the name of the entry in the cache – Polls_Settings. You can actually copy and paste the code from the ModuleConfig class of a previous module, and replace the configuration and cache entry names with those values.

The Settings File

To see what the settings file looks like, we first implemented a simple page that created an instance of ModuleSettings with the settings we wanted, and then persisted it to a file with the ModuleConfig class. This created the file with the right format and values, and spared us the need to write it by hand. This is the file content produced:

```
<?xml version="1.0"?>
<ModuleSettings xmlns:xsi="http://www.w3.org/2001/XMLSchema-instance"
                xmlns:xsd="http://www.w3.org/2001/XMLSchema">
```

```
    <ConnectionString>server=(local);database=ThePhile;uid=sa;pwd=;
    </ConnectionString>
    <LockByIP>true</LockByIP>
    <LockByCookie>true</LockByCookie>
    <LockDuration>7</LockDuration>
  </ModuleSettings>
```

We decided to name the file `Polls.Config`, but you can choose any name you want, as long as you store its path in the site-wide `web.config` file, as follows:

```
<?xml version="1.0" encoding="utf-8" ?>
<configuration>
  <appSettings>
    <add key="Polls_SettingsFile" value="/ThePhile/Config/Polls.Config" />
  </appSettings>
  ...
</configuration>
```

The Business Assembly

We create a Class Library project for the new business classes assembly, change the usual properties, and set the namespace and assembly name as `Wrox.WebModules.Polls.Business`. Also remember that we must add references to the `Core`, `Wrox.WebModules.Polls.Data`, and `Wrox.WebModules.Polls.Configuration` projects. We have two classes for this assembly, `Question` and `Option`. As we've said for the data access assembly, the code of many methods is very similar to the code of the business classes of Chapter 6. For example, the methods for loading a specified record and exposing its values through the object's public properties, returning all the records, and adding, editing, or deleting a record, are actually almost the same. All that changes is the name of the data access class to instantiate and the methods to call, and of course the number and type of parameters. We don't want to repeat here code already shown, so we'll only cover the methods that are really new to this module, namely those methods that implement the real business rules, such as checking if the user has already voted and is allowed to vote again, reading and writing cookies and IP addresses to remember a vote, etc. As always, the entire code of all the other methods is available in the code download.

The Question Class

This is the class that will be used most frequently, since it provides access to any question and the associated options and results. It also exposes methods to vote for a particular option and to check if the user can vote for the question represented by an instance of this class. In the following sections we'll see the implementation of most of the methods that are specific to this module and not as general as other methods mentioned above.

Managing the Child Options

We have a couple of methods for creating a child option, and for returning all the available child options already present. The first method does not directly access the data layer to create a new record, but it calls the `Create` method of an `Option` object. As a result it's quicker to update the business class if the data class changes, because we have less code that references it directly:

```
public DataSet GetOptions()
{
  Data.Options options = new Data.Options(settings.ConnectionString);
  return options.GetOptions(questionID);
}

// add a new child option
public Option AddOption(string optionText)
{
  Business.Option option = new Business.Option();
  option.Create(questionID, optionText);
  return option;
}
```

The GetCurrent Method

Here things start to get more interesting. In the design section we decided to return both the question and the results through a single static method, GetCurrent, which returns a DataSet with two tables. The code is as follows:

```
public static DataSet GetCurrent()
{
  Configuration.ModuleSettings settings =
                              Configuration.ModuleConfig.GetSettings();

  // get the current question's ID
  Data.Questions questions = new Data.Questions(settings.ConnectionString);
  int questionID = questions.GetCurrentID();

  // if there is no current question, return an empty DataSet
  if (questionID == -1) return new DataSet();

  // get the options for this question
  Data.Options options = new Data.Options(settings.ConnectionString);
  DataSet currPoll = options.GetOptions(questionID);

  // get the current question's details
  DataRow question = questions.GetDetailsRow(questionID);

  // clone its parent table's structure and add it to the DataSet
  currPoll.Tables.Add(question.Table.Clone());

  // import the details row into the new table
  currPoll.Tables["Questions"].ImportRow(question);

  // return the Dataset with the two tables
  return currPoll;
}
```

If there is no current question, the method creates and returns an empty DataSet. Otherwise, it first retrieves the DataSet with a table called Options containing the options for the current question. Then it retrieves the row with the details of the question, and adds a new table, Questions, to the DataSet retrieved in the previous step. It does this by cloning the structure of the question row's parent table. Finally, it imports the question's details row to the Questions table. This might sound a bit intricate, but look again at the code and read the comments, and you'll see that it's actually quite straightforward.

When we clone a table it means that we clone its structure, namely the number and type of columns it has, and all its attributes. The normal way to add a new table to a DataSet (which if you remember is a collection of tables and relationships) would be to create a new DataTable object and add all the required columns by hand. However, this would require quite a lot of code to set all the attributes (data type, size, etc.) for any column. Instead, cloning an existing table that has the structure we want to reproduce is quite a nice trick, because it only requires a single line, and brings us to the same result.

The GetDetailsRow method of the Data.Questions class calls the sp_Polls_GetQuestionDetails stored procedure and puts the results in a table called Questions. When the table is cloned, the new table is also called Questions because the attributes are copied. This explains why we can easily access it by name rather than by index when we call its Add method to add the row that describes the current question.

The AllowVote Property

This property checks whether the user can vote for the specified question. The check is done against a client cookie and the IP address stored in the database. If the user has already voted, it also looks to see if the lock period for multiple votes has expired.

```csharp
public bool AllowVote
{
  get
  {
    bool cookieOK = false;
    bool ipOK = false;

    HttpRequest request = HttpContext.Current.Request;
    int duration = settings.LockDuration;

    // if the lock period is 0, return true
    if (duration == 0) return true;

    // check the cookie if necessary
    if (settings.LockByCookie)
    {
      if (request.Cookies["Polls_Question" + questionID.ToString()] != null)
        return false;
      else
        // if the cookie is null, we're ok so far
        cookieOK = true;
    }
    else
      cookieOK = true;

    // check the ID if necessary
    if (settings.LockByIP)
    {
      Data.Votes votes = new Data.Votes(settings.ConnectionString);
      int voteID = votes.GetUserVoteID(questionID,
                                       request.UserHostAddress.ToString());
      // if GetUserVoteID returned -1, the current user has never
      // voted for this question
      if (voteID == -1)
```

```
          ipOK = true;
      else
      {
          // if a vote for this question is found, and the duration time is -1
          // it means that it will never expire --> return false
          if (duration == -1) return false;

          // otherwise check if the LockDuration time has expired
          DateTime addedDate = votes.GetDetails(voteID).AddedDate;
          ipOK = (addedDate.AddDays(duration) <= DateTime.Today);
      }
  }
  else
    ipOK = true;

  return (cookieOK && ipOK);
}
}
```

As you can see, if the lock duration is 0 it means that multiple votes are allowed with no limitations, so the procedure returns `true` straight away, without performing any further checks. Otherwise, it starts by checking if the client has a cookie ending with the specified question's ID, if we enabled cookie locking in the settings. If the cookie exists, the user has already voted and so the routine returns `false`. Otherwise, we go ahead by checking in the database, looking for a vote for the specified question with the current user's IP address, if IP locking is employed. The IP address of the current user is returned by the `UserHostAddress` property of the `HttpContext.Current.Request` class. (Note that to use this class you need to reference the `System.Web.dll` assembly, which is not added by default in Class Library projects.) If both checks go well, the method ends by returning the final value of `true`.

It is also worth noting that we do not need to check the `LockDuration` setting for the cookie. In fact, when the cookie is created (we'll see how, when, and where, in a moment) it is given an expiration time equal to the `LockDuration` setting. When that time has passed the cookie is no longer valid, and is therefore not found by the server – the check succeeds. In the database we store the date the vote was added, so we also need to check if the specified time has passed since the `AddedDate` date.

The Vote Method

The `Vote` method is the one that actually adds votes to the database. It first calls `AllowVote`, discussed above, to check if the user has already voted for this question, and if so, to check if the lock period for multiple votes has expired. If the check returns `true`, the vote is saved to the database and a cookie is created on the client to record that the current user has voted for that question:

```
public bool Vote(int optionID)
{
    // before voting, check if the user has already voted,
    // and if so check also if the lock period for multiple votes has expired
    if (AllowVote && questionID != -1 && optionID != -1)
    {
        int voteID;
        int duration = settings.LockDuration;
        if (duration == -1) duration = 365;
```

```
      // add the vote
      Data.Votes votes = new Data.Votes(settings.ConnectionString);
      voteID = votes.Add(questionID, optionID,
                              HttpContext.Current.Request.UserHostAddress);

      // add a new cookie for this question
      HttpCookie voteCookie = new HttpCookie("Polls_Question" +
                                                  questionID.ToString());
      voteCookie.Value = optionID.ToString();
      voteCookie.Expires = DateTime.Today.AddDays(duration);
      HttpContext.Current.Response.Cookies.Add(voteCookie);
      return (voteID != -1);
    }
    else
    {
      return false;
    }
  }

  public bool Vote(Option option)
  {
    return Vote(option.ID);
  }
```

The trick to handling cookies for multiple polls is to name the cookie with a fixed string (`Polls_Question` in the code above) plus the ID of the question. This way different polls have different cookies and are not overwritten by each other. The cookie's value is the ID of the option voted for: this information could be useful later if we want to remind the user of their choice. The cookie is given an expiration time, which is the current date plus a number of days (specified by the `LockDuration` setting, or 365 days if the setting is -1).

> If `LockDuration` is -1 it is meant to be forever, but we considered one year as long enough. You can of course change `LockDuration` to any value you want.

Finally, the cookie is saved to the client computer using the `Add` method of the `Cookies` collection of the current `Response` object.

The Administration User Interface

Even though we've already completed much of the work, we can't yet see any results in the browser. As with the rest of our site, designing and implementing good data and business components is of fundamental importance and has taken precedence here. Having taken care of the data and business layers we can now move on to our administration user interface. The presentation tier will directly use only the business layer to access and modify the data, and will have no dependency on the data layer. We just need to show the records and offer some way to call the business component's methods, which is a trivial task thanks to the powerful ASP.NET server controls available.

The ASPXs for this module should go into the `modules\forums` folder and be part of the main `ThePhile` project. Remember to add a reference to the `Business` and `Configuration` projects developed earlier.

Before starting to look at the code, let's see a screenshot of what we're going to produce:

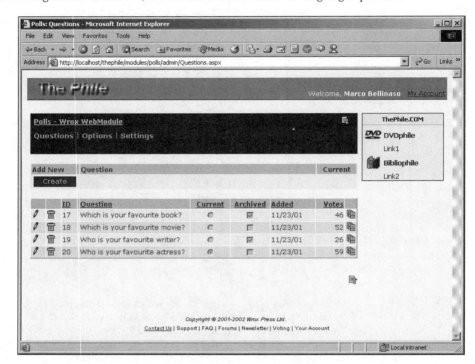

This page allows the administrator to see the available questions, change which is the current one, archive old questions, change the text, see the total number of votes for any question, and add a new question. The 'group of sheets' icon on the far right is used to jump directly to the page that displays and manages the options for the question.

Creating the Header and Footer User Controls

As in previous chapters, we need a header control and a footer control for all the pages in this administration section. The header control includes the site bar and another menu bar, as can be seen in the screenshot above. This menu bar contains the module name and links to the other administration pages. The footer bar is the same as for the other administration pages.

We add two user controls to the project and name them `AdminHeader.ascx` and `AdminFooter.ascx`. Their content is exactly the same as the header/footer we built for the `NewsManager` module in Chapter 6, except for the links of course, so refer back if you want to see the complete code. Except for the site header and footer, and the menu server control, the rest is plain HTML code for displaying the links, and a JavaScript function to show a short description when the mouse cursor hovers over a menu link. We don't need to add any code to the codebehind files, just change their namespace from the default value to `Wrox.WebModules.Polls.Controls.User`, according to the naming conventions described in Chapter 2.

The Questions Manager Page

The screenshot above shows the records in the grid in normal display mode. To add a new question the administrator clicks the **Create** button at the top-left of the main page, and this is the result:

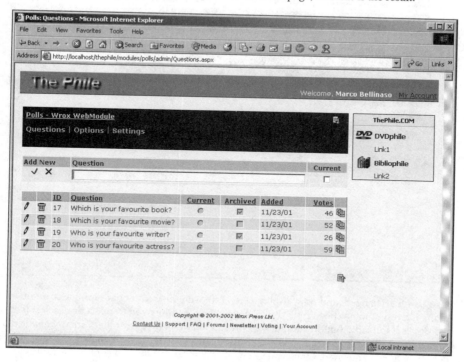

In 'new question mode' the administrator can type the text of the new question and check the checkbox if the new question is to be the current one. It is not possible to set the `Archived` attribute at this time, because it would not make sense to add a question and archive it immediately. The question is actually added to the database by pressing the green tick icon, or the operation can be cancelled by pressing the red X.

You can see that the `Current` and `Archived` attributes are displayed in the grid with a `radiobutton` and a `checkbox`, respectively. We use a `radio button` for the **Current** column because only one question can be the current one, and radiobuttons generally indicate that only one of a set of options can be selected. In this case this is more a graphical detail, because it is not possible to change the values anyway since the controls are in read-only mode. If you want to change the `Archived/Current` attributes, or edit the text of any question, press the pencil icon at the far left of the grid, and you'll get the grid changed as follows:

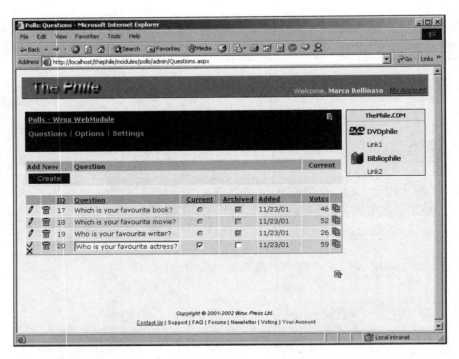

The clicked row has changed, and now displays a textbox with the current question's text, and two checkboxes. Note that the radio button has been replaced by a checkbox, to allow you to select or deselect it: it wouldn't be possible to deselect the radio button without selecting another one (and the others are not enabled anyway). Note also that some of the columns, namely ID, Added, and Votes, are not editable, because these values should not be manually amended. Once you've changed the values, you can confirm or cancel the update with the tick or the cross icon.

The Questions.aspx Page

This ASP.NET page is the place where the user interface is defined. We create Questions.aspx page in the modules\forums folder of the main ThePhile project. The page starts with the declaration of the codebehind file, the <head> section, the insertion of the header control, and the declaration of the server-side form:

```
<%@ Page language="c#" Codebehind="Questions.aspx.cs"
        AutoEventWireup="false"
        Inherits="Wrox.WebModules.Polls.Web.Questions" %>
<%@ Register TagPrefix="Polls" TagName="AdminHeader"
            src="AdminHeader.ascx" %>
<%@ Register TagPrefix="Polls" TagName="AdminFooter"
            src="AdminFooter.ascx" %>
<!DOCTYPE HTML PUBLIC "-//W3C//DTD HTML 4.0 Transitional//EN" >
<html>
  <head>
    <title>Polls: Questions</title>
    <link href="/ThePhile/Styles/ThePhile.css" rel="stylesheet" />
```

```
      <link href="/ThePhile/Styles/Navigator.css" rel="stylesheet" />
      <meta name="CODE_LANGUAGE" Content="C#">
  </head>
  <body>
    <form method="post" runat="server" ID="Questions">
      <!-- Insert the menu user control -->
      <Polls:AdminHeader ID="Menu" runat="server" />
```

Moving down into the body of the page, we come to the table for adding a new question when the **Create** button is pressed:

```
<asp:table runat="server" CssClass="Grid_General" Width="100%" >
  <asp:TableRow CssClass="Grid_Header">
    <asp:TableCell Width="85px" Text="Add New" />
    <asp:TableCell Text="Question" />
    <asp:TableCell Width="70px" Text="Current" HorizontalAlign="Center" />
  </asp:TableRow>
  <asp:TableRow ID="CreateNewRow">
    <asp:TableCell HorizontalAlign="Center">
      <asp:Button runat="server" Text="Create" ID="Create"
                  CssClass="Button" OnClick="Create_Click" Width="80px" />
    </asp:TableCell>
    <asp:TableCell ID="AddNewResultCell" ColumnSpan="2">
      <asp:Label runat="server" CssClass="Error" ID="AddNewError"
                 Text="This item was already present" Visible="false" />
    </asp:TableCell>
  </asp:TableRow>
  <asp:TableRow ID="AddNewControlsRow" Visible="false">
    <asp:TableCell VerticalAlign="Top">
      <asp:Image ImageURL="./Images/Spacer.gif" Width="15px"
                 Height="1px" runat="server" />
      <asp:LinkButton ID="AddNew" runat="server"
                 Text="<img border=0 src=./Images/OK.gif Alt='Add new list'>"
                 OnClick="AddNew_Click" />
      <asp:Image ImageURL="./Images/Spacer.gif" Width="15px"
                 Height="1px" runat="server" />
      <asp:LinkButton ID="CancelAddNew" runat="server"
                 CausesValidation="false"
      Text="<img border=0 src=./Images/Cancel.gif Alt='Cancel editing mode'>"
                 OnClick="CancelAddNew_Click" />
    </asp:TableCell>
    <asp:TableCell VerticalAlign="Top">
      <asp:TextBox runat="server" CssClass="TextBox"
                 ID="NewQuestionText" Width="100%" />
      <asp:RequiredFieldValidator runat="server"
                                   ControlToValidate="NewQuestionText"
                                   Display="dynamic">
        <br>* Question text is required
      </asp:RequiredFieldValidator>
    </asp:TableCell>
    <asp:TableCell VerticalAlign="Top" HorizontalAlign="Center">
      <asp:CheckBox runat="server" ID="NewIsCurrent" />
    </asp:TableCell>
  </asp:TableRow>
</asp:table>
```

The controls for the question's text and its current state are made invisible in the declaration above – they will be shown later from the codebehind, in the `Click` event of the **Create** button.

347

Now let's look at the central part of the page: the grid that displays and edits the records. It's very similar to what we've already covered in previous chapters, but we'll show it again here in a few separate pieces. In the following code the grid is declared, and we create the first two columns, for editing and deleting a row:

```
<asp:DataGrid ID="QuestionsGrid" runat="server"
              CssClass="Grid_General"
              HeaderStyle-CssClass="Grid_Header"
              ItemStyle-CssClass="Grid_Item"
              AlternatingItemStyle-CssClass="Grid_AlternatingItem"
              AllowSorting="True" AutoGenerateColumns="False"
              DataKeyField="QuestionID"
              OnEditCommand="QuestionsGrid_Edit"
              OnCancelCommand="QuestionsGrid_CancelEdit"
              OnUpdateCommand="QuestionsGrid_Update"
              OnDeleteCommand="QuestionsGrid_Delete"
              OnSortCommand="QuestionsGrid_Sort"
              Width="100%">

  <Columns>
    <asp:EditCommandColumn
                    ItemStyle-Width="25px" EditText="<img border=0
                    alt='Edit this question' src=./Images/Edit.gif>"
                    CancelText="<img border=0 src=./Images/Cancel.gif>"
                    UpdateText="<img border=0 src=./Images/OK.gif>"
    />
    <asp:ButtonColumn
                    ItemStyle-Width="25px" Text="<img border=0
                    alt='Delete this question' src=./Images/Delete.gif>"
                    CommandName="delete"
    />
```

The grid allows us to sort the questions, set the `QuestionID` column as the primary key for the grid, and define some event handlers. The `EditCommandColumn` is a specific column with a link to begin the editing, while `ButtonColumn` creates normal buttons or links whose `Click` event must be handled to delete the question. Here is the code for the columns that display the question's ID, text, and other attributes that were visible in the last screenshot:

```
<asp:BoundColumn HeaderText="ID" ItemStyle-Width="30px"
                DataField="QuestionID" ReadOnly="True"
                SortExpression="QuestionID"
/>
<asp:TemplateColumn HeaderText="Question"
                SortExpression="QuestionText">
  <ItemTemplate>
    <asp:Label runat="server" Text='<%# DataBinder.Eval(
            Container.DataItem, "QuestionText") %>' />
  </ItemTemplate>
  <EditItemTemplate>
    <asp:TextBox ID="EditQuestionText" runat="server"
        Text='<%# DataBinder.Eval(Container.DataItem, "QuestionText") %>'
        CssClass="TextBox" Width="100%" />
```

```
                <asp:RequiredFieldValidator runat="server"
                                   ControlToValidate="EditQuestionText"
                                   Display="dynamic">
                                   * Question text is required
            </asp:RequiredFieldValidator>
        </EditItemTemplate>
    </asp:TemplateColumn>
  <asp:TemplateColumn HeaderText="Current"
                    SortExpression="IsCurrentQuestion"
                    ItemStyle-Width="70px"
                    HeaderStyle-HorizontalAlign="Center"
                    ItemStyle-HorizontalAlign="Center">
    <ItemTemplate>
      <asp:RadioButton runat="server" Enabled="false" Checked='<%#
                    Convert.ToBoolean(DataBinder.Eval(
                        Container.DataItem, "IsCurrentQuestion")) %>' />
    </ItemTemplate>
    <EditItemTemplate>
      <asp:CheckBox ID="EditIsCurrent" runat="server" Checked='<%#
                    Convert.ToBoolean(DataBinder.Eval(
                        Container.DataItem, "IsCurrentQuestion")) %>' />
    </EditItemTemplate>
  </asp:TemplateColumn>
  <asp:TemplateColumn HeaderText="Archived" SortExpression="Archived"
                    ItemStyle-Width="70px"
                    HeaderStyle-HorizontalAlign="Center"
                    ItemStyle-HorizontalAlign="Center">
    <ItemTemplate>
      <asp:CheckBox runat="server" Enabled="false" Checked='<%#
                    Convert.ToBoolean(DataBinder.Eval(
                        Container.DataItem, "Archived")) %>' />
    </ItemTemplate>
    <EditItemTemplate>
      <asp:CheckBox ID="EditArchived" runat="server" Checked='<%#
                    Convert.ToBoolean(DataBinder.Eval(
                        Container.DataItem, "Archived")) %>' />
    </EditItemTemplate>
  </asp:TemplateColumn>
  <asp:TemplateColumn HeaderText="Added"
                    SortExpression="AddedDate" ItemStyle-Width="80px">
    <ItemTemplate>
      <asp:Label runat="server" Text='<%# DataBinder.Eval(
                    Container.DataItem, "AddedDate", "{0:MM/dd/yy}") %>' />
    </ItemTemplate>
  </asp:TemplateColumn>
  <asp:BoundColumn HeaderText="Votes" ItemStyle-Width="50px"
                    DataField="TotalVotes" ReadOnly="True"
                    SortExpression="TotalVotes"
                    ItemStyle-HorizontalAlign="Right"
                    HeaderStyle-HorizontalAlign="Right"
  />
```

The first column is defined as a normal, non-editable column that shows the ID of the question. The second column has a label with the question text when in display mode, and a textbox for modifying the text when in editing mode.

The third and fourth columns show a radio button and a checkbox, respectively, when in display mode, and both of them show a checkbox in editing mode. There isn't much difference between using a radio button or a checkbox as they both have a `Checked` property, whose value is the value of the respective field converted to a Boolean value through the `Convert.ToBoolean` method. We use a radio button for the Current column because it indicates that only one question can be the current one.

The last two columns declared in the code above are read-only columns that display the `AddedDate` and `TotalVotes` field values, respectively.

The last column on the far right shows the icon to jump to the options page:

```
<asp:HyperLinkColumn ItemStyle-Width="20px"
               DataNavigateUrlField="QuestionID"
               DataNavigateUrlFormatString="Options.aspx?QuestionID={0}"
               DataTextFormatString="<img border=0 Alt='Show options'
                                         src=./Images/Group.gif>"
               DataTextField="QuestionID"
               ItemStyle-HorizontalAlign="Center"
    />
</Columns>
</asp:DataGrid>
```

It is a non-editable hyperlink rendered as an image, and the URL which it points to is built with a string template defined in `DataNavigateUrlFormatString`: the ID of each row will replace the `{0}` marker.

The page ends with the closing tags for the `DataGrid` control, the form, and the footer control:

```
    <Polls:AdminFooter ID="Footer" runat="server" />
  </form>
  </body>
</html>
```

The Codebehind for Questions.aspx

Now we're going to write the code that drives the page's functionality, in the codebehind file automatically created by Visual Studio .NET, `Questions.cs`. The code of this file is very similar to the codebehind file we saw in Chapter 6, so we'll show the code here without repeating all the details already explained. Here is the handler that runs when the page is loaded:

```
protected void Page_Load(object sender, EventArgs e)
{
  if (!Page.IsPostBack)
  {
    // bind the page's controls
    BindGrid();
  }
}
```

The code above calls the `BindGrid` method, which actually fills the grid with the database records. Here's the code for this procedure:

```
protected void BindGrid()
{
  // get all the Questions
  DataView myDV = Business.Question.GetQuestions().Tables[0].DefaultView;

  // sort the data according to the SortExpression value
  if (QuestionsGrid.Attributes["SortExpression"] != null)
    myDV.Sort = QuestionsGrid.Attributes["SortExpression"];

  QuestionsGrid.DataSource = myDV;
  QuestionsGrid.DataBind();
}
```

The function uses the business component to retrieve all the questions, and assigns the resulting `DataView` to the `DataSource` property of the `QuestionsGrid`. The `DataView` is then sorted according to a custom attribute set by the code in the next section. By default, when the page is loaded for the first time or when the grid's `SortAttribute` is null anyway, the records are sorted by creation date. They are already returned sorted in that way by the `sp_Polls_GetQuestions` stored procedure, so we don't have to set the `Sort` property in this case.

Sorting the Questions

When a column header is clicked, the `QuestionsGrid_Sort` function is called:

```
protected void QuestionsGrid_Sort(Object sender,
                                      DataGridSortCommandEventArgs e)
{
  AddNewError.Visible = false;
  ShowAddNewControls(false);
  QuestionsGrid.EditItemIndex = -1;
  // set the SortExpression attribute that will be used to actually sort
  // the data in the BindGrid method
  QuestionsGrid.Attributes["SortExpression"] = e.SortExpression.ToString();
  BindGrid();
}
```

The function first of all hides the controls for adding a new question or displaying an error message, in case they are visible. Then it disables the editing mode of a row, if enabled. Finally it extracts the selected ordering field and saves it as a grid attribute, the one we've just used in the previous procedure. The `BindGrid` procedure is called to refresh the grid with the new order applied.

Editing and Updating Questions

Now we will implement the methods that deal with the editing and updating of rows. The first procedure hides the control for adding a record, if visible, and starts the editing mode for the selected row by setting the `EditItemIndex` property:

```
protected void QuestionsGrid_Edit(object sender, DataGridCommandEventArgs e)
{
```

```
    AddNewError.Visible = false;
    ShowAddNewControls(false);
    // start editing
    QuestionsGrid.EditItemIndex = (int)e.Item.ItemIndex;
    BindGrid();
}
```

The second procedure resets the same property to −1, which brings the grid back to the normal display mode:

```
protected void QuestionsGrid_CancelEdit(object sender,
                                        DataGridCommandEventArgs e)
{
    QuestionsGrid.EditItemIndex = -1;
    BindGrid();
}
```

The last procedure completes the updating of the row, as long as the validator controls find no error in the input values. It extracts the new values from the edit controls, updates the properties of a Business.Question object, and persists the changes by calling its Update method:

```
protected void QuestionsGrid_Update(object sender,
                                    DataGridCommandEventArgs e)
{
    if (Page.IsValid)
    {
        // get the new values from the textboxes
        string questionText = ((TextBox)e.Item.FindControl(
                                            "EditQuestionText")).Text;
        bool isCurrent = ((CheckBox)e.Item.FindControl("EditIsCurrent")).Checked;
        bool archived = ((CheckBox)e.Item.FindControl("EditArchived")).Checked;
        int questionID = (int)QuestionsGrid.DataKeys[e.Item.ItemIndex];

        // update the values
        Business.Question question = new Business.Question(questionID);
        question.Text = questionText;
        question.IsCurrent = isCurrent;
        question.Archived = archived;
        question.Update();

        QuestionsGrid.EditItemIndex = -1;
        BindGrid();
    }
}
```

Deleting a Question

This event handler has the same structure as the procedure above, but it's actually simpler because it just extracts the primary key of the clicked row, uses it to initialize a new Business.Question object, and calls its Delete method:

```
protected void QuestionsGrid_Delete(object sender,
                                          DataGridCommandEventArgs e)
{
  AddNewError.Visible = false;
  ShowAddNewControls(false);
  QuestionsGrid.EditItemIndex = -1;

  // get the ID of this record and delete it
  Business.Question question = new Business.Question(
                    (int)QuestionsGrid.DataKeys[e.Item.ItemIndex]);
  question.Delete();
  BindGrid();
}
```

Creating a Question

The last part to see is how to add a new question. When the Create button is pressed, the textbox and checkbox controls and the respective icons for confirming or canceling the operation are shown, while the Create button is made invisible. Below you can see the code for this event and the support functions that show or hide the controls according to the passed Boolean parameter:

```
protected void Create_Click(object sender, EventArgs e)
{
  // show the textboxes and buttons for adding a new record
  AddNewError.Visible = false;
  ShowAddNewControls(true);
  QuestionsGrid.EditItemIndex = -1;
  BindGrid();
}

protected void ShowAddNewControls(bool ShowControls)
{
  // show/hide the controls for adding a new record
  NewQuestionText.Text="";
  NewIsCurrent.Checked=false;

  AddNewControlsRow.Visible = ShowControls;
  CreateNewRow.Visible = !ShowControls;
}
```

The icon for adding a new list is a button with a click event procedure:

```
protected void AddNew_Click(object sender, EventArgs e)
{
  if (Page.IsValid)
  {
    // add the new record
    if (new Business.Question().Create(NewQuestionText.Text,
                              NewIsCurrent.Checked, false) < 0)
    {
      // if Add returned -1, the question was already present
      AddNewError.Visible = true;
  }

    ShowAddNewControls(false);
```

```
        BindGrid();
    }
}
```

The above code calls the `Create` method of the `Business.Question` class with the values read from the input textbox and checkbox, and the value `false` for the `Archived` field. If the method returns `true` then it makes visible the label that tells the user that the question is already present.

The `ButtonLink` control is for canceling the operation; when pressed it hides the controls for adding the question and shows the **Create** button:

```
protected void CancelAddNew_Click(object sender, EventArgs e)
{
    ShowAddNewControls(false);
}
```

This button would cause the page to be validated, as does any control that handles a server event and submits the page, and would result in an error if the textbox were empty. To avoid this problem we set its `CausesValidation` property to false when we declared it in the ASPX page.

Managing the Options

The page for managing the options of the questions has a very similar structure to the page we've just completed. It is simpler because we have less information to show, and it only adds a `DropDownList` control to select the question for which we want to see and edit the available options. The following screenshot shows the page while we're adding an option for the currently selected question:

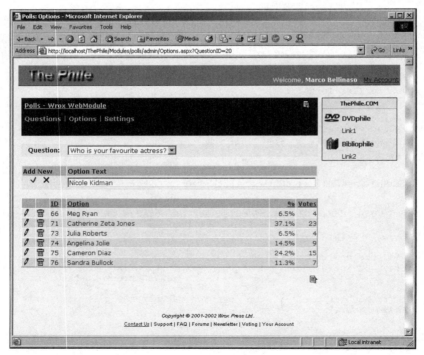

The Options.aspx Page

As we mentioned, the code for this page is similar to the previous one, so we'll only see the additions, which in this case is just the drop-down list of questions. Look at the code below to see how this is declared:

```
<asp:table Width="100%" ID="TableOptions"
           runat="server" CssClass="Grid_General">
  <asp:TableRow>
    <asp:TableCell Width="85px" HorizontalAlign="Center"
                   VerticalAlign="Top" Font-Bold="True" Text="Question:" />
    <asp:TableCell>
      <asp:DropDownList runat="server" ID="QuestionsDropDown"
                   DataTextField="QuestionText"
                   DataValueField="QuestionID"
                   CssClass="TextBox" AutoPostBack="True"
                   OnSelectedIndexChanged="QuestionsDropDown_IndexChanged"
      />
    </asp:TableCell>
  </asp:TableRow>
</asp:table>
```

The main thing to note is that the drop-down list has the `AutoPostBack` property set to `true`, which causes the form to be posted back every time the user changes the selected item. Remember that when a page is posted back its `IsPostBack` property is `true` – you can check this property to avoid filling the `DropDownList` of questions every time the form is posted back, since the control's state is maintained in subsequent calls of the page.

The rest of the page is mostly composed of the grid, which has four columns (`QuestionID`, `QuestionText`, `Percentage`, and `TotalVotes`) returned by the `sp_Polls_GetOptions` stored procedure. (Remember that `TotalVotes` and `Percentage` are calculated columns, but this does not make any difference here.) Only the question's text is an editable column, the others are read-only columns. There is really nothing in this grid that we haven't already seen in the `Questions.aspx` page and the previous chapters, so we won't repeat the code here. You can find the complete code in the download.

The Code-behind for Options.aspx

As for the ASPX page, here we'll show only the differences from the previous page. The code for loading and binding the records to the grid is the same, as well as the code that adds, edits, and deletes the options. The difference here is that we also retrieve the questions and bind them to a `DropDownList` control, selecting the question with the ID that was specified in the `QueryString` passed along with the page URL. Here is the code that does all this, in the `Page_Load` event handler:

```
protected void Page_Load(object sender, EventArgs e)
{
  // get the QuestionID from the QueryString
  string questionID = Request.Params["QuestionID"];
  OptionsGrid.Attributes["QuestionID"] = questionID;

  if (!Page.IsPostBack)
  {
    // load all the available questions in the DropDown control
    DataView myDV = Business.Question.GetQuestions().Tables[0].DefaultView;
```

```
        QuestionsDropDown.DataSource = myDV;
        QuestionsDropDown.DataBind();

        if (questionID!=null)
        {
          // select the DropDown element according to the questionID
          QuestionsDropDown.SelectedIndex = QuestionsDropDown.Items.IndexOf(
                          QuestionsDropDown.Items.FindByValue(questionID));
        }

        // (re)bind the page's controls
        BindGrid();
    }
}
```

If the ID retrieved from the `QueryString` is supplied, we select the corresponding item in the `DropDownList` after it has been filled.

Staying with the `QuestionsDropDown` control, there is also the procedure that handles the `OnSelectedIndexChanged` event:

```
protected void QuestionsDropDown_IndexChanged(object sender, EventArgs e)
{
    // reload the page to show the options for the selected question
    // This will also hide the controls to add an option if they were visible
    Response.Redirect("Options.aspx?QuestionID=" +
                            QuestionsDropDown.SelectedItem.Value);
}
```

This redirects the browser to the same page, but with the ID of the selected question, in order to load that question's options the next time `BindGrid` is called.

Modifying the Settings Online

We've used the configuration component on several occasions so far, to get the settings, but whenever we wanted to change them we had to manually edit the `Polls.Config` file. It's not that big a deal, but why not provide a new page that allows the administrator to make all the changes through a web browser? This will avoid the need for editing the file and uploading it through FTP or with the tool we built in Chapter 4. The page, `Settings.aspx`, is presented below:

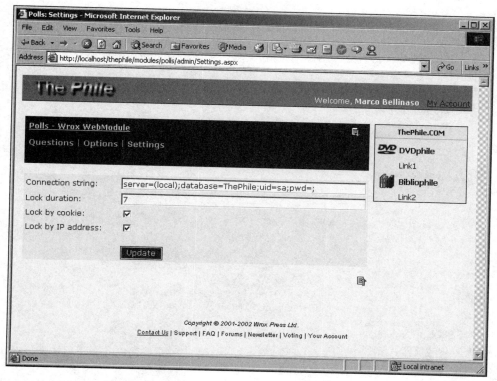

The Settings.aspx Page

This ASP.NET page is made up of a couple of textboxes, a couple of checkboxes, and the Update button, all aligned within a table. Once we've created the new Settings.aspx page, we fill it with the usual code for the page declaration, the header and the footer, and this server-side form in the middle:

```
<form method="post" runat="server" ID="Settings">
  <asp:table runat="server" CssClass="Grid_General" Width="100%">
    <asp:TableRow>
      <asp:TableCell Width="150px" Text="Connection string:" />
      <asp:TableCell>
        <asp:TextBox runat="server" Width="100%"
                     ID="ConnectionString" CssClass="TextBox" />
        <asp:RequiredFieldValidator runat="server"
                          ControlToValidate="ConnectionString" Display="dynamic">
          <br>* This field is required
        </asp:RequiredFieldValidator>
      </asp:TableCell>
    </asp:TableRow>
    <asp:TableRow>
      <asp:TableCell Text="Lock duration:" />
      <asp:TableCell>
        <asp:TextBox runat="server" Width="100%"
                     ID="LockDuration" CssClass="TextBox" />
```

```
        <asp:CompareValidator runat="server"
                            ControlToValidate="LockDuration" Type="Integer"
                            Operator="DataTypeCheck" Display="dynamic" >
          <br>* Invalid format
        </asp:CompareValidator>
      </asp:TableCell>
    </asp:TableRow>
    <asp:TableRow>
      <asp:TableCell Text="Lock by cookie:" />
      <asp:TableCell>
        <asp:CheckBox runat="server" ID="LockByCookie" />
      </asp:TableCell>
    </asp:TableRow>
    <asp:TableRow>
      <asp:TableCell Text="Lock by IP address:" />
      <asp:TableCell>
        <asp:CheckBox runat="server" ID="LockByIP" />
      </asp:TableCell>
    </asp:TableRow>
    <asp:TableRow VerticalAlign="Bottom" Height="40px">
      <asp:TableCell />
      <asp:TableCell>
        <asp:Button runat="server" Text="Update" ID="Update"
                  CssClass="Button" OnClick="Update_Click">
        </asp:Button>
      </asp:TableCell>
    </asp:TableRow>
  </asp:table>
</form>
```

The highlighted code declares the controls that show the current settings and allow changes to be made. There are two invisible controls, the validators, which ensure that the connection string is supplied and that if the (optional) lock duration is provided it is a number.

The Codebehind for Settings.aspx

The codebehind for modifying settings is composed of just two procedures. The first is `Page_Load`, which retrieves the settings from the XML file (or from the cache if this is not the first time we request them) by using the `ModuleConfig` and `ModuleSettings` classes in the `Configuration` assembly. The following code shows the current settings when the page is first loaded:

```
protected void Page_Load(object sender, EventArgs e)
{
  if (!IsPostBack)
  {
    Configuration.ModuleSettings settings =
                            Configuration.ModuleConfig.GetSettings();
    ConnectionString.Text = settings.ConnectionString;
    LockDuration.Text = settings.LockDuration.ToString();
    LockByCookie.Checked = settings.LockByCookie;
    LockByIP.Checked = settings.LockByIP;
  }
}
```

The second procedure is `Update_Click`, raised when the **Update** button is clicked. It gets the new settings from the controls, sets the properties of a new `ModuleSettings` object, and finally calls the `ModuleConfig`'s `SaveSettings` method to serialize the `settings` object to the XML file:

```
protected void Update_Click(object sender, EventArgs e)
{
  Configuration.ModuleSettings settings = new
                                  Configuration.ModuleSettings();

  // set the new properties values and update everything
  settings.ConnectionString = ConnectionString.Text.Trim();
  settings.LockByCookie = LockByCookie.Checked;
  settings.LockByIP = LockByIP.Checked;

  if(LockDuration.Text.Trim().Length > 0)
    settings.LockDuration = int.Parse(LockDuration.Text.Trim());
  else
  {
    settings.LockDuration = -1;
    LockDuration.Text = "-1";
  }

  // save the new settings
  Configuration.ModuleConfig.SaveSettings(settings);
}
```

Note that the `LockDuration` setting is not required; if it is not supplied then the default value -1 is chosen, and also shown in the respective textbox.

We're done with the administration settings now. In the next sections we're going to discuss the end-user side of the module, such as the poll box, archive page, and the Windows client.

The Poll User Control

The administration console is complete, and now we can think about the implementation of the end-user part of the module. In the previous screenshots you will have noticed that a number of votes have been cast, but so far we have no way of posting a vote. In order to be able to test the grid in the administration pages we initially added some records to the `Polls_Votes` table manually. Now it's time to build the poll user control that we'll use in the homepage or other pages of the site. The poll box we want to create is represented in the following diagram:

We add a new user control named `Poll.ascx` to the project, and enter the following code. The code is quite long, so we'll split it up and explain the individual pieces. The code below is all that is needed to create the poll box, and show the question and list of options:

```
<%@ Control Language="c#" AutoEventWireup="false" Codebehind="Poll.ascx.cs"
           Inherits="Wrox.WebModules.Polls.Web.Controls.User.Poll"%>
<asp:Table runat="server" ID="PollTable">
  <asp:TableRow>
    <asp:TableCell runat="server" ID="PollHeader"
                   HorizontalAlign="Center" />
  </asp:TableRow>
  <asp:TableRow>
    <asp:TableCell runat="server" ID="PollQuestion"
                   HorizontalAlign="Center" />
  </asp:TableRow>
  <asp:TableRow>
    <asp:TableCell HorizontalAlign="Center">
      <asp:RadioButtonList runat="server" ID="OptionsList"
                   DataTextField="OptionText" DataValueField="OptionID" />
      <asp:Label Runat="server" ID="PollError" Text="* Please select an
                 option" CssClass="Error" Visible="False" />
    </asp:TableCell>
  </asp:TableRow>
  <asp:TableRow>
    <asp:TableCell HorizontalAlign="Center">
      <asp:Button runat="server" Text="Vote" ID="Vote" CssClass="Button"
                  OnClick="Vote_Click" />
    </asp:TableCell>
  </asp:TableRow>
```

The header of the poll will be displayed by setting the `Text` property of the cell named `PollHeader`, and the question through the `PollQuestion` cell. Finally, the options are shown by the `RadioButtonList` called `OptionsList`. This works similarly to a `DropDownListBox`: it creates an item for each row in the data source and shows the content of the `DataTextField` field, and the added radio button has the value of the `DataValueField` field.

In a few lines we've already declared all the controls that show the options and post back the form with the selection. Now we need to declare other controls that show the results after the user has voted. We use a `DataList` for this, because it allows us to repeat custom HTML code or server controls for all the rows in the data source. The `DataList` control has many members in common with the `DataGrid` control, since they both inherit from `BaseDataList` – properties such as `DataKeyField`, `DataKeys`, `DataSource`, and `DataMember` and methods such as `DataBind` have exactly the same meaning in the two controls, and are used in the same way. The main difference between the two controls is that the `DataList` requires at least the `<ItemTemplate>` section, which contains the template code repeated for each item of the bound `DataSource`, while the `DataGrid` control can auto-generate HTML for rendering the data in columns. If you want to reproduce something like a grid, with multiple columns, you must do it by writing the `<table>`, `<tr>`, and `<td>` tags by yourself to create the grid layout–the `DataList` does not do that for you. Other templates supported by the `DataList` control are `HeaderTemplate`, `AlternatingItemTemplate`, `EditItemTemplate`, `SelectedItemTemplate`, `SeparatorTemplate`, and `FooterTemplate`, whose meaning should be clear (many of them are available for the `DataGrid`'s templated columns too). A very interesting property for this control is `RepeatColumns`, which allows us to specify that the templated items will be repeated in one or more columns.

For complete examples of these properties and templates refer to Professional ASP.NET 1.0 (Wrox Press, ISBN 1-861007-03-5), or Building Web Solutions with ASP.NET and ADO.NET (MS Press, ISBN 0-735615-78-0).

The `DataList` in our page is declared as follows:

```
<asp:TableRow>
  <asp:TableCell HorizontalAlign="Center">
    <asp:DataList runat="server" ID="ResultsList">
      <ItemTemplate>
        <span class='<%# CssClass %>'>
          - <%# DataBinder.Eval(Container.DataItem, "OptionText") %>
          <br>
        </span>
        <span class='<%# ResultsStyle %>'>
          <%# DataBinder.Eval(Container.DataItem, "TotalVotes",
                                            "({0} votes") %>
          - <%# DataBinder.Eval(Container.DataItem, "Percentage",
                                            "{0:N1}%)") %>
        </span>
        <hr class='<%# BarStyle %>' width='<%# DataBinder.Eval(
            Container.DataItem, "Percentage", "{0:N0}%") %>' align="left">
      </ItemTemplate>
    </asp:DataList>
  </asp:TableCell>
</asp:TableRow>
```

The `ItemTemplate` section will be repeated for every row of the data source, as we said. For each data row we create the following elements:

❑   A `<span>` container for the option's text.

❑   A `<span>` container for the option's total number of votes and the corresponding percentage. (Both values are provided by the data source, and calculated by the `sp_Polls_GetOptions` stored procedure.)

❑   An `<hr>` line, whose width is set to the `Percentage` field of the data row currently being processed by the `DataList`. This way, creating the bars that graphically show the results for the options is really a no-brainer.

So, I guess that displaying the results and the graphical bars has turned out to be simpler than you might have thought.

It's worth noting that in the table in the previous piece of code, and in the code above, we set the `class` or `CssClass` properties of the HTML and server controls to public properties defined in the code-behind. No style is hard-coded in the control itself – everything (well, the most important parts at least) can be defined by the hosting page at design time or programmatically at run-time, as we can do with any server control.

The file ends with a link to the `ShowArchive.aspx` page, and the closing tags for the parent table and the HTML form:

```
<asp:TableRow>
  <asp:TableCell HorizontalAlign="Center">
    <asp:HyperLink runat="server" ID="ArchiveLink" Text="[Archive]"
                   NavigateUrl="ShowArchive.aspx" />
  </asp:TableCell>
</asp:TableRow>
</asp:Table>
```

The Codebehind for the Poll User Control

In the codebehind for the poll user control, we change the namespace to `Wrox.WebModules.Polls.Web.Controls.User`. The class then starts with the declaration of the server-side control that Visual Studio .NET should have already added for us. Then we have to add the code for the public variables listed in the design section: the properties for the style of the header, question, results, and, most notably, the `QuestionID` property for specifying the ID of the question to load in the poll box. Here is the code:

```
private string barStyle;
private string resultsStyle;
private int questionID = -2;

public bool ArchiveLinkVisible
{
  get { return ArchiveLink.Visible; }
  set { ArchiveLink.Visible = value; }
}

public string BarStyle
{
  get { return barStyle; }
  set { barStyle = value; }
}

public string ResultsStyle
{
  get { return resultsStyle; }
  set { resultsStyle = value; }
}

public string CssClass
{
  get { return PollTable.CssClass; }
  set
  {
    PollTable.CssClass = value;
    OptionsList.CssClass = value;
  }
}

public Unit Width
```

```
  {
    get { return PollTable.Width; }
    set { PollTable.Width = value; }
  }

  public HorizontalAlign HorizontalAlign
  {
    get { return PollTable.HorizontalAlign; }
    set { PollTable.HorizontalAlign = value; }
  }

  public string QuestionStyle
  {
    get { return PollQuestion.CssClass; }
    set { PollQuestion.CssClass = value; }
  }

  public string HeaderStyle
  {
    get { return PollHeader.CssClass; }
    set { PollHeader.CssClass = value; }
  }

  public string ButtonStyle
  {
    get { return Vote.Attributes["Class"].ToString(); }
    set { Vote.Attributes["Class"] = value; }
  }

  public string LinkStyle
  {
    get { return ArchiveLink.Text; }
    set { ArchiveLink.Text = value; }
  }

  public string HeaderText
  {
    get { return PollHeader.Text; }
    set { PollHeader.Text = value; }
  }

  public int QuestionID
  {
    get { return questionID; }
    set { questionID = value; }
  }
```

It's worth noting that most style properties, such as HeaderStyle or ButtonStyle, directly map properties of the server-side control, while others, such as BarStyle and ResultStyle, need an auxiliary private property to keep the state of the respective property. This is because the controls they will be used with are dynamically built by the DataList control at runtime.

Now for the code that retrieves the data from the database, binds it to the proper controls, and either shows or hides the options or results (depending on whether the user has already voted for the question being asked):

```
public override void DataBind()
{
  PollError.Visible = false;

  // if the QuestionID is not specified, get the current question's ID
  if (QuestionID == -2)
    QuestionID = Business.Question.GetCurrentID();

  // if there is a valid question
  if (QuestionID > -1)
  {
    // get the details for the specified question
    Business.Question question = new Business.Question(QuestionID);
    // if this question does not exist, exit now
    if (question.ID == -1)
    {
      Vote.Visible = false;
      return;
    }

    // show the question text
    PollQuestion.Visible = true;
    PollQuestion.Text = question.Text;

    // get the options
    DataView options = question.GetOptions().Tables[0].DefaultView;

    // if the user has not already voted, or is allowed to vote again...
    if (question.AllowVote)
    {
      // show the radiobutton options and hide the results
      OptionsList.Visible = true;
      ResultsList.Visible = false;
      OptionsList.DataSource = options;
      OptionsList.DataBind();
      // show the Vote button only if there is at least 1 option
      Vote.Visible = (options.Count >= 1);
    }
    else
    {
      // otherwise hide the RadioButtonList + Vote button,
      // and show the results
      OptionsList.Visible = false;
      Vote.Visible = false;
      ResultsList.Visible = true;
      ResultsList.DataSource = options;
      ResultsList.DataBind();
      // add the number of total votes to the question text
      PollQuestion.Text += "<br>(" + question.TotalVotes + " votes)";
    }
```

```
    }
    else
    {
      // if there is no current question, hide the controls
      PollQuestion.Visible = false;
      OptionsList.Visible = false;
      Vote.Visible = false;
      ResultsList.Visible = false;
    }
  }
```

The core procedure is DataBind, which overrides the implementation of the base class. The code first gets the details of the specified question (if no QuestionID is supplied, it takes the current question by default). If the question is not found the procedure does not do anything else, otherwise it goes ahead by showing the question text in the respective table tell. Then, if it detects that the current user can vote (through the AllowVote property of the instance of Business.Question) it binds the question's options to the RadioButtonList control and shows it. Otherwise it hides the RadioButtonList control and binds the options to the DataList control, and shows this control instead. Also the Vote button is shown or hidden accordingly.

There is also the Page_Load event that calls DataBind if the page that hosts the control is not posted back. We could avoid having to implement the Page_Load event, and we could leave the task of calling the control's DataBind method up to the host page, as we've done for all controls in the previous pages. However, the control retrieves the connection string, gets the records, and sets all the controls' properties on its own, so it makes sense that it also actually binds the data to the proper controls without any external intervention. This is the same method we followed for the Headlines control in the NewsManagement module in Chapter 6. Here's the required code:

```
private void Page_Load(object sender, System.EventArgs e)
{
  if (!Page.IsPostBack)
    DataBind();
}
```

> It's worth noting that in the code above we called the **DataBind** methods of this control. We can't use the **Page.DataBind** method to bind the data to all the controls, because this would also affect the controls on the page that hosts the user control, and this can cause unwanted behaviors. For example, say that the parent page has a listbox bound to a table, and that during its **Page_Load** event we selected an item. If we call **Page.DataBind** from the code above, the listbox would be reloaded and would of course deselect the item previously selected.

Handling the Postback Event

The code for the Vote_Click event is straightforward, thanks to the Business.Question's Vote method that takes care of checking if the user has already voted, and stores the vote in the database. We just have to get the ID of the selected option from the RadioButtonList, and pass it to the Vote method. If no option is selected, which is the case when the options are loaded and the user does not click any of them, then the control shows an error message instead. Here's the complete code:

```
protected void Vote_Click(object sender, EventArgs e)
{
  // if there is no option selected, show the error label
  if (OptionsList.SelectedItem == null)
  {
    PollError.Visible = true;
  }
  else
  {
    if (QuestionID == -2) QuestionID = Business.Question.GetCurrentID();
    // add the user's vote
    new Business.Question(QuestionID).Vote(
                            int.Parse(OptionsList.SelectedItem.Value));
    // re-bind, to show the results this time
    DataBind();
  }
}
```

Optimizing the Poll User Control

At this point the poll user control is fully functional. There is an issue though: every time we load the page that hosts the poll box we have to query the database to get the options and their details. Say that we want to insert the poll box into the site layout, into the header or footer maybe, and show the poll box from all the pages. This means that we would slow down execution of all the pages.

The content of the poll box does not change very often (at least as long as you don't have thousands of concurrent users with a large proportion actually voting), and once published it is very likely that the available options will remain the same. The first thing that comes to mind is to employ dynamic output caching, as we did in Chapter 6, since it allows us to easily cache pages and user control output for a given amount of time. However, after considering this option, we realized that this isn't the ideal solution in this case. In fact, dynamic caching saves the output every *n* seconds, or when the parameters in the URL or the form's controls change. But it does not refresh the cache based on custom rules defined within our control's code. In our case, we have to output different HTML depending on whether the user has or has not already voted for the current question. If we use dynamic output caching, the first time the control is displayed the whole output will be cached. Say that the user that requests the page with the poll box for the first time has already voted for the current question: the cached output would be the list of results. Now a second user, who has not voted yet, loads the page with the poll box: the ASP.NET engine detects that the output for the poll box is cached and displays it. Unfortunately, it displays the version with the results, and does not allow the user to vote! And a similar problem would occur if the first user had not voted yet, the output cached would display the list of options, and this would then be displayed to subsequent users, even those who should be prevented from voting again.

Well, this is the behavior of the standard control caching, but we can always employ our own implementation. Instead of caching the complete output, we will only cache the options data retrieved from the database – this is the operation that takes the longest time, and this data is the same in both cases (whether we're showing the results or the options list). When the user votes we delete the cached data, so that it is refreshed the next time someone loads the poll box.

Storing and reading data to and from the cache is really a no-brainer, thanks to the `Cache` object. Like the `Application` object, it is has a key/value pair `HashTable` to save and retrieve data, but also adds dependency-based expiration, lock management, and resource management (meaning that cached items not used are automatically removed). A dependency can be another cache key, a file, or a timestamp. When a dependency changes or expires, the respective cache item is invalidated and removed, so that the data must be retrieved again from its real source (file, database, return value of a function, etc.) the next time we need it. As mentioned, the `Cache` object manages concurrent requests and locks on its own, and unlike the `Application` object does not need the caller to use the `Lock` and `Unlock` methods.

Below you can see the complete structure of the codebehind, with the added or modified code highlighted:

```
public abstract class Poll : System.Web.UI.UserControl
{
  // controls declaration...

  private int cacheDuration = 5;

  public int CacheDuration
  {
    get { return cacheDuration; }
    set { cacheDuration = value; }
  }

  // other properties and private variables...

  public override void DataBind()
  {
    // if the QuestionID is not specified, get the current question's ID...

    // if there is a valid question
    if (QuestionID > -1)
    {
      ...
      // get the options
      DataView options;
      // if the options for this question are not cached,
      // retrieve and cache them, adding a dependency to a timestamp
      if (Cache["Polls_Question" + question.ID.ToString()]== null)
      {
        options = question.GetOptions().Tables[0].DefaultView;
        Cache.Insert("Polls_Question" + question.ID.ToString(), options,
                null, DateTime.Now.AddMinutes(CacheDuration), TimeSpan.Zero,
                System.Web.Caching.CacheItemPriority.High, null);
      }
      else
      {
        // otherwise extract the DataView from the cache
        options = (DataView)Cache["Polls_Question" +
                                            question.ID.ToString()];
      }
```

```
      // display the options or the results...
    }
    else
    {
      // if there is no current question, hide the controls...
    }
}

protected void Vote_Click(object sender, EventArgs e)
{
    // add the user's vote...
    ...
    // reset the options cached
    ResetCache();
    // re-bind, to show the results this time
    DataBind();
  }
}

public void ResetCache()
{
  if (QuestionID == -2) QuestionID = Business.Question.GetCurrentID();
  Cache.Remove("Polls_Question" + QuestionID.ToString());
}
}
```

First of all we added a public property called CacheDuration, which allows us to specify the number of minutes for which the data is cached (five minutes is the default). Then, in Page_Load we check if the cache has a non-null entry for the current question. If so, the entry is cast to a DataView type and we can bind the data to the proper controls. Otherwise, we first retrieve the data and then insert it into the cache, specifying the expiration time by summing the CacheDuration minutes to the current time. Lastly, in Vote_Click, after adding the vote, we call ResetCache, which deletes the cached DataView, so that the updated options and results are retrieved again next time DataBind is executed. The ResetCache method has public visibility, so that the host page can call it by itself if there are special needs.

Now we have an optimized control, which only queries the database every five minutes, or whatever duration you choose with the programmable CacheDuration property. This way we speed up all the pages that host the control.

Testing the Control

To test the control we add one poll box to the Questions.aspx page of the administration section. We want to test if the control correctly shows the current question when we change it from the administration page, and if it shows the updated text. It is also useful to have it here because we can add test votes without leaving the administration console. We register the control at the top of the page, and declare one at the bottom, just before the server form closing tag:

```
<%@ Page language="c#" Codebehind="Questions.aspx.cs"
        AutoEventWireup="false"
        Inherits="Wrox.WebModules.Polls.Web.Questions" %>
<%@ Register TagPrefix="Polls" TagName="Poll" src="..\Poll.ascx" %>
```

```
<%@ Register TagPrefix="Polls" TagName="AdminHeader"
          src="AdminHeader.ascx" %>
<%@ Register TagPrefix="Polls" TagName="AdminFooter"
          src="AdminFooter.ascx" %>
<html>
  <body>
    <form method="post" runat="server" ID="Questions">
      ...

      <Polls:Poll ID="CurrentPoll" runat="server"
              CacheDuration="10"
              Width="180px"
              ArchiveLinkVisible="True"
              HeaderText="Current Poll"
              CssClass="Poll_Box"
              BarStyle="Poll_Bar"
              ResultsStyle="Poll_Results"
              HeaderStyle="Grid_Header"
              QuestionStyle="Poll_Question"
              ButtonStyle="Button"
              LinkStyle="PollLink"
              HorizontalAlign="Center"
      />

      <!-- Insert the footer -->
      <Polls:AdminFooter ID="Footer" runat="server" />
    </form>
  </body>
</html>
```

We haven't supplied the `QuestionID` property, so the control will show the current question. We've instead set the other properties for the style (font, colors, etc.) of the various parts of the poll box, and set the duration for which the results will be cached.

> *As a possible enhancement, you could extend the `ModuleSettings` class and the `Settings.aspx` page to allow the administrator to change the default cache duration online, without the need to manually change the settings in the source code and re-upload the updated file.*

We also have to modify the codebehind code, by adding the calls to `CurrentPoll`'s `DataBind` method every time we delete, add, or edit a question. This is necessary if we want the poll box to always show the current question and the updated question text. Here are the modifications:

```
public class Questions : System.Web.UI.Page
{
  ...
  protected Wrox.WebModules.Polls.Web.Controls.User.Poll CurrentPoll;

  // other procedures here...

  protected void QuestionsGrid_Update(object sender,
                                          DataGridCommandEventArgs e)
  {
    if (Page.IsValid)
```

```
    {
      ...
      QuestionsGrid.EditItemIndex = -1;
      BindGrid();

      // rebind the CurrentPoll control,
      // because the current poll might have changed
      CurrentPoll.DataBind();
    }
  }

  protected void QuestionsGrid_Delete(object sender,
                                              DataGridCommandEventArgs e)
  {
    ...
    BindGrid();

    // rebind the CurrentPoll control,
    // because the deleted poll could be the current one
    CurrentPoll.DataBind();
  }

  protected void AddNew_Click(object sender, EventArgs e)
  {
    if (Page.IsValid)
    {
      ...
      BindGrid();

      // rebind the CurrentPoll control,
      // because the new question might have been set as current
      CurrentPoll.DataBind();
    }
  }
}
```

And, finally, here is how the `Questions.aspx` page looks with the poll user control within it:

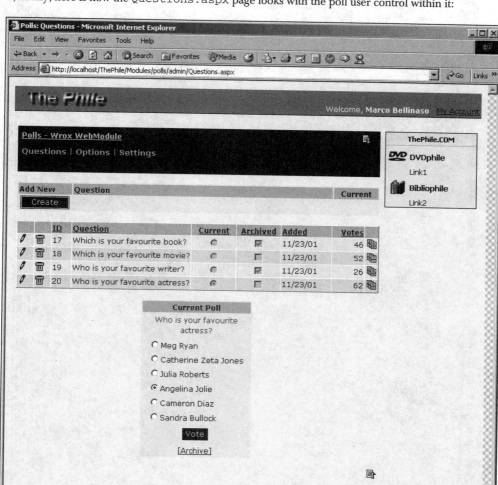

The screenshot above shows the `Polls` control with the radio buttons to allow the user to vote. The screenshot below shows the situation where the `Poll` control detects that the current user has already voted for the question, and so it automatically shows the results:

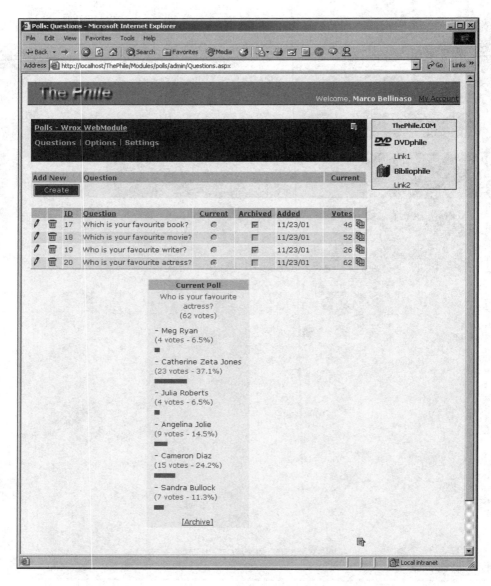

Of course, your results might be different – it's a matter of personal taste, and this was just an example. :-)

We only showed a single poll box here, but you could try creating a simple page with multiple boxes that ask different questions.

The ShowArchive.aspx Page

We've already mentioned a few times that we need a page that shows the results for the archived polls, and we added a link to it from within the poll box. Now it's time to develop the page. We want it to show all the questions, one per line, and when we click one it has to expand and display its options and results. We should be able to have multiple questions expanded at the same time if we want to. We will initially show them in 'collapsed' mode because we don't want to create a very long page, distracting the user and making it hard for them to search for a particular question. Displaying only the questions when the page is first loaded produces a clearer and more easily navigable page. The following screenshot shows the complete page with three archived polls (two expanded to show the results and one collapsed):

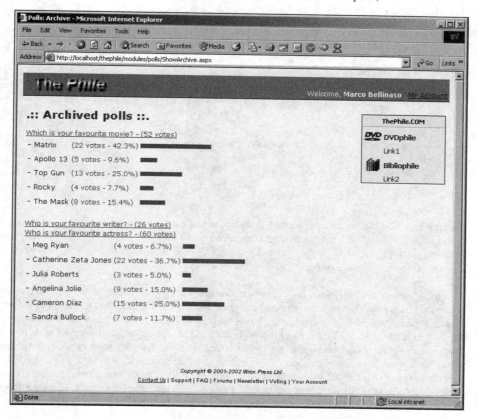

That said, here's the content of the ASPX page, ShowArchive.aspx:

```
<%@ Page language="c#" Codebehind="ShowArchive.aspx.cs"
        AutoEventWireup="false"
        Inherits="Wrox.WebModules.Polls.Web.ShowArchive" %>
<%@ OutputCache Duration="3600" VaryByParam="none" %>
<%@ Register TagPrefix="WroxUser" TagName="SiteHeader"
        Src="/ThePhile/Controls/SiteHeader.ascx" %>
<%@ Register TagPrefix="Wrox" Namespace="Wrox.ThePhile.Web.Controls.Server"
        Assembly="Wrox.ThePhile.Web.Controls" %>
```

```
<%@ Register TagPrefix="WroxUser" TagName="SiteFooter"
            Src="/ThePhile/Controls/SiteFooter.ascx" %>
<!DOCTYPE HTML PUBLIC "-//W3C//DTD HTML 4.0 Transitional//EN" >
<html>
  <head>
    <title>Polls: Archive</title>
    <link rel="stylesheet" HREF="/ThePhile/Styles/ThePhile.css" />
    <link href="/ThePhile/Styles/Navigator.css" rel="stylesheet" />
    <meta name="CODE_LANGUAGE" Content="C#">
    <script language="JavaScript1.2" type="text/javascript">
      function expandDiv(ctrl)
      {
        ctl = eval(ctrl);
        if (ctl.style.display == "none")
          ctl.style.display = "";
        else
          ctl.style.display = "none";
      }
    </script>
  </head>
  <body>
    <form method="post" runat="server" ID="Archive">
      <WroxUser:SiteHeader id="Header" runat="server" />
      <br>
      <table width="100%" border="0" cellspacing="4" cellpadding="2">
        <tr>
          <td width="100%" valign="top">
```

The code above defines the JavaScript function that expands or collapses the passed `<div>` element, inverting its state, and adds the site-wide header and menu box. Also note that we've used the `@ OutputCache` directive to cache the page output for one hour (you can change this value to suit your needs), which avoids querying the database every time the page is loaded.

The rest of the code, continued below, is a `Repeater` control that shows the question text and the total number of votes for each question. The `Repeater` control does not inherit from `BaseDataList`, but it does expose properties and methods that we've already seen in the `DataGrid` and `DataList` controls, such as `DataSource` and `DataBind`. This control has no built-in HTML layout at all; it just processes and repeats the `Item` template (the code is declared inside an `<ItemTemplate>` section) for each item of the specified source of data. It also does not have built-in support for selecting/deleting/editing items – if you need to do that you have to implement the mechanism by yourself by using the general `ItemCommand` event. This control is best suited when you don't need the advanced features of a `DataGrid/DataList` control, and want to generate as little HTML code as possible, to speed up the download from the server to the client. It is also used when you don't want to show the records in rows (for which you have to build a table by yourself, as we see in our page), but maybe you want to render the data as a continuous string, or with any other heavily customized layout.

This first `Repeater` also contains a second `Repeater` control. The `DataSource` of this nested `Repeater` is dynamically set by calling a public function declared in the codebehind, which accepts as input the ID of the question being processed by the parent `Repeater`. The called function returns a `DataView` with the child options and number of votes, which are shown as in the poll control. The only other difference is that here the nested `Repeater` is wrapped by a collapsed `<div>` element, refreshed when the question text is clicked.

```
<asp:Repeater runat="server" ID="ArchivedPolls">
  <ItemTemplate>
    <a class="Poll_Question" href="javascript:expandDiv('div<%#
                      DataBinder.Eval(Container.DataItem, "QuestionID") %>')">
      <%# DataBinder.Eval(Container.DataItem, "QuestionText") %>
      - <%# DataBinder.Eval(Container.DataItem, "TotalVotes",
                                              "({0} votes)") %>
    </a>
    <div style="display:'none'" ID="<%# "div" +
                    DataBinder.Eval(Container.DataItem, "QuestionID") %>">
    <table>
      <asp:Repeater id="MyRepeater" runat="server"
                  DataSource='<%# GetResultsSource(int.Parse(
                  DataBinder.Eval(Container.DataItem,
                  "QuestionID").ToString())) %>'>
        <ItemTemplate>
          <tr>
            <td class="Poll_Option">
              - <%# DataBinder.Eval(Container.DataItem, "OptionText") %>
            </td>
            <td class="Poll_Results">
              <%# DataBinder.Eval(Container.DataItem, "TotalVotes",
                                              "({0} votes") %>
              - <%# DataBinder.Eval(Container.DataItem, "Percentage",
                                              "{0:N1}%)") %>
            </td>
            <td width="300px">
              <hr class="Poll_Bar" width='<%# DataBinder.Eval(
                        Container.DataItem, "Percentage", "{0:N0}%") %>' >
            </td>
          </tr>
        </ItemTemplate>
      </asp:Repeater>
    </table>
    </div>
    <br>
  </ItemTemplate>
</asp:Repeater>
```

The page terminates with the site-wide footer control, and the other closing tags.

The Codebehind for ShowArchive.aspx

The following code retrieves all the questions and binds them to the `ArchivedPolls Repeater` control:

```
private void Page_Load(object sender, System.EventArgs e)
{
  ArchivedPolls.DataSource = Business.Question.GetQuestions(
                                            true).Tables[0].DefaultView;
  ArchivedPolls.DataBind();
}
```

Note that on this occasion we pass `true` to the `GetQuestions` method, because we only want the archived questions. And here is the `GetResultsSource` method that returns the child options of the specified question:

```
public DataView GetResultsSource(int questionID)
{
  return new Business.Question(
                        questionID).GetOptions().Tables[0].DefaultView;
}
```

Securing the Module

For this module we're going to protect only the administration console, and leave the archive page freely accessible. However, if you plan to employ polls to gather marketing information, or if you receive several thousands of votes (making your results accurate enough to sell them), you might want to protect the archives too. You'll just need to add a new permission, or in the `ShowArchive.aspx` page add the code to check if the current user has the `AdministerPolls` permission.

First we declare the enumeration with the single permission, under the `Wrox.WebModules.Polls` namespace, in the `Enums.cs` file of the `Core` module:

```
namespace Wrox.WebModules.Polls
{
  public enum PollsPermissions
  {
    AdministerPolls = 300
  };
}
```

Then, in the `Page_Load` event of the administration pages, we add the following code:

```
protected void Page_Load(object sender, EventArgs e)
{
  // check if the current user is allowed to administer the polls
  if (!Context.User.Identity.IsAuthenticated ||
                        !((SitePrincipal)Context.User).HasPermission(
                        (int)PollsPermissions.AdministerPolls))
  {
    // if not, redirect to the Login page
    Response.Redirect(
                "/ThePhile/Modules/Users/Login.aspx?ShowError=true", true);
  }
  ...
  }
}
```

This code takes advantage of the short-circuiting feature of C# with Boolean operators: if the current user is not authenticated the permission is not checked (it would cause an error otherwise, because the `Context.User` would not cast to `SitePrincipal`) and it redirects to the login page. It does the same if the user is logged in but without the `AdministerPolls` permission. Refer back to Chapter 5 if you need more details about the way the `Accounts.Business` classes work.

The Poll Web Service

The last thing we have to implement is the web service that allows external clients to retrieve the current question and its results from our site. In the design section we decided to return both the question and the results through a single method, `GetCurrent`, in two tables of the same `DataSet` object. The web service's method simply wraps a call to the `GetCurrent` static method of the `Business.Question` class. So, we add a new web service to the project, name it `Poll.asmx`, and edit its codebehind file. (The web services created by **Visual Studio .NET** use the `.asmx` file only to declare the respective codebehind.) Apart from the use of the `[WebMethod]` attribute, which permits remote calling of this method, the code is not particularly exciting and so we will not list it in full here:

```
...
    [WebMethod]
    public DataSet GetCurrent()
    {
      return Business.Question.GetCurrent();
    }
...
```

Testing the Web Service

After compiling the project the web service is now ready to be tested. If you browse to `Poll.asmx`, you'll get the list of the available web methods, just `GetCurrent` in this case. Click the `GetCurrent` link, and you'll see sample SOAP code for requests and responses, and a button to invoke the method. The following screenshot shows part of this window, and the window opened when the **Invoke** button is pressed, with the SOAP response that lists the question and the results:

As you can see in the foreground window, the returned `DataSet` first lists the options, and then has all the details for the current question.

The Windows Client Application

In Visual Studio .NET we add a new C# Windows Forms project to the solution. First we create a proxy class for using the `Poll` web service. We do this by adding a web reference to the project (Project | Add Web Reference). We just specify the full URL of the web service file, and Visual Studio .NET creates a proxy class to access the web service. The proxy class appears under Web References in the Solution Explorer. We rename it from `localhost` to `ThePhile`, to make its name more meaningful.

Now, through the visual designer, we drop some controls onto the form:

- ❑   A label to display the question
- ❑   A `DataGrid` to show the options and their percentages
- ❑   A timer and a button to automatically or manually refresh the results

The controls are placed on the form as shown:

The code we need to add is pretty simple. We retrieve the question and the options in a single call, then we get the question text from a table and show it in the label, and bind the other table to the grid to make it automatically display the results one per row. Here is the code you have to add to the Visual Studio .NET generated code of the form class:

```csharp
private void Viewer_Load(object sender, System.EventArgs e)
{
  FillOptionsGrid();
}

private void FillOptionsGrid()
{
  // get the dataset through the web service
  DataSet currPoll = new DataSet();
  ThePhile.Poll poll = new ThePhile.Poll();
  try
  {
    currPoll = poll.GetCurrent();
  }
  catch (Exception exc)
  {
    // if the call to GetCurrent throws an exception, disable the timer
    // show the exception's error message and close the app
    TimerRefresh.Enabled = false;
    MessageBox.Show(exc.Message, "Error",
                         MessageBoxButtons.OK, MessageBoxIcon.Error);
    Close();
  }
  Options.DataSource = currPoll.Tables["Options"];

  // set the question title
  Question.Text = string.Format("{0}     ( {1} votes )",
      currPoll.Tables["Questions"].Rows[0]["QuestionText"].ToString(),
      currPoll.Tables["Questions"].Rows[0]["TotalVotes"].ToString());

  // remove the current grid columns
  Options.TableStyles.Clear();

  // bind Options table to the Grid, and show
  // the OptionText, TotalVotes, and Percentage
  Options.SetDataBinding(currPoll, "Options");
  DataGridTableStyle ts = new DataGridTableStyle();
  ts.MappingName = "Options";
  ts.AlternatingBackColor = Color.LightGray;

  // Add the OptionText column
  DataGridColumnStyle OptionCol = new DataGridTextBoxColumn();
  OptionCol.MappingName = "OptionText";
  OptionCol.HeaderText = "Option";
  OptionCol.Width = 300;
  ts.GridColumnStyles.Add(OptionCol);

  // Add the TotalVotes column
  DataGridColumnStyle VotesCol = new DataGridTextBoxColumn();
  VotesCol.MappingName = "TotalVotes";
  VotesCol.HeaderText = "Votes";
  VotesCol.Width = 50;
  VotesCol.Alignment = HorizontalAlignment.Right;
  ts.GridColumnStyles.Add(VotesCol);
```

```
    // Add the Percentage column
    DataGridColumnStyle PercCol = new DataGridTextBoxColumn();
    PercCol.MappingName = "Percentage";
    PercCol.HeaderText = "%";
    PercCol.Width = 50;
    PercCol.Alignment = HorizontalAlignment.Right;
    ts.GridColumnStyles.Add(PercCol);

    // finally add the table to the grid
    Options.TableStyles.Add(ts);
}

private void RefreshTimer_Tick(object sender, System.EventArgs e)
{
    FillOptionsGrid();
}

private void ButtonRefresh_Click(object sender, System.EventArgs e)
{
    FillOptionsGrid();
}
```

The heart of the class is the `FillOptionsGrid` routine, which is called when the form loads, when the **Refresh** button is pressed, and when the time specified for the timer expires. As previously mentioned, the routine retrieves the `DataSet` returned by the web service's `GetCurrent` method, gets the question's text and total number of votes from the `Questions` table, and shows this information in the label. Then it binds the `Options` table to the grid, and creates columns for the option's text, total number of votes, and respective percentage, by mapping the database's columns to the grid's new columns. It's worth noting that the call to `GetCurrent` is protected inside a `try...catch` block, to catch exceptions that may occur, for example if the web service or a specific method is not found, or if the request times out. If an exception is caught we first disable the timer that updates the results by re-calling the `FillOptionsGrid` routine, and then show an error message with the exception's text – when the user closes the message box the application is terminated. If we didn't disable the timer then if the user does not close the message box soon and exits the application, the timer would continue to refresh the grid, opening further error dialogs.

Here is a screenshot of the application running:

The Web Service's Timeout and Url Properties

Before concluding the web service example it's worth introducing two very useful properties that every web service proxy exposes: `Timeout` and `Url`. The former allows us to set the interval of time before a request – a call to a method – times out. The default is 90 seconds, but you may want to choose a longer or shorter interval, according to the forecasted traffic and number of calls to the web service. The concept is exactly the same as the timeout interval for an ASP.NET page. This is a public property, so from the client code you can easily change the value as follows:

```
ThePhile.Poll poll = new ThePhile.Poll();
// set the timeout to 180 seconds
poll.Timeout = 180;
```

The `Url` property allows the consumer of the web service to change the URL to which the proxy points. When we added a reference to the web service in Visual Studio .NET, the IDE saved for us a **WSDL (Web Service Description Language) file** and created the proxy, namely the local class that allows the client to access the web service as if it were on the local computer and not on a server on the Internet. Both the WSDL file and the proxy reference the web service with the URL specified in the Add Web Reference wizard. In the WSDL file the URL is defined in the `<soap:address>` tag as follows:

```
<service name="Poll">
  <port name="PollSoap" binding="s0:PollSoap">
    <soap:address
            location="http://localhost/ThePhile/Modules/Polls/poll.asmx" />
  </port>
  ...
</service>
```

While in the proxy it's defined in the constructor:

```
public Poll() {
   this.Url = "http://localhost/ThePhile/Modules/Polls/poll.asmx";
}
```

The code above saves the URL of the web service in the public variable `Url`, which is accessible from the client code too. This means that the client can change the value of this property and point to a web service in a different location, as long as it supports the same methods and parameters of course. This is quite important, because if we have deployed the web service on several servers and we find that one server is not available, we can easily change the proxy's `Url` property and point to the web service on another working server! Here's a quick example:

```
ThePhile.Poll poll = new ThePhile.Poll();
poll.Url = "http://www.thephile2.com/Modules/Polls/poll.asmx";
```

As a last note, in this example we've referenced the web service on our local server. Of course when we deploy the site and the web service we must rebuild the proxy so that it points to the web service on the production server, or we can manually change the URL in the WSDL file and the proxy class.

> *If you want to know more about web services you can refer to Professional ASP.NET Web Services (ISBN 1-861005-45-8) or to Professional C# Web Services (ISBN 1-861004-39-7), both from Wrox Press.*

Summary

This chapter has presented a working solution for handling multiple dynamic polls on our website. The complete `Polls` module is made up of several parts:

❑   An administration console for managing the polls through a web browser

❑   Integration with the `Accounts` module to secure the administration pages

❑   A user control that enables us to show different polls in any page we want with just a couple of lines of code

❑   A web service that can be accessed by external clients to get the current poll's question and results

❑   A Windows client program that uses the web service to display the current poll and its results

This module can easily be employed in many real world sites as it is now, but of course you can expand and enhance it. Here are just a few suggestions:

❑   Add more styles properties to the poll control, and the ability to remind the user which option they voted for. Currently they can see the results, but the control does not indicate how they voted.

❑   Add a `ReleaseDate` and `ExpireDate` to the polls, so that we can schedule the current poll to change automatically.

❑ Provide the option to allow only registered users to vote. Alternatively, keep the vote open to all, but allow only registered users to see the results and/or the archive page.

❑ Expand the web service and the respective Windows client so that it can display all the archived polls as well as the current one.

In the next chapter we're going to continue the development of ThePhile.com through the addition of another easily pluggable module. This new module will be used for managing multiple mailing lists and their subscribers, and for sending out newsletters.

9

Mailing Lists

In this chapter we'll discuss the design and implementation of a complete mailing list system. This will enable users to subscribe to receive regular newsletters, and will allow administrators to manage mailing lists and newsletter content. First we'll look at what mailing lists and newsletters can offer to websites like ours, and will consider various ways of making the mailing list administrator's life as easy as possible. By the end of the chapter we'll have developed a flexible mailing list module that can be plugged into most sites. In keeping with the rest of the project, we will aim to integrate this module into our ThePhile.com site through the reuse of familiar code and architecture where appropriate.

The Problem

Throughout this book we've mentioned that the key to a successful site is having good content. This content also needs to be logically organized to ease navigability, have an attractive design, and offer some interaction with the user. The content not only has to be interesting and accurate, but to ensure that users keep visiting the site it must always be fresh and regularly updated. To help us achieve this for our ThePhile.com website, we built the NewsManager module (in Chapter 6) to allow an administrator to easily manage and publish new content (for example an article, a new product for sale, or a new design).

But even if fresh content is frequently added to the site, not every user will be aware of it. They might not visit the site daily or weekly just to see the latest updates, especially if the site is updated on a random basis with no public announcement of when new material has been added. A good way to inform the user that some new content has been added to the site is to send an e-mail **newsletter** that lists all the new resources available on the site. Many sites offer the option of subscribing to a **mailing list,** which typically represents a group of users interested in a certain kind of news. A newsletter is sent to a mailing list to inform the community of users that the site is still worth visiting.

You should always keep in mind that you're offering a service to the user, and it must be a high quality service if you don't want to lose your subscribers. This means that you need to provide *targeted* content. So, you shouldn't send out a general content newsletter if you have a large site with different sections and different types of content. For example, at ThePhile.com we cover DVDs and books, and so we have news for two different topics. We should provide at least two different mailing lists, so that the users can get what they want and avoid getting what they are not interested in, which they may perceive as spam.

It's a nice touch to personalize every e-mail message, for example with the name of the subscriber if this information is available, because this can help to build a more personal relationship with the subscriber. However, in order to persuade users to subscribe to a mailing list the subscription process should be as straightforward as possible and they should not be forced to provide additional personal details. The most common way of subscribing to a list is to type your e-mail address in a form on the home page and press submit. This will allow only the e-mail address to be used to personalize the newsletter. In order to achieve more extensive personalization you have to ask the users to provide more details, such as their first and last names. For your websites the choice is up to you, but we want our module for ThePhile.com to support both a basic and extended subscription form, so that we can cater for users with different attitudes and so that managing the mailing list is as straightforward as possible in either case.

Some website visitors don't like to submit their e-mail address even to be informed about changes to the website. To encourage people to maintain their subscriptions, and to encourage more people to sign up, a webmaster can offer something extra that is only available to the mailing list's subscribers, for example a short tip, article, or some kind of discount for one of the site's products.

The primary purpose of a mailing list system is to inform the users that some new material is available online, and therefore convince them to visit the site again. But you could also make money from your mailing lists. Say that you have several thousands of subscribers; you could sell some space in your newsletters for **advertisement spots**. These shouldn't be anything too invasive, perhaps just a two to three line description of a partner site or company, or the manufacturer of a product you sell on your site. If you provide some valuable content in your newsletters (as mentioned above, an extra article or tip), and the advertisement is short and not invasive, the users won't complain about it. If you manage to sell space in the newsletter, remember that this space is very valuable for the sponsor. As users have elected to receive the newsletter, they will often read it thoroughly, and so the advertisement will get much more attention than it would receive through a common banner ad. Research shows that the average click-through from spots in newsletters is around 4-5%, compared to around 1% or less for banner ads.

However you decide to promote your website and get more people to subscribe, you will face the problem of managing all the details of your clients, such as e-mail addresses, keeping track of the messages you send, and building a system to allow the user to subscribe or unsubscribe easily. The user must have the right to unsubscribe at any time, so we should provide facilities that allow the user to easily do this, preferably without having to re-typing their e-mail address. Some small sites manually collect subscriber e-mail addresses from an HTML form, create a group of contacts in Outlook or their messaging client, and use it to write to all the subscribers. This mostly applies to static sites, where ASP or other server-side code is not used. However, when the site starts to have a significant number of subscribers, manually adding or removing the users several times a week becomes a pain, and if the number is in the order of thousands, it is almost impossible.

The Problem Statement

This leads us to our problem statement: we risk losing traffic because we have no way of letting our users know that our content has been updated. So the aim for the chapter is to build a newsletter mailing list system so we can deliver targeted, personalized content to users who choose to subscribe. A secondary problem then arises – managing the system and personalizing newsletters could become time-consuming. So we want to include a subscription and administration system that automates most of the tasks and allows the administrator to complete the rest of the tasks much easier.

Now we know what the problems are that we want to solve, we can move on to specifying the features we want our solution to have, in other words the requirements:

❑ A user interface where users can join/leave mailing lists without needing to register on the site.

❑ An administration console for managing multiple mailing lists. It should allow the administrator to add, remove, or modify lists and their properties.

❑ The administrator should also be able to manage the archive of newsletters previously sent to each list, reading the archived messages, and copying them. The copy facility will be useful for quickly creating new messages, or for manually sending a message to a recent subscriber who has requested an old newsletter.

❑ The ability to send e-mails to subscribers in plain text or HTML format, containing the message and other information about the list (such as the name and description).

❑ In each newsletter there should be a link to enable easy unsubscription.

❑ A facility for automatically customizing each e-mail message with the name and address of the user, even within the body of the message (the user feels this as a more personal relationship with the site's staff, even if we all know that it's not really personal, since the name is automatically replaced by a machine). We will also need a backup plan in case the user decides not to supply their name.

❑ The ability for the administrator to auto-generate HTML code for a form that will collect the user's data. This feature works like a wizard – we choose the list we want to create the form for, select a few other options, and the wizard generates the code for us. This can then be copied into any (static or dynamic) page where we want to show the subscription form.

❑ The facility to set options such as the sender's name and address that will be seen by the subscribers on the e-mails they receive, a signature that will be automatically added to each message, a default subject, and subscription and un-subscription messages.

❑ We want the administrator to be able to monitor website subscribers online, contact them, and even change the website layout from anywhere is the world – all that is needed is access to a computer with a web browser and an Internet connection.

In the next section we're going to provide a more detailed discussion of the features we can implement to have a fully functional mailing list module.

The Design

From our requirements it's clear that we're going to be handling data about users and the lists they subscribe to. In keeping with the rest of the site we'll use our SQL Server database to store this information. We'll also need an interface for administrators to manage the lists, and an interface where users can subscribe. As with other modules we'll use a multi-tier approach and will make use of data access and business logic layers to keep the UI and database separate.

In this section we'll design the database tables for this module, and design the data and business layers that we'll use for managing the subscriptions from the administration console. The nice thing about the administration console is that we won't need to manually manage the group of subscribers – the application will automatically add or remove them to/from the database. For this we will make use of stored procedures called by methods in response to certain events.

Designing the Database Tables

As discussed in Chapter 2, all modules in our project require a prefix for the tables and stored procedures. For this module it will be MLists_. We need the four tables shown in the following diagram, which also indicates their relationships:

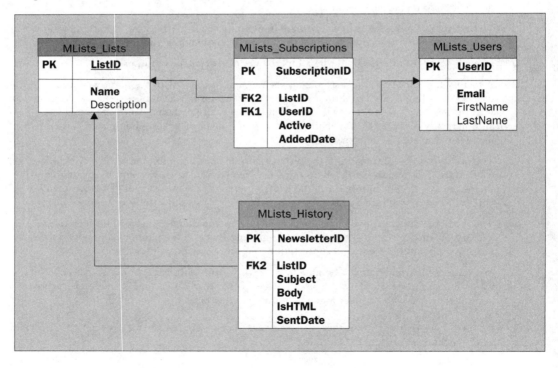

The MLists_Lists Table

The `MLists_Lists` table is used to store the information about each available mailing list:

Column Name	Type	Size	Allow Null	Description
ListID	int – Identity primary key	4	No	The unique ID for the mailing list.
Name	varchar	50	No	The name of the mailing list.
Description	varchar	250	Yes	The optional description of the mailing list.

The MLists_Users Table

The `MLists_Users` table stores the user's personal information:

Column Name	Type	Size	Allow Null	Description
UserID	int – Identity primary key	4	No	The unique ID for the user.
Email	varchar	50	No	The user's e-mail address. This column must have a `unique` constraint, to avoid multiple records with the same e-mail address.
FirstName	varchar	50	Yes	The user's first name.
LastName	varchar	50	Yes	The user's last name.

You may wonder why we need a new table for storing the user's e-mail address and name, since we already have an `Accounts_Users` table that can store this information (created in Chapter 5). That table stores information about users who have registered with the site, in order to gain access to protected areas or to personalize the site. But a visitor might not be interested in those advantages, and might just want to know when the site is updated. We can't force them to register and provide personal details if they only want to subscribe to the mailing list. Many sites follow this approach: subscribing to a mailing list often requires the e-mail address only, or at most the e-mail and subscriber's name. They have a different page that asks for a lot of personal details (most of which are not optional) that are required, for example, for shipping goods and invoicing in the case of an e-commerce site. We decided that it would be wiser to have two tables to separate registered users from those who have just subscribed to a mailing list. Furthermore, not depending on the `Accounts` module allows any site to easily plug in the mailing lists manager, even if they're already using another online manager to administer their customers/users, without requiring changes to the existing code. Of course, this does not prevent us from modifying the registration page written in Chapter 5 and allowing the user to register for both the site and the mailing list in a single step. Later we'll build a new data component that makes the addition of a subscription very easy.

Another thing you'll notice in this table is that we decided to allow the first and last names to be null. Having the first and last name would allow us to achieve some form of newsletter personalization, but most sites don't ask for this information, because users prefer to give as little information as possible. So we'll make it optional to supply this information. Later we'll see how we can replace some special marks in the newsletter with the user's information, so that they receive a newsletter customized with their name. This will contribute to making the user feel that they have a more personal relationship with the site's staff. If their name isn't supplied we'll use a generic 'name' instead, such as "List Reader".

This table does not store the lists to which the user is subscribed, because a single user can subscribe to several lists. This would require the user's data to be repeated, which is bad design, as it wastes space and makes it more difficult to update the user's details. Instead we treat each user-list pair as a subscription and store these in a separate table.

The MLists_Subscriptions Table

The `MLists_Subscriptions` table stores the subscriptions for all the lists:

Column Name	Type	Size	Allow Null	Description
SubscriptionID	int – Identity primary key	4	No	The unique ID for the subscription.
ListID	int foreign key	4	No	The ID of the list to which the user is subscribed, which should match an ID in the `MLists_Lists` table.
UserID	int foreign key	4	No	The ID of the user, which should match an ID in the `MLists_Users` table.
Active	bit	1	No	If false (0) the subscription is inactive, and the user will not receive newsletters for the `ListID` list.
AddedDate	datetime	8	No	The date of creation of this subscription.

This is the table where we maintain the relationship between the users and the mailing lists to which they have subscribed. In conjunction with `MLists_Users`, we have all the information for the subscription: for example the lists to which the user is subscribed, the e-mail and name of the subscriber, and each subscription's active state.

The `Active` column is included to allow the user to unsubscribe from a mailing list (and you must allow this), without deleting the subscription details. This is useful because you might still want to contact old subscribers in special circumstances. If a subscription record has 0 (false) in that field, it means that the subscription is inactive, namely that the user does not receive newsletters from the mailing list of that subscription. Later in the chapter we'll show how the administration console allows us to change the `Active` status of any subscription. We'll also give options for when a user wants to unsubscribe, that is, whether their subscription should be permanently deleted or just made inactive.

The MLists_History Table

The `MLists_History` table is used to store newsletters previously sent to the subscribers of a mailing list:

Column Name	Type	Size	Allow Null	Description
Newsletter ID	int – Identity primary key	4	No	The unique ID for the message.
ListID	int foreign key	4	No	The mailing list to which the message was sent.
Subject	varchar	200	No	The subject of the message.
Body	text		No	The body of the message.
IsHTML	bit	1	No	If true, it means that the message was sent in HTML format.
SentDate	datetime	8	No	When the message was sent.

The Stored Procedures that Manage the Database

To manage the database we will build a set of stored procedures, that we'll run later in the data layer classes to do everything from the addition or deletion of lists and subscriptions, to the update of single fields. Here is the complete list of the stored procedures we'll be building with their parameters:

Stored Procedure	Parameters	Description
sp_MLists_GetLists		Returns all the available mailing lists.
sp_MLists_GetListDetails	@ListID int	Returns the complete row identified by the specified ID.

Table continued on following page

Stored Procedure	Parameters	Description
sp_MLists_InsertList	@Name varchar(50), @Description varchar(250), @ListID int OUTPUT	Inserts a new list. If a list already exists with the same name, the new list is not added and the output parameter is set to -1. Otherwise @ListID will be set to the new list's ID.
sp_MLists_UpdateList	@ListID int, @Name varchar(50), @Description varchar(250)	Updates all the fields of the mailing list identified by the specified ID.
sp_MLists_DeleteList	@ListID int	Deletes the specified list.
sp_MLists_GetSubscriptions	@ListID int, @ActiveOnly bit	Returns the subscriptions (with all the details for both the subscriptions and the subscribers) for the specified list. If @ActiveOnly is 1, returns only the subscriptions where the Active field is 1.
sp_MLists_GetSubscription Details	@Subscription ID int	Gets all the details for the specified subscription.
sp_MLists_GetSubscriptionID	@ListID int, @Email varchar(50), @Subscription ID int OUTPUT	Gets the ID of the subscription for the specified mailing list, with the specified e-mail address.

Stored Procedure	Parameters	Description
sp_MLists_InsertSubscription	@ListID int, @FirstName varchar(50), @LastName varchar(50), @Email varchar(50), @Active bit, @Subscription ID int OUTPUT	Inserts a new subscription for the specified mailing list. If a subscription to this list already exists with the specified e-mail address, the new subscription is not added and the output parameter is set to -1. Otherwise @SubscriptionID will be set to the new subscription's ID.
sp_MLists_UpdateSubscription	@Subscription ID int, @FirstName varchar(50), @LastName varchar(50), @Email varchar(50), @Active bit	Updates all the fields of the specified subscription. This includes the fields of the subscriber (name and e-mail address).
sp_MLists_SetSubscriptionActive	@Subscription ID int, @Active bit	Updates only the Active field for the specified subscription.
sp_MLists_DeleteSubscription	@Subscription ID int	Deletes the specified subscription (but not the respective user, because they could be subscribed to other lists).
sp_MLists_GetNewsletters	@ListID int	Gets all the archived newsletters sent to the specified list.
sp_MLists_GetNewsletterDetails	@NewsletterID int	Gets all the details of the specified archived newsletter.

Table continued on following page

Stored Procedure	Parameters	Description
sp_MLists_InsertNewsletter	@ListID int, @Subject varchar(200), @Body text, @IsHTML bit, @NewsletterID int OUTPUT	Inserts a newsletter into the database and returns its ID. No check is performed to see if the newsletter is already present in the archive, since we can have as many newsletters with the same subject as we want. The value for the SentDate field is not passed as a parameter; the stored procedure takes care of retrieving and using the current date for that field, as the other Insert procedures do for the AddedDate fields.
sp_MLists_DeleteNewsletter	@NewsletterID int	Deletes the specified newsletter.

The stored procedures that manage the lists and the archived newsletters are pretty simple. Those that manage the subscriptions are a bit more complex, because they work on two tables, MLists_Subscriptions and MLists_Users. For example, when we retrieve all the subscriptions, using sp_MLists_GetSubscriptions, we need to *join* the two tables, in order to have rows with the complete details of the subscriptions, the parent list's ID, the active state of the subscription, and all the information of the subscribed user. The procedures that add and update a subscription also operate on the same two tables. In cases like this, having stored procedures that do the work will make it much easier to write the data component later, rather than writing SQL commands directly into the classes, because we write methods that map the stored procedures, and don't worry much about the relationships. This is even more evident when different teams are responsible for the database/stored procedure design and writing the data/business layers.

Designing the Data Services

Now that we understand what data is stored in the database tables, and we have designed a set of stored procedures to add, delete, and modify any row in the tables, we can design the data services. These are a set of classes in their own assembly and namespace (Wrox.WebModules.MailingLists.Data) that provide an object-oriented version of the stored procedures. In other words the data components have methods that exactly map the stored procedures, exposing them through a set of classes. We will look at each class in turn.

The ListDetails Class

The ListDetails class exposes three public fields that map the three fields of a row in the MLists_Lists table. This class is used as the return type for the GetDetails method in the Lists class, discussed next, that instead of returning a DataRow type returns an instance of an object that exposes the values in a more easily accessible way.

The Lists Class

This class has a set of methods that map the calls to the stored procedures that manage the mailing lists. The methods return the value of the output parameter of the respective stored procedure, or a Boolean value indicating whether the query succeeded. Here is a complete list of the methods we'll implement:

Method Name	Description
`public Lists(string newConnectionString)`	Class constructor taking the connection string as a parameter.
`public DataSet GetLists()`	Returns a `DataSet` with all the lists.
`public ListDetails GetDetails(int listID)`	Returns an instance of `ListDetails` that describes the specified mailing list.
`public DataRow GetDetailsRow(int listID)`	Returns a `DataRow` containing details of the specified list.
`public int Add(string listName, string listDescr)`	Adds a new mailing list, and returns its ID, or `-1` if the same list was already present.
`public bool Update(int listID, string listName, string listDescr)`	Updates all the fields of the specified mailing list.
`public bool Delete(int listID)`	Deletes the specified mailing list.

The SubscriptionDetails Class

This class is basically the same as `ListDetails`, but for the `MLists_Subscriptions` and `MLists_Users` tables. It has only public fields that map the physical fields of the tables returned by the `sp_MLists_GetSubscriptionDetails` stored procedure.

The Subscriptions Class

This class wraps the calls to the stored procedures that manage the subscriptions and the respective users:

Method Name	Description
`public Subscriptions(string newConnectionString)`	Class constructor taking the connection string as a parameter.
`public DataSet GetSubscriptions(int listID)`	Returns a `DataSet` with all the subscriptions for a particular mailing list.
`public DataSet GetSubscriptions(int listID, bool activeOnly)`	The same as above, but here we have the opportunity to specify that we only want the *active* subscriptions.
`public SubscriptionDetails GetDetails(int subscriptionID)`	Returns an instance of `SubscriptionDetails` that describes the specified subscription.

Table continued on following page

Method Name	Description
public DataRow GetDetailsRow(int subscriptionID)	Returns the DataRow of the specified subscription.
public int GetSubscriptionID(int listID, string email)	Returns the ID of the subscription for the specified mailing list, and with the specified e-mail address.
public int Add(int listID, string firstName, string lastName, string email, bool active)	Adds a new subscription, and returns its ID, or -1 if the same e-mail address was already subscribed for the specified list.
public bool Update(int subscriptionID, string firstName, string lastName, string email, bool active)	Updates all the fields of the specified subscription. This includes fields in both the MLists_Subscriptions and MLists_Users tables.
public bool SetActive(int subscriptionID, bool active)	Changes only the Active state of the specified subscription.
public bool Delete(int subscriptionID)	Deletes the specified subscription.

The NewsletterDetails Class

This class is the same as the two xxxDetails classes above, but this time for the archived newsletters. It has fields corresponding to all the fields of the MLists_History table.

The Newsletters Class

This class is shorter than the previous ones, because it only provides methods to retrieve, add, and delete newsletters, and doesn't provide any methods for updating them:

Method Name	Description
public Newsletters(string newConnectionString)	Class constructor taking the connection string as a parameter.
public DataSet GetNewsletters(int listID)	Returns all the newsletters for a particular mailing list.
public NewsletterDetails GetDetails(int newsletterID)	Returns an instance of NewsletterDetails that describes the specified newsletter.
public DataRow GetDetailsRow(int newsletterID)	Returns the DataRow of the newsletter identified by the specified ID.
public int Add(int listID, string subject, string body, bool isHTML)	Archives a newsletter, and returns the ID of the new record.
public bool Delete(int newsletterID)	Deletes a newsletter.

Storing and Retrieving Settings

In previous chapters we've already designed a couple of classes that retrieve and store each module's settings in an XML file. This module has quite a lot of settings to store, because we want it to be as flexible as possible. This is the list of settings that will be persisted to and retrieved from the XML file:

Setting Name	Type	Description
ConnectionString	string	The connection string that all the data classes use to access the database.
SubscribeURL	string	The complete URL of the Subscribe.aspx page that actually adds or removes a user to or from a list.
SenderName	string	The name of the news sender.
SenderEmail	string	The e-mail address of the news sender.
NewsSubject	string	The default subject for the news. The administrator will be able to append any text to this default string, directly from the page where the message is written.
Signature	string	The signature that will automatically be appended at the end of the message.
SubscrSubject	string	The subject of the e-mail sent as the confirmation message for the subscription.
SubscrMessage	string	The body of the e-mail sent as the confirmation message for the subscription.
UnsubscrSubject	string	The subject of the e-mail sent as the confirmation message for the unsubscription.
UnsubscrMessage	string	The body of the e-mail sent as the confirmation message for the unsubscription.
UnsubscrAction	UnsubscrAction Type custom enumeration	Specifies the action taken when a user unsubscribes from a mailing lists. They can be completely removed, or the subscription can just be set as inactive, by setting the respective field in the MLists_Subscription table.

Table continued on following page

Setting Name	Type	Description
SendSubscrEmail	bool	If `true`, the new subscriber will get a confirmation e-mail after subscribing to a list.
SendUnsubscrEmail	bool	If `true`, the existing subscriber will get a confirmation e-mail after unsubscribing from a list.

The `NewsSubject`, `[Un]SubscrSubject`, and `[Un]SubscrMessage` settings can contain special tags, such as `#SubscriberFirstName#` and `#ListDescription#`. These will be replaced with their respective values just before each mail is sent. We'll see more on this point later in the chapter.

Designing the Business Services

At this point we have all the calls to the stored procedures wrapped into easily accessible methods of the data access layer. Now it's time to build the business classes upon the data access classes, in order to provide a real object-oriented representation of the data and its relationships. However, the mailing list manager not only has to manage the data in the database, but it has other work to take care of too, such as actually sending out the newsletters to the active subscribers (the stored procedure only inserts the newsletter into the database, but does not send the e-mails), subscribing or unsubscribing someone and sending a confirmation message if required, and processing special list and subscription tags. One option would be to write the code to do this directly in the presentation layer: if we have data/business classes that simplify access to the database, the rest of the work will be quite easy. However, these methods are best fit in the business layer, since they are based upon business rules and the application's settings, stuff that the presentation layer doesn't need to know about. By adding methods in the business layer to also do the non-database work, in the presentation layer we'll be able to write only the code that manages the visual appearance of the site, plus a few lines to call the business assembly's methods. With this code separation we achieve better reusability and maintenance of the business rules, and it's easier to change the application's user interface, because we don't need to touch the business code.

The List Class

This class exposes most of the functionality we need: it allows us to manage the mailing lists, but also to send out newsletters, subscribe and unsubscribe someone, and return all the child records (both subscriptions and archived newsletters), although some of these methods just wrap the respective methods of the child objects.

Method Name	Description
public int ID	Read-only property that returns the ID of the list represented by the object.
public string Name	Gets/sets the list's name.
public string Description	Gets/sets the list's description.

Method Name	Description
`public List()`	Class constructor with no parameters. It only resets the properties.
`public List(int existingListID)`	Class constructor that sets the properties to describe the list identified by the input ID.
`public List(List existingList)`	Class constructor that sets the properties to describe the list identified by an existing `List` object.
`private void LoadFromID()`	Retrieves the list record identified by a private ID variable, and loads the object's properties accordingly. This method is called by the constructors, or when the data has to be refreshed.
`private void ResetProperties()`	Resets the properties.
`public int LoadFromID(int existingListID)`	Loads all the properties of the question identified by the input ID.
`public int Create(string listName, string listDescription)`	Creates a new mailing list, and sets the properties of the object to represent the new record.
`public bool Update()`	Updates the list with the new values of the public properties.
`public bool Delete()`	Deletes the list.
`public static DataSet GetLists()`	Static method that returns all the mailing lists.
`public DataSet GetNewsletters()`	Returns all the child archived newsletters.
`public Newsletter SendNewsletter(string subject, string body, bool isHTML, MailPriority priority, bool saveToDB, out int totalNewsletters)`	Sends out a newsletter to all the active subscribers of the mailing list. The last parameter is an output parameter that can be used by the caller to retrieve the number of sent newsletters.
`public Newsletter SendNewsletter(string subject, string body, bool isHTML, MailPriority priority, bool saveToDB)`	Overloads the method above, but does not have the last output parameter.
`public DataSet GetSubscriptions(bool activeOnly)`	Gets the subscribers of the list; all of them or only those that are active.
`public DataSet GetSubscriptions()`	Overloads the above method, and returns *all* the subscriptions.

Method Name	Description
`public Subscription AddSubscription(string firstName, string lastName, string email, bool active)`	Adds a new child subscription to the database.
`public Subscription Subscribe(string firstName, string lastName, string email, out string subjectText, out string messageText)`	Subscribes a new user to the mailing list. It differs from the `AddSubscription` method in that a confirmation is sent to the subscriber, if required in the settings. The output parameters are used to return the subject and body of the confirmation message.
`public bool Unsubscribe(string email, out string subjectText, out string messageText)`	Unsubscribes the user with the specified e-mail address. The output parameters are used to return the subject and body of the confirmation message.

You may be wondering why we need both the `AddSubscription` and the `Subscribe` methods. Well, the former simply wraps a call to the `Add` method of the `Data.Subscriptions` class to add a new record to the database, and is used by the administration console to manage the subscriptions. On the other hand, the `Subscribe` method adds a record to the database if the subscription is not present, or activates the existing subscription. It also sends a customized confirmation message to the user, if required. Consequently, the page that handles the mailing list subscription box uses this version and it is therefore available to any site visitor.

The Subscription Class

This is a simple class that describes a particular subscription. It allows us to update, delete, or create a new subscription, and also to subscribe/unsubscribe a user:

Method Name	Description
`public int ID`	Read-only property that returns the ID of the subscription represented by the object.
`public int ListID`	Read-only property that returns the ID of the parent mailing list.
`public Business.List List`	Returns the parent mailing list.
`public int UserID`	Returns the ID of the user.
`public bool Active`	Gets/sets the `Active` state of the subscription.
`public string FirstName`	Gets/sets the subscriber's first name.
`public string LastName`	Gets/sets the subscriber's last name.

Method Name	Description
`public string Email`	Gets/sets the subscriber's e-mail.
`public DateTime AddedDate`	Returns the date when the subscription was added to the database.
`public Subscription()`	Class constructor with no parameters. It only resets the properties.
`public Subscription (int existingSubscriptionID)`	Class constructor that sets the properties to describe the subscription identified by the input ID.
`public Subscription (Subscription existingSubscription)`	Class constructor that sets the properties to describe the subscription identified by an existing `Subscription` object.
`public Subscription(int subscrListID, string subscrEmail)`	Class constructor that sets the properties to describe the subscription with the specified e-mail address.
`private void LoadFromID()`	Retrieves the subscription record identified by a private ID variable, and loads the object's properties accordingly.
`private void ResetProperties()`	Resets the properties.
`public int LoadFromID(int existingSubscriptionID)`	Loads all the properties of the subscription identified by the input ID.
`public int LoadFromEmail(int subscrListID, string subscrEmail)`	Loads all the properties of the subscription with the specified e-mail address.
`public int Create(int subscrListID, string subscrFirstName, string subscrLastName, string subscrEmail, bool subscrActive)`	Creates a new subscription record to the database.
`public bool Update()`	Updates the current subscription with the new values of the public properties.
`public bool Delete()`	Deletes the subscription.
`public int Subscribe(int subscrListID, string subscrFirstName, string subscrLastName, string subscrEmail, out string subjectText, out string messageText)`	Creates a new subscription or reactivates a disabled one, and optionally (if required in the settings) sends a confirmation message. The last two output parameters return the subject and body of that message, customized with the list and subscriber's data.

Table continued on following page

Method Name	Description
public bool Unsubscribe(int subscrListID, string subscrEmail, out string subjectText, out string messageText)	Removes or inactivates a subscription, as specified in the settings, and optionally sends a confirmation message. The last two output parameters return the subject and body of that message.

The Subscribe and Unsubscribe methods are those used by the identically named methods of the List class. Subscribe adds a subscription for the specified mailing list if one with the same specified values is not already present, otherwise it ensures that its Active status is true. Unsubscribe removes a subscription, or deactivates it.

The Newsletter Class

The Newsletter class is even simpler than Subscription because, in addition to the usual LoadFromID, ResetProperties, and Update, it has only a Send method, and all the properties are read-only. This is because it doesn't make sense to modify a newsletter when it is archived.

Method Name	Description
public int ID	Returns the ID of the newsletter represented by the object.
public int ListID	Returns the ID of the parent mailing list.
public Business.List List	Returns the parent mailing list.
public string Subject	Returns the newsletter's subject.
public string Body	Returns the newsletter's body.
public bool IsHTML	Returns whether the newsletter is in HTML format.
public DateTime SentDate	Returns the date when the newsletter was sent.
public Newsletter()	Class constructor with no parameters. It only resets the properties.
public Newsletter(int existingNewsletterID)	Class constructor that sets the properties to describe the newsletter identified by the input ID.
public Newsletter(Newsletter existingNewsletter)	Class constructor that sets the properties to describe the newsletter identified by an existing Newsletter object.
private void LoadFromID()	Loads the properties of the option identified by a private ID variable.

Method Name	Description
`private void ResetProperties()`	Resets the properties.
`public int LoadFromID(int existingNewsletterID)`	Loads all the properties of the specified archived newsletter.
`public bool Delete()`	Deletes the newsletter.
`public int Send(int newsletterListID, string newsletterSubject, string newsletterBody, bool newsletterIsHTML, MailPriority priority bool saveToDB, out int totalNewsletters)`	Sends out a newsletter with the specified subject, body, format, and priority to all the active subscribers of the specified mailing list. The last output parameter returns the total number of newsletters sent to the mailing list.
`public int Send(int newsletterListID, string newsletterSubject, string newsletterBody, bool newsletterIsHTML, MailPriority priority, bool saveToDB)`	The same as the above version, but without the last output parameter.

The Send method requires as input all the parts of the newsletter (subject, body, priority) in order to archive the newsletter to the database. The interesting point is that the subject and body strings can contain special tags such as #ListName# or #SubscriberEmail#. These are processed and replaced with the respective values for each subscription to which the newsletter is sent. Read below for more details about the supported tags.

> *An alternative implementation of the Send method would be to set all the public parameters, and just call a Send() method without parameters. However, some properties are read-only and this would create a bit of confusion when the user has to set them. Additionally, and this is the main reason, I personally prefer to pass all the parameters in a single line, rather than having to set one property per line. This same discussion applies to the Create methods of most of the business classes, which require as input all the values for a new record, instead of using the values of the public properties.*

The Helper Class

The Helper class exposes some static methods that are not specific to any other class, but can be of general use, namely it exposes the methods to process and replace the special tags just mentioned above:

Method Name	Description
`public static string ProcessListTags(string message, int listID)`	Replaces the list's special tags with the respective values.
`public static string ProcessSubscriptionTags(string message, int subscrID)`	Replaces the subscription's special tags with the respective values.
`public static string ProcessSettingsTags(string message)`	Replaces the settings' special tags with the respective values.

You may be wondering why there are three methods instead of only one. Each method requires the subscription ID or list ID as input and performs the necessary replacements. The reason for having three methods is as follows. When we build the administration console later in the chapter, we'll see that there are occasions when we only need to parse and replace the tags for the settings and the list, and not for the current subscription. For example, when we preview a message during its preparation with the editor that we'll provide, we can't replace the tags for the subscription. This is because there is no current subscription to parse; the preview is general, not specific to a particular subscription. This means that we wouldn't have a subscription ID to pass to a unique method. Sure, we could pass a value with the special meaning of "do not replace the tags for the subscription", but at this point it is easier to use separate methods.

The tags for the list can be inserted in both the body and the subject of the newsletters we send out, while the tags for the settings and the subscription are allowed within the body only. The newsletter's subject does not need to be customized for each subscriber, so we accept this limitation by design in order to speed up the execution of the Send method. In fact, we can spare thousands of calls to the ProcessSubscriptionTags and ProcessSettingsTags methods for the subject in this way, if we have thousands of subscriptions. This is another reason why it is simpler to provide three separate methods that parse the text and replace the tags: if we had only one method for all the replacements, we would need a further parameter to tell the method if the passed text is the subject, and whether we can skip the tags for the subscriber.

But which are the tags for the lists, subscriptions, and settings? Here is the complete list:

- ❏ List tags: #ListID#, #ListName#, #ListDescription#

- ❏ Subscription tags: #SubscriptionID#, #SubscriberFirstName#, #SubscriberLastName#, #SubscriberEmail#

- ❏ Settings tags: #SenderName#, #SenderEmail#, #SubscribeURL#

The settings should be self-explanatory, except for #SubscribeURL# maybe. This tag maps the SubscribeUrl setting, and refers to the full base URL (the URL without additional parameters) of the page that takes care of subscribing or unsubscribing a user based on the parameters passed along with its URL. At the end of each newsletter we should provide an opt-out link to allow the user to easily unsubscribe. The link points to that page, with some additional parameters that specify the current e-mail address, and the fact that we want to unsubscribe them from the mailing list. So we can use this tag and the other subscription tags to dynamically build the complete opt-out link customized for each subscriber.

Designing the User Interface Services

The user interface layer of this module is simpler than for the previous ones. Some of our other modules have numerous pages for the user, reusable user controls, web services, and also Windows clients that make use of the web services. In this case, most of the module is made up of the administration console. The end-user side of things includes a box for subscribing to a mailing list, and a page that either confirms the operation or reports an error.

We could think about implementing a web service to administer the mailing lists through a Windows client, but this wouldn't be really useful. The administrator only needs to access the administration console for sending out a newsletter once a week, every two weeks, or less frequently. There isn't a huge amount of work involved in administering subscriptions, since the users can subscribe and unsubscribe by themselves, with no help from the administrator. Therefore, unless you have dozens of different mailing lists and you are sending out newsletters every day, the mailing list administration pages won't be required very often. When you have to prepare a newsletter, you'll usually use a word processor or an HTML editor to write and format the content, then you'll copy and paste it to the module's administration page and send it out. In the HTML code you can also use <img> tags that reference images on your server, and these can be uploaded through the file manager tool presented in Chapter 4. Most of the time that is actually spent is on thinking about the organization of the content, but this has nothing to do with the module implementation. Therefore, we decided we don't need a web service and a Windows client to administer the newsletters section of the database.

Let's move on and think about the subscription box. Should we build a user control so we can insert it into any page? Well, that is a possible solution, but in this case there are other factors to consider:

❑ We aren't using any server controls bound to the data.

❑ We don't need the box to be dynamically programmable.

❑ The box is a simple HTML table that requires only a few lines of normal HTML code.

❑ When a user subscribes we want to point to a different page to handle the submitted data, because we also want to print a confirmation message or show an error if the user has not supplied the required information. If we employed a user control, we would need to handle a server event and then redirect to another page to show those messages, because writing the messages directly into the box could possibly enlarge the subscription box and mess up the layout of the page that hosts the user control. We don't have this problem if we use a simple HTML form that points to a separate ASP.NET page to handle the submitted user's data and show the required messages.

❑ If we have partner sites, they may agree to host our mailing list subscription box on their own site. If they run on a Linux server or a Windows server without the .NET Framework installed, they won't be able to insert our user control box. We can avoid this problem by using HTML.

After considering all these points, we came to the conclusion that having a user control won't provide any significant advantages for this solution. In fact, it would actually make it more difficult to customize it, add JavaScript client-side validation of input, or show the confirmation/error messages. Also, a mailing list box is something that we can plug into our layout and show in every page (maybe in the right-hand column in a typical site layout). However, our web developers might have got used to two-line implementations for things like this. So instead of forcing them to manually write the dozen lines of HTML code, in the administration console we'll provide a wizard that will create the necessary code for the box for the specified mailing list. Aren't we kind to our web developers? The wizard actually auto-generates the code for a basic subscription box that the developers can customize with images, JavaScript, other colors, etc., to make it best fit with the current site's layout and styles.

The Need for Security

As we just mentioned in the last section, the end-user side of this module is very limited, and most of the module is concerned with the administration console. Therefore, all that we need to do to protect this module is to check if the current user has the `AdministerData` permission for general administration tasks (adding, editing, and deleting records), and the `SendNewsletter` permission for sending out a newsletter. We'll be using the `Accounts` module from Chapter 5 to check the permissions, as we've already done in previous chapters for other administration pages.

The Solution

This module has a very similar structure to that of previous modules. The administration console has similar pages: the page for the mailing lists (questions or categories in the previous chapters), the page for the subscribers (options and news in the previous chapters), and the page for the settings. We won't list the code for these pages, as it is so similar to the code already seen – all of the code can be found in the download. The same applies to the data component. Thanks to the `DbObject` base class of the `Core` assembly, we can use the `RunProcedure` method to run the stored procedures and return a dataset or an output parameter. As we saw in the *Design* section, our data assembly has classes that almost exactly map the stored procedures, and there is nothing new to add that wasn't already discussed in previous chapters.

So what *are* we going to see? We'll look at the code of some of the stored procedures (to better understand the relationships between the tables), the business classes, the subscription box, and the pages required for subscribing.

Working on the Database

Looking at the diagram and the descriptions of the tables we provided earlier, you should have no problems building the tables for our SQL Server database and the relationships. (All three one-to-many relationships should have the **Enforce Relationship for INSERTs and DELETEs** options selected.) However, as for the previous chapters, you can go to the Wrox site and download the database backup with all the tables, stored procedures, triggers, and also some data that will allow you to test the module straight out of the download.

Creating the Stored Procedures and Triggers

In this section we won't cover the code of all the stored procedures, since in previous chapters we've already seen how the procedures for deleting and updating a record work. However, we'll show a few of the procedures for working with subscribers, because they are a bit more complex as they involve joins and relationship constraints.

Retrieving Subscriptions

Here's the code for the `sp_MLists_GetSubscriptions` procedure. It joins the `MLists_Subscriptions` and `MLists_Users` table, to return either all the details of the subscriptions for the specified mailing list, or just the details of those users with an active subscription:

```
CREATE PROCEDURE sp_MLists_GetSubscriptions
                @ListID int,
                @ActiveOnly bit
AS

IF @ActiveOnly = 0
  BEGIN
  SELECT SubscriptionID, MLists_Users.UserID, Active, FirstName, LastName,
                                    Email, AddedDate, ListID
    FROM MLists_Users
    INNER JOIN MLists_Subscriptions
      ON MLists_Users.UserID = MLists_Subscriptions.UserID
    WHERE MLists_Subscriptions.ListID = @ListID
  END
ELSE
  BEGIN
  SELECT SubscriptionID, MLists_Users.UserID, Active, FirstName, LastName,
                                    Email, AddedDate, ListID
    FROM MLists_Users
    INNER JOIN MLists_Subscriptions
      ON MLists_Users.UserID = MLists_Subscriptions.UserID
    WHERE MLists_Subscriptions.ListID = @ListID
        AND MLists_Subscriptions.Active = 1
  END
GO
```

There are two distinct SELECT statements, with or without the WHERE clause for the active subscriptions. The two tables are joined on the UserID field that is present in each table.

The sp_MLists_GetSubscriptionDetails procedure is very similar, it just has an additional WHERE clause for the specified SubscriptionID.

Retrieving Subscriptions by ID

This procedure, sp_MLists_GetSubscriptionID, also joins the two tables, as above, but only for the purpose of returning the information for the subscription with the specified e-mail address that points to the specified mailing list. If a row is found we return its SubscriptionID, or -1 otherwise:

```
CREATE PROCEDURE sp_MLists_GetSubscriptionID
                @ListID int,
                @Email varchar(50),
                @SubscriptionID int OUTPUT
AS

SELECT @SubscriptionID = SubscriptionID
  FROM MLists_Users
  INNER JOIN MLists_Subscriptions
    ON MLists_Users.UserID = MLists_Subscriptions.UserID
  WHERE MLists_Subscriptions.ListID = @ListID
        AND MLists_Users.Email = @Email

IF @SubscriptionID IS NULL
  SET @SubscriptionID = -1
GO
```

Inserting Subscriptions

`sp_MLists_InsertSubscription` is the most complex procedure. It has to add a row in both tables, but it also has to check that the subscription does not already exist. If it does not, it has to check if a user with the specified e-mail address already exists (which is the case when the user is already subscribed to another mailing list). If so, it gets their ID and uses it for the `UserID` field of the new row it creates in `MLists_Subscription`. Otherwise it first adds a new row in `MLists_Users`, gets the ID of the new row, and then adds a row in `MLists_Subscriptions`. The code below is well commented, so you should have no problems understanding the execution flow:

```
CREATE PROCEDURE sp_MLists_InsertSubscription
                @ListID int,
                @FirstName varchar(50),
                @LastName varchar(50),
                @Email varchar(50),
                @Active bit,
                @SubscriptionID int OUTPUT
AS

DECLARE @CurrSubscription int
DECLARE @CurrUser int

-- see if the subscription already exists
SELECT @CurrSubscription = SubscriptionID
  FROM MLists_Users
  INNER JOIN MLists_Subscriptions
    ON MLists_Users.UserID = MLists_Subscriptions.UserID
  WHERE MLists_Subscriptions.ListID = @ListID
        AND MLists_Users.Email = @Email

-- if not, go ahead
IF @CurrSubscription IS NULL
  BEGIN

  -- the subscription does not exist, but check if the user already exists
  SELECT @CurrUser = UserID
    FROM MLists_Users
    WHERE MLists_Users.Email = @Email

  -- if the user is not present, add it
  IF @CurrUser IS NULL
    BEGIN
    -- insert the User
    INSERT INTO MLists_Users
                (FirstName, LastName, Email)
                VALUES (@FirstName, @LastName, @Email)
    -- save the new UserID
    SET @CurrUser = @@IDENTITY

    IF @@ERROR > 0
      BEGIN
      RAISERROR ('Insert of User failed', 16, 1)
      RETURN 99
      END
```

```
      END

   -- add the new subscription
   INSERT INTO MLists_Subscriptions
               (ListID, UserID, Active, AddedDate)
               VALUES (@ListID, @CurrUser, @Active, GETDATE())
   -- save the new ID to be returned
   SET @SubscriptionID = @@IDENTITY

   IF @@ERROR > 0
     BEGIN
     RAISERROR ('Insert of Subscription failed', 16, 1)
     RETURN 99
     END

   END
ELSE
   SET @SubscriptionID = -1
GO
```

Deleting Subscriptions

To delete a subscription we have a simple stored procedure, sp_MLists_DeleteSubscription, defined as follows:

```
CREATE PROCEDURE sp_MLists_DeleteSubscription
                  @SubscriptionID int
AS

DELETE FROM MLists_Subscriptions WHERE SubscriptionID = @SubscriptionID
GO
```

As you can see, this code only deletes the record in the MLists_Subscription table, and does not delete the respective user in the MLists_Users table. The same user can be subscribed to more than one mailing list, so if we wanted to delete it, we should first ensure that there are no other subscriptions that refer to it. This would be simple to do, and could be done from within the stored procedure above. However, if we deleted a subscription by directly executing a DELETE query, without calling the helper stored procedure, no check would be performed, and unused users could remain in the database. To be sure that the user is deleted and can have no more subscriptions when we delete a subscription, either via the stored procedure or with a direct query, we can write a **trigger**. This is the code to create it:

```
CREATE TRIGGER DeleteUser ON [dbo].[MLists_Subscriptions]
FOR DELETE
AS

DELETE MLists_Users
  FROM MLists_Users AS u
  JOIN Deleted AS d
    ON u.UserID = d.UserID
  LEFT JOIN MLists_Subscriptions AS s
    ON s.UserID = d.UserID
  WHERE s.UserID IS NULL
```

This trigger is executed when one or more records are deleted from the `MLists_Subscription` table. When records are deleted, they are copied into the `Deleted` table, a table managed by SQL Server behind the scenes, and that exists only within the scope of the trigger. Therefore, we can retrieve the deleted subscriptions from the `Deleted` table, join the two tables as you see above, and detect which users are no longer subscribed to any mailing list and can therefore be deleted.

> *If you want to know more about triggers, you can read about them in Professional SQL Server 2000 (Wrox Press, ISBN 1-861004-48-6).*
>
> *Note that if we were using the Users table of the Accounts module to store the users' contact information for the subscriptions, we wouldn't have this trigger. Although they aren't subscribed to anything they might still use the site and so we should keep their account in the database.*

Implementing the Data and Configuration Assemblies

At this point we should build the data and configuration assemblies, following the structure designed earlier. However, as we mentioned, the code required has the same structure as the respective assemblies of the previous chapters, with just the following differences:

- ❏ The names of the methods and stored procedures in the data component
- ❏ The site-wide `web.config`'s custom key that stores the settings file name
- ❏ The entry name for the cached settings in the configuration component

The data component is an assembly named `Wrox.WebModules.MailingLists.Data`, the configuration assembly and namespace is `Wrox.WebModules.MailingLists.Configuration`, the new custom key for `web.settings` is `MailingLists_SettingsFile`, and the cache entry is `MailingLists_Settings`. You can refer back to Chapter 5 to see how these two assemblies are structured, and you can find the complete code for this module in the download.

Implementing the Business Layer

Just like the data assembly, some of the methods of the business layer are the same as in other modules. For example, those that load and reset the properties, and those that create, delete, and update a record. But there are also some things that are specific to this module, such as the methods for sending out a newsletter, subscribing/unsubscribing a user, and processing the special tags. We'll just look at these new methods here. In the *Design* section you can read the complete declaration of them all, and you can understand how they are implemented by looking at the respective methods in some of the previous chapters.

We start off by adding a new Class Library to the solution, name it `MailingLists.Business`, set its properties (set the assembly and default namespace name to `Wrox.WebModules.MailingLists.Business`) and edit its `AssemblyInfo.cs` file to specify the assembly key file. From reading the previous chapters you should already know how to complete all this without the need for further details, so let's go ahead and start coding the classes.

The Subscription Class

If you still have the default `Class1.cs` file in the project, rename it to `Subscription.cs`. The methods we're going to show for this class are `Subscribe` and `Unsubscribe`. These are also used by the corresponding methods of the `List` class.

The Subscribe Method

The `Subscribe` method takes care of all the details for the subscription of a new user. It checks if the user is already present on the chosen mailing list, but in inactive mode. In that case it sets the user as active, otherwise it adds a new record. Then, if required in the settings, it sends a confirmation message to the subscriber. Sending the notification e-mail requires a couple of classes of the .NET Framework, `MailMessage` and `SmtpMail`, which we'll explain when discussing the `Send` method of the current class. For now just be aware that they are needed to send e-mails.

The notification message can be personalized with the name, e-mail address, and other user or list information, thanks to the special tags explained earlier which are replaced by the methods of the `Helper` class that we'll see shortly. The subject and the body of the confirmation message are also returned to the caller through two output parameters, in case the caller wants to print them on the page (that's exactly what we'll be doing later). Here's the code:

```
public int Subscribe(int subscrListID, string subscrFirstName,
                     string subscrLastName, string subscrEmail,
                     out string subjectText, out string messageText)
{
  subjectText = "";
  messageText = "";
  if (subscrEmail.Trim() == "") return -1;

  // get the subject/body of the subscription message
  subjectText = settings.SubscrSubject;
  messageText = settings.SubscrMessage;

  // get the subscription for this list, with the specified e-mail, if any
  Business.Subscription subscription = new Business.Subscription(
                                           subscrListID, subscrEmail);
  // if the subscription already exists...
  if (subscription.ID != -1)
  {
    // set it to active
    subscription.Active = true;
    subscription.Update();
  }
  else
  {
    // otherwise add the subscription
    subscription.Create(subscrListID, subscrFirstName, subscrLastName,
                                      subscrEmail, true);
  }

  // replace the tags of this new subscriber
  messageText = Helper.ProcessSubscriptionTags(
                                    messageText, subscription.ID);
```

```csharp
    // replace the list's and settings tags
    subjectText = Helper.ProcessListTags(subjectText, subscrListID);
    messageText = Helper.ProcessListTags(messageText, subscrListID);
    messageText = Helper.ProcessSettingsTags(messageText);

    // if a confirmation e-mail is required
    if (settings.SendSubscrEmail)
    {
      // create a new message
      MailMessage mailMsg = new MailMessage();
      mailMsg.From = settings.SenderName + " <" + settings.SenderEmail + ">";
      // set the "To" field to the subscriber's e-mail
      mailMsg.To = subscrEmail;
      // set the Subject/body to the subject/body created
      // for the confirmation page
      mailMsg.Subject = subjectText;
      mailMsg.Body = messageText;
      // send the mail
      SmtpMail.Send(mailMsg);
    }

    if (subscription.ID == -1)
      ResetProperties();
    else
      LoadFromID(subscription.ID);

    return subscriptionID;
}
```

In order to save a round trip to the database, we could also add an overloaded version of `ProcessSubscriptionTags` that accepts a `Subscription` object instead of the subscription's ID, and pass in the existing `Subscription` object. But as this method isn't called very often (unless we have 100 users registering every minute) the effect on performance will not be significant.

The Unsubscribe Method

The `Unsubscribe` method has the same structure as `Subscribe`. It first checks if the specified subscriber is present: if not, the method returns `false`, otherwise it sets the subscription as inactive (the subscriber won't receive any future newsletters for this mailing list), or completely removes the record from the database, according to the options set by the administrator. It also sends the confirmation message if required:

```csharp
public bool Unsubscribe(int subscrListID, string subscrEmail,
                        out string subjectText, out string messageText)
{
    subjectText = "";
    messageText = "";
    if (subscrEmail.Trim() == "") return false;

    // get the subscriptions for this list, with the specified e-mail, if any
    Business.Subscription subscription = new Business.Subscription(
                                               subscrListID, subscrEmail);
```

```
    // if the subscription does not exist...
    if (subscription.ID == -1)
    {
      subjectText = "There is no subscription with the specified e-mail
                                                   address";
      messageText = "";
      return false;
    }

    // get the subject/body of the subscription message
    subjectText = settings.UnsubscrSubject;
    messageText = settings.UnsubscrMessage;
    // replace the tags of this subscription. This has to be done
    // BEFORE removing the subscription
    messageText = Business.Helper.ProcessSubscriptionTags(messageText,
                                                   subscription.ID);

    // remove or inactivate the subscription,
    // according to the UnsubscrAction setting
    if (settings.UnsubscrAction == Configuration.UnsubscrActionType.Remove)
      subscription.Delete();
    else
    {
      subscription.Active = false;
      subscription.Update();
    }

    // replace the list's and settings' tags
    subjectText = Helper.ProcessListTags(subjectText, subscrListID);
    messageText = Helper.ProcessListTags(messageText, subscrListID);
    messageText = Helper.ProcessSettingsTags(messageText);

    // if a confirmation subscrEmail is required
    if (settings.SendUnsubscrEmail)
    {
      // create a new message
      MailMessage mailMsg = new MailMessage();
      mailMsg.From = settings.SenderName + " <" + settings.SenderEmail + ">";
      // set the "To" field to the subscriber's subscrEmail
      mailMsg.To = subscrEmail;
      // set the subject/body to the subject/body created
      // for the confirmation page
      mailMsg.Subject = subjectText;
      mailMsg.Body = messageText;
      // send the mail
      SmtpMail.Send(mailMsg);
    }

  ResetProperties();
  return true;
}
```

You can see that in both these methods we use the static methods of the `Helper` class to process and replace the special tags. In this second case, this is still required because even if the subscription is being deleted and the user won't receive any more newsletters from that mailing list, we need to show and/or send a last personalized confirmation message. We'll see the implementation of those helper methods shortly, but let's first have a look at the `Newsletter` class.

The Newsletter Class

The core of the `Newsletter` class is the `Send` method, which sends the newsletter to all the active subscribers for the specified list. The e-mails are sent through the default SMTP service installed with Windows 2000 Server, so we don't need anything special or any third party server to send the messages. All we need is a reference to `System.Web.dll`, which is not added by default for this type of project. Before starting with the implementation of the methods, ensure that you've also added a reference to the `Core` project, inherited from `BizObject`, and added a `using` directive for the `System.Web.Mail` namespace.

How to Send E-mails with the .NET Classes

In the `Subscribe` and `Unsubscribe` methods shown above we've used a couple of classes from the `System.Web.Mail` namespace to send the notification e-mails. Before going ahead with the `Send` method that actually sends out all the newsletters, it's worth taking a closer look at those classes.

The most important class is `SmtpMail`, which allows e-mail messages to be sent through the use of the **Collaboration Data Objects** (**CDO**) for Windows. The e-mails are delivered through any third party server specified by the static property `SmtpServer` or, if this property is not set, through the default SMTP Server installed with Windows 2000 Server. In our case we'll always use the default server, so there is no need to supply a value for this property. The method that we actually use to send a mail is `Send`, which has two overloaded versions. The first one is declared as follows:

```
public static void Send(string from,
                        string to,
                        string subject,
                        string messageText);
```

This version accepts as input all the parameters needed to send an e-mail, namely the e-mail address of the sender and the receiver, and the subject and body text. The method is static, so we don't need to create an instance of the class to use it. Here's an example of its usage:

```
SmtpMail.Send("myemail@thephile.com", "youremail@thephile.com",
              "Test",
              "Hello! This is just to test the Send method");
```

This version works fine if we only want to send a message in plain text, and we don't need anything more than those four parameters. But what if we want to create an HTML e-mail, set its priority, and the CC and BCC properties? Well, for this there is the second overloaded version of the `Send` methods, defined as follows:

```
public static void Send(MailMessage message);
```

Here the method takes as input a `MailMessage` object (the second class mentioned above), which has properties such as `From`, `To`, `Cc`, `Bcc`, `Subject`, `Text`, `Priority`, `BodyFormat`, and `Attachments`. The meaning of these properties is clear; in the implementation of the `Unsubscribe/Subscribe` methods we've already seen how to create and use a `MailMessage` object and send the respective mail, and we'll see similar code again in the next section, for the implementation of `Newsletter.Send`. The only property that's worth a further example is `Attachments`, because it is not used anywhere in our module. Say that we've already created an instance of `MailMessage` called `mailMsg`, and set its basic properties (sender, recipient, subject, and text). The following code shows how to add a couple of attachments:

```
mailMsg.Attachments.Add(new MailAttachment(@"C:\file1.doc"));
mailMsg.Attachments.Add(new MailAttachment(@"C:\file2.bmp"));
```

We add new `MailAttachment` items through the `Add` method of the `Attachments` collection. The constructor of the `MailAttachment` class takes as input the path of the file to add to the e-mail. As a last step, the mail is sent with:

```
SmtpMail.Send(mailMsg);
```

The Send Method

The `Send` method requires as input the destination mailing list's ID, the newsletter's subject, body, format, and priority, and a parameter that tells whether the newsletter has to be archived to the database or not. It returns the number of sent e-mails through the last (output) parameter. Here is the complete code:

```
public int Send(int newsletterListID, string newsletterSubject,
            string newsletterBody, bool newsletterIsHTML,
            MailPriority priority, bool saveToDB,
            out int totalNewsletters)
{
  // reset the ID of the newsletter identified by this object
  newsletterID = -1;

  // replace the list's tags in the subject
  newsletterSubject = Helper.ProcessListTags(newsletterSubject,
                                              newsletterListID);
  // replace the list's and settings' tags in the body
  newsletterBody = Helper.ProcessListTags(newsletterBody, newsletterListID);
  newsletterBody = Helper.ProcessSettingsTags(newsletterBody);

  // add a new record in the newsletters archive, if required
  if (saveToDB)
  {
    Data.Newsletters news = new Data.Newsletters(settings.ConnectionString);
    newsletterID = news.Add(newsletterListID, newsletterSubject,
                                newsletterBody, newsletterIsHTML);
  }

  // create a new mail message and set the common properties
  MailMessage mailMsg = new MailMessage();
```

```
    mailMsg.From = settings.SenderName + " <" + settings.SenderEmail + ">";
    mailMsg.Priority = priority;
    mailMsg.BodyFormat = (MailFormat)Convert.ToInt16(newsletterIsHTML);
    mailMsg.Subject = newsletterSubject;

    // get all the active subscribers of this list
    DataTable dt = new Business.List(
                        newsletterListID).GetSubscriptions(true).Tables[0];
    for(int i = 0; i < dt.DefaultView.Count; i++)
    {
      // replace the subscriber's special tags with their values
      mailMsg.To = (string)dt.DefaultView[i]["Email"];
      mailMsg.Body = Helper.ProcessSubscriptionTags(newsletterBody,
                              (int)dt.DefaultView[i]["SubscriptionID"]);
      // send the mail to this subscriber
      SmtpMail.Send(mailMsg);
    }

    // load the data for the sent newsletter in the current object
    if (newsletterID != -1)
      LoadFromID();
    else
      ResetProperties();

    // return the number of sent newsletters through an output parameter
    totalNewsletters = dt.DefaultView.Count;

    // return the ID of the newsletter added to the archive,
    // or -1 if it has not been added
    return newsletterID;
}
```

This code does quite a lot of things, so let's break it down:

❏ The special tags for the list and the general settings are replaced with their values.

❏ If required, the newsletter is archived to the database through the Data.Newsletters class.

❏ A new MailMessage object is created, and its properties that are common for all the subscribers are set.

❏ A Business.List class instance is used to get all the active subscribers for the specified mailing list, through the GetSubscriptions method.

❏ For each subscription returned by the query, it replaces the subscription's special tags, sets its e-mail address as the destination address for the mail object, and sends the mail.

❏ The number of sent messages is saved and returned to the caller through the output parameter.

This method does not support attachments for the newsletters, but it would be quite easy to add a parameter array with the path of the files to send, and attach them through the MailMessage's Attachments collection (of course you would need to update the presentation layer as well, though).

One last thing that's worth noting in the code is that after sending the newsletter we call the `LoadFromID` method to set the object's properties with the values of the new record. This is exactly what we do in the `Create` methods of any other business class. Here the name of the method is different and we also do different work, but we still add a record to the database (if `saveToDB` is `true`) and so we also update the object's state before terminating the method.

For the sake of completeness, let's also look at the overloaded version of the `Send` method. This version takes the same parameters except for the last one, and it's useful because it is quicker to call if we're not interested in the number of sent messages. Here's the code:

```
public int Send(int newsletterListID, string newsletterSubject,
             string newsletterBody, bool newsletterIsHTML,
             MailPriority priority, bool saveToDB)
{
  int totalNewsletters;
  return Send(newsletterListID, newsletterSubject, newsletterBody,
           newsletterIsHTML, priority, saveToDB, out totalNewsletters);
}
```

It just calls the first version we wrote, and passes as the last parameter a variable declared with a private scope. The `Send` method is also called by another business class (`List`) from its `SendNewsletter` method.

The Helper Class

The `Helper` class is the easiest to implement, as it only exposes three very short static methods. The `ProcessListTags` method retrieves the details of the specified list through an instance of `Business.List`, and then replaces the special tags:

```
public static string ProcessListTags(string message, int listID)
{
  Business.List list = new Business.List(listID);

  message = message.Replace("#ListID#", listID.ToString());
  message = message.Replace("#ListName#", list.Name);
  message = message.Replace("#ListDescription#", list.Description);

  return message;
}
```

`ProcessSubscriptionTags` does the same, but for the subscription tags:

```
public static string ProcessSubscriptionTags(string message, int subscrID)
{
  // if the subscriber does not exist, replace with empty strings
  if (subscrID==-1)
  {
    message = message.Replace("#SubscriptionID#", "");
    message = message.Replace("#SubscriberFirstName#", "");
    message = message.Replace("#SubscriberLastName#", "");
    message = message.Replace("#SubscriberEmail#", "");
```

```
    }
    else
    {
      // otherwise get the details of this subscriber
      Business.Subscription subscription =
                                    new Business.Subscription(subscrID);

      // and replace the tags
      message = message.Replace("#SubscriptionID#", subscrID.ToString());
      // replace #SubscriberFirstName# with the subscriber's first name
      // if the first name value is not null,
      // otherwise replace with "List Reader"
      message = message.Replace("#SubscriberFirstName#",
        subscription.FirstName!="" ? subscription.FirstName : "List Reader");
      message = message.Replace("#SubscriberLastName#",
        subscription.LastName);
      message = message.Replace("#SubscriberEmail#", subscription.Email);
    }

    return message;
}
```

In the code above there is one detail that's especially worth noting. If the subscriber's first name is empty, the #SubscriberFirstName# tag is replaced with "List Reader". This is because we might ask the subscriber to type and submit only the e-mail address, or even if we asked for their name they could choose not to supply it (as long as we don't make it required of course, but that's not a good choice usually). The conclusion is that we might easily have subscriptions without the first/last names. If we then sent a newsletter with the #SubscriberFirstName# tag, someone would receive the message with a null string where their name should be (for example "Dear , how's it going?", instead of something like "Dear Marco, how's it going?"). To prevent this, we replace the tag with "List Reader" if the first name is not provided, so that the message would be "Dear List Reader, how's it going?". That is a more acceptable message.

> It's better not to replace #SubscriberFirstName# with "List" and
> #SubscriberLastName# with "Reader", as you might think at first, because we may use only
> the first tag in the newsletter. However, if we use both, it's very probable that we won't have e-mails
> with "List Reader" plus a non-null last name (for example "Dear List Reader Bellinaso, ..."),
> because if the first name is not supplied then it's very likely that the last name won't be either.
> (Also, we might ask for the full name with a single field, and the value would be stored as first
> name only).

Lastly, ProcessSettingsTags processes and replaces the settings tags, retrieved through an instance of ModuleSettings:

```
public static string ProcessSettingsTags(string message)
{
    Configuration.ModuleSettings settings =
                                    Configuration.ModuleConfig.GetSettings();
    // replace the tags
    message = message.Replace("#SenderName#", settings.SenderName);
    message = message.Replace("#SenderEmail#", settings.SenderEmail);
    message = message.Replace("#SubscribeURL#", settings.SubscribeUrl);

    return message;
}
```

The Administration User Interface

The administration console is made up of a set of pages that allows us to add, remove, and edit the mailing lists, their subscriptions, and the subscribers' personal details. It also allows us to send out newsletters and consult the archive, and a few other things. The following screenshot shows the `Lists.aspx` page, which lists and manages the available mailing lists:

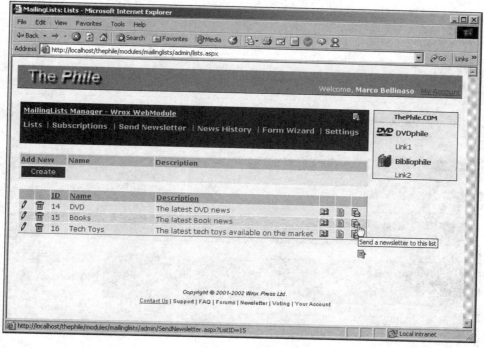

You can see that, in addition to the ID, name, and description of each mailing list, the grid also displays some icons, which allow us to directly jump to other pages to do something to the mailing list of the clicked row. Here is a list of the grid's icons with a description of the actions they perform:

Icon	Description
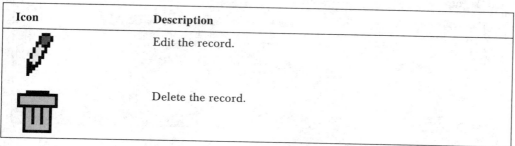	Edit the record.
	Delete the record.

Table continued on following page

Icon	Description
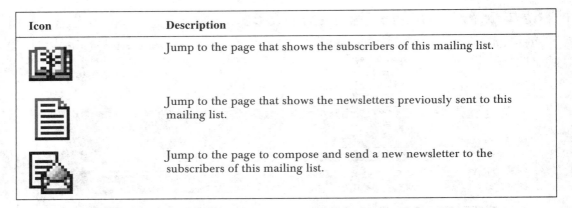	Jump to the page that shows the subscribers of this mailing list.
	Jump to the page that shows the newsletters previously sent to this mailing list.
	Jump to the page to compose and send a new newsletter to the subscribers of this mailing list.

When you click the book icon in the table above you jump to the page to manage the subscriptions, `Subscriptions.aspx`, which looks like the following screenshot:

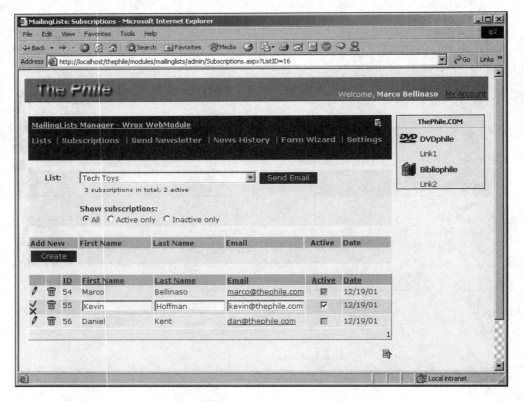

The code for these two web forms should be familiar if you've read the previous chapters. Maybe the only interesting new detail is that we use a `RegularExpressionValidator` control to validate the e-mail address for a new subscription or a subscription being edited. Here is how we define the textbox and the validators:

```
<asp:TextBox runat="server" CssClass="TextBox" ID="NewEmail" Width="100%" />
<asp:RequiredFieldValidator runat="server" ControlToValidate="NewEmail"
                            Display="dynamic"><br>* Email is required
</asp:RequiredFieldValidator>
<asp:RegularExpressionValidator runat="server"
                            ValidationExpression=".*@.*\..*"
                            ControlToValidate="NewEmail"
                            Display="dynamic">
                            <br>* This Email address is not valid
</asp:RegularExpressionValidator>
```

The expression .*@.*\..* means that the string must begin with a number of characters (.*), then it must contain a '@' character, some more characters, a period (escaped as \.), and finally more characters. For example, marco@thephile.com is a valid e-mail address, while marco@thephile or marco.thephile.com are invalid addresses.

The following tables summarize the most commonly used syntax constructs for the **regular expressions**. First of all let's see how to express the characters that we want to match:

Character Escapes	Description
ordinary characters	Characters other than .$^{[(|)*+?\ match themselves.
\b	Matches a backspace.
\t	Matches a tab.
\r	Matches a carriage return.
\v	Matches a vertical tab.
\f	Matches a form feed.
\n	Matches a newline.
\	If followed by a non-ordinary character (one of those listed in the first row), matches that character. For example, \+ matches a + character.

In addition to single characters, we can specify a class or a range of characters that can be matched in the expression. That is to say, we might want to allow any digit or any vowel in a position, and exclude all other characters. The following character classes enable this:

Character Class	Description
.	Matches any character except \n.
[aeiou]	Matches any single character specified in the set.
[^aeiou]	Matches any character not specified in the set.
[3-7a-dA-D]	Matches any character specified in the specified ranges (in the example the ranges are 3-7, a-d, and A-D).

Character Class	Description
\w	Matches any word character, that is, any alphanumeric character or the underscore (_).
\W	Matches any non-word character.
\s	Matches any whitespace character (space, tab, form-feed, new line, carriage return, or vertical feed).
\S	Matches any non-whitespace character.
\d	Matches any decimal character.
\D	Matches any non-decimal character.

Also, we can specify that a certain character or class of characters must be present at least once, or between two and six times, etc. The quantifiers are put just after a character or a class of characters, and allow us to specify how many times the preceding character/class must be matched:

Quantifier	Description
*	Zero or more matches.
+	One or more matches.
?	Zero or one matches.
{N}	N matches.
{N, }	N or more matches.
{N,M}	Between N and M matches.

To recap everything with another easy example, say that we have the expression `[aeiou]{2,4}\+[1-5]*`: this means that a string to correctly match this expression must start with two to four vowels, have a + sign, and terminate with zero or more digits between 1 and 5.

> *Regular expressions are a very powerful tool to validate the content of a control because they can be very detailed and complex. Furthermore, you can use them to do other advanced tasks, such as replacing or extracting the occurrences that match the expression, as we'll see in practice in the next chapter. Entire books have been written to teach how to use regular expressions, such as Teach Yourself Regular Expressions in 24 Hours (SAMS Press, ISBN 0-672319-36-5).*

You have to be aware, however, that the regular expression used to validate the e-mail address in the module only checks that the address is well formed. There's nothing to prevent someone from subscribing with an e-mail address that does not exist. To limit this you can at least improve the regular expression with other rules, such as checking that the domain name is at least two characters long and that it does exist, and that the extension is supported (consult www.icann.org to get a complete list). There are other rules, and although we kept it simple in our example, you'll find that a complete regular expression could be much longer than ours. If regular expressions are not enough for you (and they are not if you want to check the existence of a domain, for example), you can use a `CustomValidator` and write your own function to validate a value.

However, even with the most complete expression and other methods you can't be 100% sure that the address exists. The user can write an address with a real domain name, a real extension, but with a made-up name before the @. When the messages are sent out, you won't get any errors or exceptions at that time – the SMTP server does its work without letting you know about the result. However, messages sent to non-existent addresses usually come back to the sender with an error message saying that the message couldn't be successfully delivered because the address does not exist. These error messages are sent to the server's postmaster and then forwarded to the site's administrator. At this point, when you get such a message you can manually remove the address from the database. Alternatively you could write a program that parses the incoming messages to find the error messages, and automatically deletes the non-existent e-mail addresses by using the business classes of the `MailingList` module. This is beyond the scope of this book, and it is usually only provided by professional modules that have to be able to handle tens or hundreds of thousands of e-mails, and automate any possible process. For most sites, though, our module is enough, and deleting the erroneous addresses from the database once a month or so is not such a big issue (how often you should do this actually depends on the frequency of your newsletters).

Sending out Newsletters to Subscribers

The console has a simple newsletter editor, basically a form with a textbox for the body, and the common fields you find in any e-mail client, such as Subject, To, Format, and Priority. You can type a newsletter, preview it, and finally send the message out to the selected mailing list's active subscriptions. The screenshot below represents the `SendNewsletter.aspx` page with the message preview:

You can see that the settings tags (such as #SubscribeURL#) and the list tags (such as #ListName#) were processed for the preview, while the subscription tags were not. This is because they have different values for every subscription, and are actually processed only when the newsletter is sent to each subscriber.

The code for presenting the page is simple enough, so we won't show it. Instead, we'll have a look at the code-behind that shows the message preview, and actually sends out and archives the newsletter. First of all, in Page_Load there is some code that fills the DropDownList with the available mailing lists, and sets the default subject and signature as specified in the settings file. Then, when the **Preview** button is pressed, the following event handler is executed on the server:

```
protected void Preview_Click(object sender, EventArgs e)
{
    string msgText = Body.Text;
    int listID = int.Parse(ListsDropDown.SelectedItem.Value);

    // replace the list's and settings, special tags with their values
    msgText = Business.Helper.ProcessListTags(msgText, listID);
    msgText = Business.Helper.ProcessSettingsTags(msgText);

    // encode the body if the format is not HTML
    if (FormatDropDown.SelectedIndex==0)
    {
      msgText = HttpUtility.HtmlEncode(msgText);
      // replace the new lines with <br>, to show the new lines in the Label
      msgText = msgText.Replace("\n", "<br>");
      // remove carriage returns
      msgText = msgText.Replace("\r", "");
    }

    // show the body in the preview label
    MsgPreview.Text = msgText;
    MsgPreview.Visible = true;
}
```

This code replaces the special list and settings tags with their respective values, and if the selected format is plain text it encodes the text (for example <b> become <b>), replaces the new-lines with a <br> tag, and removes the carriage returns, because '\n' and '\r' characters are not recognized by HTML. Finally, it displays the body in the preview label.

The code for the **Send** button is even simpler, because the Newsletter business class does all the work required for processing the tags and sending out the mails. This is the code for the button's Click event:

```
protected void Send_Click(object sender, EventArgs e)
{
    Server.ScriptTimeout = 3600;

    // send the newsletter and eventually save it to the DB
    int numSent;
    Business.List list = new Business.List(
                            int.Parse(ListsDropDown.SelectedItem.Value));
    list.SendNewsletter(Subject.Text, Body.Text,
```

```
                    (FormatDropDown.SelectedIndex==1),
                    (MailPriority)PriorityDropDown.SelectedIndex,
                    ArchiveNewsletter.Checked, out numSent);

    // show the number of sent mails
    MsgPreview.Text = string.Format(
                            "<b>{0} mail(s) have been sent</b>", numSent);
    // if the newsletter has been archived, say this
    if (ArchiveNewsletter.Checked)
      MsgPreview.Text += "<br><b>The newsletter has been archived</b>";
      MsgPreview.Visible = true;
}
```

The last parameter of this method returns the number of mails that have been sent, and this is displayed at the bottom of the page, as a confirmation message. The only point that's worth noting here is the first line of code:

```
Server.ScriptTimeout = 3600;
```

Sending a single message is a very quick task, but if you have thousands of subscribers this may take a while: several minutes or even some hours for large messages. Those of you who are already familiar with traditional ASP programming will know that by default a page has 90 seconds to execute the scripting code and to send all the generated HTML code to the browser. The IIS administrator can change this value or we can hardcode it into the page, which is exactly what we do here. We set the maximum time to complete the execution to an hour, but you can change it to a value that you consider to be long enough for your needs. If you have many thousands of subscriptions, you may even consider deploying the MailingLists module on a separate server, to avoid serious problems with the services that run on the primary server. You can have the module's engine on a server and the subscription box on another server, as long as the subscription box points to the Subscribe.aspx page on the first server. However, if you have a really large base of subscribers, some web hosting companies can offer a dedicated server with specific software that can handle tens or hundreds of thousands of e-mail addresses. This software should be able to process your newsletters asynchronously and provide some fault tolerance, by using transactions and messaging services such as MSMQ. It goes without saying that these extra services are quite expensive, and are not required for most sites.

Here is an example of the message generated, as received in Outlook Express:

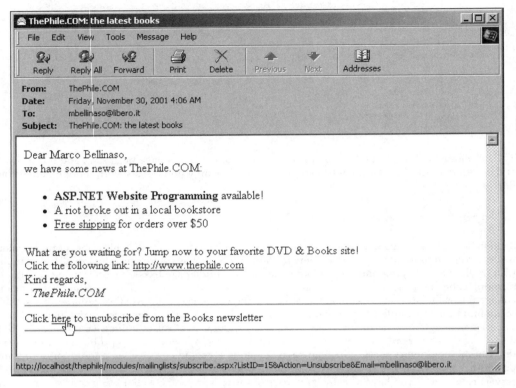

In the status bar of the window above you can see the URL pointed at by the link under the mouse cursor. It redirects to the `Subscribe.aspx` page with some parameters indicating that the user with the specified e-mail address wants to be unsubscribed from the specified mailing list. We'll be looking at this page and the required parameters shortly.

Managing the Newsletters Archive

The newsletters archive page, NewsHistory.aspx, displays all the messages previously sent to any mailing list, in plain text or HTML, according to the format they were sent in. Here is a screenshot of the page:

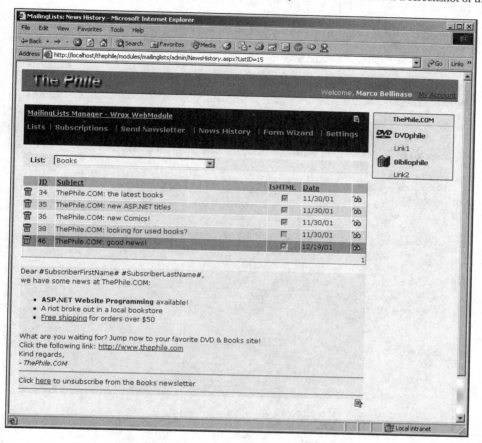

The code for the DataGrid has already been covered earlier in the book, so we'll skip it here. In this case the grid is even simpler because it does not have to handle the editing mode or additions of new rows. The code for displaying the newsletters is almost the same as the code shown in the previous section to display the preview of a message before sending it out.

Modifying the Settings Online

The `Settings.aspx` page makes use of the configuration classes to retrieve and show the current settings, and persist the new settings changed by the user. This is the user interface:

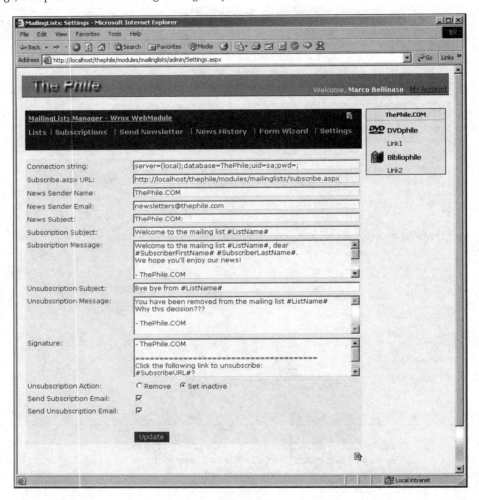

This is probably one of the simplest pages to write. It has a series of textboxes, some of which require a value and can't be left empty, and a few other controls. We've already seen the settings page for other modules. The one for this module is the longest, as this module has quite a lot of options, but it works in exactly the same way. In `Page_Load` we retrieve an instance of `ModuleSettings` through a call to the shared method `Configuration.ModuleConfig.GetSettings`, and fill the textboxes and other controls with the respective `ModuleSettings` properties. When the **Update** button is pressed we create a new instance of `ModuleSettings`, set its properties with the values currently present on the page, and call the shared method `Configuration.ModuleConfig.SaveSettings` to persist the new settings to the XML file.

Creating a Subscription Form for the User

All the pages to manage mailing lists and subscriptions, send e-mail messages, and change the settings are finally complete. So what's left? The subscription form to allow the end user to subscribe from the public part of the site, of course!

Instead of writing the HTML code for each mailing list (a boring task), it would be much better to add a further page that automates this operation. This involves generating the HTML code for the specified mailing list subscription form, as demonstrated in the following screenshot of our `FormWizard.aspx` page:

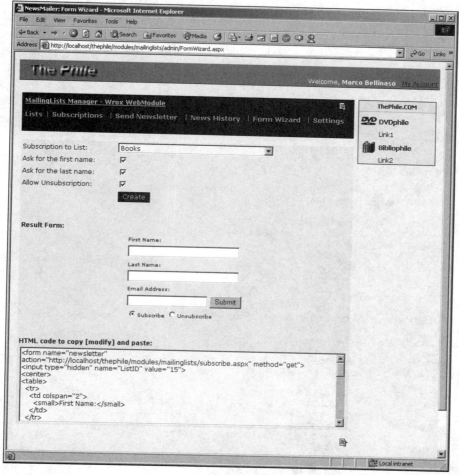

The administrator selects the mailing list for which they want to create the subscription form, specifies if the fields for the first and last name are required (these fields are not mandatory for a subscription, so the form can work without them), and chooses whether the form will have two option buttons to allow the user to subscribe and unsubscribe. When the Create button is pressed the HTML code is generated and appears within the textbox at the bottom, and a preview of the form is shown in the center of the page. At this point the administrator can copy the HTML and paste it into any HTML page.

The first part of the page, which has the dropdown list and the checkboxes, is built as usual, with the controls aligned using a table. The second part of the table shown above (the "Result Form:" part) is invisible by default, and is only displayed when the user presses the **Create** button. As this code consists almost entirely of ASP.NET controls, the likes of which we have seen many times before, we will not show the code here.

The code-behind for this page simply uses the database to fill the dropdown list with the available mailing lists, and gets the URL of the Subscribe.aspx page from the settings file. The rest of the code, the Create_Click event handler, builds the HTML string, the content of which depends on the options selected by the administrators in the top of the page. Here's the code for this event handler:

```
protected void Create_Click(object sender, EventArgs e)
{
  string formHTML="";

  formHTML += string.Format("<input type=\"hidden\" name=\"ListID\"
                       value=\"{0}\">", ListsDropDown.SelectedItem.Value);
  formHTML += "\n<center>\n<table>";
  // add the First Name choice if the AskFirstName CheckBox is checked
  if (AskFirstName.Checked)
  {
    formHTML += "\n<tr>\n<td colspan=\"2\">";
    formHTML += "\n<small>First Name:</small>";
    formHTML += "\n</td>\n</tr>";
    formHTML += "\n<tr>\n<td colspan=\"2\">";
    formHTML += "\n<input type=\"text\" name=\"FirstName\" size=\"30\">";
    formHTML += "\n</td>\n</tr>";
  }
  // add the Last Name choice if the AskLastName CheckBox is checked
  if (AskLastName.Checked)
  {
    formHTML += "\n<tr>\n<td colspan=\"2\">";
    formHTML += "\n<small>Last Name:</small>";
    formHTML += "\n</td>\n</tr>";
    formHTML += "\n<tr>\n<td colspan=\"2\">";
    formHTML += "\n<input type=\"text\" name=\"LastName\" size=\"30\">";
    formHTML += "\n</td>\n  </tr>";
  }
  // add the Email Address field and the Submit button
  formHTML += "\n<tr><td><small>Email Address:</small></td></tr>";
  formHTML += "\n<tr>\n<td><input type=\"text\" name=\"Email\"
          size=\"20\"></td>";
  formHTML += "\n<td><input type=\"submit\" value=\"Submit\"></td>";
  formHTML += "\n</tr>";
  // add the Unsubscribe choice if the respective checkbox is selected
  if (AllowUnsubscription.Checked)
  {
    formHTML += "\n<tr>\n<td colspan=\"2\">";
    formHTML += "\n<small><input type=\"radio\" name=\"Action\"
          value=\"Subscribe\" checked>Subscribe";
    formHTML += "\n<input type=\"radio\" name=\"Action\"
          value=\"Unsubscribe\">Unsubscribe</small>";
    formHTML += "\n</td>\n</tr>";
  }
  formHTML += "\n</table>\n</center>";

  // show the table just created
  ResultForm.Text = formHTML;

  // get the settings
  Configuration.ModuleSettings settings =
                              Configuration.ModuleConfig.GetSettings();

  // add the <form> tag and show the HTML code in the TextBox
```

```
formHTML = string.Format("<form name=\"newsletter\" action=\"{0}\"
                                   method=\"get\">\n{1}\n</form>",
                                   settings.SubscribeUrl, formHTML);

ResultFormHTML.Text = formHTML;

// show the result table and the HTML code
TableResult.Visible=true;
}
```

First of all the code creates the text for a hidden field in which the ID of the selected mailing list is stored. Then it creates the table and textboxes for the first and last name (if required, as indicated by the respective checkboxes) and the e-mail address, and finally the **Submit** button. As a last step, if the **Allow Unsubscription** checkbox is selected, it also adds two radio buttons to let the user specify if they want to subscribe or unsubscribe. The administrator may not want to add the **Unsubscribe** option to the form to prevent someone from unsubscribing someone else just by typing an e-mail address. Sure, they could do this anyway with the special unsubscription URL (the one which is often added at the bottom of each newsletter), but it is more difficult and less likely to be done by accident.

The HTML code just created is displayed in the `ResultForm` label to give a preview of the result. The pasted code is not a real form though, and if we press the **Submit** button nothing happens, because we didn't add the `<form>` tag. This tag wraps the previously created `FormHTML` string, specifying the `Subscribe.aspx` page as the target for the post operation, and then the closing tag is appended at the end of the string. The final string is set as the text of the textbox control, to let the user easily copy it.

In the following screenshot you can see a few examples of forms produced by this page:

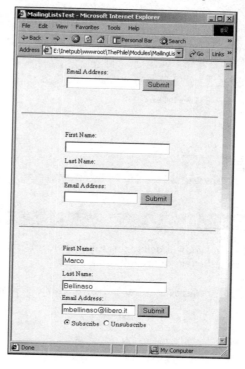

The first form in the above screenshot was produced by leaving all three options unchecked. The second was produced by selecting the first two options (ask for the first and last name), while the third was produced by checking all three options.

Since the code produced is simple HTML, you can customize the result as you wish: for example you may want to change the colors, the font, the width of the textboxes, add an image as a border or background, or a comment informing the client about the name of the mailing list they are subscribing to. A very useful change would be to add a JavaScript function to ensure that the e-mail address field is not empty before actually submitting the form.

Subscribing to a Mailing List

So far we've seen the entire application from the administrator's point of view, but what about the end user? We're now going to show how a visitor can come to our website and subscribe to a mailing list. The page with the subscription form can be located anywhere, even on a different server, because it points to the full URL of Subscribe.aspx stored in the settings.

It's now time to test one of the subscription forms shown in the last screenshot to subscribe a new user (we used the third form and chose the Books mailing list). If the Send Subscription Email setting option is selected in the administrator's page, which it is by default if you use the provided settings file, the subscriber receives the confirmation e-mail message customized with their information:

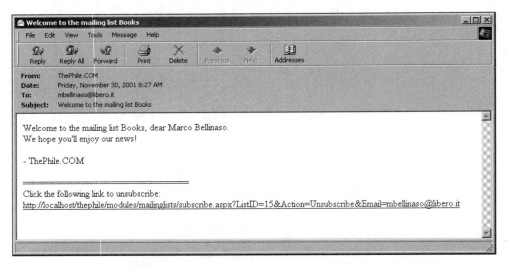

The last line is a link that, if clicked, will delete this subscriber from the mailing list. This link is dynamically built by replacing the tags of the following string:

```
#SubscribeURL#?ListID=#ListID#&Action=Unsubscribe&Email=#SubscriberEmail#
```

As you can guess from reading the string, what differentiates between a subscription and unsubscription is the `Action` parameter, which in this case is set to `Unsubscribe`. The link for the subscription is the same string but without the `Action` parameter, or with that parameter set to anything other than `Unsubscribe`. The other parameters of the link are the ID of the mailing list (stored in the hidden field in the form) and the e-mail address of the subscriber.

The confirmation e-mail is sent only if the respective setting is enabled. However, you always get a confirmation web page, containing the same text as the mail. The same applies to the unsubscription process. To also test this operation, click the link of the previous e-mail message – a browser instance will open and a message will be displayed, as follows:

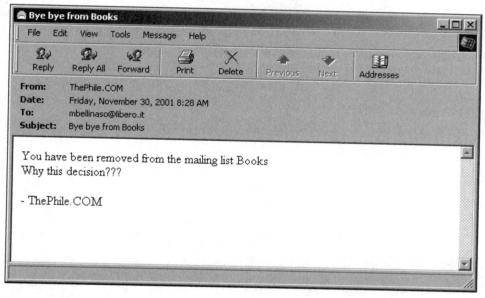

You would get exactly the same result by selecting the `Unsubscribe` option in the HTML form. Obviously, you can check if the subscriber is actually added or removed by viewing the `Subscriptions.aspx` page in the administration console.

The Subscribe.aspx Page

This page has the shortest code we have seen so far in this chapter. Except for the site header/footer and menu box, the controls we're interested in are the following:

```
<asp:Label ID="Subject" runat="Server" CssClass="SubscrSubject"
          Visible="false" />
<br>
<asp:Label ID="Message" runat="Server" CssClass="SubscrMessage"
          Visible="false" />
<asp:Label runat="server" ID="EmailRequired" Visible="false"
          Text="The Email address is required" CssClass="Error" />
```

There are three labels: one for the confirmation subject, one for the message body, and one for an error message in case the e-mail address is not specified. All these labels are invisible by default. They will be shown after the user subscribes or unsubscribes, according to the result of the operation.

The Code-behind for Subscribe.aspx

All the code of this code-behind class is located in the `Page_Load` procedure, because everything is done when the page is loaded – there aren't any forms or controls that raise other events. The complete code of this event handler is as shown:

```csharp
protected void Page_Load(object sender, EventArgs e)
{
    // get the ListID, FirstName, LastName, Email and the action to perform
    // from the QueryString generated by the HTML form
    int listID = int.Parse(Request.Params["ListID"]);
    string firstName = Request.Params["FirstName"] + "";
    string lastName = Request.Params["LastName"] + "";
    string email = Request.Params["Email"] + "";
    string action = Request.Params["Action"] + "";

    if (email.Trim()=="")
    {
        // if the Email was not specified, show the error message
        // and do not proceed
        EmailRequired.Visible = true;
    }
    else
    {
        string subjectText;
        string messageText;

        // remove/inactivate or add/activate a subscription,
        // according to the Action param
        Business.List list = new Business.List(listID);
        if (action == "Unsubscribe")
            list.Unsubscribe(email, out subjectText, out messageText);
        else  // subscribe or activate the user
            list.Subscribe(firstName, lastName, email, out subjectText,
                                                       out messageText);

        // show the message that confirms the action
        Subject.Text = subjectText;
        Message.Text = messageText.Replace("\n", "<br>");
        Subject.Visible = true;
        Message.Visible = true;
    }
}
```

In the first lines the target list's ID and the subscriber's name and address are extracted from the query string and saved in local variables to make it easier to use them later in the procedure. Before going ahead with any other operation, the code checks if the e-mail parameter is empty. If it is then the `EmailRequired` error label is shown and the rest of the procedure is not executed. If the execution does proceed, we call the `Subscribe` or `Unsubscribe` method of the instance of `Business.List` for the target mailing list, according to the `Action` parameter. As we've seen earlier, these methods will take care of all the details and will operate according to the settings stored in the XML file. They will also return the confirmation message, so that we can show it on the page as an instant confirmation.

Securing the Module

In the *Design* section we decided that two permissions are adequate to provide security for the module: one for general administration, and the other for sending out a newsletter. We define these permissions in a new enumeration in the `Enum.cs` file of the `Core` module, as follows:

```
namespace Wrox.WebModules.MailingLists
{
  public enum MailingListsPermissions
  {
    AdministerData = 400,
    SendNewsletter = 401
  };
}
```

Then we limit access to the administration pages by adding the following code at the beginning of the `Page_Load` event handler (remember that you must add a reference to the business component of the `Accounts` module for it to work):

```
protected void Page_Load(object sender, EventArgs e)
{
  // check if the current user is allowed to administer lists/subscriptions
  if (!Context.User.Identity.IsAuthenticated ||
                          !((SitePrincipal)Context.User).HasPermission(
                          (int)MailingListsPermissions.AdministerData))
  {
    // if not, redirect to the Login page
    Response.Redirect(
                  "/ThePhile/Modules/Users/Login.aspx?ShowError=true", true);
  }
  ...
}
```

As we've already seen in some of the previous chapters, in the code above we first check if the user is authenticated: if not, the second half of the `if` block is not processed (thanks to short-circuiting) and we redirect to the login page (with the `ShowError` parameter set to `true`, to cause the login page to show an error message telling the user that they do not have the necessary permissions to load the page). Otherwise we check if the current user has the `AdministerData` permission, by casting `Context.User` to `SitePrincipal` (which implements the `IPrincipal` interface) and calling its `HasPermission` method. If the specified permission is not found in the user's profile, the user is redirected to the login page, as if they were not authenticated. Otherwise the execution of the page continues, and the data is retrieved from the database and shown in the grid and the other controls.

The code for protecting `SendNewsletter.aspx` is almost the same; the permission just needs to be changed from `AdministerData` to `SendNewsletter`. We don't need to add anything to the `Subscribe.aspx` page, as it must be freely accessible by the visitor when they post a subscription.

Summary

The aim of this chapter was to show how to design and build a full-featured mailing list manager that could be used as-is for many websites. We've implemented an administration console that allows us to:

❑ Add, edit, and delete mailing lists and their associated subscriptions.

❑ Create and send newsletters (both in plain text and HTML format) and consult the archive of previously sent messages.

❑ Modify the settings online.

❑ Auto-generate the HTML code for the subscription box.

Administration aside, we've developed the page that actually handles the subscription process. This used the business components developed at the beginning of the implementation section. Finally, we've used the Accounts business classes to ensure that only users with the appropriate permissions can administer the data and send out newsletters.

By doing all this we've learnt some new techniques in this chapter, most notably:

❑ How to use the SmtpMail and MailMessage classes to send e-mails with the Windows SMTP Server.

❑ The use of regular expressions to validate e-mail addresses (or, in general, any other string) against a given pattern.

As for any other module presented in this book, you can add further features to make it even more powerful. Here are just a few ideas:

❑ Add the ability to create and handle subscription forms that allow the user to subscribe to *multiple* mailing lists in one step, giving their e-mail address only once. This would simply require a few changes to the HTML form that you paste in your pages, and to the Subscribe.aspx page that processes the data posted to the server. Adding a subscription to more than one list is really just a matter of a few lines of code, thanks to the business layer classes that handle the actual subscription process.

❑ Allow each user to choose whether to receive the newsletters in HTML or plain text format, and send different newsletters according to that choice.

❑ Add the ability to send attachments with the newsletters. This can be very useful if you want to send HTML newsletters with images. Currently, you can send mails with images by referencing the full URL of the image on your server, but it would be better to send them along with the message.

❑ Add a search engine to the administration console, which allows a specified e-mail address or contact name to be easily found. This would be useful if the administrator wants to see or change the properties of a particular subscriber.

❑ Add a double check on the subscription/unsubscription process. This consists of sending a notification e-mail to the subscriber, asking them to confirm that they want to subscribe/unsubscribe fto/from the mailing list. The action will only be taken if they click a link to confirm. This feature is really useful if you want to be sure that someone does not subscribe someone else by posting a false e-mail address. You can't be 100% sure that this won't happen anyway, since (as always) someone could hack the link format and make false confirmations, but it's better than doing no checks at all!

❑ Add the option to have multiple administrators, with different rights. For example, a basic administrator could only see the current mailing lists and subscribers, a second level of administrator could also send out new newsletters, and an advanced administrator would have full rights, with permission to add, remove, and modify the mailing lists and subscribers.

In the last few chapters we've developed modules to strengthen the site-to-user communication, such as the polls module and this mailing lists manager. In the next chapter we're going to implement a module to manage forums, the most important form of user-to-user communication system.

10

Forums and Online Communities

A successful site should build a community of loyal visitors. Internet users like to feel part of a community of people with the same interests, to discuss their favorite subjects, and to ask questions and reply to those of others. Community members will return often to meet other people that they've already chatted with, or to find comments and opinions about their interests. In this chapter we'll outline some of the advantages of building such a virtual community. We'll then identify the goals for our website community, and step through the design and implementation of a new module for setting up and managing discussion boards (forums).

The Problem

User-to-user communication is important in many types of website. For example, in a content-based site relating to programming resources, programmers need to ask questions about problems they are facing and hear suggestions from their peers. e-Commerce sites benefit from allowing users to review products online.

Two ways to provide user-to-user communication are opinion polls and discussion boards. We looked at opinion polls in Chapter 8. In this chapter we will talk about discussion boards, or **forums**.

Forums act as a source of content, and provide an opportunity for visitors to participate and contribute. Visitors can browse the various messages in the forums, post their questions and topics, reply to other people's questions, and share ideas and tips.

For our ThePhile.com site, we can offer discussion boards about books and DVDs. We will also want sub groups within that, so that it is easier for visitors to read about what they are specifically interested in. For example, if we have a books category we can have sub forums for programming books, classic literature, novels, and publishing.

Early web-forum systems often threw up long lists of messages on a single page, which took ages to load. We want to avoid this by displaying lists in pages, with each page containing a set number of messages.

Our website already has a way to identify users (the `Accounts` module we developed in Chapter 5), and our forums should support that. But we should also give users the opportunity to create a **profile**, so that they can post messages without revealing their true identity. These profiles should include a public name, an avatar image (a small picture that represents the user), a signature, and a homepage URL.

The administrator must be able to add, remove, or edit categories, forums, topics, and replies, and change the module's settings. If you're wondering what the difference is between a category and a forum, let's say that a category is a container for multiple forums. For example, we can have two categories: Books and DVD. The Books category can contain the following forums: programming books, books for children, school course books, spy stories, etc. The DVD category, on the other hand, will have child forums such as PC games, action movies, horror movies, cartoons, etc. In practice, a category allows better organization and keeps together forums with related subjects.

Cross-Site Scripting

One problem with forums is when users enter HTML or JavaScript code that somehow impairs the site. This could range from making the page look irritating (remember `<blink>`?), including large or offensive images, or automatically redirecting the browser to other sites. However, giving readers access to some simple tags can make the site far more user friendly.

The problems we're trying to solve here are relatively simple. Our site will be nothing like the massive forum systems such as Slashdot or Plastic. In the site's design, we will try to get the best of both worlds – give users the flexibility to present their messages well, without allowing them to damage the site.

The Design

As usual, we will design our data layer first and work up to the presentation layer. The configuration system is quite important in this module, so we will look at the design for that before considering the business layer.

The Database

The design begins with the database tables needed to store all the categories, forums, topics, replies, and members. The prefix for the tables and stored procedure for this module is Forums_. We have five new tables (we also use Accounts_Users, created in Chapter 5), shown in the following diagram:

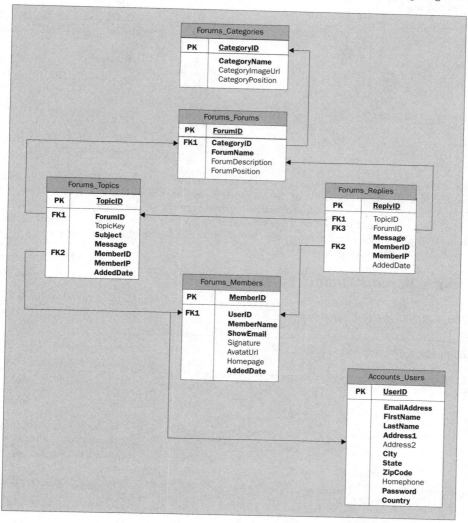

In the next sections we'll be explaining each table in detail, but remember that – as usual – you can download the complete database backup with the required tables, stored procedures, views, etc. from the Wrox site.

The Forums_Categories Table

The Forums_Categories table is used to store the name and image for the forum categories. It is structured as follows:

Column Name	Type	Size	Allow Null	Description
CategoryID	int – Identity primary key	4	No	The unique ID for the category.
CategoryName	varchar	100	No	The name of the category.
CategoryImage Url	varchar	100	Yes	The optional URL of the category's descriptive image.
CategoryPosition	int	4	Yes	The ordinal position of the category. Later we'll return the categories ordered by this field, in ascending order.

At first, the CategoryPosition column might seem useless, but it's actually very handy. It allows the administrator to decide the position of the categories when they are all shown in a web page. For example, you may want to show a particular category at the top of the page, because it reflects the subject of the site's main business. We can't just use the ID column to order the categories, because it is an Identity column that's auto-incremented. It reflects the order in which the categories were created and not necessarily their importance.

The Forums_Forums Table

The Forums_Forums table stores information on specific forums, and their relationship with the parent categories. It is structured as follows:

Column Name	Type	Size	Allow Null	Description
ForumID	int – Identity primary key	4	No	The unique ID for the forum.
CategoryID	int foreign key	4	No	The ID of the parent category, matching a record in the Forums_Categories table.
ForumName	varchar	100	No	The name of the forum.
ForumDescription	varchar	250	Yes	An optional description of the forum.
ForumPosition	int	4	Yes	The ordinal position of the forum, used to control display order.

The Forums_Topics Table

The `Forums_Topics` table stores all the topics for all the forums. When a new topic is introduced, the message is stored in this table. Then responses are posted as replies to this message – our chat room does not allow true threading at this stage. `Forums_Topics` has the following columns:

Column Name	Type	Size	Allow Null	Description
TopicID	int – Identity primary key	4	No	The unique ID for the topic.
ForumID	int foreign key	4	No	The ID of the parent forum, matching a record in the `Forums_Forums` table.
TopicKey	varchar	15	Yes	An optional key for the topic.
Subject	varchar	100	No	The subject/title of the topic.
Message	text	0	No	The text of the topic.
MemberID	int foreign key	4	No	The ID of the member who authored this message. It matches a record in the `Forums_Members` table (presented shortly).
MemberIP	varchar	15	No	The IP address of the member who authored this message.
AddedDate	datetime	8	No	When the message was added to the database.

Two columns, `TopicKey` and `MemberIP`, are worth some more explanation. `TopicKey` enables us to associate a particular topic to other resources, such as a news article. It can contain the ID (but in string format) of a news article, or some identifier (of string type) of another resource, such as the ISBN for a book, for example. Later we'll see in practice how to employ this column to integrate the module with other parts of the site.

The `MemberIP` column stores the IP address of the member who submitted the topic. We already have the `MemberID` column to identify members, and can ban them if they post offensive messages. If a user posts something illegal, we might need to resort to legal means to identify them. Although difficult, it is sometimes possible to use IP to trace a specific user. In any case, it will act as a deterrent for serious misuse.

The Forums_Replies Table

Forums_Replies is similar to Forums_Topics, but stores messages sent in reply to the topics:

Column Name	Type	Size	Allow Null	Description
ReplyID	int – Identity primary key	4	No	The unique ID for the reply.
TopicID	int foreign key	4	No	The ID of the parent topic, matching a record in the Forums_Topics table.
ForumID	int foreign key	4	No	The ID of the parent forum. It matches a record in the Forums_Forums table.
Message	text		No	The text of the message.
MemberID	int foreign key	4	No	The ID of the member who authored this message. It matches a record in the Forums_Members table, presented below.
MemberIP	varchar	15	No	The IP address of the member who authored this message.
AddedDate	datetime	8	No	When the message was added to the database.

As you can see, this table has almost the same columns as Forums_Topics, except for TopicKey and Subject, which are not present here. We could just use one table for the topics and the replies, but using two separate tables makes retrieving a list of topics for a forum faster. We also want to calculate further columns for topics and replies, and this is much easier if they are stored in separate tables.

ForumID may seem unnecessary, since we could retrieve the parent forum's ID from the Forums_Topics table joined through the TopicID value. However, repeating the ForumID here helps us count the number of replies for the specified forum, which we will want to do later when displaying the page with the available forums.

It's also worth noting that this structure does not support **threaded discussions**, such as the newsgroup discussions that you can browse through your mail client. Threaded discussions allow a reply to any post, as a new topic or as a reply to an existing topic, and are represented through a tree structure. The structure for non-threaded discussions only allows replies directly to the main topic – there is no field in the database to keep a reference to another reply. The replies will be shown to the reader sorted by creation date, from the oldest to the newest. Both these two types of forum systems, threaded or not, have their pro and cons. Threaded discussions make it easier to follow replies to previous posts, but non-threaded discussions make it easier to follow the discussion with the correct temporal order. Furthermore, non-threaded discussions usually allow a previous reply to be quoted, making it quite easy for the reader to follow the discussion even if the referenced message is a number of posts above the new reply. I don't know if it is because non-threaded forums are a little easier to develop, but our investigations of the discussion boards used in quite a lot of popular sites show that non-threaded discussions seem to be used most often, so we've decided to go that way too.

The Forums-Member Table

The `Forums_Members` table stores the profiles of the registered forums' members:

Column Name	Type	Size	Allow Null	Description
MemberID	int - Identity primary key	4	No	The unique ID for the member.
UserID	int foreign key	4	No	The ID of the respective site's account that matches a record in the `Accounts_Users` table.
MemberName	varchar	15	No	The member's name.
ShowEmail	bit	1	No	If `true`, the e-mail address will be visible in the posts of this member.
Signature	varchar	300	Yes	The signature text, added at the bottom of every message from this member.
AvatarUrl	varchar	100	Yes	The URL of an image that will be shown together with the member name in all the member's posts
Homepage	varchar	100	Yes	The URL of the member's homepage, if any.
AddedDate	datetime	8	No	The date when the user registered a profile for the forums.

This table is joined to the `Accounts_Users` table of the `Accounts` module, developed in Chapter 5, on the `UserID` column. This table contains information specific to forums, while other information such as the user's first and last name, e-mail address, etc., are already present in the `Accounts_Users` table. This also means that the user must create an account for the site first, and then register for the forums. This is good because this way the user is not required to insert the same information twice, but neither do we need to have a unique but larger table if the user does not want to use the forums. Of course, you can change the site's registration page to require all the information in a single place, and store the value for both tables.

Database Views

We need to return more information than that stored in the tables above, including the number of topics and posts (topics plus replies) to the forums, and the date of the most recent post to a forum or topic. We will provide this through views with dynamically calculated columns, so that it's easier to access the data from the stored procedures without repeating the required SQL code in all of them. We'll build some **views** for retrieving the data in `Accounts_Users` and `Forums_Members` in a single `SELECT` statement, so that we don't need to write the `JOIN`s in the stored procedures, and it's easier to modify them if we need to do so. We'll see all the details about the added columns and the required `JOIN`s in the *Solution* section.

Stored Procedures

As usual, we'll use stored procedures to keep our application efficient and simplify the data layer. The complete list of the stored procedures that we'll build later is presented below.

Managing the Categories

We will build the following stored procedures for managing categories:

Stored Procedure	Description
sp_Forums_GetCategories	Returns all the available categories.
sp_Forums_GetCategoryDetails	Returns the complete row identified by the specified ID.
sp_Forums_InsertCategory	Inserts a new category. If a category already exists with the same name, the new category is not added and the output parameter is set to −1. Otherwise @CategoryID will be set to the new category's ID.
sp_Forums_UpdateCategory	Updates all the fields of the category identified by the specified ID.
sp_Forums_DeleteCategory	Deletes the specified category.

Managing the Forums

These procedures are the same as above, but this time for the Forums_Forums table:

Stored Procedure	Description
sp_Forums_GetForums	Returns all the forums underneath the specified category.
sp_Forums_GetForumDetails	Returns the complete row identified by the specified ID.
sp_Forums_InsertForum	Inserts a forum and returns its ID. If a forum with the same name already exists, returns −1.
sp_Forums_UpdateForum	Updates the specified forum record.
sp_Forums_DeleteForum	Deletes a forum.

Managing the Topics

The procedures for the Forums_Topics table are slightly more complex:

Stored Procedure	Description
sp_Forums_GetTopics	Returns all the topics of the specified forum.
sp_Forums_GetTopicsByPage	Returns the topics for the specified virtual page of the specified forum. The last parameter is the number of topics that make up a page.

Stored Procedure	Description
sp_Forums_GetTopicDetails	Returns the complete row identified by the specified ID.
sp_Forums_GetTopicID	Returns the ID of the topic identified by the specified key.
sp_Forums_InsertTopic	Inserts a new topic and returns its ID. Nothing is done to check if a topic with the same subject is already present, as this is perfectly possible in a forum.
sp_Forums_UpdateTopic	Updates a topic record. Note that not all fields can be updated, in fact we don't want to allow anybody to change the ID or the IP address of the user who posted the topic.
sp_Forums_DeleteTopic	Deletes the specified topic.

The most notable procedure here is sp_Forums_GetTopicsByPage, that instead of returning *all* the topics returns only the topics for a virtual page. We've already seen that it's important to display long discussions in pages. If we paginate the records through the auto pagination feature of the DataGrid or DataList controls, all the records are retrieved, and then only the records for the current page are shown. This works fine if we have a few records but it becomes inefficient when we have thousands of topics to retrieve. The sp_Forums_GetTopicsByPage procedure only returns the records of a specified page with a specified size, wasting no time retrieving records that we won't show.

sp_Forums_UpdateTopic doesn't update the member's ID and IP, because it is only the administrator who will update a topic – we want to preserve the information about the original sender. If an administrator wants to change the IP or member ID, they must use a SQL query through the online database manager presented in Chapter 4.

Managing the Replies

These procedures are very similar to the procedures above, but work against the Forums_Replies table:

Stored Procedure	Description
sp_Forums_GetReplies	Returns all the replies to the specified topic.
sp_Forums_GetRepliesByPage	Returns the replies for the specified virtual page of the specified topic.
sp_Forums_GetReplyDetails	Returns the complete row identified by the specified ID.
sp_Forums_InsertReply	Inserts a new topic and returns its ID.
sp_Forums_UpdateReply	Updates the message text of the specified reply.
sp_Forums_DeleteReply	Deletes the specified reply.

Managing the Members

These procedures work against the `Forums_Members` and `Accounts_Users` tables to manage those members who are current site users with a special profile for the discussion board:

Stored Procedure	Description
sp_Forums_GetMembers	Returns all the members.
sp_Forums_GetMemberDetails	Returns the complete row identified by the specified ID.
sp_Forums_GetMemberID	Returns the ID of the member registered against the specified user account.
sp_Forums_InsertMember	Inserts a new member. If a member already exists with the same name, the new member is not added and the output parameter is set to -1. Otherwise @MemberID will be set to the new member's ID.
sp_Forums_UpdateMember	Updates the member.
sp_Forums_DeleteMember	Deletes a member.

Designing the Data Services

As usual, the data layer will consist of classes whose members map one-by-one onto the stored procedures listed above. The parameters are the same as those of the respective stored procedure. Since the meaning of the methods is also the same as the stored procedure, we won't repeat the complete list of members here.

Configuration

As in the previous module, the `Forums` module will have a configuration component that exposes two classes to load, access, and save the settings. The classes are `ModuleConfig` and `ModuleSettings`, as before.

The table below lists all of the available settings, with their meanings:

Setting Name	Type	Description
ConnectionString	string	Database connection string.
TopicsPerPage	int	The maximum number of topics per page.
RepliesPerPage	int	The maximum number of replies per page.
HtmlEnabled	bool	If true, users can use HTML tags. Usually false.

Setting Name	Type	Description
SpecialTagsEnabled	bool	If true, the users can use special tags such as [:)], [B], and [/B] to format their messages and add 'smilies'.
SmiliesFolder	string	The virtual path of the folder where the 'smilies' images are stored. These images are shown if SpecialTagsEnabled is true, and replace some special tags such as [:)].

The Business Layer

The business layer of this module is not complex, but it is fairly big: six classes, with quite a lot of members, to manipulate the data in a good object-oriented way. All the classes except for Helper, which has a single static method, expose a set of public properties that describe a specified record and then have methods such as Create, LoadFromID, ResetProperties, and Delete. It's easy to guess that the meaning of these methods is always the same, so it's not worth showing the declaration for each class here. Instead, we'll look at the complete declarations for just a representative class, Forum, and the Helper class.

The Forum Class

A Forum object represents a single forum. Here are the members of the Forum class:

Method Name	Description
public int ID	Read-only property that returns the ID of the forum represented by the object.
public int CategoryID	Returns the ID of the parent category.
public Business.Category Category	Returns a Category object that represents the forum's parent category.
public string Name	Gets/sets the forum's name.
public string Description	Gets/sets the forum's description.
public int Position	Gets/sets the forum's position.
public int Topics	Returns the total number of topics for this forum. This information is dynamically calculated by a view, as we mentioned earlier.
public int Posts	Returns the total number of posts (topics plus replies) for this forum. This information is dynamically calculated by a view, too.

Method Name	Description
`public DateTime LastPostDate`	Returns the date when the last post for this forum was added. As with the two properties above, this is a dynamically calculated value.
`public Forum()`	Class constructor with no parameters. It only resets the properties.
`public Forum(int existingForumID)`	Class constructor that sets the properties to describe the forum identified by the input ID.
`public Forum(Forum existingForum)`	Class constructor that sets the properties to describe the forum identified by an existing `Forum` object.
`private void LoadFromID()`	Loads the properties of the list identified by a private ID variable. This method is called by the constructors, or when the data has to be refreshed.
`private void ResetProperties()`	Resets the properties.
`public int LoadFromID(int existingForumID)`	Loads all the properties of the forum identified by the input ID. This method is useful when we create the object with the parameter-less constructor, or we want to change the currently loaded forum.
`public int Create(int forumCategoryID, string forumName, string forumDescription, int forumPosition)`	Creates a new forum, and sets the properties of the object to represent the new record.
`public bool Update()`	Updates the forum with the new values of the public properties.
`public bool Delete()`	Deletes the forum.
`public DataSet GetTopics()`	Returns all the child topics.
`public DataSet GetTopics(int pageNumber)`	Returns the child topics for the specified page. This method is employed for the custom pagination. The number of topics per page is retrieved internally through the configuration component.
`public Topic AddTopic(string topicKey, string subject, string message, int memberID)`	Adds a child topic and returns a `Topic` object that represent the new record.

This class allows us to create, edit, and delete any forum, and to access its properties. It also provides direct access to all the properties and operations of the parent category, by exposing the `ParentCategory` property of type `Category`. Lastly, it has methods to directly retrieve the child topic or add a new topic. It's not like the data access classes, where each class has methods to retrieve, add, edit, and delete only the records of the respective database table, and has no relationships with the other classes. The business classes really provide an object-oriented way to access records, by returning and linking to instances of other business classes.

The Helper Class

This class has a single static method, `ProcessSpecialTags`, which processes a given text string and replaces the special tags with the respective HTML tags. It's time to decide which tags we want to support, so here's the complete list:

❑   `[B]sometext[/B]` is replaced with `<b>sometext</b>`.

❑   `[I]sometext[/I]` is replaced with `<i>sometext</i>`.

❑   `[U]sometext[/U]` is replaced with `<u>sometext</u>`.

❑   `[:)]`, `[:D]`, `[8)]`, `[:(]`, `[:o]`, `[:x]` are all replaced with 'smilies' images, whose folder's path is stored in the settings file and is exposed by `ModuleSettings.SmiliesFolder` of the `Configuration` library.

❑   `[URL]http://www.thephile.com[/URL]` is replaced with `<a href="http://www.thephile.com" target="_blank">http://www.thephile.com</a>`.

❑   `[EMAIL]marco@thephile.com[/EMAIL]` is replaced with `<a href="mailto:marco@thephile.com ">marco@thephile.com</a>`.

❑   `[QUOTE]sometext[/QUOTE]` is replaced with `<blockquote>sometext</blockquote>`, and is used to indent the `sometext` part. This tag is still supported when `ProcessSpecialTags` is `false`, because quoting a message must always work – the other tags will still appear on screen.

Designing the User Interface Layer

All of the modules from previous chapters have two separate user interfaces: one for administrators, and one for normal users.

With the `Forums` module, we want administrators to see similar things to normal users. Instead of building a separate administration system, we will simply give users with special privileges access to features hidden from other users. Here are the relevant permissions, and the special facilities they will get:

❑   `AdministerCategories`: the user is allowed to add, edit, or delete categories and forums

❑   `ModerateForums`: the user is allowed to add, edit, and delete topics and replies

❑   `EditSettings`: the user is allowed to edit the module's settings

That said, the following diagram describes all the various execution paths that an end-user can follow in the forums application. This is useful to determine what pages to build:

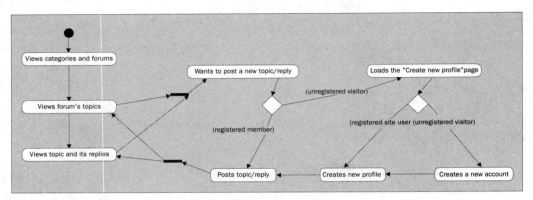

As you can see, first the user views the available categories and forums in one page, then in another page views the topics for the selected forum. One level below, again, and they read the complete topic and its replies. From the list of topics or from the complete topic the users may want to post their own message to the current forum, or to post a reply to the current topic. When they try to load the page to post the message, if they already have a profile for the Forums module the page loads correctly and they can post the message. Otherwise they are redirected to the page to register a new profile. But we already know that to create a new profile, a site account must be already present. This check is done when the registration page loads, and if the user is not logged in or the account is not present at all, the user is redirected immediately to the Login page developed in Chapter 5, where there is also a link to create the new account. Otherwise the profile is created, and the message sent.

This shows that we need to develop the following new pages:

❑   Default.aspx: lists categories and respective forums

❑   Forum.aspx: lists all topics in a selected forum

❑   Topic.aspx: displays a topic and its replies (in pages)

❑   PostMessage.aspx: posts a new topic or a reply to an existing topic

❑   MyProfile.aspx : creates or edits the user's profile

❑   Settings.aspx: enables the administrator to edit the module's settings online, without the need to manually edit and upload the settings file.

The Solution

We've already developed several modules throughout the book, and we know the path to follow. We start by creating the database tables and the stored procedures, then we continue with the data and business classes, and finish with the ASP.NET pages for the presentation layer. In practice, we'll follow exactly the order of the design section. Much of the code required here is very similar to that of previous chapters, which was shown in great detail. So we'll skip the discussion of the common code, and try to focus on the new stuff.

Creating the Database Tables

We create the tables and relationships, and set all relationships to enforce cascade updates and deletes – except for the relationship between `Forums_Replies` and `Forums_Members`. This is because we already have a relationship between `Forums_Topics` and `Forums_Members`, and one between `Forums_Replies` and `Forums_Topics`.

When a member is deleted, all topics by that member are deleted, and all the replies of that topic are deleted as well. SQL Server can't handle a cascade delete of the same row when rows from two different tables are deleted, which would happen if we enforced a cascade update between `Forums_Replies` and `Forums_Members`. And exactly the same applies for the cascade update. So, when a member is deleted its topics are deleted, the replies of those topics are deleted, and we must ensure that the replies authored by that member for other topics are deleted as well. This can be done using a `DELETE` trigger, created on the `Forums_Members` table as follows:

```
CREATE TRIGGER DeleteForumsReplies ON [dbo].[Forums_Members]
  FOR DELETE
  AS

    DELETE Forums_Replies
      WHERE MemberID = (SELECT MemberID FROM Deleted)
```

Deleting all records of a user is an extreme measure. In most cases we would prevent a user from accessing the site by revoking all their permissions, but would leave their database entries intact.

Creating the Views

We now need to create views to add dynamically calculated columns, and create standard joins between tables.

The v_Forums_Forums View

This view joins the `Forums_Categories` and `Forums_Forums` table to return rows with information on the forums and their parent category as well. It also adds these calculated columns:

- ❑ `ForumTopics`: the total number of topics for the forum
- ❑ `ForumPosts`: the total number of posts (topics + replies) for the forum
- ❑ `LastPostDate`: the date when the last post for the forum was added

Here's the code used for this view:

```
SELECT Forums_Categories.CategoryID, Forums_Categories.CategoryName,
       Forums_Categories.CategoryImageUrl,
       Forums_Categories.CategoryPosition, Forums_Forums.ForumID,
       Forums_Forums.ForumName, Forums_Forums.ForumDescription,
       Forums_Forums.ForumPosition,
  (SELECT COUNT(*)
    FROM Forums_Topics
    WHERE Forums_Topics.ForumID = Forums_Forums.ForumID) AS ForumTopics,
```

```
(SELECT COUNT(*)
   FROM Forums_Topics
   WHERE Forums_Topics.ForumID = Forums_Forums.ForumID) +
      (SELECT COUNT(*)
         FROM Forums_Replies
         WHERE Forums_Replies.ForumID = Forums_Forums.ForumID) AS ForumPosts,
(SELECT MAX(AddedDate)
   FROM (SELECT ForumID, AddedDate FROM Forums_Topics
      UNION ALL
      SELECT ForumID, AddedDate FROM Forums_Replies) AS dates
   WHERE dates.ForumID = Forums_Forums.ForumID) AS ForumLastPostDate
FROM Forums_Categories INNER JOIN Forums_Forums
ON Forums_Categories.CategoryID = Forums_Forums.CategoryID
```

Except for the join between the two tables, it's pretty simple. The interesting thing is the code that calculates the other dynamic column. Let's see the code piece by piece. Here's the SQL that counts the topics for the forum:

```
(SELECT COUNT(*)
   FROM Forums_Topics
   WHERE Forums_Topics.ForumID = Forums_Forums.ForumID) AS ForumTopics
```

To count the number of posts, we copy the code above and add similar code to count the replies, then sum the two values:

```
(SELECT COUNT(*)
   FROM Forums_Topics
   WHERE Forums_Topics.ForumID = Forums_Forums.ForumID) +
      (SELECT COUNT(*)
         FROM Forums_Replies
         WHERE Forums_Replies.ForumID = Forums_Forums.ForumID) AS ForumPosts
```

The last column, LastPostDate, is the most complex to calculate:

```
(SELECT MAX(AddedDate)
   FROM (SELECT ForumID, AddedDate FROM Forums_Topics
      UNION ALL
      SELECT ForumID, AddedDate FROM Forums_Replies) AS dates
   WHERE dates.ForumID = Forums_Forums.ForumID) AS ForumLastPostDate
```

Here we extract the ForumID and AddedDate values from the Forums_Topics and Forums_Replies tables. All these values are placed in a temporary table by the UNION operator. The view then gets the date of the final post by calculating the latest date among the values in the temporary table, using the MAX function.

The v_Forums_Members View

This view joins the `Accounts_Users` and `Forums_Members` table, to view all user information together. Here's the code:

```
SELECT Forums_Members.MemberID, Forums_Members.UserID,
       Forums_Members.MemberName, Forums_Members.ShowEmail,
       Forums_Members.Signature, Forums_Members.AvatarUrl,
       Forums_Members.Homepage, Forums_Members.AddedDate,
       Accounts_Users.EmailAddress AS Email
  FROM Forums_Members INNER JOIN Accounts_Users
  ON Forums_Members.UserID = Accounts_Users.UserID
```

The v_Forums_Topics View

This joins the members and forums tables, and calculates the date of the last post for a topic. This way, in a single virtual table we can see all the information on topics, their authors, and their parent forums and categories. All this data will be retrieved by stored procedures and returned to the ASP.NET pages. Here's the complete code of the view:

```
SELECT v_Forums_Forums.CategoryID, v_Forums_Forums.CategoryName,
       v_Forums_Forums.CategoryPosition, v_Forums_Forums.ForumID,
       v_Forums_Forums.ForumName, v_Forums_Forums.ForumDescription,
       v_Forums_Forums.ForumPosition, v_Forums_Forums.ForumTopics,
       v_Forums_Forums.ForumPosts, Forums_Topics.TopicID,
       Forums_Topics.TopicKey, Forums_Topics.Subject,
       Forums_Topics.Message, Forums_Topics.AddedDate,
 (SELECT COUNT(*)
   FROM Forums_Replies
   WHERE Forums_Replies.TopicID = Forums_Topics.TopicID) AS TopicReplies,
 (SELECT MAX(AddedDate)
   FROM Forums_Replies
   WHERE Forums_Replies.TopicID = Forums_Topics.TopicID) AS
                                                TopicLastReplyDate,
 (SELECT MAX(AddedDate)
   FROM (SELECT TopicID, AddedDate FROM Forums_Topics
   UNION ALL
   SELECT TopicID, AddedDate FROM Forums_Replies) AS dates
   WHERE dates.TopicID = Forums_Topics.TopicID) AS TopicLastPostDate,
       Forums_Topics.MemberID, v_Forums_Members.UserID,
       v_Forums_Members.MemberName, v_Forums_Members.ShowEmail,
       Forums_Topics.MemberIP,
       v_Forums_Members.Signature, v_Forums_Members.AvatarUrl,
       v_Forums_Members.Homepage, v_Forums_Members.Email,
       v_Forums_Forums.ForumLastPostDate
  FROM v_Forums_Forums INNER JOIN Forums_Topics
    ON v_Forums_Forums.ForumID = Forums_Topics.ForumID INNER JOIN
    v_Forums_Members ON Forums_Topics.MemberID = v_Forums_Members.MemberID
```

The v_Forums_Replies View

The code in this view is much simpler than in the previous one, because it has no columns to dynamically calculate – it just joins `Forums_Replies` with `v_Forums_Members`, `v_Forums_Forums`, and `Forums_Topics`:

```
SELECT v_Forums_Forums.CategoryID, v_Forums_Forums.CategoryName,
       v_Forums_Forums.ForumID, v_Forums_Forums.ForumName,
       Forums_Topics.TopicID, Forums_Topics.TopicKey,
       Forums_Replies.ReplyID, Forums_Replies.Message,
       Forums_Replies.MemberID, Forums_Replies.AddedDate,
       Forums_Replies.MemberIP, v_Forums_Members.UserID,
       v_Forums_Members.MemberName, v_Forums_Members.ShowEmail,
       v_Forums_Members.Signature, v_Forums_Members.AvatarUrl,
       v_Forums_Members.Homepage, v_Forums_Members.Email
  FROM Forums_Topics INNER JOIN Forums_Replies
    ON Forums_Topics.TopicID = Forums_Replies.TopicID
   INNER JOIN v_Forums_Forums
      ON Forums_Topics.ForumID = v_Forums_Forums.ForumID
     INNER JOIN v_Forums_Members
        ON Forums_Replies.MemberID = v_Forums_Members.MemberID
```

Creating the Stored Procedures

The stored procedures we need are similar to those in other modules. They add, edit, delete, and return records for all our tables. The following procedure returns all the topics of the specified forum:

```
CREATE PROCEDURE sp_Forums_GetTopics
                @ForumID int
AS

SELECT TopicID, Subject, AddedDate, TopicReplies, TopicLastReplyDate,
       TopicLastPostDate, MemberID, MemberName, Email, ShowEmail
  FROM v_Forums_Topics WHERE ForumID = @ForumID
  ORDER BY TopicLastPostDate Desc
GO
```

You see that even if the v_Forums_Topics view exposes many more columns, namely all the details of the parent forum and category, we don't need to return them all, and we take advantage of the fact that we don't need to calculate columns such as TopicReplies, TopicLastReplyDate, and TopicLastPostDate. The records are sorted by the TopicLastPostDate field in descending order, because we'll be displaying the topics from the one with the newest post to the one with the oldest post. Returning the details of a topic is just a matter of returning the complete row of the same view:

```
CREATE PROCEDURE sp_Forums_GetTopicDetails
                @TopicID int
AS

SELECT * FROM v_Forums_Topics WHERE TopicID = @TopicID
GO
```

The only procedure that really has something new is sp_Forums_GetTopicsByPage, which returns only a virtual page of topics, not all of them.

The sp_Forums_GetTopicsByPage Procedure

This procedure is quite long, but it's well worth showing it split up in pieces, explaining a few lines of code at time. We first create a temporary table, with the fields we want to retrieve from v_Forums_Topics, plus a new ID column that we declare as IDENTITY, so that its value is automatically set with an auto-increment number for each record we add:

```
CREATE PROCEDURE sp_Forums_GetTopicsByPage
                @ForumID     int,
                @PageNumber  int,
                @PageSize    int
    AS

    -- create a temporary table with the columns we are interested in
    CREATE TABLE #TempTopics
    (
      ID                  int IDENTITY PRIMARY KEY,
      TopicID             int,
      Subject             varchar(100),
      AddedDate           datetime,
      TopicReplies        int,
      TopicLastReplyDate  datetime,
      TopicLastPostDate   datetime,
      MemberID            int,
      MemberName          varchar(15),
      Email               varchar(50),
      ShowEmail           bit
    )
```

Then we copy all the records of v_Forums_Topics to this #TempTopics table:

```
INSERT INTO #TempTopics
(
  TopicID,
  Subject,
  AddedDate,
  TopicReplies,
  TopicLastReplyDate,
  TopicLastPostDate,
  MemberID,
  MemberName,
  Email,
  ShowEmail
)
SELECT
  TopicID,
  Subject,
  AddedDate,
  TopicReplies,
  TopicLastReplyDate,
  TopicLastPostDate,
  MemberID,
  MemberName,
  Email,
  ShowEmail
FROM
  v_Forums_Topics WHERE ForumID = @ForumID ORDER BY TopicLastPostDate Desc
```

Now we have to calculate the ID of the first and last record to retrieve, and return that range of records from the temporary table. The #TempTopics table with the IDENTITY ID column is necessary because we need a column whose IDs ascend from one to the total number of records, without holes in the middle. We can't use the TopicID column to do this, because we could have deleted records. Here is the code:

```
-- declare two variables to calculate the range of records to extract for
-- the specified page
DECLARE @FromID int
DECLARE @ToID int
-- calculate the first and last ID of the range of topics we need
SET @FromID = ((@PageNumber - 1) * @PageSize) + 1
SET @ToID = @PageNumber * @PageSize

-- select the page of records
SELECT TopicID, Subject, AddedDate, TopicReplies, TopicLastReplyDate,
       TopicLastPostDate, MemberID, MemberName, Email, ShowEmail
  FROM #TempTopics WHERE ID >= @FromID AND ID <= @ToID
GO
```

The first and last ID in the range are calculated according to the current page and the page's size parameter, and the returned records as sorted by `TopicLastPostDate` in descending order, as we saw for the `sp_Forums_GetTopics` procedure.

Later, in the client code, we'll need to know the number of pages in order to build the links that allow the user to navigate through all the topics. This information could be returned as an output parameter by this stored procedure, but we decided that this was not needed. Instead, the number of pages is calculated on the client, in the presentation layer. If you look back at the `v_Forums_Forums` view, you'll see that we return the total number of topics of any forum, and that value is exposed by a property of the `Forum` class. Therefore, from the client we can get that number, and also the number of topics per page, retrieved from the settings, so it's really straightforward to get the number of pages.

Implementing the Data Layer

As we mentioned above, the data layer is made up of classes whose members exactly map all the stored procedures listed in the design section. For this reason, it's not worth showing the code here – the only difference from previous chapters is the name of the stored procedures and the respective parameters.

The data layer consists of a new project, called `Forums.Data`, which is included in the `ThePhile` Visual Studio .NET solution. The assembly and the namespace are called `Wrox.WebModules.Forums.Data`, and it needs a reference to the `Core` assembly since it inherits from `DbObject`. The full implementation is in the code download.

Implementing the Configuration Layer

As for the data layer, the implementation of the configuration assembly (`Wrox.WebModules.Forums.Configuration`) is similar to the respective components already developed for other modules. What changes here is the file name in the `GetSettingsFile` private function, the name of the cache entry to where the settings are stored to be retrieved quicker, and of course the properties of the `ModuleSettings` class. However, these are all simple changes and are not really worth another complete discussion here. You can refer back to see the implementation of the main methods `GetSettings` and `SaveSettings`.

Here is a sample settings file, to see how it is structured and to use as a test:

```xml
<?xml version="1.0"?>
<ModuleSettings xmlns:xsd="http://www.w3.org/2001/XMLSchema"
                xmlns:xsi="http://www.w3.org/2001/XMLSchema-instance">
  <ConnectionString>
    server=(local);database=ThePhile;uid=sa;pwd=;
  </ConnectionString>
  <SmiliesFolder>./Images/Smilies</SmiliesFolder>
  <TopicsPerPage>5</TopicsPerPage>
  <RepliesPerPage>5</RepliesPerPage>
  <HtmlEnabled>false</HtmlEnabled>
  <SpecialTagsEnabled>true</SpecialTagsEnabled>
</ModuleSettings>
```

Of course, we also need to add a custom key in the `web.config` file, with the path of the settings file:

```xml
...
<appSettings>
  <add key="NewsManager_SettingsFile" value="~/Config/NewsManager.Config" />
  <add key="Forums_SettingsFile" value="~/Config/Forums.Config" />
  ...
</appSettings>
...
```

Implementing the Business Layer

The structure of the classes is not new in this component, either. However, since the business assembly is the core of the module, we'll show at least one of the typical classes, `Forum`, as an example. We'll also look at the `Helper` class as it has business logic that is really specific to this module. First of all, we create the new Class Library project, and name it `Wrox.WebModules.Forums.Business`. Then we edit the `AssemblyInfo.cs` file to set some attributes and specify the key file, and add references to the `Data`, `Configuration`, and `Core` projects.

The Forum Class

At this point, we can start coding the `Forum.cs` class. First, we declare the namespace and class:

```csharp
using System;
using System.Data;
using System.Data.SqlClient;

namespace Wrox.WebModules.Forums.Business
{
  public sealed class Forum : Wrox.WebModules.Business.BizObject
  {
```

The class is defined as `sealed` (which means it can't be inherited) since we know we won't need to create derived classes.

Next, we declare private variables and the public properties that read, and sometimes write, to them. There's no point in looking at all of these here – let's move straight onto the constructors and methods.

The Constructors

We have three constructors for each class. The first simply sets member variables to their default state, ready to create a new forum. The second loads the specified forum, and populates the class members appropriately. The final one initializes the variables by loading the record identified by an existing Forum object. Here's the code:

```
public Forum()
{
   settings = Configuration.ModuleConfig.GetSettings();
   ResetProperties();
}

public Forum(int existingForumID)
{
   settings = Configuration.ModuleConfig.GetSettings();
   forumID = existingForumID;
   LoadFromID();
}

public Forum(Forum existingForum)
{
   settings = Configuration.ModuleConfig.GetSettings();
   forumID = existingForum.ID;
   LoadFromID();
}
```

Each constructor creates and saves to a private variable an instance of ModuleSettings, with the current module's settings. This way any other methods can access the settings from the private variable without retrieving them every time.

Resetting and Initializing the Variables

Each constructor calls a private method to populate the variables. If we are loading an existing forum record then we set this object's ForumID variable, and call LoadFromID:

```
private void LoadFromID()
{
   Data.Forums forums = new Data.Forums(settings.ConnectionString);
   Data.ForumDetails details = forums.GetDetails(forumID);

   forumID = details.ForumID;
   categoryID = details.CategoryID;
   name = details.Name;
   description = details.Description;
   position = details.Position;
   topics = details.Topics;
   posts = details.Posts;
   lastPostDate = details.LastPostDate;
}
```

If we are creating a blank forum, we just want to set our variables to appropriate starting values:

```
private void ResetProperties()
{
  forumID = -1;
  categoryID = -1;
  name = "";
  description = "";
  position = 0;
  topics = 0;
  posts = 0;
  lastPostDate = new DateTime();
}
```

We also have a public overload of `LoadFromID`, which takes a forum ID and populates the object based on that ID. In reality it just stores the ID and calls the private `LoadFromID`, as does the constructor:

```
public int LoadFromID(int existingForumID)
{
  forumID = existingForumID;
  LoadFromID();
  return forumID;
}
```

This last method is useful when you have an existing `Forum` instance that already represents a record. If you no longer need that object but need to manipulate another record, instead of creating a new object or destroying and recreating the one you have, just load another record to the existing object by calling this method.

Adding, Updating, or Deleting Forums

To create, update, and delete a record we use the respective methods of the `Data.Forums` class. Here's the business layer's `Forums.Create` method:

```
public int Create(int forumCategoryID, string forumName,
                            string forumDescription, int forumPosition)
{
  Data.Forums forums = new Data.Forums(settings.ConnectionString);
  forumID = forums.Add(forumCategoryID, forumName,
                                    forumDescription, forumPosition);
  LoadFromID();
  return forumID;
}
```

This creates a new record. The method takes every value as a parameter – the `Forum` object's properties prior to calling `Create` are ignored and lost.

The `Update` method saves the current state of the `Forum` object back to the database. The way we have designed the business layer means that some properties cannot be changed once the forum is first created – for example, we cannot move a forum to a new category once it has been created. Only fields exposed as read-write properties are editable:

```
public bool Update ()
{
  Data.Forums forums = new Data.Forums(settings.ConnectionString);
  return forums.Update(forumID, name, description, position);
}
```

If a user calls this method on a *new* Forum object, nothing will happen. The ID property would be -1, so the stored procedure would find no record to update and the method would return `false`.

The `Delete` method is also very similar, except that after deleting the row we must reset all the properties, since the record that was described by the object no longer exists:

```
public bool Delete()
{
  Data.Forums forums = new Data.Forums(settings.ConnectionString);
  bool ret = forums.Delete(forumID);
  ResetProperties();
  return ret;
}
```

Returning and Adding Child Topics

`GetTopics` uses methods in the `Data.Forums` class to obtain the topics in the current forum:

```
public DataSet GetTopics()
{
  Data.Topics topics = new Data.Topics(settings.ConnectionString);
  return topics.GetTopics(forumID);
}
```

The same applies to the overloaded version that returns the specified page of topics. However, the page size is not passed as a parameter (as it is for the method in the data layer), but is retrieved internally through the `ModuleSettings` instance saved in a private variable by the constructors:

```
public DataSet GetTopics(int pageNumber)
{
  Data.Topics topics = new Data.Topics(settings.ConnectionString);
  return topics.GetTopics(forumID, pageNumber, settings.TopicsPerPage);
}
```

The `AddTopic` method adds a child topic and returns a `Business.Topic` object describing the new record. It does not directly map to the `Data.Topic.Add` method – instead it calls the `Create` method of the `Business.Topic` class, which is similar to the `Create` method we created above for the Forum class:

```
public Topic AddTopic(string topicKey, string subject,
                                        string message, int memberID)
{
  Business.Topic topic = new Business.Topic();
  topic.Create(forumID, topicKey, subject, message, memberID);
  return topic;
}
```

Remember that topicKey is a unique name for the topic, which we can use to provide links to a given topic from other parts of the site.

The Helper Class

This class has one static method to process text into HTML format. This includes replacing the special tags (such as [b]) with HTML, replacing smilies with images, and replacing carriage returns with <br> tags. Here is the code. Note that we are using System.Text.RegularExpressions:

```
using System;
using System.Data;
using System.Web;
using System.Text.RegularExpressions;

namespace Wrox.WebModules.Forums.Business
{
  public class Helper: Wrox.WebModules.Business.BizObject
  {
    public static string ProcessSpecialTags(string text)
    {
      Configuration.ModuleSettings settings =
                        Configuration.ModuleConfig.GetSettings();
```

If we are not allowing HTML tags, and in most cases we are not, this will ensure that HTML code is *displayed* rather than *processed*. (For example, it will convert <p> to <p>, which browsers will display as <p> rather than creating a new paragragh):

```
if (!settings.HtmlEnabled)
    text = HttpUtility.HtmlEncode(text);
```

If the special tags are enabled, they are processed:

```
if (settings.SpecialTagsEnabled)
{
  string smiliesFolder = settings.SmiliesFolder;
  if (!smiliesFolder.EndsWith("/")) smiliesFolder += "/";
  // replace the bold special tags
  text = Regex.Replace(text, "\\[B\\](?<boldText>.*)\\[/B\\]",
                  "<b>${boldText}</b>", RegexOptions.IgnoreCase);
```

Other tags are handled in a similar way. We also need to replace smilies tags with <img> tags. Here's how we do this (remember we've already assigned our smiliesFolder variable):

```
// replace the smilies
text = text.Replace("[:)]", "<img src=\"" +
                    smiliesFolder + "Smile.gif\" border=\"0\"/>");
text = text.Replace("[:D]", "<img src=\"" +
                    smiliesFolder + "LargeSmile.gif\" border=\"0\"/>");
```

The process is the same for other smilies. Next the URLs:

```
// replace the URL tag
text = Regex.Replace(text, "\\[URL\\](?<url>.*)\\[/URL\\]",
                "<a href=\"${url}\" target=\"_blank\">${url}</a>",
                RegexOptions.IgnoreCase);

// replace the EMAIL tag
text = Regex.Replace(text, "\\[EMAIL\\](?<email>.*)\\[/EMAIL\\]",
                "<a href=\"mailto:${email}\">${email}</a>",
                RegexOptions.IgnoreCase);
}
```

Outside of the `if` block, we replace the quote tags. Quoting is enabled even if the special tags are not:

```
text = Regex.Replace(text, "\\[QUOTE\\]",
            "<font size=\"1\"><blockquote>quote:<hr height=\"1\" noshade>",
            RegexOptions.IgnoreCase);
text = Regex.Replace(text, "\\[/QUOTE\\]",
                "<hr height=\"1\" noshade></blockquote></font>",
                RegexOptions.IgnoreCase);
```

Finally, we need to replace the new line and carriage return characters. HTML will ignore carriage returns, so we need to use <br>:

```
text = text.Replace("\n", "<br>");
text = text.Replace("\r", "");

return text;
    }
  }
}
```

We use .NET's **regular expression** support to help with replacing the text (refer back to Chapter 9 for an introduction to the basic regular expressions syntax rules). Using the `String` object's `Replace` method would be insufficient because it does not handle case-insensitive situations very well.

The `System.Text.RegularExpressions` namespace contains classes for working with regular expressions, and `Regex` is a principal one. This class has several methods for searching substrings, splitting a string into an array, and replacing strings. We use the `Replace` method to execute a case-insensitive search, by passing `RegexOptions.IgnoreCase` as the last parameter. Look again at this piece of code:

```
text = Regex.Replace(text, "\\[QUOTE\\]",
            "<font size=\"1\"><blockquote>quote:<hr height=\"1\" noshade>",
            RegexOptions.IgnoreCase);
```

Note that [is a special character, so we escape it using \\. Replacing a substring is straightforward, but for the [URL] and [EMAIL] tags we need something more complex. Say that we have the text:

```
[URL]http://www.thephile.com[/URL]
```

We want to transform it to:

```
<a href="http://www.thephile.com" target="_blank"> http://www.thephile.com</a>
```

We have to extract the URL and place it inside the <a> tag for the href attribute, leaving it between the opening and closing tags. Using the regular expressions engine we can do everything in a single line, covering the whole text. Look at the code that does the magic:

```
text = Regex.Replace(text, "\\[URL\\](?<url>.*)\\[/URL\\]",
                     "<a href=\"${url}\" target=\"_blank\">${url}</a>",
                     RegexOptions.IgnoreCase);
```

The pattern string specifies that we want to find all the block [URL]sometext[/URL], capture the sometext substring, and assign it the name url. In the replacement string, the captured url substring is recalled through $(url), and placed as the value for the href attribute as well as the link text between <a> and </a>.

Regular expressions can do much more than this, and are often used for string validation. We've actually shown a couple of examples when validating ZIP codes in Chapter 5, or e-mail addresses in Chapter 9. For more information on regular expressions, see a book such as *Teach Yourself Regular Expressions in 24 Hours* (SAMS Press, ISBN 0-672319-36-5).

The Presentation Layer

We can finally start to write the presentation layer, and see the results of our hard work. We've already decided that we won't have a separate administration section – we will display different options on the pages depending on the user's permissions.

To give an idea of the final pages, here is the Forums homepage in 'standard' mode:

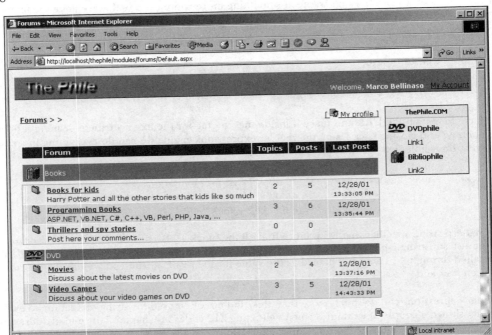

We can see how this page uses our business layer objects – we have our two categories, and our topics with their message counts and last dates calculated. Let's look at how we built this page.

The Categories and Forums Page

The page shown above is `Default.aspx`. Its structure is quite complex, because it has to modify itself for the current user, and because it has two 'levels' – the categories and their child forums.

The early part of the ASPX file is concerned mainly with administration features, hidden from most users – so we will start by looking at them.

Administration Features

The code is quite long, so we'll pick out highlights. To make the system more user-friendly, and reduce the chance of accidental edits, we will use JavaScript alerts to confirm forum and category deletions:

```
<script language="javascript">
   function DeleteForum(id)
   {
     if (confirm('Are you sure that you want to delete this forum and all
                                         its discussions?'))

     {
       document.forms['Forums'].elements['paramID'].value = id;
       __doPostBack('DeleteForum', '');
```

```
      }
    }

    function DeleteCategory(id)
    {
      if (confirm('Are you sure that you want to delete this category and
                                            all its sub-forums?'))
      {
        document.forms['Forums'].elements['paramID'].value = id;
        __doPostBack('DeleteCategory', '');
      }
    }
  </script>
```

We used the built-in __doPostBack method to fake the user clicking on a button called DeleteForum or DeleteCategory. For this to work we need to have buttons that would expose the click event – then we can add event handlers in the codebehind. We define the buttons, hidden, first thing in the page:

```
  </head>
  <body>
    <form ID="Forums" method="post" runat="server">
      <Forums:Header Runat="server" ID="Header" />
      <!-- hidden server controls for handling the events on the server -->
      <input type="hidden" ID="paramID" runat="server">
      <asp:LinkButton ID="DeleteCategory" runat="server"
                      OnClick="DeleteCategory_Click" Visible="False" />
      <asp:LinkButton ID="DeleteForum" runat="server"
                      OnClick="DeleteForum_Click" Visible="False" />
```

We used the same technique in Chapter 4, for deleting directories and files – refer back for further details about ASP.NET server event handling.

The next section defines a hidden form for editing or creating forums, and another for editing or creating categories. There is nothing complex about the code, so we won't list it here. Here is the page with the forum editor displayed:

The Forum Menu

Now we get to the main attraction – a table listing the categories with their child forums. We need a way to handle the two 'levels' of data. Here's a brief outline of what we will do:

❏ Have a main DataList where each item (record) occupies two rows. The first row contains the header for a given category (in the image above we have Books and DVD). The second row contains the topics DataGrid.

❏ The topics DataGrid contains a row for each topic under that category – so in the Books category above, the second row of the category grid contains a DataGrid for 'Books for Kids', 'Programming Books', and 'Thrillers and spy stories'.

Now let's look at the code. This section defines the overall header for the DataList, which simply contains column headings:

```
<asp:DataList ID="CategoriesList" runat="server"
              DataKeyField="CategoryID"
              OnEditCommand="CategoriesList_Edit"
              Width="100%">
  <HeaderTemplate>
    <table width="100%">
      <tr>
        <td>
          <table width="100%">
            <tr class="Forums_Header2">
              <td width="16px" runat="server"
                  Visible='<%# CanAdministerCategories %>'>
                <asp:LinkButton ID="NewCategory" runat="server"
                                OnClick="NewCategory_Click"
                                CausesValidation="False">
                  <img border="0" src="./Images/FolderNew.gif"
                              Alt="Create a new category">
                </asp:LinkButton>
              </td>
              <td width="16px" runat="server"
                  Visible='<%# CanAdministerCategories %>'>
                <asp:LinkButton ID="NewForum" runat="server"
                                OnClick="NewForum_Click"
                                CausesValidation="False">
                  <img border="0" src="./Images/Folder.gif"
                        Alt="Create a new forum">
                </asp:LinkButton>
              </td>
              <td class="Forums_Header2" width="32px"> </td>
              <td class="Forums_Header2">Forum</td>
              <td class="Forums_Header2" width="60px"
                                        align="center">Topics</td>
              <td class="Forums_Header2" width="60px"
                                        align="center">Posts</td>
              <td class="Forums_Header2" width="90px"
                                        align="center">Last Post</td>
            </tr>
          </table>
        </td>
      </tr>
    </table>
  </HeaderTemplate>
```

The `NewCategory` and `NewForum` buttons are declared within two table cells declared with the `runat="server"` attribute, and whose `Visible` attribute is bound to the value returned by `CanAdministerCategories`, a public property declared in the codebehind. We'll see the implementation of the property in the codebehind section, for now you just need to know that the property checks the permissions of the current user and returns `true` if they have the `AdministerCategories` permission.

After `HeaderTemplate`, we have the `ItemTemplate`, whose code is repeated for each record in the datasource:

```
<ItemTemplate>
  <table width="100%">
    <tr>
      <td>
        <table width="100%">
          <tr class="Forums_Header">
            <td width="15px" runat="server"
                Visible='<%# CanAdministerCategories %>'>
              <asp:LinkButton CommandName="Edit"
                          runat="server" CausesValidation="False">
                <img border="0" Alt="Edit this category"
                            src="./Images/Edit.gif">
              </asp:LinkButton>
            </td>
            <td width="15px" runat="server"
                Visible='<%# CanAdministerCategories %>'>
              <a href='<%#
                    string.Format("javascript:DeleteCategory({0});",
                    DataBinder.Eval(Container.DataItem,
                                      "CategoryID")) %>'>
                <img border="0" Alt="Delete this category"
                            src="./Images/Delete.gif" />
              </a>
            </td>
            <td width="35px" align="center">
              <asp:Image Runat="server" BorderWidth="0"
                    ImageUrl='<%# DataBinder.Eval(Container.DataItem,
                    "CategoryImageUrl") %>'
                    Visible='<%# DataBinder.Eval(Container.DataItem,
                    "CategoryImageUrl").ToString().Length > 0 %>'
              />
            </td>
            <td>
              <%# DataBinder.Eval(Container.DataItem,
                                            "CategoryName") %>
            </td>
          </tr>
        </table>
      </td>
    </tr>
```

The code above creates a table and defines the first row, with the following cells:

❑   A `LinkButton` shows the `CategoryBox` in editing mode when clicked. The cell is visible according to the `CanAdministerCategories` property.

❑   A link that calls the `DeleteCategory` JavaScript, passing the current category's ID as a parameter. The cell is visible according to the `CanAdministerCategories` property.

❑   The category's image. The `Image` server control is only visible if the length of the image URL is longer than zero (that is, there is an image to display).

❑   The category's name.

The `DataList`'s `ItemTemplate` continues with a second row – this time with a single cell. The content is a `DataGrid` control for this category's child forums. The `DataGrid` has columns for the forum's name and description, number of topics, number of posts, and the date of the most recent post. The forum's name is a hyperlink, which points to the `Forum.aspx` page – with the `ForumID` value as a parameter on the URL. There are also buttons to edit or delete the forum. The deletion requires a confirmation, through the JavaScript function as seen above. The code is quite verbose because there is so much HTML, so we will just pull out some highlights.

First, let's look at the definition of the `DataGrid`:

```
<asp:DataGrid runat="server"
              AutoGenerateColumns="False"
              CssClass="Forums_General"
              ItemStyle-CssClass="Forums_Item"
              AlternatingItemStyle-CssClass="Forums_AlternatingItem"
              DataKeyField="ForumID"
              DataSource='<%# GetForumsSource(int.Parse(DataBinder.Eval
                      (Container.DataItem, "CategoryID").ToString())) %>'
              OnEditCommand="ForumsGrid_Edit"
              ShowHeader="False"
              Width="100%">
```

Here we set the `DataGrid`'s `DataSource` to the `DataView` returned by `GetForumsSource` in the codebehind. The function takes a category ID as a parameter, and returns the child forums. We do this because we can't set the `DataGrid.DataSource` property from the codebehind – `DataGrid`s are built dynamically and have no reference to them in the codebehind. Most of the columns are not new, and only show the data without further processing, but there are a few that it is important to show:

```
<Columns>
  <asp:TemplateColumn ItemStyle-Wrap="True"
                      ItemStyle-Width="1px">
    <ItemTemplate>
      <asp:ImageButton Runat="server" CommandName="Edit"
          Visible='<%# CanAdministerCategories %>'
          ImageUrl="./Images/Edit.gif"
          AlternateText="Edit this forum" BorderWidth="0"/>
    </ItemTemplate>
  </asp:TemplateColumn>
  <asp:TemplateColumn ItemStyle-Wrap="True"
                      ItemStyle-Width="1px">
```

```
                    <ItemTemplate>
                      <asp:HyperLink Runat="server" NavigateUrl='<%#
                          "javascript:DeleteForum(" + DataBinder.Eval(
                          Container.DataItem, "ForumID") + ")" %>'
                          Visible='<%# CanAdministerCategories %>'
                          Text="<img border=0 Alt='Delete this forum'
                          src=./Images/Delete.gif>" />
                    </ItemTemplate>
                  </asp:TemplateColumn>
```

The second `TemplateColumn` defined in the code above declares a `HyperLink` that points to the JavaScript `DeleteForum` routine explained earlier, with the forum's ID as an input parameter. The routine will ask for confirmation, and if the user presses **OK** it will pass this ID to the server, indicating which forum has to be deleted.

Going ahead, we find the column with the forum's name and description. The name is rendered as a link that points to `Forum.aspx`, with the `ForumID` value passed as a parameter in the URL:

```
                  <asp:TemplateColumn>
                    <ItemTemplate>
                      <asp:HyperLink runat="server" Font-Bold="True"
                        Text='<%# DataBinder.Eval(
                        Container.DataItem, "ForumName") %>'
                        NavigateUrl='<%# "Forum.aspx?ForumID=" +
                        DataBinder.Eval(Container.DataItem, "ForumID") %>'
                        />
                      <br>
                      <asp:Label runat="server" Text='<%#
                                DataBinder.Eval(Container.DataItem,
                                "ForumDescription") %>' />
                    </ItemTemplate>
                  </asp:TemplateColumn>

                    ...declaration of the columns Topics, Posts,
                    and Last Post goes here...

                </Columns>
              </asp:DataGrid>
```

The page ends with the closing tags of the category `DataList`'s `ItemTemplate` and the `DataList`:

```
                </td>
              </tr>
            </table>
          </ItemTemplate>
        </asp:DataList>
        <br>
        <Forums:Footer Runat="server" ID="Footer" />
      </form>
    </body>
</HTML>
```

The Codebehind for Default.aspx

We start the code-behind with the basics – declaring the namespace and class, and implementing basic methods such as `Page_Load`. Here is the `Page_Load` event:

```
private void Page_Load(object sender, System.EventArgs e)
{
    // do not allow to manage categories if the user is not authenticated
    // or does not have the proper permission
    canAdministerCategories = (Context.User.Identity.IsAuthenticated &&
                              ((SitePrincipal)Context.User).HasPermission(
                              (int)ForumsPermissions.AdministerCategories));

    if (!IsPostBack)
    {
        BindList();
    }
}
```

This sets the `canAdministerCategories` variable appropriately, using the `Accounts` system we created in Chapter 5. `canAdministerCategories` is a private variable, accessed through the `CanAdministerCategories` property. Note how easy it is to get the `SitePrincipal` object from `Context.User` – we really benefit from integrating our security system with .NET's built-in authentication.

Next, we call the `BindList` method, provided we are not processing a postback. `BindList` binds the appropriate `DataView` to our `DataList` (the list of categories, which contains the `DataGrid` for child topics). Here is the code for `BindList`:

```
private void BindList()
{
    CategoriesList.DataSource =
                Business.Category.GetCategories().Tables[0].DefaultView;
    CategoriesList.DataBind();
}
```

Because there are multiple `DataGrid` instances, generated dynamically, we cannot access it as an object. So we will expose a method that our main page can call, to return a `DataView` listing topics in a given category:

```
public DataView GetForumsSource(int categoryID)
{
    // get the DataView with the forums for the specified category
    return new Business.Category(
                        categoryID).GetForums().Tables[0].DefaultView;
}
```

Adding and Editing a Category

When we want to edit an existing category, we show the box, but set the textboxes with the current properties of the clicked category. The properties are exposed by an instance of `Business.Category`, as you see below:

```
protected void CategoriesList_Edit(object sender,
                                        DataListCommandEventArgs e)
{
  // if the user cannot administer categories, redirect to the login page
  if (!canAdministerCategories) {
    Response.Redirect(
              "/ThePhile/Modules/Users/Login.aspx?ShowError=true", true);
  }

  // get the ID of the clicked category
  int categoryID = (int)CategoriesList.DataKeys[e.Item.ItemIndex];
  // get the category's details
  Business.Category category = new Business.Category(categoryID);

  // set the controls for editing the record
  CategoryName.Text = category.Name;
  CategoryImageUrl.Text = category.ImageUrl;
  CategoryPosition.Text = category.Position.ToString();
  CategoryIDCurr.Text = category.ID.ToString();
  CategoryBoxHeader.Text = "Edit category";

  // hide the forum box, if visible
  ForumBox.Visible = false;
  // show the category box
  CategoryBox.Visible = true;
}
```

Before doing anything else we must check if the current user has the permission to edit a category. If not, they are redirected to the Login page. It's true that the permissions are checked in `Page_Load`, and that if the `ForumsPermissions.AdministerCategories` permission is not present the controls for editing and deleting records are not shown, but an expert user could still hack the page by manually calling the `__doPostBack` function with the parameters to call this server event. It's quite difficult, but not impossible, to guess the required parameters, because they are dynamically generated according to the index and name of the inner columns and links.

It's also worth noting that we set the `CategoryIDCurr` textbox (that is hidden) to the category's ID. Later, when the box is submitted, this will tell us the ID of the category to update, or, if empty, will tell us that we're adding a new category.

When the administrator clicks the image button to add a new category, the page calls `NewCategory_Click`. This is similar to `EditCategory_Click`, except that all of the textboxes are blank (except `CategoryBoxHeader`, of course).

These methods display the edit box, but the real addition or update of a category is done when the box is submitted. Look at the following code:

```
// submit the box for adding/editing a category
protected void SubmitCategory_Click(object sender, EventArgs e)
{
  if (!canAdministerCategories) {
    Response.Redirect(
                "/ThePhile/Modules/Users/Login.aspx?ShowError=true", true);
  }

  int categoryPos = (CategoryPosition.Text.Length > 0 ?
    int.Parse(CategoryPosition.Text) : 0);

  // if the hidden textbox is empty, it means that we're adding a category
  if (CategoryIDCurr.Text.Length == 0)
  {
    // add a new category
    Business.Category category = new Business.Category();
    category.Create(CategoryName.Text, CategoryImageUrl.Text, categoryPos);
  }
  else
  {
    // edit a category
    Business.Category category = new Business.Category(
                                        int.Parse(CategoryIDCurr.Text));
    category.Name = CategoryName.Text;
    category.ImageUrl = CategoryImageUrl.Text;
    category.Position = categoryPos;
    category.Update();
  }

  // hide the category box
  CategoryBox.Visible = false;

  // refresh
  BindList();
}
```

As mentioned above, if the `CategoryIDCurr` textbox is empty it means that we're adding a category, otherwise we retrieve the ID and update that category with the new values. At the end of the procedure we hide the box and call `BindList` to refresh the data bound to the `DataList` control.

If the user presses the Cancel link instead of submitting the form, the box is simply hidden:

```
// cancel the box for adding/editing a category
protected void CancelCategory_Click(object sender, EventArgs e)
{
  CategoryBox.Visible = false;
}
```

Deleting a Category

To delete a category we create an instance of `Business.Category` for that category, whose ID is retrieved from the HTML hidden control set by the `DeleteCategory` JavaScript function, and call its `Delete` method:

```
protected void DeleteCategory_Click(object sender, EventArgs e)
{
  if (!canAdministerCategories) {
    Response.Redirect(
                "/ThePhile/Modules/Users/Login.aspx?ShowError=true", true);
  }

  // extract the ID of the category to delete
  int categoryID = int.Parse(paramID.Value.ToString());
  // delete the category
  Business.Category category = new Business.Category(categoryID);
  category.Delete();
  // re-bind the list to show the updated records
  BindList();
}
```

Note that here it is really crucial to check if the user has permission to delete a category. In fact, hacking the parameters for `__doPostBack` to edit a forum or category is quite complex, but hacking the page to delete a category would be a breeze: it would be sufficient to call the `DeleteCategory` JavaScript trying to pass some IDs! Therefore, before doing anything else we check the permissions, and redirect to the login page if the user is not supposed to be able to delete records.

Working With Forums

The operations to add, update, or delete a forum are very similar to the respective category methods, so we won't go through everything again – for the full code, see the code download.

The Header Control

We declared the header and footer controls (the files `Header.ascx` and `Footer.ascx`, located in the same folder together with the ASP.NET pages) at the top of `Default.aspx`, but we haven't developed them yet. The footer control has a link to jump to the top of the page, and some closing tags of the table we open in the header to create the layout with two columns (the real content on the left, and the menu on the right side column). This control is the same as the one we developed in earlier chapters (Chapters 6, 8, and 9), so we won't show it again here.

The header control, in addition to opening the layout table and adding the site-wide header and the menu box, also adds the following parts:

❑ Up to three links to navigate forum sublevels, giving links to the Forums homepage, the page listing the topics for the selected forum, and the page with the topic and its replies. This means that we can move up to higher levels in the forum's hierarchy. The link to the topic is shown when the user is reading the topic itself, and can be used to go to the first page of replies if there are more than one, but it is also shown when the user is editing a topic/reply (if the user is the administrator) and wants to go back to the topic page before submitting the changes.

❑   A link to the module's settings page, visible to users with the `EditSettings` permission only.

❑   A link to the `MyProfile.aspx` page, allowing users to edit their current profile if it already exists, or create a new one.

There's nothing new, or particularly interesting, about the ASCX file so we will move onto the codebehind. But to understand the codebehind, we need to know that the ASCX file declares four ASP.NET `HyperLink` objects – `LinkToCategories`, `LinkToForum`, `LinkToTopic`, and `LinkToSettings`. It also exposes a `Label` object called `LinkToProfileText` – we use a label here because the link's target and visibility will always be the same (`MyProfile.aspx`, and `true`), only the text will change. These links map to the links described above.

With that said, let's look at the codebehind.

The Codebehind for Header.ascx

We'll look at the codebehind class in two parts. First we will look at the `Page_Load` event, which shows the **Settings** link only if the user is authenticated and has the `EditSettings` permission. It also sets the text of the `MyProfile.aspx` link to **Register** if the user is not authenticated or does not have a forums profile, or to **My Profile** otherwise. We'll leave out the namespace and class definitions, to keep things brief:

```
private void Page_Load(object sender, System.EventArgs e)
{
  if (Context.User.Identity.IsAuthenticated)
  {
    // check if the current user is allowed to change the settings
    SitePrincipal currentPrincipal = (SitePrincipal)Context.User;
    if (!currentPrincipal.HasPermission(
      (int)ForumsPermissions.EditSettings))
    {
      // if not, hide the link
      LinkToSettings.Visible = false;
    }

    // change the title of the link to the MyProfile page depending on
    // whether the current user is registered for the forum or not
    SiteIdentity currUser = (SiteIdentity)Context.User.Identity;
    Business.Member member = new Business.Member();
    member.LoadFromUser(currUser.UserID);
    LinkToProfileText.Text = (member.ID == -1 ?
                                        "Register" : "My profile");
  }
  else
  {
    LinkToProfileText.Text = "Register";
    LinkToSettings.Visible = false;
  }
}
```

To check if the currently logged in user has a profile for the forums, we create a new instance of `Business.Member`, and try to load the member profile 'attached' to the user's ID specified with the `LoadFromUser` method. If the member is not found, the object's ID property is set to -1, and we set the link's text to **Register**.

Now let's look at the public properties that allows the host page to specify the ID of the current topic or forum shown on the page. According to the ID specified, the code shows the complete path of links from the Forums homepage through to our topic:

```
public int ForumID
{
  get { return forumID; }
  set
  {
    forumID = value;
    topicID = -1;

    Business.Forum forum = new Business.Forum(forumID);
    LinkToCategories.Text = forum.Category.Name;
    LinkToForum.Text = forum.Name;
    LinkToForum.NavigateUrl = "Forum.aspx?ForumID=" +
                                              forum.ID.ToString();
  }
}

public int TopicID
{
  get { return topicID; }
  set
  {
    forumID = -1;
    topicID = value;

    Business.Topic topic = new Business.Topic(topicID);
    LinkToCategories.Text = topic.Forum.Category.Name;
    LinkToForum.Text = topic.Forum.Name;
    LinkToForum.NavigateUrl = "Forum.aspx?ForumID=" +
                                        topic.Forum.ID.ToString();
    LinkToTopic.Text = topic.Subject;
    LinkToTopic.NavigateUrl = "Topic.aspx?TopicID=" +
                                        topic.ID.ToString();
  }
 }
 }
 }
```

The ForumID property is used by the Forums.aspx page, while TopicID is used by Topic.aspx. The PostMessage.aspx page uses either one or the other, according to whether it's being used to create or edit a topic. If it's creating a new topic the page will use the ForumID property to point to the parent forum, since there is no topic to point to. Otherwise, if the page is used to edit an existing topic, we'll use the TopicID property to show the link to that topic. We'll see the implementation of these three pages in the following sections.

The Forum.aspx Page

This page is loaded when the user selects a forum from the list on Default.aspx. It allows users to browse the selected forum's topics – represented by the ForumID parameter in the URL.

It lists topics in a DataGrid that employs the custom pagination described earlier, and shows other information such as the name of the topic's author, the number of replies, and the date of the last reply. With an administrator signed in, it looks like this:

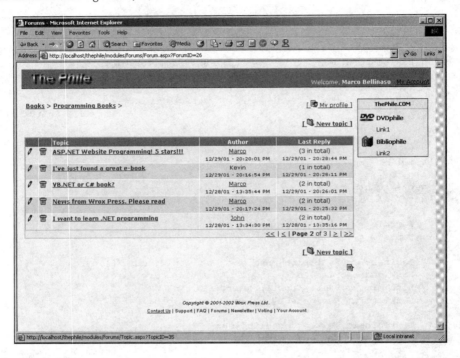

We'll show only the most interesting part of the page here: the declaration of the DataGrid and the controls for custom pagination. Let's explain the code in small pieces:

```
<table class="Forums_General" width="100%" cellpadding="0" cellspacing="0"
                                                        border="0">
  <tr>
    <td>
      <asp:DataGrid runat="server" ID="TopicsGrid"
                AllowCustomPaging="True" AutoGenerateColumns="False"
                CssClass="Forums_General" ItemStyle-CssClass="Forums_Item"
                AlternatingItemStyle-CssClass="Forums_AlternatingItem"
                HeaderStyle-CssClass="Forums_Header" DataKeyField="TopicID"
                OnDeleteCommand="TopicsGrid_Delete" Width="100%">
```

Here the grid is declared, and we say that we want to implement our own pagination by setting `AllowCustomPaging` to `true`. Here's the declaration of the grid's columns:

```
<Columns>
    <asp:HyperLinkColumn ItemStyle-Width="25px"
            DataNavigateUrlField="TopicID" DataNavigateUrlFormatString=
            "PostMessage.aspx?Action=EditTopic&TopicID={0}"
            DataTextFormatString=
            "<img border=0 Alt='Edit this topic' src=./Images/Edit.gif>"
            DataTextField="TopicID"
    />
```

This column has a link to jump to the `PostMessage.aspx` page, with parameters that indicate that we want to edit the clicked topic (later we'll see the meaning of the parameters in detail, but you should be able to guess it). Next we have a column with a link to delete the topic:

```
    <asp:ButtonColumn CommandName="delete" ItemStyle-Width="25px"
                        Text="<img border=0 Alt='Delete this topic'
                        src=./Images/Delete.gif>"
    />
```

Both these two first columns will be made invisible at runtime if the user does not have the `ModerateForums` permission. Here we can easily reference the grid from the codebehind, so there is no need to bind to a `CanModerateForums` public property, as we've done with the `CanAdministerCategories` property for the `Default.aspx` page. Instead, we can do everything from the codebehind.

Next, we add the templated columns that show the topic's subject (that is a hyperlink that points to `Topic.aspx` with the topic's ID as a parameter), the name and e-mail of the topic's author, the date when the topic was posted, the number of replies, and the date of the last one. We don't show the code here, since the structure of these columns is something we've already explained many times, but of course you can find the complete code in the download package.

At the bottom of the `DataGrid`, we add controls to move to the previous and next pages of the grid, and to view the index of the current page. The current index and the total number of pages are displayed by two separate labels, and we have four linkbuttons (first, previous, next, and last) to navigate between the pages:

```
<tr>
  <td align="right">
    <asp:LinkButton runat="server" ID="FirstPage" Text="<<"
            OnCommand="TopicsGrid_PageChanged" CommandName="FirstPage" />
    |
    <asp:LinkButton runat="server" ID="PreviousPage" Text="<"
            OnCommand="TopicsGrid_PageChanged" CommandName="PreviousPage" />
    | <b>Page
      <asp:Label runat="server" ID="PageNumber" Text="1" /></b> of
    <asp:Label runat="server" ID="TotalPages" Text="10" />
    |
    <asp:LinkButton runat="server" ID="NextPage" Text=">"
            OnCommand="TopicsGrid_PageChanged" CommandName="NextPage" />
```

```
           |
        <asp:LinkButton runat="server" ID="LastPage" Text=">>"
                OnCommand="TopicsGrid_PageChanged" CommandName="LastPage" />
      </td>
    </tr>
  </table>
```

It's worth noting that all the linkbuttons declare the same event handler for OnCommand, but they have different values for the CommandName property, to specify which link posted the form back, and to increment or decrement the index of the current page accordingly.

To conclude, at the top and bottom of the grid there are also two links that point to PostMessage.aspx, with parameters to indicate that we want to add a topic to the current forum:

```
<asp:HyperLink runat="server" ID="NewTopic2"
            NavigateUrl="PostMessage.aspx?Action=NewTopic&amp;ForumID=">
  [ <img src="./Images/Folder.gif" Alt="New topic" border="0"> New topic ]
</asp:HyperLink>
```

Note that the ID of the current forum is not specified, as it will be added to the NavigateUrl value from the codebehind.

The Forum.aspx Codebehind

The codebehind starts with the usual Page_Load procedure. It first checks the permissions of the current user, and hides the first two columns of the grid (those for editing or deleting a record) if they don't have the ModerateForums permission. It also extracts the ForumID parameter from the QueryString, and sets the ForumID property of the Header control:

```
private bool canModerateForums;

protected void Page_Load(object sender, EventArgs e)
{
  // check if the user has the permission to moderate the forums
  canModerateForums = (Context.User.Identity.IsAuthenticated &&
                          ((SitePrincipal)Context.User).HasPermission(
                          (int)ForumsPermissions.ModerateForums));

  // get the ForumID from the QueryString
  string forumID = Request.Params["ForumID"];

  if (!Page.IsPostBack)
  {
    // set the hyperlinks to jump to the parent category
    NewTopic1.NavigateUrl += forumID;
    NewTopic2.NavigateUrl = NewTopic1.NavigateUrl;
    Header.ForumID = int.Parse(forumID);
    // bind the data to the grid
    TopicsGrid.Attributes["ForumID"] = forumID;
    BindGrid();

    // hides the first 2 columns for editing/deleting a record, if the
```

```
    // current user does not have the permission to do that
    TopicsGrid.Columns[0].Visible = canModerateForums;
    TopicsGrid.Columns[1].Visible = canModerateForums;
  }
}

public bool CanModerateForums
{
  get { return canModerateForums; }
}
```

Binding the Records and Handling the Custom Pagination

Before looking at the `BindGrid` procedure that retrieves and binds the data to the grid, let's look at how the custom pagination works. When one of the page-navigator links is clicked, we calculate the new index of the page to show, and call `BindGrid` to refresh the grid. To identify the clicked link, we check the `CommandName` property of the `CommandEventArgs` object passed as a parameter to the event handler, and update the current index accordingly. Here's the code:

```
protected void TopicsGrid_PageChanged(object sender, CommandEventArgs e)
{
  if (PageNumber.Text.Trim().Length == 0) return;

  switch (e.CommandName)
  {
    case "FirstPage":
      PageNumber.Text = "1";
      break;
    case "PreviousPage":
      PageNumber.Text = (int.Parse(PageNumber.Text) -1).ToString();
      break;
    case "NextPage":
      PageNumber.Text = (int.Parse(PageNumber.Text) +1).ToString();
      break;
    case "LastPage":
      PageNumber.Text = TotalPages.Text;
      break;
  }

  // show the new page
  BindGrid();
}
```

Note that when the user clicks the link to move to the last page, the index is calculated by taking the value displayed by the `TotalPages` label. The value of that label is set by `BindGrid`, which occurs before the user can change the page – so we can be sure that the label is displaying a value.

The `BindGrid` method retrieves the records of the current page (the index is retrieved from the other label) by calling the `GetTopics` method of a `Business.Forum` object for the current forum. It also updates the `TotalPages` label, and enables or disables the links to navigate through the grid's pages according to the current index. (For example, if we're on the last page, the links to the last page and the next page are disabled.) Here it is:

```
protected void BindGrid()
{
  // get the ForumID value from the Grid's attributes.
  // if null, redirect to the Default.aspx page
  if (TopicsGrid.Attributes["ForumID"] == null)
    Response.Redirect("Default.aspx", true);

  // get the current forum's ID
  int forumID = int.Parse(TopicsGrid.Attributes["ForumID"]);
  // get the number of topics per page
  int pageSize = Configuration.ModuleConfig.GetSettings().TopicsPerPage;

  // get the current forum page
  int pageNumber = (PageNumber.Text == "0" ?
    1 : int.Parse(PageNumber.Text));

  // retrieve and bind the records to the grid
  Business.Forum forum = new Business.Forum(forumID);
  DataSet topics = forum.GetTopics(pageNumber);
  TopicsGrid.DataSource = topics.Tables[0].DefaultView;
  TopicsGrid.DataBind();

  // show the total number of pages
  int totalPages = (int)Math.Ceiling((double)forum.Topics/pageSize);
  if (totalPages == 0) totalPages = 1;
  TotalPages.Text = totalPages.ToString();
  // enable/disable the links to navigate through the pages
  FirstPage.Enabled = (pageNumber != 1);
  PreviousPage.Enabled = (pageNumber != 1);
  NextPage.Enabled = (pageNumber != totalPages);
  LastPage.Enabled = (pageNumber != totalPages);
}
```

The last method used to show the records is GetAuthorText, which returns the HTML link pointing to the e-mail of the topic's author if their ShowEmail property is true, or simply displays their name:

```
public string GetAuthorText(object memberName, object eMail,
                                                 object showEmail)
{
  // return the member Name only or a link to its e-mail address,
  // according to the ShowEmail value
  if (!Convert.ToBoolean(showEmail))
    return memberName.ToString();
  else
    return string.Format("<a href=\"mailto:{0}\">{1}</a>",
      eMail.ToString(), memberName.ToString());
}
```

Deleting a Topic

Deleting a topic is a simple task, and it is something that we've already shown in previous chapters for other DataGrids. We first check if the current user is allowed to moderate the forum, and if so we retrieve the ID of the record from the grid's DataKeys collection, create a Business.Topic object for that topic, and call its Delete method:

```
protected void TopicsGrid_Delete(object sender, DataGridCommandEventArgs e)
{
  // if the user cannot moderate forums redirect to the login page
  if (!canModerateForums) {
    Response.Redirect(
                "/ThePhile/Modules/Users/Login.aspx?ShowError=true", true);
  }

  // delete this topic
  Business.Topic topic = new Business.Topic(
                            (int)TopicsGrid.DataKeys[e.Item.ItemIndex]);
  topic.Delete();
  BindGrid();
}
```

The Topic.aspx Page

Topic.aspx shows the selected topic (identified by the TopicID parameter in the URL), and all its replies. The list is divided into pages in a similar way to the Forum.aspx page we just looked at. We use a DataGrid to list the replies, and a set of server controls aligned through a table with a single row for the topic.

Here is a screenshot of the finished page as a moderator sees it, with some replies to the topic. The third reply quotes the previous one, and the messages have some HTML formatting. Although the first message looks similar to the others, it is taken from the topics table, and implemented in a different way to the replies. It is shown only on the first page of the discussion, in the following pages the users will only see the replies. They will still see the topic's subject in the navigation link at the top of the page:

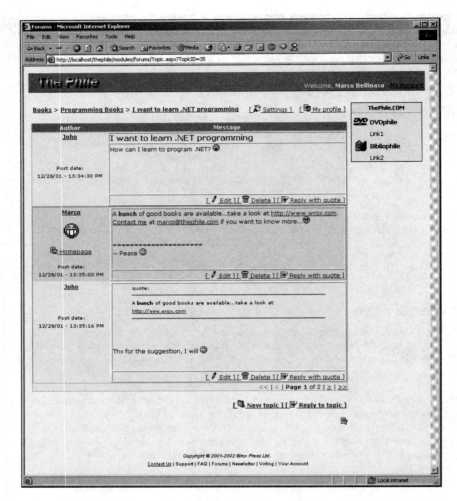

Below you see a partial declaration of this table and the controls to display all the topic's parts (subject, body, author name, homepage, e-mail address, date, etc.):

```
<table runat="server" id="TopicTable" class="Forums_General" width="100%"
                           cellpadding="0" cellspacing="0" border="0">
  <tr>
    <td class="Forums_Item" align="middle" width="160">
      ...in this column show the author's name, e-mail, web site
      and the date of the post...
    </td>
    <td class="Forums_Item">
      <table width="100%" height="160" cellpadding="1" border="1">
        <tr height="20">
          ...show here the message and the author's signature...
```

```
        </tr>
        <tr height="20">
          <td align="right">
            <asp:HyperLink Runat="server" ID="EditTopic">
              [ <img border=0 alt='Edit this topic'
                                      src=./Images/Edit.gif> Edit ]
            </asp:HyperLink>
            <asp:LinkButton Runat="server" ID="DeleteTopic"
                                      OnClick="DeleteTopic_Click">
              [ <img border="0" alt="Delete this topic"
                                src="./Images/Delete.gif"> Delete ]
            </asp:LinkButton>
            <a href="<%= "PostMessage.aspx?Action=NewReply&TopicID=" +
                      Request.QueryString["TopicID"] + "&QuoteTopicID=" +
                      Request.QueryString["TopicID"] %>">[
                <img src="./Images/Reply.gif" Alt='Reply with quote'
                                      border="0"> Reply with quote ]
            </a>
          </td>
        </tr>
      </table>
    </td>
  </tr>
</table>
```

No control is bound to a `DataSource`. We'll set the controls' content from the codebehind, control by control, since we have references to them.

The structure of the `DataGrid` follows the pattern of the table above – it has two `TemplateColumn` objects that extract from the data to display from the `DataSource`. Here it is:

```
<asp:DataGrid Runat="server" ID="RepliesGrid" AllowCustomPaging="True"
      AutoGenerateColumns="False" CssClass="Forums_General"
      HeaderStyle-CssClass="Forums_Header" DataKeyField="ReplyID"
      OnDeleteCommand="RepliesGrid_Delete" ShowHeader="False" Width="100%">
  <Columns>
    ...add here a templated column that shows the author's name, e-mail,
    website, and the date of the post...
    <asp:TemplateColumn>
      <ItemTemplate>
        <table width="100%" height="160px" cellpadding="1" border="1">
          <tr>
            ...show here the message and the author's signature...
          </tr>
          <tr height="20px">
            <td align="right">
              <asp:HyperLink Runat="server"
                      NavigateUrl='<%#
                      PostMessage.aspx?Action=EditReply&ReplyID=" +
                      DataBinder.Eval(Container.DataItem, "ReplyID") %>'
                      Visible='<%# CanModerateForums %>'>
                [ <img border=0 Alt='Edit this reply'
```

```
                               src=./Images/Edit.gif> Edit ]
                </asp:HyperLink>
                <asp:LinkButton CommandName="delete" runat="server"
                               Visible='<%# CanModerateForums %>'>
                               [ <img border="0" Alt="Delete this reply"
                               src="./Images/Delete.gif"> Delete ]
                </asp:LinkButton>
                <asp:HyperLink runat="server"
                       NavigateUrl='<%#
                       "PostMessage.aspx?Action=NewReply&TopicID=" +
                       Request.QueryString["TopicID"] + "&QuoteReplyID=" +
                       DataBinder.Eval(Container.DataItem, "ReplyID") %>'>
                       [ <img src="./Images/Reply.gif" alt='Reply with quote'
                       border="0"> Reply with quote ]
                </asp:HyperLink>
            </td>
          </tr>
        </table>
      </ItemTemplate>
    </asp:TemplateColumn>
  </Columns>
</asp:DataGrid>
```

We declare a `HyperLink` to jump to `PostMessage.aspx` and edit the reply, and a `LinkButton` to delete the reply, but these are visible according to the `CanModerateForums` property, defined in the code-behind. There is also another link to `PostMessage.aspx`, used for replying to a comment and quoting from the original message. The difference between the links that point to `PostMessage.aspx` is the list of parameters attached to the URL: the `Action` parameter is `EditReply` or `NewReply`, and in the latter case the optional `QuoteReplyID` parameter indicates whether we want to post a simple reply or we want to quote an existing one. We'll say more about these and the others parameters when we talk about the `PostMessage.aspx` page.

One last thing before moving ahead to the codebehind: we don't directly display the `Message` and `Signature` values as they are retrieved from the database, but pass them through `ProcessTags` – the method we created to encode the HTML.

The page ends with links to navigate between the `DataGrid` pages, and one more link to reply without quoting any message. The pagination controls are the same as those in the `Forum.aspx` page, so there is no need to show them again here.

The Codebehind for Topic.aspx

The codebehind of this page has to take care of binding the data to the replies grid and topic controls, and handling the custom pagination. We'll start looking at the code from `Page_Load`, as usual. The method begins by checking if the current user has the right to modify forums:

```
private bool canModerateForums;

protected void Page_Load(object sender, EventArgs e)
{
    // check if the user has the permission to moderate the forums
```

```
canModerateForums = (Context.User.Identity.IsAuthenticated &&
                     ((SitePrincipal)Context.User).HasPermission(
                     (int)ForumsPermissions.ModerateForums));

string topicID = "-1";
```

Next, we obtain the `ForumID` from `Request.QueryString`, which contains the URL parameters. Then we set properties on the **EditTopic** link, depending on the user's permissions and the selected topic:

```
if (Request.QueryString["TopicID"] != null)
  topicID = Request.Params["TopicID"];

// show or hide the Edit and Delete topic links, according to
// the permissions of the current user
EditTopic.NavigateUrl = "PostMessage.aspx?Action=EditTopic&TopicID=" +
                                          topicID.ToString();

EditTopic.Visible = canModerateForums;
DeleteTopic.Visible = canModerateForums;
```

Remember, we want to be able to link to topics from other parts of the site. To do this we allow a topic to have a `TopicKey` – a string that we can use to identify a topic. If a user follows a link based on `TopicKey`, we want to obtain the `TopicID` and redirect the user. Redirecting to the same page but with the `TopicID` parameter is not a big waste of time, because everything happens on the server and there are no round trips, and it makes it easier to load the topic when the pages is loaded or posted back. In fact, if we just used the key to obtain the ID, and assigned the ID to a local variable, we would need to do this every time the users go to another page of replies, since the URL would still have the key as its parameter and not the ID. In reality we could persist the obtained ID between postbacks in the `StateBag` hashtable, accessible through the `ViewState` property, but at this point it's easier and faster to just redirect to the same page with the ID as the parameter. Here is the code:

```
if (!Page.IsPostBack)
{
  Business.Topic topic;

  // if the TopicKey value is not null, find the topic with
  // that key and redirect to it
  if (Request.QueryString["TopicKey"] != null)
  {
    topic = new Business.Topic(
      Request.QueryString["TopicKey"].ToString());
    // if found, redirect to it, otherwise redirect to Default.aspx
    if (topic.ID != -1)
      Response.Redirect("Topic.aspx?TopicID=" +
                                          topic.ID.ToString(), true);
    else
      Response.Redirect("Default.aspx", true);
  }
```

Otherwise, we set properties on the HyperLink objects and page position appropriately and bind the data to the DataGrid:

```
    else
    {
        // set the links for posting a new topic/reply
        topic = new Business.Topic(int.Parse(topicID));
        NewTopic.NavigateUrl += topic.Forum.ID.ToString();
        NewReply.NavigateUrl += topic.ID.ToString();
        // set the navigation bar TopicID
        Header.TopicID = int.Parse(topicID);

        // if there is the paramter idicating to show the last page, set
        // the number in the label. This will be read
        // in the BindGrid procedure
        if (Request.QueryString["Display"] != null &&
            Request.QueryString["Display"].ToString().ToLower() == "lastpage")
        {
            int pageSize =
                        Configuration.ModuleConfig.GetSettings().RepliesPerPage;
            int totalPages = (int)Math.Ceiling((double)topic.Replies/pageSize);
            PageNumber.Text = totalPages.ToString();
        }

        // bind the data to the grid
        RepliesGrid.Attributes["TopicID"] = topicID;
        BindGrid();
    }
}
}

public bool CanModerateForums
{
    get { return canModerateForums; }
}
```

Now we can go on with the BindGrid procedure, in which the custom pagination management is similar to the respective procedure in Forum.aspx. However, here we must also show or hide the table containing the Topic record – we only want it to display on the front page. Let's look at the code:

```
protected void BindGrid()
{
    // get the ForumID value from the Grid's attributes.
    // if null, redirect to the Default.aspx page
    if (RepliesGrid.Attributes["TopicID"] == null)
        Response.Redirect("Default.aspx", true);

    // get the current forum's ID
    int topicID = int.Parse(RepliesGrid.Attributes["TopicID"]);
    // get the number of topics per page
    int pageSize = Configuration.ModuleConfig.GetSettings().RepliesPerPage;
```

```
// get the current replies page
int pageNumber = (PageNumber.Text.Length == 0 ?
  1 : int.Parse(PageNumber.Text));

// retrieve and bind the records to the grid
Business.Topic topic = new Business.Topic(topicID);
DataSet replies = topic.GetReplies(pageNumber);
RepliesGrid.DataSource = replies.Tables[0].DefaultView;
RepliesGrid.DataBind();

// show the total number of pages
int totalPages = (int)Math.Ceiling((double)topic.Replies/pageSize);
if (totalPages == 0) totalPages = 1;
TotalPages.Text = totalPages.ToString();
// enable/disable the links to navigate through the pages
FirstPage.Enabled = (pageNumber != 1);
PreviousPage.Enabled = (pageNumber != 1);
NextPage.Enabled = (pageNumber != totalPages);
LastPage.Enabled = (pageNumber != totalPages);

// show also the topic, if this is the first page
if (pageNumber == 1)
{
  BindTopicControls(topicID);
  TopicTable.Visible = true;
  // if this is the first page, also swap the styles for the Item and
  // AlternatingItem of the DataGrid, because the Topic has the Item style
  RepliesGrid.ItemStyle.CssClass = GridAlternatingItemStyle.Text;
  RepliesGrid.AlternatingItemStyle.CssClass = GridItemStyle.Text;
}
else
{
  TopicTable.Visible = false;
  RepliesGrid.ItemStyle.CssClass = GridItemStyle.Text;
  RepliesGrid.AlternatingItemStyle.CssClass =
                                    GridAlternatingItemStyle.Text;
}
}
```

If the page to show is the first one, the TopicTable is shown (otherwise the topic is hidden), and we also call BindTopicControls with the ID of the current topic. This retrieves the required data and sets the labels, links, and other controls. Here's the code for this method:

```
private void BindTopicControls(int topicID)
{
  // retrieve all the topic's info
  Business.Topic topic = new Business.Topic(topicID);
  Business.Member author = topic.Member;

  // show the data
  TopicAuthor.Text = GetAuthorText(author.Name,
                                    author.Email, author.ShowEmail);
```

```
TopicAuthorAvatar.ImageUrl = author.AvatarUrl;
TopicAuthorAvatar.Visible = (author.AvatarUrl.Length > 0);
TopicAuthorHomepage.NavigateUrl = author.Homepage;
TopicAuthorHomepage.Visible = (author.Homepage.Length > 0);
TopicDate.Text = string.Format("{0:MM/dd/yy}", topic.AddedDate);
TopicTime.Text = string.Format("{0:HH:mm:ss tt}", topic.AddedDate);
TopicSubject.Text = topic.Subject;
TopicMessage.Text = Business.Helper.ProcessSpecialTags(topic.Message);
TopicAuthorSignature.Text = Business.Helper.ProcessSpecialTags(
                                                     author.Signature);
}
```

Before concluding the discussion for this page, here's the code for `ProcessTags`, which simply wraps a call to the `ProcessSpecialTags` static method of the `Business.Helper` class:

```
public string ProcessTags(object rawText)
{
   return Business.Helper.ProcessSpecialTags(rawText.ToString());
}
```

The code for deleting a `DataGrid`'s reply or the topic itself has nothing new or particularly interesting, so we won't show the code for that part – for full details see the code download.

The PostMessage.aspx Page

This page is used to edit an existing message, or to post a new topic or reply. It has a simple table with some textboxes, some of which are made visible or invisible according to the action we're taking. For example, we cannot specify subjects for replies, so if we're replying we should not see the `Subject` textbox. And the textbox for the topic's key should be visible only when the moderator is adding a new topic, and invisible to normal users. We will handle this in the codebehind. Here is the code for the ASP.NET page:

```
<%@ Page language="c#" Codebehind="PostMessage.aspx.cs"
         AutoEventWireup="false"
         Inherits="Wrox.WebModules.Forums.Web.PostMessage" %>
<%@ Register TagPrefix="Forums" TagName="Header" src="Header.ascx" %>
<%@ Register TagPrefix="Forums" TagName="Footer" src="Footer.ascx" %>
<!DOCTYPE HTML PUBLIC "-//W3C//DTD HTML 4.0 Transitional//EN" >
<HTML>
  <HEAD>
    <title>Forums</title>
    <meta name="CODE_LANGUAGE" Content="C#">
    <link href="/ThePhile/Styles/ThePhile.css" rel="stylesheet" />
    <link href="/ThePhile/Styles/Navigator.css" rel="stylesheet" />
    <script language="javascript">
      function InsertTag(tagcode)
      {
        document.PostMessage.Message.value += tagcode;
      }
    </script>
  </HEAD>
```

```
<body>
  <form ID="PostMessage" method="post" Runat="server">
    <Forums:Header Runat="server" ID="Header" />
    <br>
    <asp:Table Runat="server" ID="MessageBox" Width="500px"
              HorizontalAlign="Center" CssClass="Forums_General">
      <asp:TableRow CssClass="Forums_Header">
        <asp:TableCell Runat="server" ID="MessageBoxHeader"
                      HorizontalAlign="Center" Font-Bold="True" />
      </asp:TableRow>
      <asp:TableRow Runat="server" ID="SubjectRow">
        <asp:TableCell>
          <b>Subject:</b>
          <asp:TextBox ID="Subject" Runat="server" MaxLength="100"
                      Width="100%" CssClass="TextBox" />
          <asp:RequiredFieldValidator Runat="server"
                          ControlToValidate="Subject" Display="Dynamic">
            * This field is required
          </asp:RequiredFieldValidator>
        </asp:TableCell>
      </asp:TableRow>
      <asp:TableRow Runat="server" ID="KeyRow">
        <asp:TableCell>
          <b>Key:</b>
          <asp:TextBox ID="Key" Runat="server" MaxLength="15"
                      Width="100%" CssClass="TextBox" />
        </asp:TableCell>
      </asp:TableRow>
      <asp:TableRow Runat="server" ID="SpecialTagsRow">
        <asp:TableCell>
          <a href="javascript:InsertTag('[B] [/B]')">
            <img src="./Images/EditorBold.gif" alt="Bold">
          </a>
```

There are similar JavaScript calls for all the supported tags. Let's just jump to the end of the toolbar:

```
        </asp:TableCell>
      </asp:TableRow>
      <asp:TableRow>
        <asp:TableCell>
          <b>Message:</b>
          <asp:TextBox ID="Message" Runat="server" MaxLength="100"
                      TextMode="MultiLine" Rows="15" Width="100%"
                      CssClass="TextBox" />
          <asp:RequiredFieldValidator Runat="server"
                          ControlToValidate="Message" Display="Dynamic">
            * This field is required
          </asp:RequiredFieldValidator>
        </asp:TableCell>
      </asp:TableRow>
      <asp:TableRow>
        <asp:TableCell HorizontalAlign="Right">
```

```
                <asp:LinkButton ID="SubmitMessage"
                            OnClick="SubmitMessage_Click" Runat="server">
                  [ <img border="0" src="./Images/OK.gif" Alt="submit"> Submit ]
                </asp:LinkButton>
                 
                <asp:LinkButton ID="CancelMessage" OnClick="CancelMessage_Click"
                            CausesValidation="False" Runat="server">
                  [ <img border="0" src="./Images/Cancel.gif"> Cancel ]
                </asp:LinkButton>
              </asp:TableCell>
            </asp:TableRow>
          </asp:Table>
          <br>
          <Forums:Footer Runat="server" ID="Footer" />
        </form>
      </body>
    </HTML>
```

In addition to the textboxes we also have a row with images that, when clicked, call the custom `InsertTag` JavaScript function that adds the specified text tags to the message textbox, to help users who don't know or don't remember them. This toolbar is only visible when special tags are allowed by the module's settings. However, we don't care about the visibility of the controls in this page, as everything will be done from the codebehind.

The Codebehind for PostMessage.aspx

This codebehind can seem complex, because we have to handle different actions according to the `Action` parameter passed along with the URL, as well as the usual `ForumID`, `TopicID`, `ReplyID`, `QuoteTopicID`, and `QuoteReplyID` parameters that we've used in the previous pages. To recap, here's a list of the possible values for the `Action` parameter, their respective meanings, and the companion parameters:

❑ `NewTopic`: posts a new topic to the forum identified by the `ForumID` parameter.

❑ `EditTopic`: edits the topic identified by the `TopicID` parameter.

❑ `NewReply`: posts a new reply to the topic identified by the `TopicID` parameter. Checks if the `QuoteTopicID` or `QuoteReplyID` parameter is specified, and if so quotes the respective message.

❑ `EditReply`: edits the topic identified by the `ReplyID` parameter.

The textboxes for the subject and message text are set to empty, or populated with the values of the topic or reply accordingly to the parameters above. However, before doing this, the page checks whether the current user is authenticated: if not, they are redirected to the login page, to log in or create a new account. Otherwise in `Page_Load` we also check if the current user is registered for the forums system: if not they are redirected to the `MyProfile.aspx` page to create a new profile. All this translates to the following code:

```
private int forumID;
private int topicID;
private int replyID;
```

```
private bool canModerateForums;
SiteIdentity currUser;
Business.Member currMember;

private void Page_Load(object sender, System.EventArgs e)
{
  // if the user is not authenticated, redirect to the login page
  if (!Context.User.Identity.IsAuthenticated)
  {
    Response.Redirect("/ThePhile/Modules/Users/Login.aspx", true);
  }

  // retrieve the current user/member
  currUser = (SiteIdentity)Context.User.Identity;
  currMember = new Business.Member();
  currMember.LoadFromUser(currUser.UserID);

  // if the user is not registered for the forum,
  // redirect to the profile page
  if (currMember.ID == -1)
  {
    Response.Redirect("MyProfile.aspx", true);
  }

  // check if the user has the permission to moderate the forums
  SitePrincipal currentPrincipal = (SitePrincipal)Context.User;
  canModerateForums = currentPrincipal.HasPermission(
                                  (int)ForumsPermissions.ModerateForums);

  // if the user wants to edit a topic or reply, but does not have the
  // permission to do so, redirect to the login page
  if (Request.QueryString["Action"].ToString().ToLower().StartsWith("edit")
    && !canModerateForums)
  {
    Response.Redirect("/ThePhile/Modules/Users/Login.aspx?ShowError=true",
                                                                   true);
  }

  // extract the ForumID, if specified
  if (Request.QueryString["ForumID"] == null)
    forumID = -1;
  else
    forumID = int.Parse(Request.QueryString["ForumID"]);

  // extract the TopicID, if specified
  if (Request.QueryString["TopicID"] == null)
    topicID = -1;
  else
    topicID = int.Parse(Request.QueryString["TopicID"]);

  // extract the ReplyID, if specified
  if (Request.QueryString["ReplyID"] == null)
    replyID = -1;
  else
```

```
      replyID = int.Parse(Request.QueryString["ReplyID"]);

if (!Page.IsPostBack)
{
   // show/hide the icons for the special tags, according to the settings
   SpecialTagsRow.Visible =
               Configuration.ModuleConfig.GetSettings().SpecialTagsEnabled;
```

After adding or updating a message, we redirect back to the page that originally called
PostMessage.aspx. The URL can't be retrieved through the Request.UrlReferrer property,
because when the button is clicked and the form posted back, the referrer becomes the
PostMessage.aspx page itself. To solve this simple problem, we save the original referrer's URL into
the ViewState collection. We will retrieve it in Submit_Click, and redirect to that page:

```
      ViewState["ReferrerUrl"] = Request.UrlReferrer.ToString();

Business.Forum forum = new Business.Forum(forumID);
Business.Topic topic = new Business.Topic(topicID);
Business.Reply reply = new Business.Reply(replyID);

// show the fields and the navigation path, according to the
// action to complete, and the forum/topic/reply ID
switch(Request.QueryString["Action"].ToString().ToLower())
{
  case "newtopic":
    SubjectRow.Visible = true;
    KeyRow.Visible = canModerateForums;
    MessageBoxHeader.Text = "New topic";
    Header.ForumID = forumID;
    break;

  case "edittopic":
    SubjectRow.Visible = true;
    KeyRow.Visible = canModerateForums;
    MessageBoxHeader.Text = "Edit topic";
    Subject.Text = topic.Subject;
    Key.Text = topic.Key;
    Message.Text = topic.Message;
    Header.TopicID = topicID;
    break;

  case "newreply":
    SubjectRow.Visible = false;
    KeyRow.Visible = false;
    MessageBoxHeader.Text = "New reply";
    Header.TopicID = topicID;

    // a topic or another reply can being quoted by
    // this new reply, check it is the case
    int quoteTopicID;
    int quoteReplyID;
    // extract the QuoteTopicID, if specified
```

```
          if (Request.QueryString["QuoteTopicID"] == null)
            quoteTopicID = -1;
          else
            quoteTopicID = int.Parse(Request.QueryString["QuoteTopicID"]);
          // extract the QuoteReplyID, if specified
          if (Request.QueryString["QuoteReplyID"] == null)
            quoteReplyID = -1;
          else
            quoteReplyID = int.Parse(Request.QueryString["QuoteReplyID"]);

          // if a topic is being quoted, add it to the MessageBox
          if (quoteTopicID != -1)
          {
            Business.Topic existentTopic = new Business.Topic(quoteTopicID);
            Message.Text += string.Format("[QUOTE]{0}[/QUOTE]",
                                                   existentTopic.Message);
          }
          // if a reply is being quoted, add it to the MessageBox
          if (quoteReplyID != -1)
          {
            Business.Reply existentReply = new Business.Reply(quoteReplyID);
            Message.Text += string.Format("[QUOTE]{0}[/QUOTE]",
                                                   existentReply.Message);
          }

          break;

        case "editreply":
          SubjectRow.Visible = false;
          KeyRow.Visible = false;
          Message.Text = reply.Message;
          MessageBoxHeader.Text = "Edit reply";
          Header.TopicID = reply.Topic.ID;
          break;
      }
    }
  }
```

When the form is submitted we again check the Action parameter and create or edit a record, as follows:

```
protected void SubmitMessage_Click(object sender, EventArgs e)
{
  Business.Forum forum = new Business.Forum(forumID);
  Business.Topic topic = new Business.Topic(topicID);
  Business.Reply reply = new Business.Reply(replyID);

  switch(Request.QueryString["Action"].ToString().ToLower())
  {
    // create a new topic
    case "newtopic":
      int newID = forum.AddTopic(Key.Text, Subject.Text,
```

```
                                            Message.Text, currMember.ID).ID;
      Response.Redirect("Topic.aspx?TopicID=" + newID.ToString(), true);
      break;

    // edit an existing topic
    case "edittopic":
      topic.Key = Key.Text;
      topic.Subject = Subject.Text;
      topic.Message = Message.Text;
      topic.Update();
      break;

    // add a new reply
    case "newreply":
      topic.AddReply(Message.Text, currMember.ID);
      // add the parameter to the Referrer Url to
      // jump to the last page of the topic
      if (!ViewState["ReferrerUrl"].ToString().ToLower().EndsWith(
                    "&display=lastpage"))
                    ViewState["ReferrerUrl"] += "&Display=LastPage";
      break;

    // edit an existing reply
    case "editreply":
      reply.Message = Message.Text;
      reply.Update();
      break;
  }

  // redirect to the referrer page
  Response.Redirect(ViewState["ReferrerUrl"].ToString());
}
```

> Note that in this procedure there is no need to check if the user is trying to edit a
> record and has the right permissions to do that. This is already checked in
> **Page_Load**, which is called before this event, even if the page is posted back, as in this
> case. Therefore, if the user is not allowed to edit a record but tries to do it, this will be
> recognized when the page loads, and the execution will not get to
> **SubmitMessage_Click**. The browser will instead be redirected to the login page.

If we're adding a reply, we redirect to the referring page, but add a `Display=LastPage` parameter at
the end of the URL, so that the `Topic.aspx` page (the only page with links to post a reply), shows the
last page of replies – which will include the message just posted.

The `CancelMessage_Click` procedure, executed when the user presses the Cancel button, simply
makes the browser jump back to the referrer page:

```
protected void CancelMessage_Click(object sender, EventArgs e)
{
  // go back to the referrer page
  Response.Redirect(ViewState["ReferrerUrl"].ToString());
}
```

Here is a screenshot of the complete page, when a moderator is adding a new topic (only moderators can set the topic's key):

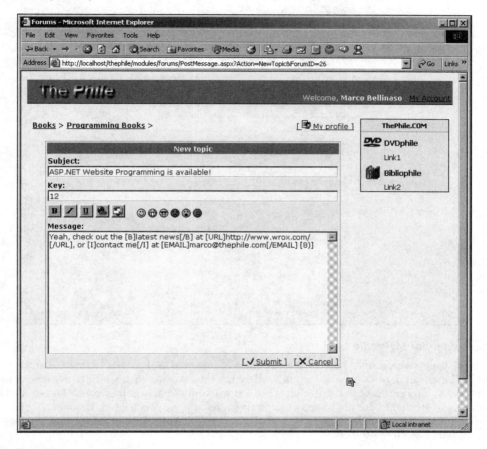

The MyProfile.aspx Page

This page allows a registered member to change their profile, namely the signature, the avatar URL, the homepage URL, and the flag indicating whether the e-mail address can be publicly shown. The member name is shown in a disabled textbox, since it can't be changed – if the user wants a different name, they must first create a new account for the site and then create a new profile for the forum. The code for the ASPX page is simple – there is just the declaration of a table and the textboxes, as you see from the following screenshot:

The Codebehind for MyProfile.aspx

When the page loads, it first checks if the current user is logged in. If not, it can mean that they are a registered user but currently not logged in, or they have not registered at all. In both cases, a user can't create or edit a forums profile if they don't own a site account first, or if they aren't logged in. Thus, the browser is redirected to the site's Login.aspx page, to log in or create a new account. If the current user has been authenticated, the page is rendered to create or edit a profile, depending on whether they have one already. Here's the code:

```
SiteIdentity currUser;
protected System.Web.UI.WebControls.Table Table1;
Business.Member currMember;

private void Page_Load(object sender, System.EventArgs e)
{
  // if the user is not authenticated, redirect to the login page
  if (!Context.User.Identity.IsAuthenticated)
  {
    Response.Redirect("/ThePhile/Modules/Users/Login.aspx", true);
  }

  // retrieve the current user/member
  currUser = (SiteIdentity)Context.User.Identity;
  currMember = new Business.Member();
  currMember.LoadFromUser(currUser.UserID);
```

```
if (!IsPostBack)
{
  // save the referrer Url
  ViewState["ReferrerUrl"] = Request.UrlReferrer.ToString();

  // if the member's ID is not -1, we have to edit the current
  // profile so load the current properties and disable the
  // textbox with the member name
  if (currMember.ID != -1)
  {
    // load the profile of the current member
    ProfileBoxTitle.Text = "Edit profile";
    Name.Text = currMember.Name;
    Name.Enabled = false;
    Signature.Text = currMember.Signature;
    AvatarUrl.Text = currMember.AvatarUrl;
    Homepage.Text = currMember.Homepage;
    ShowEmail.Checked = currMember.ShowEmail;
  }
  else
  {
    Name.Text = currUser.FirstName + " " + currUser.LastName;
    // ensure that the member name is no longer that 15 chars
    if (Name.Text.Length >15) Name.Text = Name.Text.Substring(0, 15);
    ProfileBoxTitle.Text = "Register";
  }
}
```

To check if the current user has a profile we create an instance of Business.Member, and try to load the profile through LoadFromUser. If the ID property is set to -1 it means that a profile has not been created yet, so the textboxes are all enabled and we set the username textbox to the first 15 letters of the user's first name plus last name. If a profile already exists, the textbox for the member name is disabled, and the other textboxes are set with the member's current properties.

When the user clicks the Submit button, the code in the Click event handler creates or updates a profile, depending on whether the textbox for the member name is enabled or not:

```
protected void Submit_Click(object sender, EventArgs e)
{
  // if the textbox with the name is disabled, it means that we're editing
  // an existing member, otherwise create a new one
  if (!Name.Enabled)
  {
    // update the profile of the current member
    currMember.Signature = Signature.Text;
    currMember.AvatarUrl = AvatarUrl.Text;
    currMember.Homepage = Homepage.Text;
    currMember.ShowEmail = ShowEmail.Checked;
    currMember.Update();
  }
  else
```

499

```
{
  // create a new member
  Business.Member member = new Business.Member();
  if (member.Create(currUser.UserID, Name.Text, ShowEmail.Checked,
    Signature.Text, AvatarUrl.Text, Homepage.Text) == -1)
  {
    // if a member with this name is already present,
    // show the error message
    ErrorMessageRow.Visible = true;
    return;
  }
}

// redirect to the referrer page
Response.Redirect(ViewState["ReferrerUrl"].ToString());
}
```

When the profile has been created or updated, the browser is redirected to the page that originally redirected to Profile.aspx, in the same way as PostTopic.aspx.

Summary

In this chapter we've built a forums system from scratch. We've seen how to integrate other modules such as the Core and the Accounts modules, as well as ASP.NET's built-in authentication. Our Forums module supports multiple categories and sub-forums, displays topics and replies through custom pagination, enforces the user currently registered to the site to also create a forums' profile with their username, signature, avatar, and homepage, and supports or prevents the use of HTML code and other special tags.

We've written quite a lot of code to fuel the discussion board system. Below we just list the most important techniques that this chapter should have taught you:

❑ Creating nested data bound controls: in the Default.aspx page we showed how to create a DataGrid inside a DataList to represent a parent-child relationship.

❑ Custom implementation of the Delete command for the DataList and DataGrid in Default.aspx, namely the JavaScript popup box that asks for a confirmation and calls __doPostBack to generate an event on the server.

❑ How to implement the DataGrid's custom pagination, by using a stored procedure that returns the specified page of records, the DataGrid's AllowCustomPaging property, and custom controls to navigate through the pages.

❑ Using regular expressions and the RegEx class to extract and replace string patterns.

However, we've really only scratched the surface of the features we could implement for a professional forum. Below we list some of the features they offer, in case you want to enhance our module with some more advanced functionality:

❑ Email notification of forum activity, or even e-mail message digests – eventually we could integrate the web forum with an e-mail discussion list.

❑ Add some kind of preview or revision system for users to edit their own messages.

❑ Banning certain words, and using regular expressions to replace them with acceptable alternatives.

❑ An administration console, that allows administrators to browse members, edit their profiles, or ban them from the forum.

❑ A feature that allows moderators to move a topic to another forum.

❑ Threaded discussions, where it is possible to follow a particular thread within a topic, rather than seeing all messages arranged by date.

❑ Allow all users to submit topics for approval.

❑ Allow users to see what forums contain the current hot topics, where a hot topic is one that has been posted to most frequently in a given time period. This generates cross-forum interest.

❑ Private forums, where only restricted members can read and post messages.

We've now implemented all of the modules for our website, and in the next chapter will look at how we can deploy it as a live site.

11

Deploying the Site

Now that we have developed our website, we need to **deploy** it – prepare and distribute the site so that users can access it.

The release of ASP.NET forces us to reconsider many preconceptions about the deployment of websites. For example, we need to get used to the possibility of running multiple copies of the same site on a single server, sharing different versions of identically named DLLs. Another thing that developers might find incredible is XCopy deployment, which allows a developer to deploy an application by simply copying files to the target location. There's no need to use the Registry or any complex COM registration.

In the past, deploying a large-scale web application could become a nightmare. Most enterprise web sites were comprised of dozens (or more) COM and COM+/MTS components. Maintaining the information on all of those components in the Registry and making sure that the information was updated properly when upgrading to a new version was an incredibly difficult task. ASP.NET allows entire websites to be configured with simple XML text files, and components to automatically register themselves in COM+. There's no need to look to the registry for anything in deployment of ASP.NET, completely alleviating one of the biggest ASP deployment headaches.

This chapter will discuss the general issues surrounding the deployment of ASP.NET websites and the various approaches we can take. We will describe the deployment techniques we used for ThePhile.com.

The Problem

Our problem for this chapter is deploying our fully functional website to our production server.

It is a common practice to develop a site on a *development* server, then deploy to a *staging* server, and finally after a successful test on the staging server, deploy to the *production* server. We want a solution that will allow us to deploy the entire functioning site to a production server. However, we also want to be able to easily deploy the code to multiple machines so that we can test it in various scenarios. In our solution, our production server is hosted by Wrox, but it could just as easily be a segment of disk space allocated to us by a website hosting company.

So, in this chapter we want to explore the various ways we can deploy ASP.NET websites and then choose the one that best suits our needs. The chapter will provide some useful information about ASP.NET deployment that will help decide which method is most appropriate for different organizations.

The Design

There are two parts to deploying the website: the database and the application. First of all, we will discuss how to deploy the database. Then we will move on to look at the web application itself.

Deploying the Data Store

A data store for a website can be anything from a set of XML files or simple Access database, to a complex SQL Server or Oracle database. Each of the website deployment options has a different set of limitations and advantages for database deployment. However, since database deployment is an important topic all on its own, we'll discuss it here rather than split up the discussion among the different installation scenarios.

Deploying a database is easiest when we own the machine to which it needs to be deployed. We can use whatever deployment scenario is most convenient for copying our particular data store. For SQL Server or Oracle there are several options, including:

❑ Making a backup of the development database and restoring from that backup on another machine.

❑ Transferring data structures and data between linked servers in some fashion, perhaps using script files.

We often don't fully control the database server. Web hosting companies often set up a single database with a certain quota of disk space, for example. In situations like this, our options are more limited. We probably can't restore from a backup, because we won't have access to Enterprise Manager against the host's database servers. Even if we do have access to Enterprise Manager, we might not have the right permissions to perform a database restore. In these cases, we are limited to using text queries to create the data structures and load the data.

For an Access database, the file just needs to be copied to a certain directory and the file is deployed. It doesn't matter what server access we have. This does pose a serious danger: if an unwanted intruder happens to find out that your Access database is available in a public internet directory, they'll be able to download it. You'll want to keep the MDB file somewhere non-obvious and preferably in a private location, so that only code from your application can access the file.

Consult your SQL Server, Oracle, or Access manual for the various options available for transferring your database from your development PC to a deployed production environment.

For automated deployment, where we create an installation program for our website, we have another option. We can take the scripts that recreate the data structures required for the application, and can have our installer execute them at install-time, guaranteeing that the data structures will be available before the application is run for the first time.

Preparing the Site for Deployment

There are three main scenarios that we will consider for deploying our ASP.NET website:

- ❑ XCopy deployment
- ❑ A specialized type of XCopy deployment for deploying a website to a hosted server that we have little control over
- ❑ Using Visual Studio .NET to create an installation program that will perform the installation and deployment process automatically

While there are a great number of variations in the ways to deploy an ASP.NET website, all of them will derive from a combination of the above three. We will discuss each of these methods in detail and explain the benefits and drawbacks of each, and then apply that information to our situation in terms of deploying ThePhile.com.

The following diagram shows a sample website directory structure. It includes a list of some DLLs that the sample application might be using. The directory structure contains everything that is required to run the application, except the database. There are no Registry entries to be made:

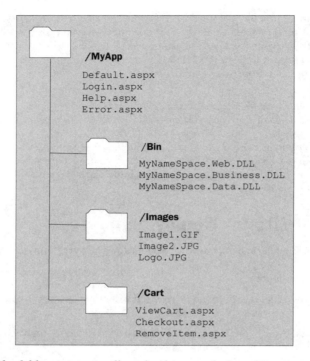

During development, the folder structure will not be this neat. In fact, things can get downright messy. In ThePhile's development folder, we have many copies of the same DLL and source code for all classes, even supposedly secret business and data layer classes. Deploying all this would waste our disk space and pose a security risk. We should only deploy the files required to execute the application – one copy of each DLL, and only source code for classes that compile on the fly.

Visual Studio .NET enables us to copy a web project to a new location. While at first it might not appear all that beneficial to copy a web project, there is a subtle feature that comes in extremely handy. On the Copy Project dialog box, accessible from the Project menu, there is a radio button that allows us to exclude source code files from the destination copy of the application. Choosing "Only files needed to run this application" when copying the project creates a copy of the entire solution, without the source code files. This includes all supporting assemblies (which will be copied to the \bin directory), all .aspx pages, all .ascx controls, and all .asmx files, as well as all images and other non-code items associated with the project. This copy can then be used as the source for all of the deployment options that we will discuss in this chapter.

If we are copying to a location that has not been set up as a web folder, Visual Studio .NET will do everything it can to create the new site. If the site already exists, make sure that its FrontPage extensions are configured properly to allow Visual Studio .NET to make whatever changes are necessary.

Once we have created a 'clean' copy the website, we can carry out one of the available deployment options.

In fact, using this method we can create a clean copy on our host's machine in one go – we just need to ensure that the host is running FrontPage Extensions.

Manual (XCopy) Deployment

XCopy deployment is a painless way to install .NET software. It gets its name from a DOS command for copying whole folders, including its subfolders, to a different location. In DOS this was often all you needed to do to install software in new locations – create an exact copy of the folder structure. Because of COM component registration, and other OS complications, this often doesn't work in Windows. .NET brings the facility back.

In the case of ASP.NET, when a codebehind class or an ASP.NET page makes a request involving an external assembly, that request is directed to the web application's \bin directory.

When using Visual Studio .NET to build a web application, compiled codebehinds will be placed in a file called Web.dll, which will be placed in the \bin directory. Therefore when ASP.NET handles a request for a page with a codebehind class, that class is obtained from the Web.dll file.

With XCopy, we only need to copy all of the files from the 'clean' application directory and all related subdirectories to the deployment location and the application is deployed.

The benefit of the XCopy approach is that it is incredibly simple, quick, and relatively painless. The downside is that it is manual. We end up deploying websites by manually dragging and dropping folders and files. If you are in control of both your clean application and the machine you are deploying to, this approach is fine. If you plan on bundling your site for distribution to a wider audience, this approach might not be suitable and you may instead have to build a deployment project in Visual Studio .NET. This latter approach is the one we took when deploying ThePhile.com, and is described in the *Solution* section.

When using XCopy there is one extra thing that must be done. XCopy only copies the files. In order for the newly deployed web application to work properly, we need to make sure that IIS has been configured properly.

Configuring IIS for your Application

Although we've hyped XCopy deployment, in ASP.NET it is not an entirely hands-free process. We can't simply copy our files to a directory and expect the directory to magically become a web application. We still need to configure IIS to replicate our local configuration. In some cases you won't have direct access to IIS and will need to communicate your needs to the host's IT staff. If this is the case, knowing the IIS issues will make it far easier to explain what you need.

To get a web application working properly, we need an IIS application to be running and serving HTTP requests for the application's virtual directory. The **IIS Virtual Directory Creation Wizard** can help do this.

Here we will set up a folder in IIS that will allow us to deploy by XCopy. First, open up the Internet Services Manager console. Expand the node for your computer, select the "Web Sites" node, and choose "New | Virtual Directory" to start this wizard.

From there, you will be prompted for an alias name (for example, `ThePhile` or `MyApp`) for the virtual directory. Then you will be asked for the physical directory to which the virtual directory should point. This will be where you manually copied your directory structure, or an empty directory if you are going to copy the files in later. Select the folder to which you copied your 'clean' website and proceed to the next step. Here you specify what permissions you would like to create for the application. Leave the checkboxes set at their default values: only **read** and **script (ASP) execution** should be allowed. These permissions are sufficient to run an ASP.NET website.

If you already have a web application created for this website, and you want to deploy to the existing IIS application, the procedure varies slightly. First, you still need to make sure that you have a clean deployment source, with no legible source code in it. Secondly, you should delete any existing files in the web application. If you created a virtual directory with IIS, or if you created a web application using VS .NET, there will be some default 'clutter' in the directories that you can get rid of before copying your files into the directory. From there, your `web.config` file will take care of the rest of the administrative tasks for your web application. With ASP.NET you no longer have to worry about other kinds of configuration methods, because all required settings are controlled by `web.config`.

Deploying to a Hosting Service

We do not all work for large corporations that can provide Internet connectivity, bandwidth, databases, and servers capable of hosting the .NET Framework and storing web pages. In these cases a hosting service comes in handy.

The Visual Studio .NET start page contains a link to a current list of participating .NET web hosting services. There are standard and premier services listed here. The standard services usually provide a web application, some limited storage space, and possibly some data access method. Premier services often offer e-commerce initiatives, larger disk space allowances, dedicated servers, and other services more useful to businesses than individual programmers. Premier services also tend to give us more control over the web and database server configurations.

Each will vary in the services they provide, the fees they charge, and the methods they support for updating the website. It's a good idea to prepare for the least amount of supported functionality in order to make your deployment plan flexible, just in case you have to suddenly change providers (a surprisingly common event).

The first thing we need is a 'clean' version of the website to be deployed. As discussed earlier, this means either manually removing sensitive source code from the web directories, or using the project copy feature in Visual Studio .NET to do this for us.

Typically, the hosting services will provide a single web application to do with as we please. For example, we might end up with a web application running at www.hostingcompany.com/myapp. If the web hosting company also provides DNS resolution, we might be able to get that particular application to be the destination for an address, for example www.myapplication.com.

To deploy an application to a hosting service, we follow the typical XCopy model, except that the destination machine is not our own, and is often an FTP site provided by the web hosting company. This works fine, allowing us to copy our files as we please. The two main differences between standard XCopy deployment and deploying to a web hosting company are:

❑ With XCopy deployment, we control our own IIS configuration manually. By deploying to a web host, the web host is in control of the IIS configuration and any changes to our application's IIS configuration often go through their technical support department.

❑ When using traditional XCopy deployment, we can use Visual Studio .NET to develop directly against the web application. However, with a web hosting company, FrontPage extensions may not be available, so we have to use VS .NET to develop the solution in an offline fashion and then FTP the files to the server later.

Before deciding on a particular web hosting company, read as much technical information about the process by which pages get uploaded to the site, their technical support policy, and any uptime guarantees they may have. Do not put a critical application on a web-hosting site unless they guarantee a reasonable level of uptime.

Because the technical support department controls our site's configuration, *always* check it before agreeing to anything. Check references, and if possible get information from other people currently running applications on their site. When looking for a hosting service, you should check out what kind of access you would have to your database (for example, if they allow Enterprise Manager), and what kind of application control you would have (for example, will they allow you to have more than one application or must you run everything from the same root application?).

Another thing to consider are the resources that your application will use. If you're designing your application with deployment to a third party server in mind, there are some design and architecture decisions that you might want to consider. Resources are generally limited or entirely restricted in availability on hosting servers. For example, most applications will typically not have access to the Event Log. Even if the application has access to it, you won't, so you would be unable to see the results of your application's log. In cases like this, you'll want to design your code to require the least amount of environment-specific resources so that you can be prepared for deployment to a variety of environments.

Automated Deployment (Building Installers)

Automated deployment is obviously the preferred solution, but it isn't always available. If you have built a web site to sell to a client, those clients need to easily install the site on their own servers. For example, if you have developed a support call center application using ASP.NET and are selling that application, you will need some robust, easy-to-use way for the clients to install and set up that application.

In the past, this was accomplished by using a tool such as InstallShield or WISE Installmaster. These tools would allow you to create scripts that dictated which files were copied during the installation. They also registered COM components and handled creation of COM+ applications. These tools are complex and take some time to fully master their use.

Visual Studio .NET provides a built-in method for creating installation programs. Visual Studio .NET allows us to create CAB files, self-installing executable files and even MSI files for use with the Microsoft Windows Installer package. While using these installers is a good solution and helpful, it only works if you actually have access to the console of the server on which you're installing the application. This pretty much rules out this method for building deployment scenarios to web hosting companies, but is still an excellent idea for providing shrink-wrapped software to clients or departments within a company.

The Solution

Wrox Press will host the final version of ThePhile.com, so we do not need to enlist the services of a web hosting company. This makes a deployment project in Visual Studio .NET an appropriate choice. We will create two – one with the source code and one without.

In this section we'll cover indepth the steps involved in creating a deployment project for ThePhile.com, which will result in a Windows Installer file to distribute for deploying ThePhile.

First, we open up Visual Studio .NET and choose the option to create a new project. Then we highlight the **Setup and Deployment Projects** option in the left pane, and the right pane shows the following options:

The following are the different types of setup and deployment projects available:

❑ **Setup Project** – this will create a blank installation project. It will be up to us to choose all of the various activities and files for the installer. This is typically recommended for those programmers who know ahead of time what activities need to be performed and which files need to be copied.

❑ **Web Setup Project** – this is similar to the blank Setup Project, except it comes with a few settings and directories already created to guide us in the right direction for installing a website.

❑ **Merge Module Project** – this is a slightly more advanced project for creating merge modules for use with the latest versions of the Windows Installer. Merge Modules are an advanced technique that we won't discuss here.

❑ **Setup Wizard** – this is basically a frontend to all of the other project types. We will choose this one – it's easy and it guides us step-by-step through creating the appropriate type of setup project.

❑ **Cab Project** – this project builds a Windows installation cabinet file. This is another advanced technique. Find out more on Cabinet files in the .NET Framework SDK and Windows documentation.

For our purposes, we're going to create a new project called `ThePhileSetup`, using the **Setup Wizard** option. We enter our new project's filename and click **OK**. Once we've done this, we're presented with a dialog that looks like this:

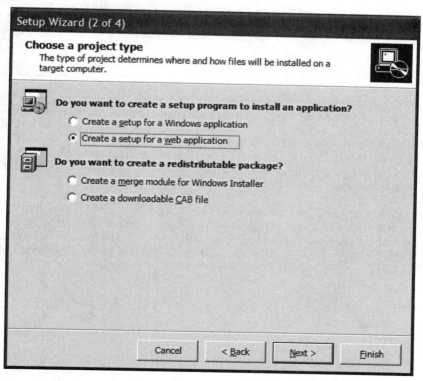

The Setup Wizard guides us through creating a new setup project. It asks a couple of user-friendly questions, and then creates a variety of blank template projects that we can expand as needed. The previous dialog asks whether the setup is for a Windows application, a web application, a merge module, or a downloadable CAB file. These options should look familiar from the New Project panel. We'll choose web application and click Next. After Visual Studio .NET does some initial setting up, we're presented with a Project view:

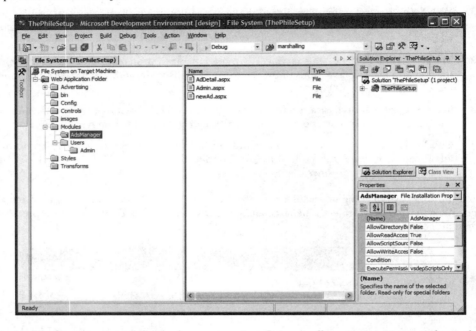

This is the File System view of the deployment project. It is actually quite intuitive – it shows the state of the file system we would like to exist *after* the installation. In our case, once the installation is over we want to place the above directory structure under a web application created in the Web Application Folder. The main benefit of using Visual Studio .NET's deployment projects, beyond the ease of use, is that we don't have to leave Visual Studio .NET to create the setup projects. The beauty of this model is that we only need to create an image of our final destination in the File System tab. To do this, we drag and drop directories and files into the file system tree and it's ready to go.

The setup project designer is far more powerful than it might first appear. If you right-click the project itself and choose View, you will be able to modify all kinds of details about the deployment project. This includes the user interface, registry settings, and much more. For example, the following screenshot shows the top left corner of a window for editing the user interface tree of a deployment project:

As you can see, the interface is incredibly easy and straightforward to understand. There are two sets of user interfaces, one for standard users and one for those users with administrative rights on the machine to which the project is being deployed. You can also change views, program prompts, and embed commands in the deployment project.

In short, creating a deployment project is so amazingly easy in Visual Studio .NET that there is no reason not to use this feature to its fullest. Unless you already own, and are extremely proficient in, another third party installation tool, this method is the best. Visual Studio .NET can automatically 'build' your project, resulting in an MSI file or a CAB file. This used to be a black art, but Visual Studio .NET illuminates it.

When we've created our two projects (one with source, one without), building them will result in two files: `ThePhileSetup.msi` and `ThePhileSourceSetup.msi`. The first file will deploy the entire website without any source code. The second file will deploy the website complete with source code, plus a Visual Studio .NET client solution file and project file.

To launch the installation program we just created, double-click the MSI files. This assumes that you have the latest version of the Windows Installer on your machine. If you are deploying to a location that might not have the latest installer, there is an option to package the installer itself with your MSI files when you build the installation projects.

Summary

We have seen how to deploy and install ASP.NET websites. We've discussed some of the issues that tend to arise during deployment and the various options available for installation. After having read this chapter, you should be familiar with the following types of deployment and their associated issues and concerns:

- ❑ XCopy deployment
- ❑ Deployment to a hosted environment
- ❑ Automated deployment using VS .NET deployment projects

12

The End

This is the end of the book but it is not the end of the road. By now you should have played with the site, both by browsing the code in Visual Studio .NET, and playing with the site on your local machine.

You should also have seen how and why we built the site the way we did, and how to use those techniques on your own website.

Get Building

The next step is to start building your site. This book will have given you a framework, and some modules to use or modify. Now you will want to tailor our modules and pages to fit the needs of your site.

We also hope that you will build your own modules in our framework. A lot of our design went into making it easy to add new modules – we don't want it to go to waste! You will be able to link your modules to our central accounts system, modify our header and footer controls, and so on. This book will provide a reference for building your own modules employing similar techniques.

Join Our Community

We don't want you to develop alone. This book will have its own forum at p2p.wrox.com where you can discuss it with us and other readers. This is a great place to get help with problems, share ideas, and find out if other people have written the module you need. Or you can just show off the sites you've developed! This service is free to all readers.

Through P2P, we hope to build up a list of the best websites built with the help of this book. If you do anything really impressive, we might even ask you to write a book about it!

Read More

This book has touched on a large number of subjects: web services, server controls, security, ADO.NET, and more. If you want to find more about any of these subjects, there are several Wrox books that will help.

Web Services

This book has presented a couple of very simple web services. *Professional ASP.NET Web Services* contains lots of detailed information on web services and how to develop them. It looks at a variety of issues, including how XML is used to transmit the data, how to send complex data types, and how to ensure web services support thousands of users.

Security

Our site uses the extensibility of the ASP.NET security framework to give us a flexible accounts system. *Professional ASP.NET Security* delves deeper into these topics, showing how we can build our own custom security frameworks. It also contains many tips on ensuring code is secure.

ADO.NET

Data access and manipulation have played a major part in developing our website. Efficient use of databases is one of the best things we can do to ensure performance and scalability. *Professional ADO.NET* covers a wide range of data handling techniques, while *Professional SQL Server 2000* gives information on setting up and using SQL Server in the most effective way.

Professional Server Controls

Our site uses server controls in a number of places. Building good controls puts us in an excellent position to reuse functionality and save development effort. *Professional ASP.NET Server Controls* looks at how to build solid, reusable and flexible controls for your ASP.NET projects.

We hope that you have enjoyed this book, and that it will prove useful as you develop ASP.NET websites.

Index

A Guide to the Index

The index is arranged hierarchically, in alphabetical order, with symbols preceding the letter A. Most second-level entries and many third-level entries also occur as first-level entries. This is to ensure that users will find the information they require however they choose to search for it.

Notes

Notes